Theoretical Issues in Sign Language Research

Theoretical Issues in Sign Language Research
Volume 2: Psychology

Edited by
Patricia Siple and Susan D. Fischer

The University of Chicago Press
Chicago and London

Patricia Siple is associate professor of psychology and director of the linguistics program at Wayne State University. Susan D. Fischer is associate professor of communication research at the National Technical Institute for the Deaf. Together they have edited *Theoretical Issues in Sign Language Research*, volume 1, *Linguistics*.

The University of Chicago Press, Chicago 60637
The University of Chicago Press, Ltd., London

00 99 98 97 96 95 94 93 92 91   5 4 3 2 1

Library of Congress Cataloging-in-Publication Data
Theoretical issues in sign language research.
   Includes bibliographical references.
   Includes index.
   Contents: v. 1. Linguistics. — v. 2. Psychology.
   1. Sign language.   I. Fischer, Susan D.
II. Siple, Patricia
HV2474.T44   1990   419   90-10997
ISBN 0-226-25149-7 (v. 1 : alk. paper)
ISBN 0-226-25150-0 (pbk. : v. 1 : alk. paper)
ISBN 0-226-25151-9 (v. 2 : alk. paper)
ISBN 0-226-25152-7 (pbk. : v. 2 : alk. paper)

To Our Families of Friends

Contents

Foreword

It is a pleasure to see the language of my father-in-law and mother-in-law receive the research attention it deserves. We have arrived at a point in history when sign languages are being increasingly accepted by linguists as languages with their own grammatical structure. Now more than ever, it is critical that we continue to apply rigorous standards to the conduct of sign language research and the analysis of the linguistic and cultural characteristics of sign languages.

This book of scholarly essays is a significant addition to our field. The contributions it contains bode well for the continued development of the state of the art of sign language research.

James J. DeCaro

Introduction

Patricia Siple and Susan D. Fischer

Little more than a decade ago, when the study of sign language was in its infancy, psychological research focused on whether the processing mechanisms employed to acquire and use sign language were analogous to those for spoken language. The primary reason for these studies was to bolster the argument that sign languages like American Sign Language (ASL) were indeed languages. With building acceptance of language status, several books and papers began to examine theoretical implications of sign language research (e.g., Klima and Bellugi 1979; Siple 1978a; Wilbur 1979). With this theoretical emphasis, the study of sign language began to take its place in basic psychology books and journals.

The primary theoretical issue addressed by these early psycholinguistic studies—the universality of language mechanisms—has held, and continues to hold, a central place in psycholinguistics research. Universal features of language are often viewed as the features that make language unique to humans. Whether specific acquisition and processing mechanisms generalize across modality is an important test of universality. To the extent that language mechanisms are modality specific, they may represent properties of the sensory and motor systems used for perception and production rather than properties unique to language processing. The general conclusion from psycholinguistic studies of sign language is that very few processes are modality specific. Overwhelmingly, these studies have shown that the major structures and processes involved in language comprehension and production, as well as the stages and processes of language acquisition, are modality independent or universal (Klima and Bellugi 1979; Kyle and Woll 1985; Lane and Grosjean 1980; Newport and Meier 1986; Siple 1978a; Wilbur 1987).

Contemporary sign language research continues to probe the modality question. With the abundance of evidence for universal language mechanisms, however, much of present-day sign language research focuses on a related issue: the fundamental question of the relative contributions of biology and input to language acquisition and use. Previous studies tended to investigate native sign language acquisition (e.g., acquisition of ASL by deaf children of deaf parents) and sign language processing by individuals who acquired a sign language as a native language, because these were the types of studies needed to establish universals. Input in these situations is similar in quality and quantity to that for spoken language acquisition, except for language modality; children acquiring the language are typical except for their deafness. Universality of language mechanisms in these situations is generally taken to indicate that the universal mechanisms reflect the biologically given machinery necessary for language acquisition and use. It is, of course, also possible that universality stems from similarly structured and experienced learning environments across languages, nations, and cultures, though this is less likely. Language processes that generalize within modality most likely reflect an indirect biological component of language acquisition and use, since they implicate the operations of sensory and production systems involved in language perception and production. Specific language input is necessarily the predominant contributor to the acquisition and use of processes found in one language or only a few languages.

Current sign language research, as represented by the chapters in this volume, examines a broad range of input situations and acquisition by typical and atypical learners to establish the boundary conditions, both environmental and biological, for language acquisition and processing. With this focus of sign language research, current studies address not only broader theoretical issues in language acquisition, but applied issues as well, bringing the research closer to the educator and clinician. Sign language acquisition and use are examined for signed English and simultaneous communication environments, which are typical language-learning environments for many deaf children. These studies provide the opportunity to examine the nature and effects of the unique, often heterogeneous, input deaf children experience. In addition, the study of atypical learners' acquisition of sign language should provide new insights into the biology-input relationship.

Only two chapters deal with native sign acquisition, and only one of these, the first in the book, concentrates exclusively on universals. Reilly, McIntire, and Bellugi examine the universality of acquisition strategies for facial expression components of ASL. Facial expression, often likened to intonation in spoken languages, conveys specific grammatical information in ASL. The authors conclude that though the production modality used to convey specific grammatical information may be modality specific, the strategies used to acquire these mechanisms are universal, generalizing across modality.

Siple and Akamatsu also investigate the acquisition of ASL in a native sign language environment, but the children acquiring ASL are a set of fraternal twins. Studies of twins' acquisition of spoken languages often show a generalized delay that has been attributed to reduced input for twins as well as to biological factors related to twin birth. Siple and Akamatsu show that the emergence of language is not delayed for this set of fraternal twins, one hearing and one deaf, compared with singletons acquiring ASL. Thus the demands of receiving visual-gestural input do not further delay language; in fact the visual-gestural modality may compensate for potential reduced input to twins, reducing or eliminating delay in the emergence of language.

Whereas input is adequate for native language acquisition in the first two chapters of this volume, Mylander and Goldin-Meadow examine the other end of the continuum, the creation of language structure by children in an environment with little or no input. They report on part of a long-term investigation of the development of gestural language systems by deaf children of hearing parents who do not use signs with them. Previous studies have demonstrated syntactic regularity in the sign combinations of these children; this one asks whether there is internal structure within the signs and how far any internal structure compares with that used in morphological systems of native sign languages like ASL. Mylander and Goldin-Meadow demonstrate that a child with little or no input creates and uses a morphological system similar to, but less complex than, that of ASL, and that development follows a course similar to that of children acquiring sign languages. It appears, then, that the units of morphological analysis are universal within the visual-gestural language modality and that both the forms used and the development of the system result in large part from the biological makeup of the child, without need for an input model.

Few deaf children grow up in a native sign language environment, and few are in the situation described by Mylander and Goldin-Meadow. Instead, most deaf children experience great variability in language input from their environment. Most parents and teachers of deaf children are hearing. Growing numbers of these parents and teachers are using some form of signed English and simultaneous communication (signed and spoken English produced together). The signed language in these forms of communication is clearly derived; it is not a "natural" language. The grammar of the language is in principle the grammar of English, but the lexical items are heavily borrowed from, and developed from the vocabulary of, a native sign language like ASL. Studying signed forms of English and of simultaneous communication provides the opportunity to explore important theoretical questions concerning language acquisition and use when the input language itself is less than optimal. Simultaneous communication provides the unique opportunity to study the production and reception of language produced simultaneously in two modalities, vocal and manual. Is it possible to produce adequate language input in this situation, given the additional processing demands of preparing the message in two modalities and coordinating the two output modalities? Or does the human language system limit the "talker" to one modality? When two modalities are involved, at what point in production are they independent, and when is there interaction between them? In a signed English environment, do deaf children learn and use this derived language, or does it constitute inadequate input? If they do not use signed English, how do they communicate?

These issues are more than just theoretical, since for most deaf children in the United States this is the language used in school, and for a growing number of them this is their first and primary language input. Several of the remaining chapters address these issues.

Two chapters take the general position that signed English may be inadequate as language input because of a loss of speed or processing efficiency, and they examine deaf children's language output for deviations from the signed English input. Gee and Mounty, working within the nativization framework, investigate the signing of deaf children whose input was highly variable and included varieties of signed English as well as ASL and ASL-like language. Under the nativization hypothesis, variable, and thus inadequate, input will lead children to construct language forms based on internal, biologically determined norms. In the Gee and Mounty study, deaf children with hearing parents and variable input tend to favor ASL forms and to invent ASL-like forms similar to the forms used by deaf children of deaf parents. The selected forms, they argue, conform to internal, biologically given norms. This tendency toward nativization interacts with input and social environment, however, to produce clear differences in language style for the two types of children.

Supalla examines the signed productions of deaf children receiving strict signed English input at school and no signed input from their hearing parents. He finds that even though the teachers use correct, sequentially produced signed English the vast majority of the time, the children spontaneously invent forms that involve spatial principles like those found in native sign languages. Taken together, the essays by Mylander and Goldin-Meadow, Gee and Mounty, and Supalla provide strong support for underlying biologically given mechanisms that favor the use of spatially based forms in sign language production.

To receive sign language as input, the child must become aware that signing is occurring and must visually attend to it. Swisher examines the extent to which deaf children visually attend to their hearing mothers' signing during simultaneous communication. She finds that these children often miss some of what is being signed because their visual attention is not directed toward the signer during all or part of the interaction. Visual-manual communication requires different attention-getting mechanisms than aural-oral communication. Swisher argues that hearing mothers do not spontaneously use appropriate methods to get the child's attention before initiating signing. These mechanisms are used by deaf parents and are learned in native sign language environments, but they must be taught to hearing adults learning to sign. Thus the adequacy of signed English and simultaneous communication input for language acquisition can be assessed only when appropriate attention-getting mechanisms are also used.

Three chapters specifically address the adequacy of simultaneous communication and signed English input for language acquisition and processing. Fischer, Metz, Brown, and Caccamise question whether the simultaneous use of two production modalities in simultaneous communication affects the intelligibility of the two components of the message. These authors find that when deaf college students are very fluent in signed and spoken English, they are just as intelligible when using simultaneous communication as when signing or speaking alone. The intelligibility of a message need not be compromised when it is conveyed simultaneously in the same language, but in two modalities, if the senders are fluent in each language mode.

Wodlinger-Cohen examines in detail the completeness of the message and the degree of overlap for the two modalities of simultaneous communication for teachers and mothers and the children receiving their bimodal input. She finds that hearing adults can achieve a high degree of fluency in simultaneous communication, producing the same message, morpheme by morpheme, in each modality. Furthermore, this input appears to be adequate for acquisition by deaf children. The children in Wodlinger-Cohen's study also display good fluency in simultaneous communication, though departures, when they occur, are not random. Departures from signed English in the children's productions occur more often at some stages of development than others. These departures appear to reflect conversational strategies rather than inadequate language development.

Depending on the circumstances, there are situations in simultaneous communication when two messages are not equivalent. Maxwell, Bernstein, and Mear explore the relation between the two modes in simultaneous communication at both the morpheme and the message levels. When mismatches occur at the morpheme level, the message level is not compromised. They conclude that there is a synergy between the two modes at the message level so that the conversational message is complete.

Fingerspelling, using a sequence of hand configurations to spell words letter by letter, is used in both ASL and signed English. Thus deaf children have a third mode of communication to acquire. Padden examines the acquisition of fingerspelling by deaf children of deaf parents and asks whether fingerspelling is learned as a separate system, independent of signing and writing. Padden finds that deaf children, although they are aware of the different modes early in development, do not treat them as separate and independent but integrate them. Interactions occur in all directions; elements of signs are found in fingerspelling and writing, and elements of writing make their way into signing. Once again, the presence of more than one input mode produces an integrated system of language rather than competing systems compartmentalized by mode.

Mayberry and Waters investigate universality of the memory processes employed in language processing and the effects of language input experience on the use of those language processes. They examine how age and language background affect short-term memory for lists of signs and fingerspelled words. Input experience produces quantitative rather than qualitative effects on short-term retention. Short-term memory processes used for language appear to be universal, but quantitative differences may occur between modes. The rate of rehearsal may differ, for example, as a function of mode.

The last two chapters examine sign language acquisition by nondeaf, atypical children who have demonstrated language delay in the spoken modality. Abrahamsen, Lamb, Brown-Williams, and McCarthy study signed English acquisition by mentally retarded children exposed to bimodal, simultaneous input, and Bonvillian and Blackburn explore acquisition in similar settings by autistic children. The results of these studies demonstrate that adding signed input produces better acquisition in some retarded and autistic, language-delayed children but not in others. Determining the factors influencing language acquisition in these atypical situations provides important data for sorting out the interaction between input characteristics and what the child brings to the language acquisition task.

Each of the essays in this volume addresses issues in psycholinguistics, including universals of language acquisition and processing and the interrelation of input and characteristics of the learner in language development. Some of the chapters are purely theoretical, with potential applied implications. Others are applied, but at the same time they address important theoretical questions. We believe this book provides a unique opportunity for theoreticians, researchers, educators, and clinicians to have access to interrelated research that speaks directly or by implication to their fields of study.

Many of the chapters in this book use a gloss notation for signs that has evolved over the years. The following conventions are common for all the essays; differences are noted in the text of individual chapters:

SIGN	Signs are glossed in small capitals.
LOOK-FOR	One sign that requires a gloss of several English words has those words connected by hyphens. This may be a monomorphemic sign, such as LOOK-FOR, or a morphologically complex sign such as THREE-HUNDRED or PERSON-FALL.
J-O-K-E	Fingerspelled word

#EARLY

A gloss preceded by # denotes a finger-spelled loan sign (Battison 1978), a finger-spelled word that has become a sign through the addition of movement and smoothing out of medial letters.

EAT^MORNING

A caret between two signs indicates that they form a compound.

$\overline{\text{MOTHER, BOY NOT CRAZY-ABOUT}}$

A line above a sign or sign sequence indicates the scope of the facial expression or other nonmanual behavior named above the line.

This book could not have been completed without a great deal of support. First we thank the Alfred P. Sloan Foundation for the grant that permitted us to hold the conference this volume is partially based on and that helped in its preparation. We also thank the National Technical Institute for the Deaf at Rochester Institute of Technology, particularly the people in the Word Processing Center and the Media Center, who helped with typing the text into the computer and with preparing some of the illustrations. Thanks are also due to the referees who helped to hone these papers at three different stages of preparation. Finally, we thank our friends and families for their moral support.

1 Baby Face: A New Perspective
on Universals in Language
Acquisition

JUDY SNITZER REILLY, MARINA L. MCINTIRE, AND URSULA BELLUGI

1.1 Introduction

Twenty years ago Jean Piaget, Werner Leopold, or Roger Brown would not likely have foreseen that the careful observation of babies' brows would be fruitful in the elaboration of developmental psycholinguistic theory. Yet we propose to investigate the nature of the language learning mechanism through the unusual route of studying facial expressions in deaf toddlers.

As in spoken languages, facial expressions in American Sign Language (ASL) convey affective information; more interesting, however, very similar facial expressions also mark certain grammatical structures. Liddell (1980), Baker-Shenk (1983), and Coulter (1979), among others, have provided compelling evidence that specific facial expressions function as grammatical devices in the adult grammar. The apparent isomorphy of these grammatical behaviors with affective facial expressions provides a unique opportunity to elucidate the nature of the language learning process and the relation of language to another communicative system: affect. If these language behaviors are extensions of affective competence, we might expect to find evidence of direct transfer of facial expressions from the affective domain into the grammar. Or it may be that these linguistic facial expressions are acquired as whole chunks, much more like intonation in spoken language, to which they have often been compared. A third possibility, since these facial expressions function as part of the grammar, is that they will be acquired in a manner consonant with the acquisition of morphology in spoken languages, as described in Slobin (1986).

Data from the acquisition of signed languages allow us not only to verify the universality and resilience of the child's ability to acquire language, regardless of modality or articulators (hands, face, and so forth), but also to

We are grateful to the deaf parents and their children in our studies as well as to the staff of the California School for the Deaf in Fremont, California. We also wish to thank Geoffrey Coulter, David Perlmutter, and Laura Petitto for their comments on an earlier version of this chapter. This research was supported in part by a grant from the John D. and Catherine T. MacArthur Foundation Research Network on the Transition from Infancy to Early Childhood to Judy Reilly, and by National Institutes of Health grants HD13249, NS15175, and NS19096 to Ursula Bellugi at the Salk Institute for Biological Studies.

9

explore the limits and boundaries of this mechanism. By examining the acquisition of grammatical facial behaviors, we can learn more about the nature of the language learning mechanism and the processes underlying it.

In a review chapter, Newport and Meier (1986) discussed findings on ASL acquisition from a wide variety of research reports, including those of Bellugi and Klima (1982b), Launer (1982a), Loew (1982), Meier (1982), Petitto (1983b), and Supalla (1982), among others. These studies argue that the acquisition of ASL by deaf children of deaf parents is remarkably consonant with the acquisition of spoken language, with respect to strategies and stages. These data are devoted to the acquisition of manual behaviors, focusing primarily on phonology and morphology and the processes involved in their acquisition. A pertinent question they raise is, What are the processes underlying the acquisition of nonmanual behaviors in ASL? As they point out, the study of this issue (facial expression in deaf children) may allow a new perspective on the contrasts between linguistic and nonlinguistic development.

Our current work addresses this issue. In a recent study of the early stages of language acquisition in deaf children of deaf parents (Reilly, McIntire, and Bellugi 1990), we found that facial expression used for *affective* purposes serves as a transition into the facial morphology of the *grammar* of ASL. With this current study, then, we examine the acquisition of certain facial expressions by young deaf children of deaf parents, with two goals in mind: (1) to expand our general understanding of the language learning process underlying an unusual layer of structure specific to a visual language; and (2) to begin to identify those language learning principles that are universal across languages and language modalities and raise new issues with respect to some that may be modality specific.

First we review grammatical facial expression in ASL, including a brief discussion of three relevant grammatical structures in the adult model; second, we discuss data collection and transcription. We then present the acquisition data and finally our discussion and conclusions.

1.2 Facial Expression in American Sign Language

Recent reports have described a wide range of nonmanual behaviors and their syntactic functions: Liddell (1980) on relative clauses; Baker-Shenk (1983) on questions; Baker and Cokely (1980) on a general overview including lexical, adverbial, and syntactic nonmanual markers; Baker and Padden (1978) and Liddell (1986) on conditionals; and Coulter (1979) on topics and conditionals. We begin by describing some of the characteristics of nonmanual (facial) behaviors found in the adult grammar of ASL. (A brief description of relevant nonmanual behaviors and their notation techniques appears in appendix A.)

Briefly, grammatical nonmanual behaviors can be divided into three types. First are those facial markers that are obligatory with single lexical items, as in (1.1) and (1.2):

(1.1)   SEARCH (eye gaze)

                neg+th
(1.2) $\overline{\text{NOT-YET}}$ (tongue thrust)

Second are those nonmanual adverbials that combine freely with predicates, for example, 'mm' and 'th,' as in (1.3) and (1.4):

                           th
(1.3)   YESTERDAY, ME $\overline{\text{SLEEP}^{\wedge}\text{SUNRISE}}$
        'Yesterday, I overslept (unintentionally).'

                         mm
(1.4)   YESTERDAY, ME $\overline{\text{SLEEP}^{\wedge}\text{SUNRISE}}$
        'Yesterday, I slept in (with pleasure).'

Finally there are syntactic markers, for example, topics and conditionals, as in (1.5) and (1.6):

               t
(1.5) $\overline{\text{BOOK THAT}}$, ME FINISH READ
        'That book? I've read it.'

                 cond
(1.6) $\overline{\text{INSULT DENNIS}}$, HIT-YOU WILL ME
        'If you insult Dennis, I'll hit you!'

Notice that sentence (1.6), without the conditional nonmanual marking, can be read as two sequential assertions:

(1.6′)   INSULT DENNIS, HIT-YOU WILL ME
          'You insulted Dennis and I'm gonna hit you!'

Hence it is solely the nonmanual behaviors that signal that (1.6) is a conditional sentence.

1.2.1 Affective and Grammatical Facial Expression

It has been suggested that grammatical facial behaviors in ASL share some characteristics with intonation in spoken languages. Like facial expression, intonation plays a variety of grammatical and paralinguistic roles, and though there are some kindred functions, the two are not identical. Like intonation, facial behaviors play both affective and linguistic roles.

Liddell (1980) and Baker-Shenk (1983) have pointed out that the scope of linguistic facial behaviors is highly constrained and rule governed; in contrast, affective scope tends to be inconsistent and highly variable (Baker-Shenk 1983). That is, grammatical facial behaviors have a very clear and specific onset and offset pattern, and their coordination with manual signs is crucial in indicating the scope of such linguistic behaviors, as in (1.7) below:

(1.7)　LAST-YEAR MY C-P-A TAX FIGURE-OUT
　　　　'Last year my CPA did my taxes haphazardly (and I had to pay a fine).'

Affective facial actions, by contrast, are inconsistent in their use and inconsistent in their onset and offset patterns and in their apex shapes. Example (1.8) is one possible pattern for affective nonmanual behaviors:

(1.8)　TRUE++ ME EXCITE SEE-you

Moreover, in hearing children, sentence intonation contours are used communicatively before the one-word stage (Weir 1962; Dore 1975) and appear to be acquired as whole prosodic envelopes or matrices (Bruner 1975). In contrast, nonmanual markers for topics and wh- questions do not appear in our data until the children reach the age of 3 years (Reilly, McIntire, and Bellugi, 1990); full mastery of timing and scope take even longer. Further, conditional nonmanual marking still poses problems at age 7, $3\frac{1}{2}$ years after the first conditionals appear, as we will discuss below.

1.2.2 Topics, Conditionals, and Questions in Adults

A promising area for examining the acquisition of nonmanual behaviors is the mapping of semantic and syntactic functions onto the facial marker raised eyebrows (Action Unit [AU] 1+2). Our choice of this particular form is motivated by its multifunctionality: affectively, it is a critical marker of surprise (Ekman 1972); communicatively and paralinguistically, it signals a question or request (Ekman 1979). The same form serves several grammatical functions: it is a major component of the obligatory markers for yes/no questions, topics, and conditionals.

To illustrate, first of all, it is a nonmanual morphological marker for yes/no questions, for example, (1.9):

(1.9)　YOU LIKE CHOCOLATE YOU
　　　　'Do you like chocolate?'

Second, it marks topics, as in example (1.10):

$$\overline{\qquad}^{\,t} \qquad \overline{\qquad}^{\,neg+th}$$
(1.10)   LIBRARY, ME GO-TO NOT-YET
         'Oh, the library—I haven't gone yet.'

Finally, it constitutes part of the antecedent of a predictive conditional sentence, as in (1.11):

$$\overline{\qquad}^{\,cond}$$
(1.11)   EAT BUG SICK WILL YOU
         'If you eat bugs, you'll get sick.'

Each of these structures is signaled by, among other things, raised brows (AU 1+2) (see app. B for a listing and description of all the action units discussed in this chapter). These structures are further distinguished by the scope of the nonmanual signal, the plane of the face, and whether the upper eyelids are retracted (AU 5). Conditionals may additionally be marked with a manual sign, for example, #IF, JUDGE, or SUPPOSE. (See Baker and Padden 1978; Liddell 1986; and McIntire, Reilly, and Bellugi 1987 for further discussion of adult conditional forms.) In the following section we focus on three of the various linguistic contexts of AU 1+2 (topics, conditionals, and yes/no questions) and review their acquisition. We leave the domains of affective and communicative use for another time and place.

1.3 Data Collection and Transcription

Our subjects are ten deaf children ranging in age from 1;0 to 7;5. All the children are learning ASL as a first language and have deaf parents and deaf siblings. The data are all interactive, involving deaf caregivers, deaf siblings, and deaf researchers; they are part of the ongoing sign language acquisition studies at the Salk Institute. The data from these same children have formed the basis for analyses of acquisition of different formal devices in ASL (verb agreement, classifier morphology, syntax), enabling comparison across domains.

To assess accurately the grammatical competence of our subjects, we have collected both experimental and naturalistic, quasi-longitudinal data. We believe these two types of data complement and balance one another. That is, experimental tasks allow us to elicit structures that seldom occur in conversation, for example, conditionals.

We have transcribed twenty-eight naturalistic videotapes (thirty to sixty minutes in length) in five deaf children, ages 1;0 to 4;0, using Ekman and Friesen's Facial Action Coding System (see below and app. B). An imitation task was administered to five additional deaf children, ages 3;5 to 7;5.

Table 1.1   Some of the Stimulus Sentences in the Imitation Task

<pre>
            ____________ topic
ICE-CREAM,   CHOCOLATE ME LOVE
            ________ cond
ME BIRD,   ME FLY
            ___________________________ wh-q
WHO BUILD HOUSE WHO
          ___ topic
PIG,   SCARED
            ________ cond
#IF RAIN,   UMBRELLA
</pre>

Table 1.1 presents a sample of the sentences the children were asked to copy. In addition to the imitation task, children performed several conditional elicitation tasks adapted from English (Reilly 1982). In this chapter, we report only on the imitation results.

Encouraged by the research of Charlotte Baker-Shenk, we have used Ekman and Friesen's (1978) Facial Action Coding System (FACS), a comprehensive, anatomically based system for coding facial expressions. FACS uses forty-six numbered "action units" to transcribe the firing of individual muscles of the face. We focused our transcription on the children's facial behaviors, both affective and grammatical, especially in contexts where we would expect linguistic facial markers—for example, topics, conditionals, questions, negative structures, and those individual lexical items in ASL that require specific co-occurring eye gaze or nonmanual behaviors. We noted the presence of any facial gesture as well as its scope and timing with respect to the manually signed utterance. (See app. B for a complete list and description of action units discussed here.) Only repeated slow-motion viewing of videotapes and frame-by-frame microanalysis, using Ekman and Friesen's Facial Action Coding System, allows coding of these subtle distinctions.

1.4 Acquisition of Topics, Conditionals, and Questions in ASL

Let us now look at the actual acquisition sequence for topics and conditionals, and the mapping of AU 1+2 onto the appropriate grammatical structures. With respect to early topics, it is difficult to assess whether a child has any notion of the concept "topic" before it is marked nonmanually. At the early stages, before children begin to develop a device for marking topic with AU 1+2, if the subject of the child's sentence is also (intended as) a topic, topicalized sentences are indistinguishable from normal declaratives. Thus the sequence of signs in (1.12)—with no nonmanual signal—could be interpreted only one way:

(1.12)   MOTHER EAT BANANA
          'Mommy (is) eat(ing) a/the banana.'

However, the child could have intended: 'Oh, Mom?—she('s) eat(ing) bananas.' It is only when an object noun phrase is preposed, as in (1.13), that we might infer the child is beginning to develop a notion called "topic."

(1.13)   BANANA MOTHER EAT
         'Banana, Mommy (is) eat(ing) it.'

Even so, this preposing of an object noun phrase is only suggestive and carries with it no inescapable evidence of the child's compentence.[1] In sum, the most convincing evidence that children control the structure "topic" comes from their first explicitly marked productions. These first topics appear in our data at age 3;0 and generally consist of single signs, as in (1.14) and (1.15):

(1.14)   Kate (3;0):

         AU 1+2+5
          WOLF BLOW BLOW COLLAPSE
         'That wolf, he blew and blew (until the house) fell down.'

(1.15)   Corinne (3;4):

                 AU 1+2+5
         STRAW-HOUSE WOLF BLOW
         'The straw house, the wolf blew (on it).'

Let us now turn to conditionals. We are assuming that before children explicitly mark a grammatical structure, they control some of the underlying semantic notions marked by that structure. For example, before children produce morphologically marked conditionals, we see evidence that they "control," at some level, some of the basic notions intrinsic to conditionals. For example, in our data there are examples of juxtaposed causally related simple propositions from children at about age 2;6, as in (1.16):

(1.16)   Kate (2;8):

                 AU 1+2
         BITE YOU SPANK ME
         '(If) I bite you, (will you) spank me?'

This is comparable to what we find in children learning spoken languages (Reilly 1982, 1986; Bowerman 1986). From these juxtaposed propositions,

1. Obviously this is a complex area that deserves further attention. The situation is complicated by the use of directional verbs, the presence or absence of the referents, definiteness and indefiniteness, and so on.

we can infer that the child, at some level, understands the following: temporal sequencing of two events, their potential causal relationship, and some notion of possibility (the child did not in fact bite her mother).

The next step in the development of conditionals is the appearance of the first morphological marker. Gabriel, age 3;3, was participating in the imitation task. The experimenter signed:

(1.17)   (a) Experimenter:

                                        cond.
        ‾‾‾
        SUPPOSE MILK SPILL, MOTHER ANGRY
        'If the milk gets spilled, Mom'll get angry.'

      (b) Gabriel (3;3) responded:

                          AU 45
        MOTHER ANGRY/   MOTHER ANGRY #IF MILK SPILL,
        MOTHER ANGRY

He virtually ignored the facial morphology, except for the clausal break (AU 45 is a blink), and substituted one manual conditional marker (#IF) for another (SUPPOSE). By virtue of his sign substitution, we infer that he understood the conditional. We know that Gabriel already uses facial expression to mark topics and, of course, to indicate affective states. What puzzled us, then, was his choice of a manual marker (#IF) over the nonmanual morphology.

Further evidence of this strategy, in which the use of manual markers precedes the use of nonmanual markers, comes from the naturalistic data. Jane, at age 3;11 in (1.18), introduces the antecedent of a conditional with a manual sign, IF/JUDGE. There is some evidence of a head tilt, but its scope is limited to IF, and there is no AU 1+2. For an adult, both the head tilt and the raised brows (AU 1+2) co-occur with the entire antecedent clause. (In this spontaneously produced utterance, Jane is talking about the necessary preparations for painting.)

(1.18)   Jane (3;11):

        AU 55 (head tilt)
        ‾‾‾‾‾‾‾‾‾‾‾‾‾‾‾
               IF INDEX-lf SOMETHING INDEX-rt PAPER-ON-WALL,

         neg   neg
        ‾‾‾‾‾‾‾‾‾   ‾‾‾‾‾‾‾‾‾
        AU 10+15   AU 4
        CAN'T PAINT WOW CAN'T
        'If it's there on the wall over there, or paper on the wall over
        there, you can't paint on it at all.'

Similar responses occur in the imitation task. At age 3;7, Trina imitated the manual sign in conditional stimuli but ignored the facial signals, as in (1.19):

(1.19)   Experimenter:

<u>   AU 1+2+55 AU 45</u>
SUPPOSE RAIN, UMBRELLA
'If it rains, (you need an) umbrella.'

Trina (3;7):

         AU 45
SUPPOSE RAIN   UMBRELLA

Once again, the child signals the clause break with AU 45, a blink, but fails to use other facial morphology with the antecedent. In addition, Trina responded correctly only to the manually marked conditional stimuli in this task. Significantly, when faced with conditional stimuli without manual markers, she interpreted them not as conditionals, but as two simple propositions, as in (1.20):

(1.20)   Experimenter:

<u>   </u> AU 1+2+55 AU 45
MILK SPILL   MOTHER ANGRY
'If the milk spills, Mother'll be mad.'

Trina:

     <u>AU 4+9</u>
MAMA ANGRY   MILK SPILL
'Mama's mad; [because?] the milk spilled.'

(AU 4+9 are furrowed brows and wrinkled nose, affective facial behaviors signaling anger.) Trina's responses in (1.19) and (1.20) suggest that she does not produce conditional nonmanual morphology. Indeed, it appears that she does not yet even perceive the experimenter's facial signals to be marking a conditional. In sum, in both naturalistic and imitation situations, the children first interpret and produce conditionals primarily, even exclusively, with manual markers, even though they already use the nonmanual form (AU 1+2) in other affective and grammatical contexts.

The conditional data are intriguing. Naturally occurring conditionals, however, are rare in all the cross-linguistic data for both children and adults. We were puzzled by the dichotomy and determined to investigate another area of syntax to help resolve the issue. A similar, though not identical, situation occurring with questions offers an opportunity to assess the generality of this acquisition profile.

As Baker-Shenk (1983) has documented in her microanalytic study, both yes/no and wh- questions are marked with facial morphology. Yes/no questions are marked with raised brows (AU 1+2) and a slightly forward head (AU 57) (see also Liddell 1980); wh- questions are marked with furrowed brows (AU 4). In addition, wh- questions also include a wh- word manual sign, such as HOW, WHAT, or WHY. Thus yes/no questions are similar to topics and wh- questions are like conditionals. In the former case (yes/no questions and topics), the only grammatical marker is a nonmanual signal. For wh- questions, as with conditionals, the language provides a set of potentially redundant markers. The acquisition of wh- and yes/no questions provides another context in which to investigate and possibly confirm the apparent initial preference for manual over nonmanual markers in those instances where the language appears to offer redundant morphology. An advantage of questions is that, unlike conditionals, they appear both early and frequently in the naturalistic data.

We have found that the children begin to signal yes/no questions with raised brows at about age 1;3 and that caregivers respond to them as such. Children begin to produce wh- questions (with wh- word signs) at about age 1;6, but these are virtually unmarked on the face until the children are about age 3;6. Except at the earliest stage, where there is evidence of a gestalt type of strategy, wh- questions are consistently produced with "blank faces" from age 1;8 to about age 3;6, as in (1.21) and (1.22):

(1.21)   Corinne (1;6):
         WHERE DOLL
         'Where's (my) dolly?'

(1.22)   Corinne (2;3):
         WOLF WHERE
         'Where's the wolf?'

Specifically, between the ages of 1;6 and 3;0 for one child and 1;6 and 3;6 for two others, we have forty-five self-generated instances of wh- questions. In forty-three of these utterances the children produce wh- questions using only manual markers (wh- word signs). This is consonant with the conditional acquisition sequence: when children have the option, lexical manual markers take developmental priority over bound facial morphology. Knowing the children's fluency with facial expression, we saw the need for further explanation of these findings. We looked to the literature from spoken language acquisition for insight into this apparent paradox: Why do these children fail to use formal devices (linguistic facial expressions), which appear to be already within their competence, in favor of manual signs in the early stages of language acquisition?

1.5 Discussion

One current model of language acquisition is that proposed by Slobin (1986). Using cross-linguistic language acquisition data, Slobin (1973) first compiled an inventory of strategies, or operating principles, that children use to approach the language learning task. He has further discussed how these operating principles accommodate language-particular features. In his recent work he has expanded and integrated these operating principles to formulate a description of the language making capacity that will, for any given child, in any language learning environment, construct an early basic child grammar. Slobin's model is rich and detailed, accounting for data from many language families. Because of its broad perspective, we thought it might provide an explanation for our puzzling data.

One of Slobin's operating principles is particularly relevant and presents a specific hypothesis for how multifunctional structures are acquired—the principle of unifunctionality. Plurifunctionality occurs in many spoken languages (cf. Karmiloff-Smith 1979; Slobin 1986) and presents similar problems to children of various language communities. Slobin's operating principle, unifunctionality, states that if a single form signals two similar but distinct meanings, the child will initially seek distinctive means to mark the two notions. This appears to be precisely the strategy the children in our study followed in acquiring topics and conditionals.

As we have discussed, the form AU 1+2 (raised brows) plays a major role in marking both topics and conditionals in ASL. Moreover, both of these structures, topics and conditionals, can be viewed as having similar focusing functions. Citing data from Hua, a Papuan language, Haiman (1978) argues compellingly that conditionals are topics, and Coulter (1979) presents data from American Sign Language noting that the markers for topics and conditionals share the feature raised brows. Coulter further proposes that this is a morphemic unit representing a backgrounding function.

Topics and conditionals in ASL represent similar focusing functions, and AU 1+2 (raised brows) plays a significant role in their nonmanual morphology. Conditionals can also include a manual conditional sign. When children learning ASL begin to produce topics, the sole morphological marker is nonmanual. When they begin to produce conditionals, however, they have access to several signaling devices: they can use facial morphology (as for topics and yes/no questions) or one of the manual signs that introduce conditionals.

As we indicated above, young deaf children learning ASL's complex facial morphology along with manual signs and their modifications first mark topics with the facial marker AU 1+2, but they mark conditionals first with a manual sign. That is, children initially appear to seek distinctive means to mark the two structures, even when the same form plays a significant role in their sig-naling. This, then, is one way of accounting for our findings. Deaf children learning ASL morphology follow Slobin's operating principle of unifunc-tionality, even when it extends across different layers of structure (manual and facial signals).

These findings are consonant with other acquisition studies focusing on ASL's complex inflectional and derivational system, as well as its spatialized syntax (see Newport and Meier 1986 for a review of these studies). Taken together, the accumulated studies suggest that deaf children use strategies in acquiring ASL that are strikingly similar to those found in the acquisition of spoken languages, despite the radical differences between signed and spoken language. In addition, our study demonstrates the remarkable breadth of the language learning mechanism in its ability to process these unusual behaviors as grammatical units.

In spite of the explanation offered by Slobin's model, we are still left with a puzzle: Why is there such a strong tendency to prefer the manual marking over the facial marking in the early stages of acquiring a structure? Why does the acquisition of grammatical facial morphology itself appear to pose such a hurdle for young deaf children as part of a linguistic system: We suggest some clues here, but we are still pursuing answers to this question.

Research on affect (Ekman 1972; Izard 1971) and on affective development (Campos et al. 1983) provides compelling evidence that facial expressions for emotion are universal and that all infants use their faces consistently to convey and to interpret affective information by the age of 1 year, before any of the grammar of language is acquired. Given that facial expression plays such an important communicative role for babies (Stern 1977), and notwithstanding Slobin's principles, we propose the following points in relation to the interest-ing developmental preference for manual signals over facial expression for grammatical purposes that we find in young children.

It is clear that faces are extremely salient for babies. Initially, the primary role for facial expression is affective, not linguistic; the child is predisposed to consider facial expression as affective. In fact, as we have discussed previ-ously (Reilly, McIntire, and Bellugi 1990), affective knowledge of facial ex-pression initially serves as a transition into the facial morphology of ASL. Thus, in the early stages of acquisition, when children are "given a choice," they choose manual over facial behaviors to convey linguistic information. In sum, it appears that their *first* hypothesis may be that hands are for language and faces are for affect.

In addition to an infant's apparent predisposition to interpret facial expres-sion as affective rather than linguistic, physiology and the environment may conspire and converge to confirm in at least four ways the child's early hy-pothesis that hands are the primary linguistic articulators. First, hands are bigger than eyebrows; manual movement is larger and capable of many more contrasts than eyebrow movement. Thus an interlocutor's hands may be linguistically more salient than eyebrow movements. Second, children can see their own hands and thus have visual as well as kinesthetic feedback. The feedback for facial expression is solely kinesthetic. Third, it may be difficult to integrate two co-occurring channels.

Fourth, and perhaps most interesting, deaf mothers signing to their toddlers under the age of 2 frequently omit obligatory grammatical facial marking. For example, ASL motherese consistently omits the grammatical facial morphology for wh- questions when signing to toddlers (Reilly and Bellugi 1988). (Launer 1982a found similar lack of morphology to distinguish noun-verb pairs in ASL motherese to toddlers under 2 years of age.) The mother's primary goal is to communicate with her child. That she chooses manual signals over facial expression to convey wh- questions suggests that she considers hands the primary articulators.

We propose, then, that young deaf children exposed to the multilayered system of ASL, a language that uses hands, face, and body for marking formal linguistic distinctions, begin by hypothesizing that the hands are the primary articulators for language and only later begin to analyze and use the distinctive facial expressions that constitute linguistic markers of grammatical constructs.

1.6 Summary

What can we infer from these acquisition data? First, all these instances provide strong support for the view that children learning signed languages use the same strategies and principles as children learning spoken languages, despite the major differences between the two types of language. What is perhaps most striking is that the particular facet of language we have focused on—grammatical facial expression—is unique to signed languages. It is clearly a modality-specific component of language. Yet the strategies involved in acquiring facial morphology are similar to those found across the world's spoken languages.

This raises a second point: the impressive resilience of the language learning mechanism, irrespective of the modality in which language is conveyed or the available articulators. The language learning mechanism is incredibly flexible in its ability to accept and process as linguistic these unusual surface behaviors. In contrast, we have seen a rigidity in the inability of this acquisition mechanism to take advantage of apparently relevant formal and semantically similar linguistic information (topics).

In this chapter we have seen one way Slobin's operating principles apply, regardless of the modality of the language. Furthermore, we have extended earlier discussions of the acquisition of ASL to an added layer of structure in the language: the acquisition of grammaticized facial expressions. From this investigation of the acquisition of a signed language in light of Slobin's operating principles, we suggest that in addition to universal principles and the language-particular features a child must accommodate, the modality in which the language is conveyed plays a significant role in language learning. Modality not only influences how universal principles are applied, it may also serve as a source of independent operating principles once the grammar is under way. One candidate we would propose for such a modality-specific operating principle is: Pay attention to faces for linguistically significant information.

As Newport and Meier (1986) suggest, a particular issue is raised with respect to the acquisition of grammaticized facial expression in ASL. Unlike most formal devices in spoken language, grammaticized facial expressions derive from a clearly nonlinguistic system (that is, nonlinguistic facial expressions). These linguistic facial expressions have their basis in the facial expressions used for affect (see Reilly, McIntire, and Bellugi 1990). In parallel studies, we are comparing the acquisition of linguistic facial expressions with the acquisition of affective facial expressions. These studies of the acquisition of facial behaviors in American Sign Language address in a new way some very fundamental questions about the contrasts between linguistic and nonlinguistic development in children.

In general, despite radical differences in language modality, we find that deaf and hearing children show a dramatically similar course of development even in the unique domain presented here. What is impressive from these studies is the remarkable resilience of the mechanisms children bring to bear on language acquisition, whether the input is in streams of linearly ordered segments of sound or in the complex simultaneously organized movements of the hands and arms—with an intriguing added layer of complexity of structure in linguistic facial signals.

Appendix A: Description and Meaning of Cited Nonmanual Grammatical Signals

Adverbial Markers

'th': carelessly, inexpertly (tongue protrudes slightly, jaw slightly open: AU 19+26)

'mm': regularly, normally, comfortably (lips closed and everted, chin boss raised: AU 17)

Syntactic Markers

'neg': negation (head shake; brows may be lowered and furrowed; frown and nose wrinkle optional: AU 4+9+51, 52) 'q': yes/no question (brows raised; eyes widened; head slightly forward; AU 1+2+5+57)

'wh-q': wh- question (brows furrowed; head slightly forward: AU 4+57)

't': topicalized noun phrase (brows raised; head slightly tilted: AU 1+2+55 or 56)

'rc': relative clauses (brows raised; head slightly back; upper lip raised: AU 1+2+10+58)

'cond': antecedent of a conditional sentence—the IF clause (brows raised; head slightly tilted followed by a blink at the clause juncture: AU 1+2+55 or 56 . . . AU 45)

Appendix B: Action Units Referred to in Text

Taken from FACS: Ekman and Friesen (1978).

AU 1	Inner brow raise
AU 2	Outer brow raise
AU 4	Brow lower
AU 5	Upper lid raise
AU 9	Nose wrinkle
AU 10	Upper lip raise
AU 12	Lip corner pull
AU 15	Lip corner depress
AU 45	Blink
AU 51	(Head) turn left
AU 52	(Head) turn right
AU 53	Head up
AU 54	Head down
AU 55	Head tilt left
AU 56	Head tilt right
AU 57	Head forward
AU 58	Head back

2 Emergence of American Sign Language in a Set of Fraternal Twins

PATRICIA SIPLE AND C. TANE AKAMATSU

2.1 Introduction

Studies of twins often provide a unique way to address questions concerning the relative contributions of biological factors and socioenvironmental factors in development. Initially, beginning with the work of Galton, these studies focused on comparisons within twin pairs to determine the contribution of heredity to cognitive and personality characteristics. More recently, twins have been compared with singletons to study the interaction of biological and social contributions more generally (Mittler 1971). Here we focus on a rare twin situation to understand more fully the factors governing language acquisition. We report the emergence of American Sign Language (ASL) acquisition in a set of twins, one hearing and one deaf, who are the firstborn children of deaf parents whose primary language in the home is ASL.

It is generally reported in the literature for spoken language acquisition that twins are delayed in language development. We will review this literature on twin language effects for spoken languages and describe the theories proposed to account for these effects. We will then consider the twin sign language situation, present initial data from our case study, and compare these data with those reported for spoken languages. The comparison will provide evidence regarding the generality of twin language acquisition effects across modality and thus contribute to sorting out theories of twin language effects and the origins of language acquisition.

2.2 Twin Language Acquisition

2.2.1 Twins versus Singletons

Mittler (1971), after reviewing several studies of intellectual ability in twins, concluded that twins score approximately five points lower than singletons on standardized tests. This conclusion is confirmed by more recent

The work reported here was supported by a grant-in-aid from Wayne State University to Patricia Siple. We deeply appreciate the cooperation of the family described here; they made the project a rewarding one for each of us.

25

studies. Fischbein (1978), in a large Swedish study, Zazzo (1978), administering the Stanford-Binet to French children, and Wilson (1975, 1977), reporting WPPSI and WISC results from the Louisville twin study, report lower average scores for twins than for matched controls or siblings. Most of these authors suggest these differences are due to the generally accepted fact that twins are delayed in language development. Indeed, when verbal tests are compared with nonverbal or performance tests (Watts and Lytton 1981; Wilson 1975, 1977; Zazzo 1978), deficits occur only for the verbal tests. These results appear to be generally the same for identical, same-sex fraternal, and opposite-sex fraternal twins (Fischbein 1981; Wilson 1981).

Several studies have focused more specifically on twin language; they can be divided into two general types. In one type, standardized tests of verbal ability have been administered to large samples of twins and singletons. These provide a general picture of the deficit. Other researchers have carried out case studies or studied smaller samples to describe twin performance for specific aspects of language acquisition.

2.2.2 Standardized Test Comparisons

When twins are compared with singletons on standardized tests of intellectual or verbal ability, the results indicate that twins are typically delayed in general language development compared with matched singletons. Koch (1966) administered Thurstone's Primary Mental Abilities Test to ninety pairs of 5- to 7-year-old twins and matched singletons. Deficits were found for all twin groups only on the verbal subtest, a test of vocabulary and general information. In fact, twins' performance on the perceptual subtest tended to be better than that of singletons. Interviews with mothers and teachers supported these findings. Mittler (1970, 1971) administered the Illinois Test of Psycholinguistic Abilities (ITPA) to two hundred sets of 4-year-old twins and one hundred matched singletons. The ITPA consists of nine subtests measuring different language abilities. Compared with singletons, twins were found to be delayed approximately six months on all subtests, with no particular pattern of deficit. Similar results were found for performance on the Peabody Picture Vocabulary Test, but no differences were found on two nonverbal tests. Whereas Koch found some sex and twin-type differences, Mittler found none; all twin groups showed the same deficit.

2.2.3 Specific Language Abilities

Delays and deficits have been reported for many aspects of language acquisition. These include the emergence and rate of growth of language use, speech characteristics, semantic and syntactic development, and conversational and interactional patterns.

On average, the emergence of language is delayed for twins. Day (1932), in her pioneering study of twins, reported that the age of first words is later for twins than for singletons. Mothers reported a marked delay of first word use in 29 percent of the twins studied by Koch (1966). In Mittler's (1970) study, first words emerged later than 18 months of age for over 30 percent of the twins studied. This marked delay persists through the first five years. Mean utterance length is shorter for twins than for singletons from 2 to 5 years of age, and the absolute difference increases with age (Day 1932). In Day's study, utterance length for 48-month-old twins was equivalent to that for 30-month-old singletons. This difference decreases from 6 to 10 years of age, but twins from lower socioeconomic levels continue to show a significant deficit compared with matched singletons (Davis 1937).

Articulation is often poorer in twins. Day (1932) reported more incomprehensible responses in twins than in singletons. Mothers of twins rated their children's speech as less mature than did mothers of singletons (Lytton 1980). About half of the twins in Koch's (1966) study were judged to have poor articulation, and mothers reported an unusual persistence of baby talk in 40 percent of the twins. Davis (1937) found that rated articulation was markedly inferior for $5\frac{1}{2}$-year-old twins, with the twin-singleton differences becoming much smaller after 6 years of age. When a standardized test of articulation was administered to twins aged 3 to 8 (Matheny and Bruggemann 1972), twins scored below the norms at all ages.

Vocabulary growth also appears to be slower in twins, and twins may acquire words in different form classes differently from singletons. Day (1932) and Tomasello, Mannle, and Kruger (1986) found in their language samples that twins used fewer words overall and fewer different words than singletons. According to Day, twins use a smaller number of verbs, adjectives, pronouns, conjunctions, and prepositions (particularly at 2 to 3 years of age), about the same number of nouns (except possibly at 2 years), and more adverbs and interjections. Older twins continue to use fewer different words than singletons (Davis 1937). Davis also reported that twins used slightly fewer personal pronouns and showed a tendency to use relatively fewer first-person pronouns and more possessive forms. More recent studies, however, indicate that twins are not delayed in the correct use of personal pronouns (Savic 1980; Waterman and Shatz 1982), but they often develop a name for the twin pair together and treat the referent as a singular item both in verb agreement and in pronoun use (Malmstrom and Silva 1986; Waterman and Shatz 1982).

Twins may show some delay in aspects of syntax acquisition and sentence construction, though there is disagreement in this area. Both Day (1932) and Koch (1966) reported that young twins make a greater number of morphological and syntactic errors than singletons. In Day's study, twins' acquisition of individual forms from 2 to 5 years of age showed the same pattern as that of singletons, but use of the forms either began later (use of compound, complex, and elaborated sentences) or peaked slightly later (use of single sentences and omission of the verb, subject, or both). No differences in any of these categories were found for older twins (Davis 1937), however, nor were differences found on a standardized test of syntactic ability (Munsinger and Douglass 1976). Even for younger twins (32 to 33 months), Conway, Lytton, and Pysh (1980) found no differences between twins and singletons in the complexity of their subject noun, predicate noun, or verb phrases. Twins did, however, show a smaller percentage of use of more complete (subject + verb) sentences, which may be related to overall utterance length.

Twins have been reported to use secret language, especially when the two are alone, and extreme use of a secret language (autonomous language or cryptophasia) has been associated with severe language disturbance (Luria and Yudovich 1971; Wallace 1986). Twins often do use autonomous language to some extent; Mittler (1970) reports its use in 47 percent of the twin pairs in his study, and Savic (1980) suggests that it occurs in approximately 40 percent of twins. Reevaluating the data of Luria and Yudovich and considering her own, Savic contends that autonomous language is no more than baby talk that the twins use with each other.

Communication and interaction patterns have indeed become the focus of most recent twin studies. Differences might well be expected here, since twins are nearly always together when interactions occur, whereas singletons' inter- actions occur in more varied environments. In communication situations with parents, twins talk less overall, respond less to parental speech, initiate fewer interactions with parents, engage in fewer conversations, and use fewer turns in those conversations than do singletons (Conway, Lytton, and Pysh 1980; Lytton 1980; Lytton, Conway, and Sauve 1977; Tomasello, Mannle, and Kruger 1986). Twins maintain interactions with their twin partners as early as 27 months, as do nontwin dyads (Billman and Shatz 1984; Keenan 1974; Keenan and Klein 1975). Twins' interactions differ from those of nontwins, however. Twins, for example, depend more on repetition to keep interactions alive (Billman and Shatz 1984; Keenan 1977) and sometimes say the same thing together or complete each other's utterances (Savic 1979, 1980; Savic and Jocic 1975).

In sum, language acquisition is generally delayed in twins compared with matched singletons. The differences appear to be primarily in frequency, rate, and length factors. Qualitative differences appear in some areas. Twins appear to differ in some aspects of conceptual development and in their early patterns of interaction.

2.2.4 Theories of Twin-Singleton Differences

Two general classes of theories have been proposed to account for twin lan- guage effects—biological and environmental. Prenatal and perinatal complications are known to be greater for twins (MacGillivray, Nylander, and Corney 1975), and these complications are related to language delay for singletons (Siegel 1982). Yet prematurity, low birthweight, and other such factors seem to account for less language variance in twins than in singletons (Mittler 1970) and simply cannot explain many findings (Conway, Lytton, and Pysh 1980; Koch 1966; Tomasello, Mannle, and Kruger 1986). Environmental factors clearly play a role in twin-singleton differences.

Because of the unique nature of the twin environment, two types of factors—twin-twin and adult-twin—must be addressed. Several investigators have attributed twin language delay to the twin-twin relationship (e.g., Day 1932; Luria and Yudovich 1971; Zazzo 1978), arguing that because twins have a close relationship, they have less need to communicate, especially with the adults in their environment. This isolation from a parental language model and early dependence on each other's imperfect language model are thought to delay normal language acquisition. One would expect similar results with closely spaced siblings (Zajonc and Markus 1975), with multiple births providing the extreme case.

A second possibility exists, however—that twin language effects are due to changes in the adult-child relationship as a function of the twin environment (Bornstein and Ruddy 1984; Conway, Lytton, and Pysh 1980; Lytton 1980; Lytton, Conway, and Sauve 1977; Tomasello, Mannle, and Kruger, 1986). Because there are nearly always two children present and the activities involved in caring for twins are much greater than for singletons, parents may spend less time communicating with twins, or they may change the nature of the interactions they have with them. Whereas the other explanations of twin effects predict primarily quantitative effects (with the exception of twin-twin interactions themselves), this alternative could lead to both quantitative and qualitative twin-singleton language differences.

Each of these theoretical positions regarding twin language effects has some support in the literature. Biological factors account for some portion of the variance in twin-singleton differences (Conway, Lytton, and Pysh 1980; Koch 1966; Mittler 1970, 1971; Tomasello, Mannle, and Kruger 1986). The use of private language by twins suggests the importance of twin-twin factors (Luria and Yudovich 1971; Zazzo 1978), and twin-twin conversation may indeed be unique (Billman and Shatz 1984; Keenan 1974, 1977; Malmstrom and Silva 1986; Savic 1979, 1980; Savic and Jocic 1975; Waterman and Shatz 1982). Finally, parental input factors also account for a portion of the variance in twin-singleton differences (Bornstein and Ruddy 1984; Conway, Lytton, and Pysh 1980; Tomasello, Mannle, and Kruger 1986). Parents of twins speak less to their children overall, initiate fewer conversations with them, use shorter, less complex sentences with them, and react less to twins' utterances (Bornstein and Ruddy 1984; Conway, Lytton, and Pysh 1980; Lytton 1980;

Tomasello, Mannle, and Kruger 1986). In fact, parental input factors appear to account for more of the variance in twin-singleton differences than biological factors (Conway, Lytton, and Pysh 1980) or underlying cognitive factors (Bornstein and Ruddy 1984).

2.3 Twin Sign Language Acquisition: A Case Study

The present study is an initial report of a longitudinal, observational study of the language acquisition of a set of twins acquiring American Sign Language from their deaf parents. Of primary concern is whether twin language effects, established for the acquisition of spoken languages, generalize across modality. With just one set of twins, we can only begin to approach this question. The relative rarity of the situation, however, and our general lack of knowledge in this area make an extensive case study the method of choice.

2.3.1 Sign Language and Twin Language Effects

The degree to which twin language effects are expected to generalize across language modality depends on the specific factors producing the effects. Biological factors would be expected to show similar effects, independent of language mode, though twin pairs with deaf members might be expected to exhibit a greater prevalence of prenatal and perinatal at-risk conditions. Prematurity and Rh incompatibility are greater among children born deaf and are among the leading causes of deafness. Deafness in children born to deaf parents is likely to be due to genetic factors, however, and these children are less likely to have other at-risk conditions than children whose deafness is due to nongenetic causes (Mindel and Vernon 1971). Deaf children, on average, have performance IQ scores equivalent to those of hearing children (Vernon 1967), and both deaf and hearing children acquire ASL in much the same way that hearing children acquire a spoken language (Bellugi and Klima 1972; Fischer 1974b; Orlansky and Bonvillian 1985; Schlesinger and Meadow 1972; Siple 1978c; Wilbur and Jones 1974).

Environmental factors, on the other hand, might well be expected to combine with the use of ASL as the primary language in the home to produce unique twin language effects. These differential effects would more likely be associated with adult-child interactions than with twin-twin factors, however.

If twin-twin factors are of primary importance in twin language effects, then little difference might be expected as a result of the nature of the language modality. In a sign language environment, twins would still have each other as language models, would have the opportunity to develop a close relationship, and would certainly have the ability to develop and use a private language. One twin-twin factor must be considered for possible effects on twin language: hearing status. The twins we have observed differ in hearing status.

One is deaf, the other is hearing. Whether hearing status has effects on native sign language acquisition has yet to be determined. It is also unclear whether differential hearing status affects the twin-twin relationship. If hearing status is a factor in twin language acquisition, however, twin-twin differences might be expected along with any overall twin effect.

To the extent that parental factors and adult-child interactions affect twin language acquisition, differences might be expected in acquisition in a sign language environment owing to the nature of sign language communication. In the twin language literature, the reduced interaction between parents and twins has been attributed to the increased activities necessary to care for the physical needs of two children, reducing the time available for each child (Lytton 1980). In this context, shorter and different utterances and interactions would be expected from parents of twins because they would be more involved in the act of caretaking. In fact, Tomasello, Mannle, and Kruger (1986) report that mothers of twins use proportionally more directive utterances and fewer comments and questions than do mothers of singletons. Because of the visual-manual nature of sign language, these parental factors might be expected to differ. To interact at all with sign language one must have visual contact and the use of the hands. It is therefore harder to communicate and also engage in other activity. These requirements of the visual-manual communication channel would be expected to further reduce input to twins. Once communication is initiated, however, the eye contact itself may lead to a greater commitment to interaction, leading to more complex, longer utterances and interactions.

Our study compares the ASL acquisition of a set of twins with reports of singleton ASL acquisition. Because we are in the early stages of the study, this first report concentrates on the emergence of the use of ASL by these children. Our initial results suggest that studies of this kind will help us better understand the nature of language acquisition in general and twin language acquisition in particular.

2.3.2 *The Family*

A family living in the Detroit suburban area has provided the opportunity for this study. Both parents have been deaf from birth and use ASL as their primary language. Their firstborn children are opposite-sex fraternal twins, one deaf and one hearing. ASL is the language of the home, and the parents feel strongly that the children should learn ASL as their native language. Thus the early language acquisition of both children is of monolingual ASL.

The twins were born ten days prematurely, and the hearing twin had a slight birth defect that was surgically corrected. Within a week of birth, crude hearing tests and parental observations indicated that the boy, whom we call K,

Table 2.1   Bayley Developmental Index for J (Hearing) and K (Deaf)

Age in Months	Mental		Motor	
	J	K	J	K
9	93	86	87	92
15	124	140	106	118

was deaf and the girl, referred to as J, was hearing. These observations were confirmed by audiological testing at four months and nine months, indicating that K was profoundly deaf while J's hearing was in the normal range. It seems reasonable to assume that the cause of deafness for K is hereditary, since there are no other handicapping conditions, the parents were deaf from birth, and both parents have deafness in their families. The father is second-generation deaf; both of his parents and all of his siblings are deaf. The mother has hearing parents, but one set of grandparents is deaf and three of her seven siblings are deaf or hard of hearing.

Standardized testing was carried out at 9 and 15 months, using the Bayley Scales of Infant Development, to determine whether the development of the twins fell within the normal range and to ascertain whether there were any developmental differences between the deaf twin and hearing twin. At 9 months this standardized testing was carried out by an unfamiliar examiner in a clinic unfamiliar to both parents and children. At 15 months the examiner was now known to the family and the tests were administered at home.

Scores for each administration of the Bayley are given in table 2.1. The twins, J and K, clearly fall within the normal range on both the Mental and Motor scales of the Bayley. A relatively high degree of concordance is expected for fraternal twins over the first three to four years (Wilson 1983), and this is seen for K and J. In fact, Wilson shows greater twin-twin correlations than age-to-age correlations over the first two years, and we see similar results here, though the age differences may be due to examiner and environmental familiarity differences over the two testing sessions.

2.3.3 Data Collection

Data collection for the project began when the twins were 9 months of age. Monthly observational videotaping began at that time, with a total of two hours of observation videotaped at each session. These sessions consisted primarily of adult-child interactions during play sessions and at mealtime; we also filmed occasional periods of the children at play. This preliminary report covers the sessions when the twins were 9 through 24 months of age.

From 9 months through 17 months, the events filmed were determined by the family interactions and the participation of one experimenter. At 18 months, a part of the filming was standardized. Each month we introduced a selection of picture books from the Brimax collection, and in a separate period we initiated a play session based on the Fisher-Price kitchen set.

Additional information concerning the twins' language use was reported in informal interviews with the parents. We estimated vocabulary size based on parental reports, from 14 to 18 months of age. At 17 and 18 months the parents' memory for vocabulary was prompted by the use of a standard list of words babies understand.

2.3.4 Analysis, Results, and Discussion

The strategy we have used is to select measures of the emergence of language for which significant delay has been reported for twins' spoken language acquisition. In these areas, data from the twins K and J will be compared with reports in the literature of singleton ASL acquisition.

For spoken languages, it is generally agreed that periods of babbling and vocal gesturing precede the first use of words, with a transition from non-specific babbling to babbling related to the language environment occurring at 6 to 7 months of age. The first actual spoken words are reported to occur between 10 and 14 months (deVilliers and deVilliers 1978; Orlansky and Bonvillian 1985). For sign language acquisition the same sequence of events occurs, but there is disagreement about whether the transitions occur at the same ages.

The transition from gesture to symbol in early language development has recently received a great deal of attention. Investigators of spoken language acquisition have suggested that early use of speech is not truly symbolic and that the transition from vocal gesture to word symbol is a slow process (Bates et al. 1979; Bates, Camaioni, and Volterra 1975). Early in this transition process, manual gestures as well as vocal gestures play a role in spoken language acquisition. In a sign language environment, it is the manual gestures that form the basis for language acquisition, with a transition from the use of manual gestures to signs as symbols occurring at the same time and in the same way as the transition from vocal gesture to word symbol (Bates et al. 1979; Goldin-Meadow and Morford 1985; Volterra 1983; Volterra and Caselli 1985). Studies using more traditional criteria for the emergence of first words and signs indicate that the appearance of signs for children in a signing environment occurs earlier than the appearance of words for hearing children in a speech environment (Orlansky and Bonvillian 1985; Schlesinger and Meadow 1972). First sign use occurs between 5.5 and 12 months, whereas first word use occurs between 10 and 14 months.

For the twins J and K, manual babbling had been produced for some time before the beginning of our testing at 9 months, according to parental interviews. At 8 months the hearing twin, J, produced manual gestures or signs (depending on the criteria employed) for MILK and MAMA, but these dropped out of use after a few appearances. BYE-BYE was used regularly by both twins at the urging of their parents from 8 months of age. At the beginning of our videotaping at 9 months, neither child used signs reliably, but each twin used simple pointing gestures and imitated BYE-BYE when going off for a nap. Deictic pointing and clear manual gestures were produced by both twins at 10 months, but especially by K, the deaf twin. K clearly pointed to and then reached for a sandwich and later a bottle. J pointed to the tray of her high chair, and pounded on it, while being fed by her father. Before eating, K used a 5 hand, palm out, near his mouth, which his mother interpreted as the sign EAT. At 11 months, deictic pointing gestures increased greatly and were used in complex interactions by both twins. Both children also produced clearly identifiable signs; when a light was turned on, both children signed LIGHT, for example.

This early sign use and deictic pointing by K and J suggest that the emergence of language for this set of twins occurs well within the age range reported for similar language activities by hearing and deaf singletons acquiring sign language. Age of first sign use varies greatly, depending on the criteria employed, but the early productions of J and K occur within the age ranges reported by Orlansky and Bonvillian (1985) and Schlesinger and Meadow (1972). Less variability has been reported for deictic pointing, and in this domain the pointing gestures of K and J are very similar to those reported for singletons acquiring sign language at the same age (Caselli 1983; Petitto 1985a).

Because of the variability and difficulty of determining meaningful first sign or word use, some researchers have suggested other criteria for establishing the emergence of language. Nelson (1973) suggested that the age of attaining a ten-word vocabulary is a better index of early language development, since this is less influenced by parents' overinterpretation of early vocalizations. Volterra (1983), on the other hand, argues that the emergence of combinatorial abilities, along with symbolic use of words or signs, is a better index of linguistic ability. Delay has been reported in each of these areas— vocabulary growth and increase in utterance length—for twins acquiring spoken languages. We will consider each in turn for J and K.

From 14 to 18 months of age, we elicited the vocabulary of each twin from the parents at our monthly filming sessions. At 17 months an explosion in vocabulary had occurred and we used a standardized list to aid the parents' recall of each child's sign production. The number of signs given for each twin and the number of overlapping signs are shown in table 2.2.

These estimates of vocabulary size are compared with data reported by Schlesinger and Meadow (1972) and Orlansky and Bonvillian (1985) for single children acquiring sign language. As table 2.2 demonstrates, vocabu-

Table 2.2   Comparisons of Vocabulary Size for Sign Language Acquisition

Age in Months	J	K	K and J Overlap	Schlesinger and Meadow[a]	Orlansky and Bonvillian[b]
12[c]	3	4			9.5
13[c]	4	5			
14	8	6	4		
15	20	23	19	19	
16	17	21	12		
17	76	77	71		
18	86	90	81	106	48.2

[a] Vocabulary reported for Ann, a child studied by Schlesinger and Meadow (1972).
[b] Average vocabulary size of thirteen children studied by Orlansky and Bonvillian (1985).
[c] Vocabulary estimates for K and J at 12 and 13 months are based on actual signs seen in the filming session rather than on parental interviews.

lary growth for the twins is very similar and parallels that for singletons. There is no evidence of delay owing to the twin situation. Interpolating from these data, J and K reached a ten-sign vocabulary at an average of 14.2 months. This is one month later than the 13.2-month average reported by Orlansky and Bonvillian (1985) but well within the range of 10 to 17 months they report for thirteen children. Note also that we have not included pointing and attention-getting gestures in our count, even though the twins used them appropriately and in different ways, because of the difficulty of distinguishing gestural use from symbolic use. Thus our vocabulary counts almost certainly underestimate the twins' language ability.

Combinatorial abilities also appear on schedule for K and J when their productions are compared with data from singletons in ASL linguistic environments. The early combinations of J and K include pointing gestures and are similar to those reported by other investigators (Caselli 1983; Hoffmeister 1977; Petitto 1985a; Volterra 1983; Volterra and Caselli 1985). Such combinations were recorded as early as 11 months. Examples for J, the hearing twin, include:

(2.1)   When her father turned on a lamp, J produced
　　　　LIGHT　　POINT
　　　　　　　to light

(2.2)   When her mother asked her if she wanted milk, J produced
　　　　POINT　　MILK
　　　　to mother

The signs of K, the deaf twin, were much more precise at this time. Examples of his combinations at 11 months include:

(2.3)   When a ball was near Tane, out of K's reach, he produced
POINT   POINT
to Tane to ball

(2.4)   When his mother had the ball in her hands, K produced
WANT   POINT
            to ball

This last utterance was repeated three times. Combinations containing deictic pointing predominated in the utterances of each twin over the next several months.

Utterances containing two signs were recorded for K at 16 months and for J at 17 months. Examples of K's combinations at 16 months include:

(2.5)   Closing a book, he signed
FINISH   BOOK

(2.6)   Wanting Tane to give a toy bottle to Pat, he produced
MILK   POINT   POINT
        to Tane to Pat

(2.7)   Wanting Tane to sit with him in a chair, he signed
CHAIR/SIT   WITH   POINT
                        to Tane

At 17 months, J produced similar combinations. These included:

(2.8)   While her father was turning a flashlight on and off, she signed
LIGHT   HOT

(2.9)   When K started crying during lunch, J produced the following
            monologue:
POINT   CRY
to K

POINT   CRY
to K

CRY   WHAT

CRY   WHAT
hands over ears

Later during lunch at 17 months, K produced the following string of
utterances:

(2.10)   While his mother was at the sink getting a washcloth, K
           produced
           PEAR
           repeated nine times

           POINT
           to refrigerator

           PEAR   POINT
                   to refrigerator

           PEAR   POINT
           repeated twice   to refrigerator

           His mother came to his high chair and washed off the tray, and K
           signed

           PEAR   EAT   PEAR
           three times   five times   two times

           PEAR   EAT

           PEAR

           PEAR   EAT   PEAR   EAT   PEAR   EAT
                   twice twice   twice   four times

These last twelve signs were produced in rapid succession without pausing.
The emergence of sign combinations at 16 and 17 months is remarkably similar to data reported for singletons acquiring ASL. Schlesinger and Meadow
(1972) report that Ann produced her first two-sign combinations at 17 months,
and Orlansky and Bonvillian (1985) found that two-sign combinations
emerged at an average age of 17.1 months for the thirteen children they
observed.

No secret language has been noted between the twins, and they communicated very little with each other during our taping sessions through their first
two years. What communication did occur took the form of action (e.g., playing with objects together or grabbing the other's toy) rather than of gesture or
utterance.

2.4 Conclusions

Measures of the emergence of language use in this set of twins, acquiring ASL from their deaf parents, indicate that they are not delayed in language development. First communicative gestures and signs appeared when they would be expected for singletons; vocabulary growth from 12 to 18 months occurred at the same rate as reported for singletons acquiring ASL; and combinatorial abilities were present in the twins' productions at the point when they have been reported for singleton ASL acquisition. Although the results of this case study should in no way be viewed as definitive, they do provide suggestions about the possible influence of twinness, hearing impairment, and the use of sign language on language acquisition.

These results, and those reported more generally for twin language acquisition, may best be understood within the framework of a transactional model of development (Sameroff 1975; Sameroff and Chandler 1975). From a transactional point of view, biological and environmental factors, varying in their severity, interactively determine developmental outcome; and both biological and environmental components vary over time rather than being constant influences on development. A very severe birth defect or a terrible environment by itself may produce a poor developmental outcome. Moderate biological or environmental difficulties may produce no adverse effects if other components are not also deficient or stressed but, rather, are compensatory. When a general self-righting tendency is added to the model, a great deal of conflicting developmental data can be understood. Several factors, for example, are correlated with language difficulty or delay, including genetics, prenatal and perinatal conditions, home environment, family size, and multiple births. None of these necessarily affect language acquisition, however. Twin language effects have been shown to be greater the lower the social class (e.g., Davis 1937; Matheny and Bruggemann 1972) and the more impoverished the adult input (Bornstein and Ruddy 1984; Conway, Lytton, and Pysh 1980; Tomasello, Mannle, and Kruger 1986), for example. Little or no twin language delay has been found by some investigators when the twins studied came from "well-situated" families that were attentive to their children (e.g., Savic 1980), whereas reports of extreme language delay are associated with a poor home environment (e.g., Luria and Yudovich 1971; Wallace 1986).

Our concern here is with the combined effects of twinness, deafness, and a sign language environment. Should a sign language environment be viewed as a negative, neutral, or positive factor for language development? What about deafness? The literature on sign language acquisition suggests that the effects of these factors are neutral to positive (e.g., Fischer 1974b; Orlansky and Bonvillian 1985; Schlesinger and Meadow 1972; Volterra and Caselli 1985). Do these results hold when the risk factor of twinness is added to the situation?

In this unique family, one twin is deaf and the other is hearing. A comparison of the twins with each other can therefore be used to assess the role of hearing status. In the data presented, little or no difference exists between J and K. In fact, although their general personalities differ greatly, the similarity of language development is striking. Hearing status appears to play a neutral role in this language acquisition situation, at least in its early stages. At some time in the future J will begin to acquire spoken English as a second language, and this would be expected to affect her continuing acquisition of ASL. In fact, J's parents have provided spoken language input for her from birth through television and auditory tapes. This passive exposure has not stimulated the production of spoken language in this hearing child with deaf parents (see also Moskowitz 1978).

The risk factor of twinness itself seems to be multifaceted, having biological, twin-twin, and adult-twin components. In the present study, the birth of the twins was not atypical. They were ten days premature, and one had minor surgery shortly thereafter to correct a slight defect. Neither of these minor conditions would be expected to affect language development. The home environment of J and K is like that of the twins studied by Savic (1980); the parents are well educated and are attentive to their children. This supportive and attentive home environment may be related to the lack of evidence for any "special" relationship between the twins leading to a secret language. Since no special twin-twin relationship seems to exist in this situation, no language delay would be predicted because of this factor.

The major difference between this set of twins and others that have been studied lies in their home language environment. The parents of K and J use ASL exclusively when at home. In this sign environment, the twins K and J showed no language delay. In spoken language acquisition, twins receive reduced language input from their parents, and this has been associated with language delay (Bornstein and Ruddy 1984; Conway, Lytton, and Pysh 1980; Lytton 1980; Tomasello, Mannle, and Kruger 1986). A sign language environment should be expected to further reduce the amount of input to the child. Since eye contact is necessary for sign reception, any signing that occurs outside the child's visual field or without the child's visual attention will not be taken in. Compared with a spoken language environment, fewer utterances will be "heard" or "overheard." When the requirements of the visual communication channel are combined with the demands of caring for twins, an even greater reduction in language input should result, and this reduced input might be expected to produce language delay. This expected delay fails to occur, we suggest, because of other requirements for sign communication: the hands of the signer must be relatively free, and the signer must get the child's visual attention before the child can be addressed. Thus, once sign communication has been initiated, a greater commitment to the interaction has been made than is necessary for oral communication. The hands have been cleared and visual contact has been established. Because of these requirements, we argue that the use of sign language leads to better adult-child interactions and that these better interactions compensate for reduced input.

The use of ASL in the twins J and K emerged right on schedule. The appearance of first signs, the rate of vocabulary growth, and the first use of sign combinations in these twins occurred at ages typical of those reported in the literature for singletons acquiring ASL. Although language delay might have been predicted because of reduced language input owing to the combined effects of twinness and the requirements of visual-manual communication, no delay occurred. We suggest that the requirements of visual-manual communication lead to better-quality interactions once communication has been initiated and that the quality of these interactions compensates for any reduced input. Studies of twins' spoken language acquisition indicate that having a same-aged sibling in the environment can produce qualitative differences in the development of communication and interaction apart from any quantitative delay (e.g., Billman and Shatz 1984; Keenan 1977; Savic 1979, 1980; Savic and Jocic 1975; Waterman and Shatz 1982). It remains to be seen how language modality and hearing status affect these aspects of twins' language acquisition.

3 Home Sign Systems in Deaf Children: The Development of Morphology without a Conventional Language Model

CAROLYN MYLANDER AND SUSAN GOLDIN-MEADOW

3.1 Levels of Structure in Early Child Language: The Role of the Language Model

The language model a child is exposed to quite obviously affects the outcome of the language learning process. The young child learns English when exposed to English, Samoan when exposed to Samoan, American Sign Language when exposed to American Sign Language, and so on. It is possible, however, that properties of language differ in their sensitivity to the language model, and that even though the development of certain properties of language depends on the presence of a language model, the development of other properties does not. If so, a child who is exposed to no language model or to an impoverished language model might be expected to develop certain linguistic properties but not others. Sachs and her colleagues (Sachs, Bard, and Johnson 1981; Sachs and Johnson 1976) studied the language development of a hearing child exposed to an impoverished model of English by his deaf parents and found that the child developed some of the properties of English but failed to develop others. The child's dearth of linguistic input thus had differential effects on his language development, suggesting that a language model may not be equally essential for the development of all properties of language.

We have explored the importance of the language model to the development of various properties of language by observing children who are not exposed to a conventional model. The children we study are deaf, with hearing losses so severe that they cannot naturally acquire oral language. In addition, these children are born to hearing parents who have chosen not to expose them to a conventional sign language. We have shown that these children, despite their impoverished language learning conditions, develop a gestural communication system with some—but not all—of the properties of language found in the communication systems developed by young children learning language from conventional language models (Feldman, Goldin-Meadow, and Gleit-

This research was supported by grant BNS 8407041 from the National Science Foundation. We thank Julie Gerhardt, John Lucy, Rachel Mayberry, and William Meadow for their thoughtful comments on earlier drafts of this chapter.

man 1978; Goldin-Meadow 1979, 1982; Goldin-Meadow and Feldman 1977; Goldin-Meadow and Mylander 1983, 1984). Our work has focused primarily on isolating those properties of language whose development can proceed without the guidance of a conventional language model—what we have called the "resilient" properties.

The heuristic we have adopted in describing the deaf children's gestural communication systems has been to determine which of the properties of early child language can be found in their gesture systems. Our previous work has demonstrated that the gesture systems our deaf subjects develop are comparable in many respects to early child language. In particular, the deaf children develop gestures that function as words do in the systems of hearing children learning conventional spoken languages and as signs do in the systems of deaf children learning conventional signed languages such as American Sign Language (ASL). The children in our studies produce two types of gestures: deictic signs used to refer to people, places, or things (e.g., a pointing sign at a snack), and characterizing signs used to refer to actions or attributes (e.g., a fist held at the mouth accompanied by chewing [EAT]).[1] In addition, the deaf children combine their signs into strings that function like the sentences of early child language in two respects: (1) The deaf children's sign sentences express the semantic relations typically found in early child language, with characterizing signs representing the predicates and deictic signs the arguments of those semantic relations. (2) The deaf children's sign sentences are structured like the sentences of early child language; specifically, there are order and deletion patterns identifiable across signs (or words) in a sentence (e.g., the sign for the patient role [snack] is likely to precede the sign for the act predicate [EAT]). Thus in our previous work we have found that deaf children, even without the benefit of a conventional linguistic model, can develop gestural communication systems with structural properties at the level of the sentence.

By age 3;6, however, children acquiring a conventional spoken language or a conventional sign language begin to develop structure at a second level—the level of the word or sign. Typically, children pass through an initial period during which they learn the words or signs of their language as unanalyzed wholes or "amalgams" (MacWhinney 1978; Newport 1984). During the next period they begin to learn that a word or sign can be composed of parts, each of which is meaningful. For example, initially a child might use the word "untie" appropriately but not be aware that the word is composed of two parts, "un" and "tie." Later, however, the child learns that "un" is a separable piece of the word associated with a particular meaning (to undo the result of an action), an insight reflected in an overgeneralized use of "un" (e.g.,

---

1. Characterizing signs are represented in small capitals; for example, EAT represents a jabbing motion toward the mouth.

"unclothes" = to take the clothes off a baby; Bowerman 1982). At this stage the child gains productive control over the parts of words, knowing the parts themselves and how they combine to form words, and thus has structure not only at the level of the sentence but also at the level of the word.

The purpose of this study is to determine whether the gesture systems created by our deaf subjects are structured at this second level, the level of the word or sign. We ask whether structure exists within signs as well as across signs and therefore whether a child can develop a system with structure at both the word/sign level and the sentence level without the benefit of a conventional language model. Thus our goal is to determine whether the deaf children in our studies display a hierarchy of structured levels in their gesture systems; in other words, we want to determine whether hierarchical structure is a "resilient" property of language.

3.1.1 Background on Deafness and Language Learning

Sign languages of the deaf are autonomous languages that are not derivative from the spoken languages of hearing cultures (Bellugi and Studdert-Kennedy 1980; Klima and Bellugi 1979; Lane and Grosjean 1980). A sign language such as ASL is a primary linguistic system passed down from one generation of deaf people to the next and is a language in the full sense of the word. Just as in spoken languages, ASL is structured at syntactic (Fischer 1975; Liddell 1980; Lillo-Martin and Klima 1990; Padden 1983), morphological (Fischer 1973b; Fischer and Gough 1978; Klima and Bellugi 1979; Newport 1981; Supalla 1982; Supalla and Newport 1978), and "phonological" (Battison 1974; Coulter 1990; Lane, Boyes-Braem, and Bellugi 1976; Liddell 1984; Liddell and Johnson 1989; Padden and Perlmutter 1987; Sandler 1986; Stokoe 1960; Wilbur 1986) levels of analysis.

Deaf children born to deaf parents and exposed from birth to a conventional sign language such as ASL have been found to acquire that language naturally; that is, in acquiring sign language these children progress through stages similar to those of hearing children acquiring a spoken language (Caselli 1983; Hoffmeister 1978; Hoffmeister and Wilbur 1980; Kantor 1982b; Newport and Ashbrook 1977; Newport and Meier 1986). Thus in an appropriate linguistic environment—in this case a signing environment—deaf children appear not to be handicapped with respect to language learning.

However, 90 percent of deaf children are not born to deaf parents who could provide early exposure to a conventional sign language. Rather, they are born to hearing parents who, quite naturally, tend to expose their children to speech (Hoffmeister and Wilbur 1980). Unfortunately, it is extremely uncommon for deaf children with severe to profound hearing losses to acquire the spoken language of their hearing parents naturally, that is, without intensive and specialized instruction. Even with instruction, deaf children's acquisition of speech is markedly delayed compared with either the acquisition of speech by hearing children of hearing parents or the acquisition of sign by deaf children of deaf parents. By age 5 or 6, despite intensive early training programs, the average profoundly deaf child has only a very reduced oral linguistic capacity (Conrad 1979; Meadow 1968; Mindel and Vernon 1971). In addition, unless hearing parents send their deaf children to a school where sign language is taught, these children are not likely to be exposed to conventional sign input. In such unpropitious circumstances, these children might be expected to fail to communicate at all or perhaps to communicate only in nonsymbolic ways. This turns out not to be the case.

Previous studies of deaf children of hearing parents have shown that these children spontaneously use gestural symbols to communicate even if they are not exposed to a conventional sign language model (Fant 1972; Lenneberg 1964; Moores 1974; Tervoort 1961). These gestures are conventionally referred to as "home signs." Most of our previous work has focused on the structural aspects of deaf children's home signs, in particular on structure across signs in a sentence—structure at the "syntactic" level. In this chapter we focus on structure across components, called "morphemes," within a sign—structure at the "morphological" level. Our search for morphological structure in the deaf children's gesture systems is guided particularly by recent research on morphology in ASL. We begin by reviewing the findings of this literature that are relevant to our analyses.

3.1.2 Morphological Structure in ASL

Early research in ASL suggested that verbs in ASL, unlike verbs in spoken languages, appeared to be continually varying forms constructed on the basis of analogue representations of real-world events (DeMatteo 1977). In other words, ASL verbs were thought not to be divisible into component parts, but rather were considered unanalyzable lexical items that mapped, as wholes, onto events in the world. Subsequently, verbs in ASL (particularly the mimetic verbs of motion) have been more accurately described as combinations of a limited set of discrete morphemes (McDonald 1982; Newport 1981; Supalla 1982).

For example, to describe a drunk's weaving walk down a path, an ASL signer would not represent the idiosyncrasies of that drunk's particular meanderings but would instead use a conventional morpheme representing random movement (a side-to-side motion) in conjunction with a conventional morpheme representing change of location. Mimetic verbs in ASL have been shown to be constructed from discrete sets of morphemes and to include, at a minimum, a motion morpheme combined with a handshape morpheme (McDonald 1982; Newport 1981; Supalla 1982).

Morphemes in ASL (as in spoken languages) have been organized into frameworks or matrices of oppositions, referred to as "paradigms" (cf. Matthews 1974). For example, the motion for "linear path" (representing change of location along a straight path) can be combined with any number of handshapes representing agents or actors (e.g., inverted V = a human; a bent inverted V = an animate nonhuman; thumb + two fingers held sideways = a vehicle). These combinations create a set of signs whose meanings are predictable from the meanings of the individual motion and handshape elements (a human moves along a straight path, an animate nonhuman moves along a straight path, a vehicle moves along a straight path). In another example, a different motion form (e.g., "arc path," representing change of location along an arced path, such as jump forward) can be combined with any of these same handshape morphemes to create a set of signs whose meanings are also systematic combinations of the component parts of each sign (e.g., a human jumps foward, an animate nonhuman jumps forward, a vehicle jumps forward). Thus many of the verbs of ASL can be described in terms of a combination of handshape and motion morphemes that together form complete paradigmatic sets.

3.2 Morphology in Home Signs: Structure within the Sign

To determine whether our deaf subjects' signs can also be characterized by systematic combinations of meaningful forms, we selected one of our original subjects (David) and analyzed the characterizing signs (the mimetic signs) he produced in naturalistic play sessions videotaped in his home when he was aged 2;10, 2;11, 3;0, 3;3, 3;5, 3;11, and 4;10.[2] These ages span the age range during which both deaf (Supalla 1982) and hearing (MacWhinney 1976) children learning conventional languages have typically already begun to acquire certain morphemic distinctions.

The videotapes of David were coded initially at the sign level according to a system described in detail in Goldin-Meadow (1979) and Goldin-Meadow and Mylander (1984).[3] We then coded each characterizing sign produced during

2. Two of the types of characterizing signs David produced during these videotapes are omitted from the analyses presented here and will be described in a forthcoming report; (1) 243 signs that were conventional in that they occur in the spontaneous gestures accompanying the speech of hearing adults and children in our culture (e.g., a flat hand extended palm up to mean "give," or two fists held together and then rotated away from each other to mean "broken"); and (2) 68 signs in which the motion sign traces the extent or outline of an object.

3. In our previous analyses of sentence-level structure in the deaf children's gestures, we glossed all characterizing signs as predicates, assigning act predicate meanings to signs that mirrored the actions on or by objects (e.g., EAT) and assigning attribute predicate meanings to signs that mirrored the perceptual characteristics of objects (e.g., ROUND; see Goldin-Meadow and Mylander 1984, 23–26, for the rationale behind these coding decisions). For the present analysis, we code the meaning of each sign twice: (1) We first code the sign in terms of the characteristics of the object that the sign is used to refer to (either the object involved in the actions of act predicates

these sessions in terms of its handshape and motion. Reliability between two independent coders ranged from 85 percent to 95 percent for handshape and from 83 percent to 93 percent for motion.

To determine whether the deaf child's signs were divisible into handshape and motion morphemes, we reviewed David's entire corpus of characterizing signs and asked whether the set of signs met the following three criteria for structure at the morphological level:

1. Is there a limited set of discrete handshape and motion forms in the child's corpus of signs? That is, are the forms categorical rather than continuous?

2. Is a particular handshape or motion form consistently associated with a particular meaning (or set of meanings) throughout the corpus of signs? That is, is each handshape and motion form meaningful?

3. Does a particular handshape or motion form/meaning pairing appear in more than one sign? That is, is a particular form/meaning pairing an independent morpheme that can combine with other morphemes in the system? Is the system combinatorial?

We begin by analyzing the forms and meanings of the handshapes David used in his signs and then the forms and meanings of the motions in those signs. We next describe the combinations of handshapes and motions that occurred in the corpus of David's signs. Finally, we focus on how those handshape/motion combinations David developed changed over the two-year period spanned by this study.

3.2.1 Handshape Morphemes

Handshape Forms

Following Supalla (1982) and McDonald (1982), we coded each handshape according to four dimensions: the shape of the palm, the distance between the fingers and the thumb, the number of fingers extended, and the presence or

---

or the object described in attribute predicates). We take this object information to be relevant to the meanings of handshape forms (cf. table 3.2). (2) We also code the sign in terms of the characteristics of the action the sign is used to refer to (the action in act predicates), and we take this information to be relevant to the meaning of motion forms (cf. table 3.4). All attribute signs were, by definition, produced without motion. We arbitrarily assigned the meaning "exists" or "is" as a placeholder for the no-motion component of these signs in the morphological analysis in table 3.4. The absence of motion in attribute signs may, of course, be meaningless. If so, attribute signs would be glossed only in terms of the object characteristics they portray (e.g., ROUND, CURVED, BULKY) and would therefore be included in table 3.2 (handshape meanings) but not table 3.4 (motion meanings).

absence of spread between the fingers. At first we coded handshapes continuously along each dimension without establishing a priori either discrete categories or boundaries. Thus, for example, we wrote down the exact distance (in inches) between the fingers and thumb of a particular handshape and did not try to force that handshape into a limited set of thumb-finger distances. We found, however, that David used only a restricted number of values on each of the four dimensions. Table 3.1 displays the five most frequent handshapes David used on these tapes, described in terms of the relevant dimensions. These five handshapes accounted for 98 percent of all of the handshapes David produced ($N = 473$).

The remaining 2 percent of David's handshapes not represented in table 3.1 were: V (two fingers spread apart and extended), L (thumb and forefinger extended at right angles to each other), thumb (thumb extended), F (thumb and finger touching with the other three fingers extended in the "okay" sign), and W (three fingers spread apart and extended). Each of these infrequently produced handshapes was used to represent only one object throughout the tapes (e.g., the V was used to represent scissors, the L was used to represent a gun). We saw no evidence that these handshapes participated in a generative way in David's sign system, so we eliminated them from further analyses.

Handshape Form/Meaning Mapping

We next determined whether David's handshapes mapped in any systematic way onto categories of meanings. We found that David used his handshapes in two ways: to represent a HAND as it manipulates an object, or to represent the OBJECT itself. For example, to describe a picture of a knife, David produced a fist handshape (with a back-and-forth movement), which mirrors a cutter's hand manipulating a knife and thus is an instance of a HAND handshape. In contrast, to describe the same picture of the knife, in a separate sentence David produced a palm handshape held perpendicular to the table (with the

Table 3.1   Description of Handshape Forms

Handshape Form	Description
Fist	Fingers and thumb curled into palm
O	Index finger or four fingers bent toward thumb with one-half inch or less between thumb and finger(s)[a]
C	Index finger or four fingers bent toward thumb with three inches between thumb and finger(s)[a]
Palm	Four fingers extended
Point	Index finger extended

[a] If only the index finger was bent toward the thumb in the O and C handshapes, the other three fingers were either curled into the palm or held sloppily in an untensed manner.

same back-and-forth movement), mirroring the flat shape of the knife itself and therefore meeting the criterion for an OBJECT handshape. The same handshape could be used with either a HAND or an OBJECT meaning in David's system. For example, David used a C handshape to describe a cup where the handshape mirrored a hand grasping the diameter of the cup [HAND], and (rotated ninety degrees) to describe a turtle where the handshape mirrored the curved back of the turtle [OBJECT].

To determine the meaning of each handshape form, we first listed all the objects represented by each handshape form used with either a HAND or an OBJECT meaning in the one-motion signs (signs that contained only a single motion) David produced during one session, the session at age 3;11. We then determined whether the set of objects associated with a particular handshape form could be said to share a common attribute or set of attributes. If so, we took that common core to be the meaning of the particular handshape form. We then used these form/meaning pairings to code the videotapes of the six remaining sessions.

Table 3.2 describes the meanings found to be associated with the HAND and OBJECT handshape forms in the session at age 3;11, as well as examples of the objects represented by each handshape form/meaning pairing. Table 3.2 also presents the total number of different types of objects represented by each form/meaning pairing and, in parentheses, the total number of times each form/meaning pairing was used throughout the seven videotaped sessions.[4] We found that 368 (95 percent) of the 387 handshapes David produced in his one-motion signs during the seven videotaped sessions could be classified into the form/meaning categories listed in table 3.2. In addition, sixty-eight (91 percent) of the seventy-five handshapes in David's two-motion signs (signs that contained two motions concatenated without a break so that both appeared to be within the same sign) were also found to conform to the form/meaning categories established on the basis of the one-motion signs produced during the 3;11 session. Note that the palm and point handshapes were each used to represent more than one class of objects (e.g., the OBJECT palm was used to represent [1] flat, wide objects, [2] many small particles, and [3] vehicles and animate objects); each of these classes is considered a distinct morpheme. Exceptions to table 3.2 consisted of form/meaning mismatches, such as a fist form used to represent a small, *short* (rather than a long) object (e.g., a knob on a toy), or a palm form used to represent a round inanimate object (e.g., a ball moving forward).

4. Numbers reported for handshape (table 3.2) reflect signs in which handshape was codable regardless of whether the corresponding motion could be seen and coded. Similarly, numbers reported for motion (table 3.4) reflect signs in which motion was codable, again independent of whether the corresponding handshape could be coded. Numbers reported for handshape and motion combinations (tables 3.5 and 3.6) reflect signs in which both handshape and motion were codable.

Table 3.2   Meanings of Handshape Forms

	HAND Morphemes			OBJECT Morphemes	
Form	Meaning	Types (tokens)		Meaning	Types (tokens)
Fist	Handle small, long object (e.g., spoon, drum-stick, balloon string, handlebar)[a]	19 (70)		Bulky object (hammer-head, block)	2 (3)
O	Handle small object (e.g., crank, shoelace)[a]	31 (102)		Round compact object (e.g., round hat, tree ball, bubble)	6 (17)
C	Handle large object (e.g., cup, horn, guitar neck)[a]	11 (20)		Curved object (e.g., cowboy's legs around a horse, turtle)	5 (7)
Palm	Handle flat surface (e.g., sides of toy bag, chair back)	12 (30)		Flat wide object (e.g., fish, flag, bird wings)	9 (43)
	Handle many small surfaces (xylophone keys)	1 (3)		Many small particles (e.g., snow)	6 (9)
				Vehicle or animate object (e.g., car, sister, Santa, plane)	13 (26)
Point	Handle small surface (trigger)	1 (2)		Thin straight object (e.g., straw, bubble wand, pinwheel)	6 (12)
				Object of any shape (e.g., bear, penny, Susan)	13 (24)

Note: The table contains the handshapes found in David's one-motion signs during the seven video-taped sessions. The first number represents the different types of objects represented by the handshape, and the number in parentheses represents the total times the handshape was used for that meaning.
[a] Small = two inches or less in diameter; large = more than two inches in diameter; long = more than five inches in length.

It is important to note that David's HAND morphemes were not always accurate representations of the way a hand grasps a particular object in the real world, nor were his OBJECT morphemes precise mimetic reconstructions of real-world objects. For example, the same HAND form (the fist) was used to represent grasping a balloon string, a drumstick, and handlebars—grasping actions that require considerable variety in diameter in the real world. David therefore appeared not to distinguish objects of varying diameters within the fist category. However, he did distinguish objects with small diameters *as a set* from objects with large diameters (e.g., a cup, a guitar neck, the length of a straw), which were represented by a C hand.

As another example, David used the same OBJECT form (the O) to represent a round hat, a Christmas tree ball, and a bubble—objects that vary in width in the real world. David again did not appear to distinguish objects with varying widths within the O category, but rather appeared to categorize them all as small round objects. However, David did distinguish these small, round objects *as a set* from larger curved objects (e.g., a turtle's back, a cowboy's legs around a horse), which were represented by a C hand. Overall, David thus appeared to consign handshapes to discrete categories rather than to utilize analogue representations of "real-world" objects.

3.2.2 Motion Morphemes

Motion Forms

We found that David used eight different types of motions, as well as a no-motion form, in his signs (table 3.3). The motions were defined in terms of the type of trajectory traced by the hand (linear path, arced path, circle) or the motions of the hand in place (revolve, open/close, bend, wiggle). In addition, arcs were distinguished in terms of length of path (seven inches or less vs. more than seven inches) and directionality (unidirectional vs. bidirectional). These motion forms account for 100 percent of the signs David produced during these sessions ($N = 514$).

Motion Form/Meaning Mapping

To determine whether each of David's nine motion forms was associated with a particular class of meanings, we began by listing all the actions David represented with each of the nine motion forms in the one-motion signs he produced during the session at age 3;11. We then determined whether the actions associated with a particular motion form shared certain common attributes. If so, we took that common core to be the meaning of the particular

Table 3.3   Description of Motion Forms

Motion Form	Description
Linear	Hand moves in a straight path
Long arc	Hand moves unidirectionally in an arced path more than seven inches in length
Short arc	Hand moves unidirectionally in an arced path seven inches or less in length
Arc to and fro	Hand moves bidirectionally in an arced path of any length
Circular	Hand moves in circle; wrist or fingers revolve
Open/close	Hand or fingers open and/or close
Bend	Hand or fingers bend
Wiggle	Fingers wiggle
No motion	Hand held in place

Table 3.4   Meanings of Motion Forms

Type of Motion	Form	Meaning	Types (tokens)	
Change of location	Linear	Change of location by moving along a path	16	(34)
	Long arc	Change of location by moving along a path, typically to or from a particular end point	19	(24)
Change of position	Short arc	Reposition (or reorient) in place; reposition to affect another object; or reposition with respect to another object or place	33	(71)
	Arc to and fro	Reposition by moving back and forth	29	(114)
	Circular	Reposition by moving in a circle or rotating around an axis	15	(37)
Change of shape	Open/close	Open/close, expand/contract, or flicker on/off	9	(16)
	Bend	Bend at a joint	2	(5)
	Wiggle	Wiggle back and forth	2	(3)
No change	No motion	Hold in place or exist	29	(91)

Note: The table contains the motions found in David's one-motion signs during the seven video-taped sessions. The first number represents the different types of actions represented by the motion, and the number in parentheses represents the total times the motion was used for that meaning.

motion form and used the resulting set of form/meaning pairings to code the videotapes from the remaining six sessions.

Table 3.4 presents the meanings of the motion forms David produced in his one-motion signs during the session at age 3;11, as well as the total number of different types of actions represented by each form/meaning pairing (and, in parentheses, the total number of times each motion form/meaning pairing was used) over the course of the seven videotaped sessions.

We found that David used his motion forms to represent four types of change in the state of an object: change of location, change of position, change of shape, and no change. He used the linear and long arc forms to represent *change of location* along a path, either of an object (or a person) moving on its own (that is, an intransitive motion; e.g., bubble go up, we go down) or an object being moved by a person (transitive motion; e.g., move coat, scoop spoon). Although both forms were used to represent change of location, the long arc was typically used to represent a change of location bounded by a particular end point (e.g., penny arc forward [toward a bank]), while the path represented by the linear form could be either open ended (e.g., bubble go upward), or bounded by an end point (e.g., we go down [to the bottom of the stairs]).

David used the arc to and fro, circular, and short arc forms to represent the *change of position* either of an object (or a person) repositioning itself (that is, an intransitive motion; e.g., wheel tip over), or an object being repositioned by a person (a transitive motion; e.g., turn over clay). A change of position involved bidirectional repositioning around a center point (the arc to and fro form; e.g., wings flap, jiggle handlebars side to side), unidirectional repositioning around an axis or center point (the circular form; e.g., wheel rotate, turn crank), or unidirectional repositioning having no center point (the short arc form). There were three types of meanings conveyed by the short arc form: repositioning in the same spot (e.g., wheel tip over), repositioning an object to affect another object (e.g., swing hammer [to knock tower], shake envelope [to release contents]), or repositioning an object with respect to another object or a place, either to remove the object (e.g., pick up bubble jar [off table]) or to place the object (e.g., hook tree lights [onto Christmas tree], push down box lid [onto bottom of box]).

David used the open/close, bend, and wiggle forms to represent the *change of shape* either of an object altering its own form (an intransitive motion; e.g., bubble expands, fish bends [to swim]), or a hand altering its shape on an object (a transitive motion, e.g., hand closes [around toy bulb], fingers wiggle [to strike piano keys]). The open/close form was used to represent an object (or hand) opening or closing (e.g., claw closes), expanding or contracting (e.g., bubble expands), or flicking on and off (e.g., tree lights flicker). The bend form was used to represent an object bending at a joint (e.g., fish bends). The wiggle form was used to represent an object (or hand) wiggling (e.g., snow flutters).

Finally, David used the no-motion form to represent *no change* in an object as it is held in place (e.g., hold bubble wand [at mouth]) or as it exists (e.g., puzzle board exists, bubble exists).

We found that 395 (90 percent) of the 439 motions in the one-motion signs David produced during the seven videotaped sessions could be classified according to the form/meaning pairings listed in table 3.4. In addition, 69 (92 percent) of the 75 motions in David's two-motion signs conformed to the form/meaning pairings established on the basis of the one-motion signs produced during the session at age 3;11. Exceptions to table 3.4 consisted of form/meaning mismatches, such as a short arc form used to represent the path of a change of location (e.g., a turtle moving forward along a path), or a long arc form used to represent an object repositioning itself (e.g., a wheel tipping over in place).

3.2.3 Handshape and Motion Combinations

We have shown that David's signs can be described in terms of handshape morphemes (handshape form/meaning pairings) and motion morphemes (motion form/meaning pairings). We now attempt to demonstrate that the signs themselves were in fact composites of hand and motion morphemes rather than one unanalyzed whole—that is, that handshape and motion are separable units. Since signs are composed of hands moving in space, it is not possible to find handshapes that are actually separated from their motions. Nevertheless, if we find a handshape that is not uniquely associated with one sign but rather is combined with several different motions in different signs, we then have evidence that the handshape may be an independent unit in David's system. Similarly, if a motion is combined with different handshapes in different signs, we infer evidence for the separability of that motion. We will consider first David's HAND handshape morphemes in combination with motion morphemes and then David's OBJECT handshape morphemes in combination with motion morphemes.

HAND *Handshape Morphemes Combined with Motion Morphemes*

Table 3.5 displays the number of types of events represented by each pairing of a HAND handshape with one of the nine motions; the numbers in parentheses represent the total number of times a particular handshape occurred with a particular motion. The table contains David's one-motion signs, excluding those that were exceptions to either table 3.2 (handshape form/meaning pairings) or table 3.4 (motion form/meaning pairings). In table 3.5 the handshapes represent an actor's hand shaped on or around a patient, and the motions represent events in which an actor manipulates a patient (transitive events).

Table 3.5   HAND Handshapes Used in Combination with Motions

	Fist	O	C	Palm (flat surface)	Palm (many surfaces)
Change of location					
Linear	—	—	—	1 (1)	—
Long arc	1 (1)	1 (1)	—	1 (2)	—
Change of position					
Short arc	6 (12)	10 (20)	2 (2)	2 (5)	—
Arc to and fro	7 (28)	7 (42)	1 (1)	5 (8)	1 (1)
Circular	1 (1)	5 (8)	4 (10)	—	—
Change of shape					
Open/close	1 (1)	2 (2)	—	—	—
Bend	—	—	—	—	—
Wiggle	—	—	—	—	1 (2)
No change					
No motion	6 (16)	9 (24)	3 (6)	—	—

Note: The first number in each entry represents the different *types* of events represented by the handshape/motion combination. The number in parentheses represents the total times the handshape/motion combination was used—the number of *tokens.* Only one-motion signs are included in the table. The point morpheme (meaning handle a small surface) is not included, since it did not occur with any well-formed motions.

Four of the six HAND handshapes occurred with at least four and as many as six of the nine motions; the two exceptions were the palm (many surfaces) morpheme and the point morpheme (not shown in table 3.5). The palm (many surfaces) morpheme occurred with only two motions, and the point morphemes did not occur with any well-formed motion morphemes. Moreover, six of the nine motions occurred with at least two and as many as five of the six HAND handshapes; the three exceptions were the linear morpheme and the wiggle morphemes, which were each used to represent a single event, and the bend morpheme, which was not used at all with HAND handshapes. Thus, most of the handshape morphemes could be found in combination with more than one motion morpheme, and vice versa. As a result, David's signs can be said to conform to a framework or system of contrasts. As an example of how the meanings of David's signs systematically contrasted with one another, the fist handshape was used in combination with the short arc motion to mean "change the position of a small, long object by hand" (e.g., pull out newspaper). The same fist handshape used in combination with a different motion (the arc to and fro) meant "move a small, long object to and fro by hand" (e.g., wave balloon string back and forth), while the same short arc motion used in combination with a different handshape (the C) meant "change the position of a large object by hand" (e.g., pick up bubble jar).

OBJECT *Handshape Morphemes Combined with Motion Morphemes*

Table 3.6 displays the number of types of events represented by each pairing of an OBJECT handshape with one of the nine motions; the numbers in parentheses represent the total number of times a particular handshape occurred with a particular motion. The table contains David's one-motion signs, again excluding the exceptions to tables 3.2 and 3.4. Three types of signs are contained in table 3.6: (1) signs describing an (intransitive) event in which an actor (animate or inanimate) propels itself and does not affect a patient, where the handshape represents a characteristic of the actor—for example, a C handshape used with a linear motion to describe a turtle moving forward; (2) signs describing a (transitive) event in which an actor affects a patient, where the handshape represents a characteristic of the patient—for example, a C handshape used with a short arc motion to describe the curved shape of a cowboy's legs as someone places the cowboy on a horse;[5] and (3) signs describing a static object—for example, a C handshape used with a no-motion

5. The orientation of the hand with respect to the motion was crucial in identifying OBJECT handshapes with transitive motions. In the example presented in the text, the fingers and palm of the C handshape point downward as the short arc motion descends, mirroring the shape of the cowboy's legs as they go around the horse. If, however, the C were perpendicular to the short arc motion (oriented as a person's hand would be if it were placing the cowboy on the horse), the handshape would be considered a HAND handshape and the sign would be included in table 3.5.

Table 3.6 OBJECT Handshapes Used in Combination with Motions

	Fist	O	C	Palm Flat Wide	Palm Vehicle Animate	Palm Particles	Point Straight Skinny	Point Neutral
Change of location								
Linear	—	—	2 (3)	1 (1)	9 (13)	—	1 (2)	3 (7)
Long arc	—	—	1 (1)	1 (1)	4 (4)	1 (1)	2 (2)	5 (7)
Change of position								
Short arc	2 (3)	2 (3)	1 (2)	1 (1)	4 (4)	1 (1)	—	3 (3)
Arc to and fro	—	1 (1)	—	5 (18)	—	—	—	—
Circular	—	—	—	—	—	—	—	2 (3)
Change of shape								
Open/close	—	—	1 (1)	1 (1)	—	2 (4)	—	—
Bend	—	—	—	1 (2)	1 (3)	—	—	—
Wiggle	—	—	—	—	—	1 (1)	—	—
No change								
No motion	—	6 (11)	1 (1)	4 (18)	—	1 (1)	3 (5)	—

Note: The first number in each entry represents the different *types* of events represented by the handshape/motion combination. The number in parentheses represents the total times the handshape/motion combination was used—the number of *tokens*. Only one-motion signs are included in the table.

form to describe the arced shape of a block. Table 3.6 contains seventy-two (56 percent) signs of type 1 (OBJECT handshapes with intransitive motions), twenty-six (20 percent) signs of type 2 (OBJECT handshapes with transitive motions), and thirty-one (24 percent) signs of type 3 (OBJECT handshapes with no motion).

Seven of the eight OBJECT handshapes occurred with at least three and as many as seven of the nine motions; the exception was the fist handshape. Similarly, seven of the nine motions occurred with at least two and as many as seven of the eight handshapes; the exceptions were the circular and wiggle motions. Thus David's signs containing OBJECT handshapes combined with motions also appeared to fit into a framework or system of contrasts. As an example of how the meanings of these signs contrasted systematically with one another, the palm (vehicle/animate) handshape was combined with the linear motion to mean "a vehicle or animate being changes location" (e.g., Santa goes down; car goes forward). This same handshape when combined with a different motion (the short arc) meant "a vehicle or animate being repositions itself" (e.g., sister sits), while the same linear motion when combined with a different handshape (the C) meant "a curved object changes location" (e.g., a turtle moves forward). The handshape morphemes in David's signs thus formed a relatively complete matrix or paradigm with the motion morphemes in the corpus of signs.[6]

3.2.4 The Development of Signs

Thus far we have suggested that a child without the benefit of a conventional language model can develop a system of signs comprising handshape and motion morphemes. We now consider the developmental steps that such a child might have taken in arriving at a handshape/motion system of contrasts.

David appeared to develop his lexicon by recruiting gestures from the actions of people and objects around him, presumably with an eye to adequately representing particular objects and events. We hypothesize that David first developed his lexical items by focusing only on the relationship between the form of the sign and the event it represented. Later, perhaps when he had accumulated a sufficient number of signs in his lexicon, David may have begun to consider his signs in relation to one another and may have organized them around any regularities that appeared in his lexicon. For example, small, long objects tend to be held by a fist—not always, but perhaps often enough so that fistlike handshapes might have predominated in the signs David created to represent handling small, long objects. He might then have made use of this trend in his lexicon and organized his system of contrasts around it.

6. As mentioned above, David also combined motions with other motions. Approximately 10 percent of the signs David produced during these seven sessions contained two or more motions. The two-motion signs are described in detail in Goldin-Meadow and Mylander, 1991.

If this hypothesis is correct, we would expect that, early on, each sign in David's repertoire might represent a single referent rather than a class of referents. For example, he might use the C handshape in combination with a circular motion to refer only to twisting a bubble jar lid and the C handshape in combination with a short arc motion to refer only to repositioning a cup. If so, each handshape/motion combination in those early sessions would be used to represent only one type of event.

After initially generating each sign in his system to map onto a particular event as a whole, David might later "analyze" his set of wholes into handshape and motion components that map onto classes of objects and actions, respectively. We would then expect that the C + circular combination, for example, would be used not only to mean "twist the bubble jar lid" but also to mean "rotate the large knob" or "move the large toy in a circle"; that is, the sign would be used to refer to a class of objects (objects with large diameters) and a class of actions (rotating or moving objects around a center point). If David were to follow this developmental path, we would expect that many of the handshape/motion combinations in his later videotaped sessions would be used to represent classes of related events rather than single events.

Table 3.7 presents the number of handshape/motion combinations used to represent a single event or a class of events for each of the seven videotaped sessions. The data are presented separately for HAND and OBJECT handshapes. Note that David used six different HAND handshape/motion combinations during the first session (age 2;10). However, each of those six combinations was used to describe a single event. It was not until the second session (age 2;11) that David first used one HAND handshape/motion combination to represent a class of events. The number of handshape/motion combinations representing classes of events subsequently increased to nine (at age 3;11). It is important to note that the appearance of handshape/motion combinations representing

Table 3.7 Number of Handshape/Motion Combinations Used to Represent a Single Event or a
Class of Events at Each Age

Age (years; months)	HAND Handshape/Motion Combinations		OBJECT Handshape/Motion Combinations	
	Representing a Single Event	Representing a Class of Events	Representing a Single Event	Representing a Class of Events
2; 10	6	—	2	—
2; 11	3	1	3	—
3; 0	1	—	1	—
3; 3	5	1	6	3
3; 5	4	5	5	—
3; 11	7	9	20	6
4; 10	7	5	9	5

classes of events in the early sessions was *not* attributable to a general increase
in the total number of signs David produced—he produced more HAND hand-
shape/motion combinations during the first session (seventeen signs at age
2;10) than he did during the second and fourth sessions (eleven signs at age
2;11 and twelve signs at age 3;3).

With respect to David's OBJECT handshapes, a comparable developmental
pattern was observed. When David first produced OBJECT handshape/motion
combinations, each of those combinations was used to represent a single
event. Subsequently, at age 3;3, David used three OBJECT handshape/motion
combinations to represent classes of events, and by 3;11 he was using six of
these signs to represent classes of events. Thus the developmental pattern seen
in both the HAND and OBJECT handshapes is consistent with the hypothesis that
David's signs are initially unrelated, unanalyzed wholes that are later organized in relation to one another to form a system of contrasts.

3.3 The Role of the Child and the Environment in the Development of Morphological Structure

3.3.1 The Resilience of Morphological Analysis

We have found that the corpus of signs David produced can be characterized as a system of handshape and motion morphemes; in particular, David's
signs were composed of a limited and discrete set of five handshapes and nine
motion forms, each consistently associated with a distinct meaning and recurring across different signs. David's signs therefore appeared to be decom-
posable into smaller morphemelike components, suggesting that his gesture
system was indeed structured at the sign level. Moreover, these structured characterizing signs formed the building blocks for the sentences he produced.
David frequently used his characterizing signs in multigesture sentences, in
combination both with deictic (pointing) signs and with other characterizing
signs. For example, in a sample of six videotapes taken between the ages of
2;10 and 3;8, 49 percent of the 482 characterizing signs David produced were
found to occur with other signs in sentence combinations. Thus his characterizing signs, which were themselves structured at one level, formed the fundamental units for structure at a second (higher) level, suggesting that the sign
system was indeed characterized by hierarchical structure.

It is important to note that David's signs did not always reflect referents in
the real world as transparently as they might have. The signs were often more
abstract and symbolic than a pantomime of a real-world object or action would
require and, as such, were not constrained by a tight fit between a sign and the
object or action it represented. For example, though in the manual modality
one can in principle represent shapes and movements along a continuous dimension, David used discrete (noncontinuous) forms to represent objects and

actions in his signs (e.g., he used the same handshape to represent holding a thin balloon string and a thicker steering wheel). When representing an object, David appeared to choose among the limited number of handshapes available in his system rather than shaping his hand to match precisely his actual grip on the object. At some level he seemed to be sacrificing the fit between a sign and its referent in order to achieve categorical representation (e.g., David used a fist handshape to represent holding a banana even though bananas require a wider hand grip). Thus, like ASL, David's gesture system does not take advantage of the possibility of continuous and transparent representation afforded by the manual modality and instead appears to be based upon categorical representation, as are all conventional languages.

In addition, as in all conventional languages, David appeared to organize his representational categories into a framework or system of contrasts. When David generated a sign to refer to a particular object or action, the form of that sign was determined not only by the properties of the referent object or action, but also by how that sign fit with the other signs in his lexicon. For example, David's motion form long arc, meaning change of location, contrasted with his motion form short arc, which meant change of position. Moreover, when the long arc was combined with a fist (meaning to handle a small, long object), the meaning of the composite sign could be derived from the meanings of the individual motion and handshape forms (i.e., change the location of a small, long object by hand) and also differed systematically from the meaning of a short arc + fist combination (which meant change the position of a small, long object by hand).

Finally, the developmental course of David's signs appears to be comparable to the development of words or signs in children acquiring conventional languages. When first generating signs, David seems to have created each sign to map onto a particular event, a stage reminiscent of the period during which children acquiring conventional languages treat their words or signs as unanalyzed wholes (MacWhinney 1978; Newport 1984). Later in development David began to use a single sign to refer to a class of events—events that involved actions sharing a common attribute (represented by the motion component of the sign) and objects sharing a common attribute (represented by the handshape component of the sign). At this point, then, David's system can be described in terms of components of sign forms mapping onto components of sign meanings, rather than the whole sign form mapping onto a global, particular event. This latter stage is comparable to the period when children acquiring conventional languages begin to analyze the words they have learned as wholes into meaningful components (Bowerman 1982; MacWhinney 1978; Newport 1984).

Our findings suggest that at some point in developing a communication system, children can begin a process akin to morphological analysis on the codes they are creating—even if they are provided with no explicit model for such analysis. Thus, despite the absence of a conventional language model, a child can develop a communication system that has morphological structure, suggesting that morphological structure is itself a "resilient" property of language.

Evidence from other studies of language learning support the notion that children impose morphological structure onto the language system they are developing even if structure of this sort is not in the language model they are receiving. For example, in spoken language, children who are exposed to pidgin languages that tend not to have morphology (structure within the word) have been found to creolize the language and in the process develop a system that has morphological structure (Kay and Sankoff 1974; Sankoff and Laberge 1973). As a second example, in sign language deaf children are often born to deaf parents who learned ASL late in life. Some of these late-learning adults develop sign systems that lack much of the morphological complexity of ASL (Newport 1984). Nevertheless, deaf children learning ASL from parents with incomplete morphological systems go on to develop sign systems with morphological structure; indeed, their morphological systems are indistinguishable from those developed by deaf children learning ASL from parents with complete morphological systems (Newport 1984).

3.3.2 The Role of the Language Model in Morphological Analysis

The corpus of signs David produced can be characterized as a system of handshape and motion morphemes. This system is comparable in broad outline to the handshape and motion system that underlies ASL. Not surprisingly, however, the system of subsign components David developed is not as complex as the morphological system underlying ASL, a conventional language that has a rich linguistic history and is shared by a wide community of signers.

Comparison with Motion Morphemes in ASL

David used nine motion forms in his signs, a set reminiscent of that isolated by Newport (1981) and Supalla (1982) in their descriptions of motion in ASL. Moreover, the meanings of David's nine motion forms fall into the same four broad categories as do the motion meanings attributed to the signs of ASL, although the details of the motion meanings differ.

First, David used two forms (linear and long arc) to represent change of location along *any* path. In ASL the type of path is specified within the change-of-location morpheme: linear path means move along a straight path, arc path means move in an arc or jump (Supalla 1982). Thus the change-of-location morphemes in ASL are more specified than the comparable morphemes in David's system.

Second, David represented change of position with three forms, short arc (= repositioning an object), arc to and fro (= change position by moving back and forth), and circular (= move in a circular path or rotate). In ASL, two forms represent change of position or orientation: end pivot means swing, and midpivot means rotate (Supalla 1982). A third ASL form, circular path, which means move in a circle, partially overlaps in meaning with David's circular form but is listed by Supalla as a change of location, not a change of orientation.

Third, David used three forms to represent change of shape (open/close, bend, and wiggle). ASL has four forms that differ in detail from David's: spread, bend-flat, bend-round, and change-diameter, each of which reflects a change in the attributes of an object (Supalla 1982).

Finally, David used his no-motion form to represent the existence of an object or holding an object in place. In ASL a distinction is made between the existence and location of an object, and that distinction is conveyed through motion: a hold movement means existence, and minimal contacting movement means location (Supalla 1982).

Comparison with Handshape Morphemes in ASL

The five predominant handshapes in David's system represent the unmarked handshapes of adult ASL systems (cf. Klima and Bellugi 1979) and are the same handshapes produced by young deaf children learning ASL from their deaf parents during their initial stages of acquisition (McIntire 1977). Since David used only the unmarked and none of the marked handshapes of ASL, he used fewer handshapes overall than are found in ASL, even in the ASL produced by young children. Nevertheless, David's use of handshapes to represent objects closely parallels the way handshapes are used in ASL.

David's handshapes represented objects in three ways. First, a set of David's OBJECT handshapes represented the visual-geometric characteristics of an object: Fist (bulky object), O (round, compact object), C (curved object), palm (flat, wide object), palm (many small particles), and point (thin, straight object). In ASL, handshapes (called size and shape specifiers; cf. Supalla 1982) are also used to represent the visual-geometric properties of an object, but the set of handshapes available in ASL is much larger than David's set. Moreover, the visual-geometric handshapes in ASL themselves consist of a group of simultaneous hand-part morphemes rather than a single handshape morpheme (Supalla 1982). For example, the number of fingers extended represents the width or depth of an object (one finger = thin or flat; two fingers = narrow or shallow; four fingers = wide or deep), while the curvature of the palm represents the shape of an object (palm straight = straight object; palm curved = round object). These components are combined within a sign in ASL to represent the width/depth *and* shape of an object (e.g., one straight finger = thin and straight object; one curved finger = flat and round object, etc.). At present we have no evidence that David's handshapes themselves consisted of a number of simultaneous morphemes rather than a single morpheme.

Second, David used one of his OBJECT handshapes to represent a semantic subcategory of objects: palm (vehicle or animate object), that is, a self-propelling object. In ASL this same category is represented, but with many more distinctions. For example, ASL has separate handshapes to represent a human, a small animal, a wheeled vehicle, an airplane, and a boat (Supalla 1982).

Finally, David's HAND handshapes represented an object indirectly by reflecting the hand grip used to manipulate the object: fist (handle a small, long object), O (handle a small object), C (handle a large object), palm (handle a large, flat surface), palm (handle many small surfaces). Again, ASL has a set of handshapes that are used in comparable ways but with many more distinctions (e.g., thumb and finger touching, with the other three fingers extended and spread = handle a wide, flattish-bottomed object; flat palm with the fingers spread = handle a flat plane; McDonald 1982).

Interestingly, when deaf children acquire ASL from their deaf parents, they tend at the earliest stages to use some handshapes comparable in form and meaning to David's. Supalla (1982) studied the development of size and shape and semantic classifiers in verbs of motion and location in three deaf children of deaf parents (ranging in age from 3;6 to 5;11). He found that all three children used what Supalla called "primitive" handshapes, the palm and the point. Two used the point for any category (as David did in his OBJECT point = any object), while the third used the point for wide, flat, and cylindrical objects. All three used the palm for animals, vehicles, and airplanes (as did David), and one used the palm for wide, flat, and cylindrical objects as well. Thus, even if provided with a conventional language model, children tend to use the same simple forms for the same general categories as David did. However, it is important to point out that, even by age 3;6, the children in Supalla's study were correctly producing the more specified handshapes for humans, animals, vehicles, and airplanes on a substantial number of the stimuli—handshapes and distinctions not seen in David's signs as late as age 4;10.

The similarities at a broad level between handshapes and motions in ASL and handshapes and motions in David's system suggest that David's set of handshapes and motions may reflect the units that are "natural" to a visual/manual language—units that may form part of the basic framework not only for ASL morphology but also for the morphologies of other sign languages. An examination of the early stages of acquisition of sign languages other than ASL might shed light on this issue, as would observations of spontaneous sign systems developed by deaf children in other cultures without access to a conventional sign language.

The deaf child in our study lacked a model of ASL—in particular, a model for the signs of ASL—which could have provided "guidance" in the extraction of subsign units. Without such "guidance," David acquired a system of subsign units with far less complexity than the morphological system of ASL. Thus, if a child like David is not exposed to a conventional language model, he is able to take only small steps toward developing a morphological system. In contrast, deaf children exposed to some model of ASL—even if that model lacks morphological analysis—have been found to develop the morphological system of ASL in *all* its complexity (Newport 1984). As might be expected, therefore, even an impoverished language model seems to make a significant difference in the nature of the morphological system the child develops.

The linguistic environment a child is exposed to thus appears to play a role in the complexity of the morphological system the child induces. Nevertheless, the fact that David could fashion a morphological system—albeit a simple one—even without the benefit of conventional linguistic input suggests that some aspects of linguistic analysis may be strongly guided by internal factors. At the very least these data suggest that, with or without a language model, children seek structure at the morphological level when developing systems for communication.

In sum, our previous work has shown that without the guidance of a conventional language model a child can develop a gesture system that has structure at the syntactic level—the level of the sentence. We report here that this same gesture system is also structured at the morphological level—the level of the word. Moreover, the forms and uses of morphological components in our subject were in several respects comparable to the forms and uses of morphological components as described for deaf children learning a conventional sign language (ASL). We suggest that hierarchical structure (or at least two hierarchical levels) appears to be a resilient property of language—a property whose development can withstand a dramatic alteration of the conditions children typically experience when learning to communicate.

4 Nativization, Variability, and Style Shifting in the Sign Language Development of Deaf Children of Hearing Parents

James Paul Gee and Judith L. Mounty

4.1 Introduction: The Nativization Framework

There are now a number of reports that deaf children of hearing parents presented with manually coded English input innovate ASL-like forms in their signing (Goodhart 1984; Gee and Goodhart 1985; Livingston 1983; Strong 1985; Suty and Friel-Patti 1982). To study this situation we have adopted, in previous work and here, Roger Andersen's "nativization hypothesis" (Andersen 1983a, 1983b; Goodhart 1984; Gee and Goodhart 1985, 1988; Mounty 1984, 1986). This hypothesis attempts to bring together, in the same conceptual framework, the processes of first-language acquisition, second-language acquisition, pidginization and creolization, depidginization and decreolization, and also language death. The nativization hypothesis proposes that there is a human biological capacity for language representing a set of internal norms for language. If the input in any language development situation is inaccessible or inadequate, for whatever reason, humans will construct their grammars on the basis of these internal norms. This process is called "nativization." If the input is accessible, however, humans will construct their grammars on the basis of the input and thus deviate more or less from their internal norms (within the limits allowed by these norms, of course). This process is

The research reported here was partially supported by a grant from the Department of Education, Office of Special Education (023-BH-40033), to James Paul Gee and Judith L. Mounty. A paper was first presented at the Conference on Theoretical Issues in Sign Language Research at the University of Rochester in June 1986. This chapter discusses the role of variability in sign language input to deaf children of hearing parents, argues for the efficacy of ASL or ASL-like input, develops "the nativization hypothesis," a hypothesis about the way ASL (and other natural sign languages) fit internal, biologically based norms for language, and finally, discusses the relationship of socially based style shifting and the acquisition of grammar in two deaf children of hearing parents. The chapter is exploratory, and the nativization hypothesis is just that—a hypothesis. For further evidence for the hypothesis readers are referred to a companion paper that was written before this essay was presented at the conference but appeared in print afterward (Gee and Goodhart 1988). Finally, this chapter is not making any general claims about style shifting in sign language, a topic that has not received nearly as much attention in the literature as it merits and needs. Rather, we claim only that looking solely at grammatical variables may obscure the developmental trajectories of deaf children of hearing parents.

called "denativization." Nativization is thus construction of grammars based on internal, biologically specified norms; denativization is construction of grammars based on the form specified by the input (for similar views in different frameworks, see Bickerton 1981; Chomsky 1986). In normal first-language acquisition the input is initially inaccessible because of the cognitive and processing limitations of the young child. Thus the child initially engages in large amounts of nativization. This is why children do not speak like adults and their initial grammars show a good deal of similarity across languages (Slobin 1977, 1982, 1983, 1986). As the child matures, the data get more accessible and the child denativizes toward the grammar specified by the input.

When a creole language first develops based on a preexistent pidgin that has itself only recently arisen, the input to the creolizing child remains inaccessible beyond early childhood. This is because there are few or no models of the superstrate language in the environment and because the pidgin constitutes inconsistent and inadequate data for the full range of functions required of a native language (Bickerton 1981, 1982, 1984). Thus the child engages in extended nativization and "invents" a new language. Since this invention is the product of extended nativization (constructing language based on internal norms), all radical creoles look a great deal alike, regardless of their substrate and superstrate languages (Bickerton 1975, 1981, 1984; for discussion, see also the comments to Bickerton 1984). If, however, speakers of the creole (as children or adults) gain access to the superstrate (by an increase in their access to native speakers, for instance), and if the superstrate is prestigious, they will gradually change the creole toward the norms represented in the input from the superstrate and the creole will "denativize" ("decreolize").

Input can be inaccessible for a wide variety of reasons: because of cognitive or processing limitations of the acquirers (e.g., children, new second-language learners), because of limited access to native speakers (e.g., pidginization), or because of psychological resistance to the input (e.g., many foreign workers in Europe; see Klein 1986). Input can also be inaccessible because it is too variable and inconsistent so that the learner cannot deduce a consistent set of rules from the input. Bickerton (1981, 1982, 1984), for instance, argues that this was the case in the development of Hawaiian creole. Children were exposed to a poorly developed and unstable pidgin spoken quite differently by speakers of different native languages (e.g., Spanish, Tagalog, Japanese, Chinese) and could not induce consistent rules (e.g., a major word-order pattern). Thus they fell back on their internal norms for language (for example, choosing subject-verb-object word order, an order that appears to be specified by our internal norms for language and that appears in most early creoles developed on the basis of nonstabilized pidgins; see also Givon 1979). Figure 4.1 and table 4.1 summarize some aspects of the nativization framework. The two poles in figure 4.1 are merely idealizations. If input were completely inacces-

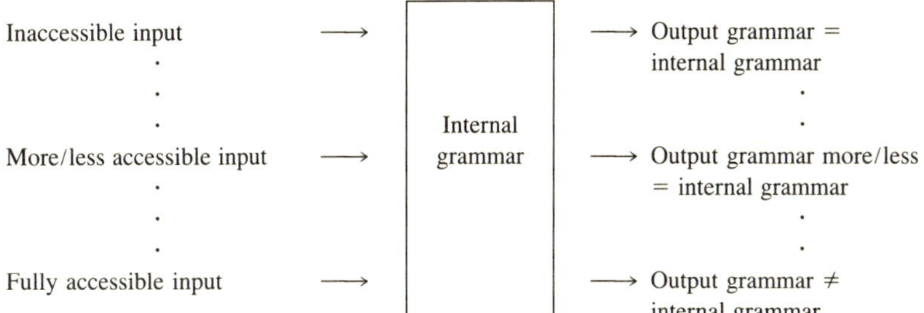

Figure 4.1. The nativization framework.

Table 4.1   Processes of Nativization and Denativization

Nativization Processes	Denativization Processes
Early first-language acquisition	Later first-language acquisition
Early second-language acquisition	Later second-language acquisition with access to native speakers
Later second-language acquisition with restricted input	
Pidginization	Depidginization
Creolization	Decreolization
Language death	

sible (the child got none at all), the human language acquisition device would not turn on; on the other hand, no matter how good the input, grammars always reflect some aspects of our internal norms for language, both in the sense that there are language universals (Comrie 1981; Foley and Van Valin 1984) and in the sense that our internal norms probably also specify the limits within which grammars differ from each other based on input (Chomsky 1986).

4.2 Nativization and Deafness

The acquisition of signed language by deaf children[1] is fertile ground for application of the nativization hypothesis (Gee and Goodhart 1985; Gee and Goodhart 1988; Mounty 1986). The well-known work by Susan Goldin-Meadow and her associates (Feldman, Goldin-Meadow, and Gleitman 1978; Goldin-Meadow and Feldman 1975, 1977; Goldin-Meadow 1979, 1982; Goldin-Meadow and Mylander 1983, 1984; Mylander and Goldin-Meadow, this volume) has brought attention to a dramatic case of inaccessible input. Deaf children with hearing parents who sign little or never to them do develop

1. One should keep in mind that even children who are not profoundly deaf will to various degrees lack full access to oral language data and thus will fall under some or all of the generalizations we make about deaf children. Such children should allow us eventually to study what happens as input gets more or less accessible in various increments.

signed linguistic structures, structures that we assume are specified by the internal norms for grammar.[2] However, these children have such poor input that one must ask whether their language acquisition device can fully engage with the process of language acquisition. Certainly they are in a position even worse than the creolizing child faced with an early, inconsistent, and highly variable pidgin. The latter child at least gets a good deal of input. But of course there are many other instances of deaf language acquisition. In fact, we can view deaf language acquisition as a continuum ranging from children who get little or no sign input, through children who get various invented systems, Manually Coded English (MCE), or Pidgin Sign English (PSE) to children who get one variety of ASL or another—for example, some deaf children of deaf parents (see Baker and Cokely 1980; Wilbur 1979; Woodward 1982 for discussion of sign varieties).[3] What complicates the matter greatly is that deaf children rarely get only one type of input. They are exposed, at various stages of their lives, to a wide variety of sources of input—in fact, to a mixture of the sign varieties above, sometimes from different people and sometimes mixed in the signing of one individual (Gee and Goodhart 1985; Mounty 1986). Deaf children of hearing parents are exposed (in addition to English-based sign) to varieties of ASL or ASL-like signing from deaf children or adults, and deaf children of deaf parents are exposed (in addition to varieties of ASL) to various varieties of manually coded English and Pidgin Sign English from hearing teachers and deaf children.[4] And this input, to both sorts of children—though a great deal of it uses ASL citation signs and thus has the same type of lexical stock—is not consistent in the grammatical rules it represents (these signing varieties do not have the same rules). Thus deaf children are exposed to highly variable and inconsistent input to a greater or lesser extent depending on individual contexts. We therefore expect to see more or less extended nativization on the part of deaf children, much as in creolizing children exposed to a variety of inputs from a highly variable pidgin and a variety of native languages (Deuchar 1983; Feldman, Goldin-Meadow, and Gleitman 1978; Fischer 1974a, 1978; Mayberry, Fischer, and Hatfield 1983; Meier 1984; Newport 1981, 1982; Woodward 1973b).

2. There may well be an important distinction to be made between cases where parents never sign and where they sign a little; it is possible that if they sign at all the influence on language acquisition may be drastic. It is an important research agenda for the future to determine, in these minimal input situations, if there is a "cutoff" point where a certain amount of input makes for a qualitative change in the nature of the language acquisition process.

3. See Mounty (1986) for a discussion on the lack of consensus on the differences between MCE and PSE.

4. It should also be said that though many English-based systems have similar rules, such systems vary a good bit in actual use. English-based input varies in the extent to which it incorporates ASL-like features or sticks to English rules. Thus, even in the English-based input itself there may be difficulties in inducing a consistent set of rules for various parts of the grammar.

Deaf language acquisition brings a set of new complexities to the nativization hypothesis, however. There is some evidence that signed English, whether an invented system or ASL citation signs put in English order, perhaps with some signs for English function words and grammatical morphemes, does not constitute accessible or adequate input. Deaf children, even when exposed to such input fairly consistently, will innovate some ASL-like forms in their signing (Goodhart 1984; Gee and Goodhart 1985; Livingston 1983; Strong 1985; Supalla, this volume; Suty and Friel-Patti 1982). Hearing parents who wish to sign such input to their deaf children often, over time, themselves innovate ASL-like forms in their signing (Swisher 1984; Mounty 1986; see also Reich and Bick 1977; Marmor and Petitto 1979; Quigley and Paul 1984 for English-based sign in the school setting and the way it often amounts to a version of PSE). Further, deaf children exposed to English-based input (of several sorts) together with samples of ASL will pick the ASL input as a model in many cases, even where there are clear alternatives in the English-based input and where that input is associated with their parents or teachers (Goodhart 1984; Mounty 1986). We can explain this if we assume that English-based sign is for some reason not fully accessible or adequate as input and will thus trigger a nativization that arrives at forms that are ASL-like. Two questions arise: Why is English-based sign inadequate? And why do deaf children, even when they have not seen the requisite ASL forms, innovate ASL-like forms based on their internal norms for language? We argued earlier (Gee and Goodhart 1985) that the answer is as follows: Children require a language that is fast and efficient (Slobin 1977; see also Slobin 1973, 1981, 1982, 1983, 1986). Given that a signed language is produced at a slower rate than an oral language (because it is made with larger muscles than oral language is; see Klima and Bellugi 1979), to be fast and efficient it must be morphologically complex (polysynthetic), not analytic (relatively isolating) like English (for this distinction between types of languages, see Comrie 1981). This may also be necessitated by the way the visual system utilizes information. In any case, signers who use sign to function fully will change the sign system they have from an analytic system like English-based sign systems to a morphologically complex system like ASL. We argue that the forms they innovate are specified at least in part by their internal norms for language within the restrictions set by the modality, and the requisite forms are in fact the ones we find in ASL. Given the conditions under which ASL itself is acquired—that is, with a small generational depth, a widely dispersed and small deaf community, and a great deal of variability in input in almost all cases—we assume that ASL must stay very close to the biological norms for language, again as these norms are expressed for the modality (i.e., analytic forms are not acceptable, being unable to fulfill Slobin's 1977 charges to language, of which two are to be fast and to be efficient). We might conclude then that some children acquire ASL forms because they make them up, some because they choose them from input that also contains less acceptable alternatives, and others because they have these forms as the main or sole alternative in their input. In all cases the result is the same and reflects the normative status of ASL.

4.3 Developmental Progression of DH and DD Children

Deaf language acquisition is thus a fertile field for the study of the trade-off between input and internal norms for language, as well as an indication of the form these internal norms take in a nonoral modality. In this light, let us look briefly at some data from a study by Wendy Goodhart (1984). Goodhart had deaf children of hearing parents (hereafter DH) and deaf children of deaf parents (hereafter DD) tell a Roadrunner cartoon story to their DH or DD peers. She counted two grammatical features of their signing that we take to be diagnostic of ASL (among many others, of course). The first feature was the number of productive verbs used with an incorporated marked handshape. These are verbs that are formed by productive sign formation rules. They are not citation forms or frozen lexical items produced as wholes from memory. ASL allows the incorporation of a classifier into these productive verbs, a classifier that stands for the entity that moves, is located, or changes state by virtue of the action of the verb (see Newport 1981, 1982; Newport and Supalla 1980; Supalla 1978a, 1978b, 1982; Padden 1983; Gee and Kegl, 1982a, 1982b, 1983a). Two examples are given in figure 4.2. In figure 4.2a a classifier for round solid objects (a 5-round handshape, open hand with bent fingertips) is incorporated into the verb stem (represented by a motion of the hand from one place to another). In figure 4.2b a classifier for vehicles (3 handshape) has been incorporated into the same verb stem (moving horizontally now). In the

(a)

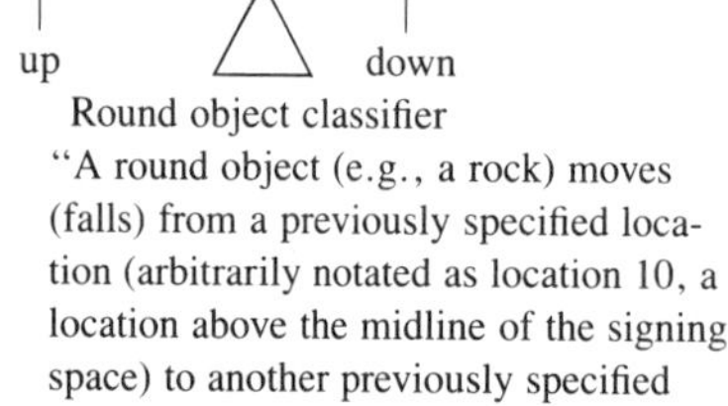

Round object classifier
"A round object (e.g., a rock) moves
(falls) from a previously specified location (arbitrarily notated as location 10, a
location above the midline of the signing
space) to another previously specified
location (location 20, a location below
location 10)"

(b)

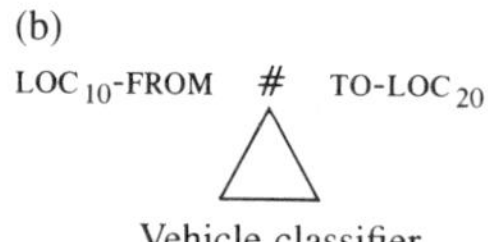

Vehicle classifier
"A vehicle (e.g., a car) moves (goes)
from a previously specified location
(location 10, e.g., representing L.A.) to
another previously specified location
(location 20, e.g., representing S.F.)"

Figure 4.2. Two examples of classifier incorporation. Two ASL clauses with productive verbs represented by the motion of the hand and incorporated classifiers represented by shape of the hand (the classifiers are placed under a triangle beneath the verb; Gee and Kegl 1982a). Adapted from Goodhart 1984, 87.

Table 4.2   Percentages of Productive Verbs with Marked Handshapes and of Verbs Showing
Agreement (out of Total Number of Verbs)

	Productive Verbs with Marked Handshapes		Verbs Showing Agreement	
Age	DD	DH	DD	DH
2–4	20*	50*	25*	25*
5–6	56.6*	56*	59*	56.7*
7–9	90.8	45.2	81.4	41.8
Adult	91.7		86.1	

Note: Percentages were obtained in cartoon retellings by deaf children of deaf parents (DD) and
deaf children of hearing parents (DH) at three age levels. Figures with an asterisk represent cases
where there is large variance about the mean, variance that is significantly greater statistically
than for those means with no asterisk.

early stages of acquisition, children use phonologically and morphophonologically easier handshapes, that is, unmarked handshapes, in these sorts of
verbs (Kantor 1982a; Supalla 1982; Goodhart 1984). For instance, they may
use a B handshape (flat hand) or a G handshape (pointing index finger), both
of which are unmarked in comparison with the marked handshapes in the example verbs above. Substituting a B handshape in figure 4.2a, for instance,
would yield the meaning "something falls" as opposed to the more specific "a
round solid object falls" with the 5-round handshape.

The second grammatical feature Goodhart counted was (spatial) agreement,
the process by which ASL agrees with the source and goal of a verb (according to some, the subject and object; see Padden 1983; Supalla 1982; Gee and
Kegl 1982a, 1982b, 1983a) by moving the motion of the verb between previously established locations assigned to the referents of the source and goal
arguments of the verb. For example, if a location in the sign space (call it
arbitrarily "LOC_{10}") has been assigned to "my home" and another location
(call it "LOC_{20}") has been assigned to "my school," then moving the hand
(with a vehicle classifier handshape) from LOC_{10} to LOC_{20} means "a vehicle
moves from my home to my school," and we want to say that the verb agrees
with the source (my home) and goal (my school) of the verb, both of which we
assume were first referred to earlier in the discourse. Agreement in ASL is of
course quite different from agreement in English (which agrees only with the
subject in the third person).

Table 4.2 below shows the percentages of productive verbs with marked
handshapes and the percentages of agreement for DH and DD at three age
levels in Goodhart's study (four or five subjects are in each cell). The percentages are out of total verbs in each text (cartoon retelling). Total number of
verbs is used as a measure of text length (on the centrality of verbs in ASL,

see Gee and Kegl 1982a, 1982b; Kegl 1985). We also give data for a DD adult whose retelling was used as a norm for the Goodhart study (a norm to compare the children with to see how close they were to a hypothesized "end state"). The DH in the Goodhart study had parents enrolled in sign language instruction where one of several English-based sign systems was taught. Thus, early in life the DH had English-based input from their parents. By age 3, however, all the children, DH and DD alike, were enrolled in either a day or a residential Total Communication school program. In this environment all the children were exposed to a highly varied linguistic environment containing various sorts of ASL (signed by deaf and hearing people with varying degrees of fluency), various varieties of Pidgin Signed English, and several types of English-based signing (see Baker and Cokely 1980; Quigley and Paul 1984; Wilbur 1979; Woodward 1973b, 1982 for discussion). Table 4.2 casts an interesting light on the question of variability in sign language acquisition. Note that the variance about the means for the 2–4 and 5–6 age groups—both DH and DD—is much larger than for the 7–9-year-olds in the case of both productive verbs with marked handshapes and verbs showing agreement. By 7–9, however, both DH and DD hit a relatively consistent group norm. We take this variance to indicate variability in the input to these children. This variability is caused either by variable types of input from a variety of sources (probably this is more the case for the DH) or by the fact that different children are exposed to different sorts of signing at home even when it is consistent (and this is probably true of the DD). We must remember that many DD have parents who were themselves DH and thus sign differently depending upon their own histories, and that most deaf children after about age 5 are exposed to a wide variety of sorts of signing. The emerging consistency out of variability we see at 7–9 reflects the nativization processes of the children as they innovate ASL-like forms, select them from the input over alternatives (see Appendix), or master them from relatively consistent input at home despite exposure to alternatives at school.

By age 7–9, DD are very close to adult norms for using productive verbs with marked handshapes and agreement in the cartoon retelling task; the DD adult used as a norm for the task above had 91.7 percent for productive verbs with marked handshapes (compared with 90.8 percent for the 7–9-year-old DD) and 86.1 percent for agreement (compared with 81.4 percent for the DD 7–9-year-olds). The DH are not near this norm. This difference is reflected in another aspect of Goodhart's data. The DD children show a clear and statistically significant developmental trend in the case of both productive verbs with marked handshapes and verbs showing agreement, increasing their output of both features in a manner consistent with age (despite the great variance at the earlier ages). The DH as a group do not show such a developmental trend. Obviously this reflects a difference in the input to DD and DH; the latter get less good (accessible/adequate) input, on the assumption that English-based sign input is less adequate than ASL-like input (where we assume the difference is one of language type—the difference between analytic and polysynthetic languages). But both DH and DD show large numbers of ASL-like forms. The DH do not, for instance, select exclusively English-based forms and forgo ASL-like agreement or productive verbs with marked handshapes. So the question is, granting that both groups are acquiring a significant amount of ASL-like morphology, What is the relation between the course of development of DD and DH?

In this regard, Goodhart stated an interesting hypothesis: she argued that the DH are on the same developmental progression as the DD but progress at a slower pace. Goodhart argued for this partly because some DH individuals in her study are closer to the DD than others and some, in fact, show evidence of full productivity for the two morphological processes she studied, attaining levels in both cases at or above those of the DD children. These children, Goodhart points out, were the ones who had gotten more ASL-like input early in life because their parents had been more involved with the deaf community—note that this does not mean they got consistent ASL input, only that they had relatively more access to ASL than the other DH, along with their substantive amounts of English-based input. The developmental progression of productive verbs with unmarked handshapes for the DD children can be summarized as follows: At age 2–4 they primarily use citation forms of verbs or emerging productive forms with an unmarked handshape; by age 5–6 they use marked handshapes incorporated into their productive verb forms, though they continue to use many productive verbs with unmarked handshapes; finally, by age 7–9 most of their verbs are productive with a marked handshape. The DH children behave differently. At age 2–4 they show more verbs with marked handshapes than the DD. This seems paradoxical, but in fact it simply reflects the input. Hearing parents and hearing teachers tend to use a large number of English-based signs (and thus at this early age DH are exposed to marked handshapes). Deaf parents, on the other hand, simplify their input to their deaf children, using phonologically and morphologically easier handshapes in their verb forms (Kantor 1982a). Hence young DD children tend to use productive verbs with an unmarked handshape at earlier ages. However, by age 7–9 the DH children have not fully acquired the process of incorporating a marked handshape into a productive verb form, though they do use a number of productive verb forms with unmarked handshapes, much like the 5–6-year-old DD children. This latter fact may reflect that they are undergoing the same developmental progression as the DD but moving at a slower pace.

It may well be true that DH children will move through the same developmental stages as DD children in acquiring ASL-like grammar, to the extent that this is supported by input and the nativization process. If this were all that was at stake—the acquisition of the grammar—then we would predict that DH children who are progressively exposed to more ASL input will eventually converge on the DD norm. However, the acquisition of grammar is not all that is at stake, as we know from numerous sociolinguistic studies over the past several decades (Labov 1972a, 1972b; Milroy 1980; Romaine 1984; Sankoff 1980). People mark their social/cultural identities through language (Ochs and Schieffelin 1984; Schieffelin and Ochs 1986). Thus one's language comes to reflect not just the overall grammar of the community, but one's identity as a member of one or more subgroups of the larger community. And this identification with one or more subcultures or social networks (Milroy 1980) is established by the control the language user has over the variable features of the grammar (e.g., the amount of /r/ deletion or missing copulas in various styles for Black Vernacular English speakers; Labov 1972b). In fact Muhlhauser (1980) argues (following Labov) that a language, to be adequate as a native language, must have variability so as to allow speakers to mark various degrees of formality (or other stylistic distinctions) by manipulating this variability. He argues that children creating a creole will add variability to the creole (that the antecedent pidgin does not have) and use it to mark different styles (e.g., they will introduce contracted forms of auxiliaries alongside full forms). We have argued above that variable input, in the sense of different sorts of input from different sources, if it is extensive and inconsistent, will trigger nativization. Here we see that any source of input, to be the basis of a viable natural language, must in fact contain some variability, though this variability, as Labov and others have shown, patterns in a consistent way across styles. We must keep these two senses of variability apart (though it is still an unsolved problem how the child recognizes the pattern behind stylistic variability in the community). While DH children are in many cases members of deaf culture, they are an identifiable subpart of it, as are DD children. On sociolinguistic grounds we do not expect their use of grammar (e.g., the strength of factors affecting the application of variable rules) to be the same, even where those grammars converge in their formal features.

To gain a deeper insight into these issues we will look briefly at two children who took part in the Goodhart study three years earlier. Both children were in the 5–6-year-old DH group, and their performances were at two extremes. One child, aged 9 three years after the Goodhart study—whom we call L—patterned like a DD child, while the other child, aged 10 three years after the Goodhart study—whom we call M—had the lowest scores of her group, being very English-based in her signing. The children have quite similar backgrounds, currently attend the same school, and are of similar intelligence. M was identified as profoundly deaf before age 2; she has an older hearing brother and a younger deaf brother. An early intervention clinic advised M's parents to a adopt a Total Communication approach, and the parents were exposed to English-based sign by professionals at the clinic. Initially the family had as input Signing Exact English (SEE 2) and signed English. Later the family had exposure to deaf adults and ASL. The parents decided to continue to use English-based input to M in the home in the hope that this would promote English speech and literacy. Despite this intention, we have discovered that over time the parents became less consistent in their use of English-based sign and began to use ASL-like inflection to express various verbal aspects, verb agreement, or plurality (Mounty 1986). At school the hearing staff generally uses ASL-based signs in English word order with signs or fingerspelling for some English function words. The other child, L, lives with his mother, who has two adult hearing children from a previous marriage. His deafness (which is equivalent to M's) was diagnosed when he was 18 months old, and the family was involved in the same early intervention program as M's family. His mother also was introduced to a combination of English-based sign and ASL through the intervention program. However, L's mother quickly decided to use ASL as well as English-based sign with him. She has a graduate background in language study, and this may have in part led her to appreciate the benefits of ASL over other forms of signing. She also became deeply involved with the deaf community. This early acceptance of ASL and the deaf community by L's mother, together with her graduate education in language, is the main difference between the two children. Thus ASL input is more accessible to L in the sense that his family situation has psychologically aided its acceptance and perhaps given him more examples of it, though both children have by now been exposed to extensive amounts of both ASL in several varieties and various varieties of English-based sign.

In table 4.3 we show the percentages of productive verbs with marked handshapes and verbs showing agreement for L and M when they were in the Goodhart study (5–6 age group) and three years later (when they were 9 and 10, respectively) on the same cartoon retelling task, done under the same con-

Table 4.3   Percentages of Productive Verbs with Marked Handshapes and of Verbs Showing Agreement (out of Total Number of Verbs)

Subject	Age	Productive Verbs with Marked Handshapes	Verbs Showing Agreement
L	5–6	85.7	82.1
L	9	36	28
M	5–6	13.3	13.3
M	10	48	38

Note: Percentages are for two DH children (L and M) as 5–6-year-old subjects in the Goodhart study and at 9 and 10 years old, respectively.

ditions. Table 4.3 is a bit surprising. At 5 years of age L had figures for both productive verbs with marked handshapes and verbs showing agreement that were very close to DD 7–9-year-old standards (90.8 and 81.4 respectively; see table 4.2). Now he has seemingly "regressed" seriously. M had been the lowest of the DH 5–6-year-olds. She has now moved her percentages of productive verbs with marked handshapes and of verbs showing agreement into line with what Goodhart's figures would lead us to expect of DH children her age. Thus she seems to be "catching up." In fact it may look as though L, who was once far ahead of M in grammatical development, is now behind her. Further, it is clear that both children are now a good deal behind the 7–9-year-old DD children Goodhart studied. The paradox here can be resolved only when we leave the purely grammatical level and turn to an analysis of these children's use of style shifting to mark out their social identities and their views of the social identities of others (for extensive discussion of the use of the notions of style and style shifting in sociolinguistics and historical linguistics, see Traugott and Romaine 1983).

To study the style shifting of these children, we had them tell the same Roadrunner cartoon used in the Goodhart study not only to each other (these are the data in table 4.3), but to a DD adult they did not know and to a hearing adult signer they also did not know. When we look at the children's performance summed across all these conditions, we see first of all that there is really little difference between them in their grammatical development at this stage. Table 4.4 below lists percentages of verbs showing agreement, productive verbs with marked handshapes, and all productive verbs (with marked or unmarked handshapes) for both children summed over all conditions (including a condition, not of concern to us here, where they signed to a DH adult). This table shows that, in terms of grammatical development, M appears to have "caught up" with L and that, as we saw also with table 4.3, they are both "behind" the older DD of Goodhart's study. But when we turn to their style-shifting behaviors, we will see that one cannot interpret figures about forms in the grammar (linguistic structures) apart from the context in which they were used and the system of style shifting they enter into. Although table 4.4 ap-

Table 4.4 Percentages of Productive Verbs with Marked Handshapes, of Verbs Showing Agreement, and of Productive Verbs (out of Total Number of Verbs)

Subject	Productive Verbs with Marked Handshapes	Verbs Showing Agreement	Productive Verbs
L	26.3	34	68.5
M	28	31.3	55.5

Note: Percentages are for two DH children (L and M) in a cartoon-retelling task summed across four conditions (to each other, to a DD adult, to a DH adult, and to a hearing adult signer).

Table 4.5   Number of Verbs, Number and Percentage of Noncanonical Verb Forms, Percentage of Verbs Showing Agreement, and Perseveration

	Peer	DD Adult	Hearing Adult
Subject L			
Total verbs	84	68	51
Total NCs[a]	31	13	3
NCs (%)	37	19	6
Verbs showing agreement (%)	38	43	12
Perseveration[b]	10 (3.2)	8 (5)	4 (2)
Subject M			
Total verbs	72	68	57
Total NCs	19	19	18
NCs (%)	26	28	32
Verbs showing agreement (%)	32	28	30
Perseveration	6 (2)	4 (2.5)	6 (3.5)

Note: Figures (percentages are out of total number of verbs) are for two DH children (L and M) signing a cartoon retelling to each other (peer), to a DD adult, and to a hearing adult signer.
[a] NCs (noncanonical verb forms) are mime and gesture.
[b] The first figure is total uses of perseveration; the figure in parentheses is the average number of signs over which classifiers were perseverated.

pears to show no real difference between the two children, differences do appear when we look at how they manipulate their grammatical resources across each condition. Here we will see that, just as L was advanced over M grammatically at 5–6 years old, he is now advanced over her at the level of style shifting.

We will now look at specific features of the children's language in each condition, chosen to represent both grammatically relevant features and ones directly relevant to the act of narrativization (Scollon and Scollon 1981; Gee 1985). The features we will discuss, shown in table 4.5 below, are as follows: each child's total number of verbs (a measure of text length), percentage of verbs showing agreement (out of total number of verbs), perseveration of classifiers (explained below), and use of "noncanonical" forms (explained below) in each condition. "Perseveration of a classifier" is a device where the signer maintains on one hand a classifier handshape that has been previously used in a productive verb while continuing to sign with the other hand. The classifier thus perseverates across several other signs (e.g., part of a two-handed sign may be perseverated while the other hand assumes a new handshape to convey another action or convey another notion). In an earlier paper (Gee and Kegl 1983b) we argued that this sort of perseveration is a topic-marking and topic-chaining device unique to ASL and is particularly effective in narrative construction. "Noncanonical form" is a cover term for "mime" and "gesture," devices that are also important for narrative construction (Loew 1984), though the use of such terms is controversial in ASL studies. In what we are calling "mime," the signer uses the full body and face to express propositional content rather than showing this content on the hands with canonical signs (either ASL or English-based). "Gesture" involves the use not of the whole body, but rather of the hands, face, or other upper body parts (e.g., shoulders) to communicate relatively straightforward ideas or emotions in forms that are not canonical signs in ASL or one of the pedagogical English-based systems. Note that in using the terms "mime" and "gesture" we are not talking about what has sometimes been called "mimetic depiction" (a misnomer for productive canonical verbs in ASL; see DeMatteo 1977). The term "mime" generally has negative connotations for some researchers, presumably because it may imply that ASL as a language is somehow less "digital" than other languages. However, Newport (1982; see also Supalla 1982) has shown convincingly that ASL is never analogue in its grammar, even in its productive verb forms used to mark movement and directions in space. And Tedlock (1983) has shown clearly that oral languages with rich traditions of oral storytelling use mimetic devices together with their normal digital grammatical devices, mimetic devices that are perfectly akin to what we are calling "mime" and "gesture" in signing (e.g., different degrees of vowel length to mark different degrees of emphasis or intensity). In fact, such mimetic devices are a hallmark of narrative in all oral language traditions we know, and what we are calling "mime" and "gesture" appear to be rich narrative devices in sign language narrative construction, devices that hearing signers can rarely use with any fluency.

Table 4.5 gives a rather clear picture of the children's behavior in each condition, though that picture must be backed up by a detailed analysis of how they signed each proposition in each retelling (Mounty 1986). In terms of the data in table 4.5, L shows a degree of patterning and consistency that M does not. L shows a regular progression across all conditions on all measures that allows us to construct a hypothesis about his style-shifting behaviors: M does not. As L moves from the peer condition to the DD adult condition to the hearing adult signer condition, he shortens his retelling (as M does also). He decreases his use of noncanonical forms incrementally, using the most to his peer M, the least to the hearing adult signer, and an intermediate number to the DD adult. In terms of verb agreement, he uses similar amounts to both deaf signers (peer and adult) but sharply decreases his agreement with the hearing signer. His use of perseveration is fairly high also in both deaf conditions but lowered to the hearing signer. In fact, both the data in table 4.5 and a close look at how L actually signs each proposition in the story to each partner (Mounty 1986) tell the same story. L appears to distinguish two dimensions along which he shifts style: formality (the peer-adult dimension) and deafness (the deaf-hearing dimension). Based on an analysis of how L signs individual propositions to each interlocutor, Mounty (1986) argues that with his peer (M)

L tends to use a good number of noncanonical forms, to role-play (Loew 1984), and to assume a good deal of shared knowledge, freely restructuring information, creatively elaborating it, and interjecting humorous comments. When signing to the deaf adult (whom he does not know) he drops some of the noncanonical forms and substitutes formal (canonical) signs, and he is more explicit in stating information rather than leaving it to inference. With the adult hearing signer he shortens his retelling, uses almost no noncanonical forms, and generally moves information off his body and face to his hands, or backs up information communicated by the body and face with overt signs. In addition, he uses fewer morphologically complex forms with the hearing signer and in this regard "simplifies" his language. Thus something like the picture in figure 4.3 emerges, where features of L's signing cross-classify the formal-informal and deaf-hearing distinctions, indicating that he can shift along at least two dimensions simultaneously. The hearing informal cell is empty because we have no condition where L signed to a hearing peer.

There is evidence, in fact, that though M does not display clear numerical evidence of style shifts, she is beginning to make the same stylistic distinctions as L. For example, consider the segment of the cartoon where the coyote walks up the inside surface of an arc-shaped tunnel to hang from the top by suction cups attached to his feet. To communicate this segment clearly in ASL, appropriate forms must be chosen to convey the following five essential elements: the tunnel, the nature of the surface (important for what comes later—the tunnel is made of blocks, and a block later falls out of the tunnel with one of the coyote's legs attached to it), that the coyote has suction cups on his paws, the difficulty of the coyote's walk up the inside surface, and finally that the coyote is hanging upside down. Only in the condition to the deaf adult does M include all these elements. With L she leaves more inferences to be drawn by the interlocutor, a general characteristic of her signing to L. In general, to the hearing signer she shortens her story, tends to repeat the elements that remain, and reinforces her facial and body information with overt signs (Mounty 1986). By looking at individual propositions we can therefore get clues that M is moving in the same direction as L. She tends to show these

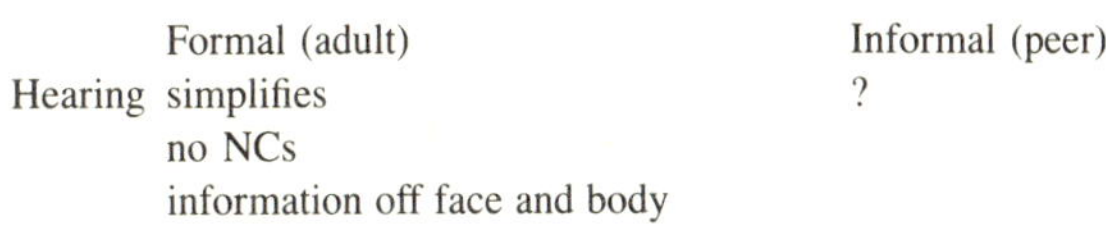

Figure 4.3. Hypothesized dimensions of style shifting for a DH child (L) in retelling a cartoon to a peer (deaf, informal), a DD adult (deaf, formal), and an adult hearing signer (hearing, formal).

shifts clearly on propositions in the story that encourage particular features relevant to the shifts (e.g., propositions that are the most heavily role-played with noncanonical forms by L in the deaf conditions are the most heavily role-played with noncanonical forms by M to the deaf signers and reduced to the hearing signer). However, she is not consistent enough across all propositions for her shifts to show up clearly in the pooled numerical data given in table 4.5. But just as she has "caught up" to L grammatically, we assume she will "catch up" stylistically. She thus appears to be on the same trajectory as L, but moving at a somewhat slower pace. We hypothesize that the rate difference between the two children is due to the input difference mentioned above—that is, the somewhat decreased emphasis on English-based sign in L's background. The similar trajectory is caused, we argue, by the ASL input the children have both been exposed to (along with much else) and the nativization process that causes these children, under such conditions, to innovate ASL-like forms and to favor ASL forms from the input over alternatives (on the issue of favoring ASL forms, see Appendix; for examples of innovated forms, not likely to have been seen by the children, see Mounty 1986; Goodhart 1984).

L, then, shows clear evidence of controlling various aspects of sign language, aspects that are typical of ASL grammar or ASL narrative style, in order to mark out stylistic distinctions between formal and informal (peer) contexts and between deaf and hearing conversational partners. M shows some indication that though she is behind L in the degree of systematicity she brings to the task of style shifting, she is following the same route. It is therefore not appropriate, and in fact can be positively misleading at this point of the children's development, solely to study their grammars. We need also to study how they bring to bear the resources of this grammar, as well as discourse devices like classifier perseveration and noncanonical forms, to mark out their social identities as DH children and to assign identities to others along such scales as formality (adult-peer) and deafness (deaf-hearing) through style shifting. Based on what we know of style shifting in various hearing communities (Labov 1972a, 1972b; Milroy 1980; Romaine 1982, 1984; Sankoff 1980), we assume that DH and DD children, having different social identities in the larger deaf community, will differ in how they marshal the resources of their grammars to mark out different styles (much like white and black speakers in the larger New York City speech community studied in Labov 1966). But since they are members of the larger deaf culture, these differences will take place in a framework of larger similarities, both in grammatical resources and in directions of style shifting (though the magnitudes in different conditions will differ). This is of course an important area for further investigation.

Keeping in mind that our study is exploratory, let us summarize our conclusions. Deaf children face a great variety of input from a variety of sources, including several varieties of English-based sign, several varieties of PSE, and several varieties of ASL signed to different degrees of fluency. This input is by no means all consistent in the rules it exemplifies, though much of it uses the same lexical stock, namely ASL citation forms. Furthermore, much of it is signed by people who do not have a sign system as their first language or who have not acquired their sign system very early in life. This variability suggests the applicability of the nativization framework. Deaf children go beyond the input and engage in extended nativization, constructing forms based on their internal norms for language in a visual modality and selecting ASL-like forms from the input as favored by these internal norms. In other work we have suggested that ASL closely reflects the human internal norms for a language in a visual modality. Given the hypothesized need for polysynthetic forms in this modality, the human biological capacity for language takes a certain form that closely resembles ASL grammar. Given ASL's small generational depth and the variable conditions under which it is acquired, ASL must stay close to the internal norms for language, commensurate with the need for nonanalytic forms. This explains why forms that deaf children innovate resemble ASL forms and why they favor ASL over other forms in the input.

The variability in input is reflected in the finding in table 4.2 that before 7 years of age deaf children (DH or DD) show a great deal of variance in their output, settling down to a relatively consistent pattern only at about age 7 or after. The efficacy of ASL input is shown by the fact that DD children, and not DH children, show a clear developmental pattern in acquiring the morphological features displayed in table 4.2. It is also shown by the fact that L was accelerated in grammatical development in comparison with M at an earlier age and is now accelerated in his discourse/style-shifting development. The only substantive difference between the two children is the somewhat greater accessibility (psychologically and perhaps in amount) of ASL as input to L, though both children have had both English-based and ASL-like input.

DH children do appear to develop grammatical forms much as DD children do, but at a slower rate. However, after the child is 7 years of age or so, looking only at grammatical development is misleading. The DH children we studied move on and learn to marshal their grammatical resources to mark out their identities as DH children in the larger deaf community and to style shift along dimensions of formality and deafness. Such style shifting is of course a universal and definitive property of anything that can rightly be called a natural language (Milroy 1980; Muhlhauser 1980; Romaine 1984). That L at age 7 used productive verbs with marked handshapes and verbs showing agreement at the level of a DD child, and that he can now style shift a variety of ASL features systematically, shows that he has had no problem acquiring ASL grammar. That his overall use of ASL grammatical forms is now lower than that of a DD child is simply indicative of his social identity as a DH child. In the end, just as it is fruitless to look only at grammatical forms as a measure of a child's language development, it is fruitless to see ASL as only what DD individuals (or even DDD) sign. ASL is a continuum of varieties used by the deaf community for the grammatical and social functions of a primary natural language. What gives this continuum its consistency and identity is not only the use it is put to by the deaf community, but the fact that it is undergirded by the nativization process—that is, by the human internal norms for language as these are expressed in this modality.

Appendix

To fully discuss the way ASL-like forms are favored in the input would take us far afield. We are not, of course, claiming that DH children (or DD children, for that matter) do not use, and stylistically shift, English-like features (e.g., "[and] then" as a narrative marker, English-like relative markers, English word order, or some English-like auxiliaries and prepositions). However, we are claiming that deaf children, when communicating in a completely fluent manner in styles they have mastery over, will either innovate or select morphologically complex verb forms, thus using a certain number of productive verb forms, incorporated marked handshapes, spatial agreement, morphophonologically fused forms, and inflectional aspect marking, resisting the more analytic (isolating) lexical and morphological aspects of English-based sign. One way we can get at the issue is as follows: we will define "vernacular" as those aspects of language used in a person's least formal, most spontaneous (least monitored) communication (using, perhaps, channel indicators of informality like rapid rate and laughter; see Labov 1972a, 1972b, 1972c). When one shifts to more formal styles, it is usually from the base defined by the vernacular, though one can of course switch entirely to a different language in a bilingual situation. The two DH children we study can be said to be showing us their vernacular when they sign to each other (and there are clear indicators of informality—laughter, elaboration, etc.). In this condition over 60 percent of their verbs are productive verb forms (61 percent for M and 71 percent for L). Such verbs are produced by productive sign-formation rules (see Newport 1982; Gee and Kegl 1982a, 1982b), involving the productive incorporation of a classifier into a verb stem, and are integral parts of ASL grammar, with no analogues in English-based sign. They are an important part of the ASL lexicon and exist side by side with citation forms of the sort listed in ASL dictionaries. Furthermore, the children show significant amounts of other features we take to be diagnostic of ASL narrative style (and not English); for example, verb agreement, role-playing, perseveration of classifiers, and noncanonical forms that enact aspects of the narrative in an integrated way with the canonical signs. The numbers of clearly English-based forms, initialized signs, or fingerspellings they use are so small in all conditions (whether signing to each other, a deaf adult, or a hearing signer) that they are not worth counting (except for prepositions, one or two for each child across conditions). Thus we can say that their vernacular is a form of ASL, not English, and that they have systematically favored this as their base language (though we could perfectly well imagine versions that are English-based, given the input they have been exposed to). A social, rather than linguistic, way we can put the point is that in setting up their vernacular they have favored their deaf identity over their identity in the English wider hearing culture (though we argue that there are linguistic and not just social reasons for this). When they style shift—for example, to a hearing signer—they do mark out the different identity of the interlocutor, but not by switching out of something that is recognizably a form of ASL (and not English-based sign). For example, about half their verbs are still productive forms (47 percent and 61 percent, respectively) and English-based verb or noun citation forms are still so low as to be uninteresting. We see in the text how they mark the style shift to the hearing signer. We are thus arguing that they are in fact style shifting on an ASL base. Of course they do use English-based features (e.g., prepositions, but they use these also in their vernacular, as does a DD adult whose performance was used as a norm for the retelling task we used). The issues are obviously complicated and have not been well studied (partly hampered by the misapplication of the notion of "native speaker," made popular by early work in generative grammar, to the ASL situation in such a way as to ensure that only DD children were thought to sign ASL, even though many of them were exposed to much English-based sign and had parents who themselves had hearing parents and learned sign relatively late). We are also aware of the controversy surrounding the notion of the vernacular (see, e.g., Romaine 1984, but also Gee 1989).

5 Manually Coded English: The Modality Question in Signed Language Development

SAMUEL J. SUPALLA

5.1 Introduction

In this chapter I address whether the structure of a spoken language (e.g., English) can be successfully incorporated into the signed medium. This question is especially relevant because Manually Coded English (MCE) is a recent development in American deaf education, used with thousands of children. The rationale behind the development of MCE lies in the assumption that there are no modality constraints specific to how signed languages should be structured. Indeed, four versions of MCE have been developed. However, evidence presented here, and in the forthcoming Supalla and Newport (n.d.), will show that MCE exhibits serious problems in being learned by children. Instead of acquiring and mastering MCE, deaf children exposed only to MCE change it into a spatially based structure more similar to American Sign Language (ASL) and other natural signed languages. These findings suggest that deaf children create their own linguistic structure to meet general modality constraints on signed (versus spoken) languages. Such devised linguistic structures afford us an insight into understanding natural signed languages in general.

Here I present a study of deaf children exposed only to MCE, with no exposure to other signed languages, who were asked to describe simple events in whatever way they chose. This was therefore a study of the spontaneous signing, outside the classroom, of children exposed only to MCE. I focus on how deaf children change the MCE input (from nonspatial to spatial) and provide an overview of the devised linguistic structures involved. Full details of these devised structures will be presented in Supalla and Newport (n.d.). Before describing the study, however, I will review our previous understanding regarding modality's role in signed language development.

In the United States, the natural language that has arisen in the visual/

This research was supported by National Institutes of Health grant NS16878 to Elissa Newport and Ted Supalla. I thank Elissa Newport for her editing and invaluable suggestions on earlier drafts of this chapter, Ted Supalla for his input on the development of tests, and Rudolph Troike and Howard Maclay for their suggestions on earlier drafts.

gestural modality is American Sign Language (ASL). Its symbol transmission occurs primarily in front of the signer's body, and the signing space and movement within the space command a formal role in the language's grammatical structure (Klima and Bellugi 1979; Petitto 1985b). Use of space and movement was once thought to be only a pantomime and thus not specifically linguistic in nature. Linguistic research has shown, however, that ASL has not taken advantage of potentially rich iconic representations provided by the visual mode; instead, its spatially based structure forms an abstract system that must be considered fundamentally linguistic in nature (Coulter 1980; Newport 1981; Supalla 1982).

In studies of the acquisition of ASL versus spoken language, the visual modality has no distorting effect on learning among deaf children; their acquisition patterns are found to be strikingly similar to those of their hearing counterparts. The two grammatical systems under investigation here—personal pronouns and verb-agreement inflection in ASL acquisition—undergo a learning process in ASL as expected in natural language acquisition. Petitto (1983a) showed that deaf children acquiring ASL personal pronouns display errors similar to those of hearing children, despite the transparency of the pointing gestures (see also Hoffmeister 1978; Bellugi and Klima 1982a; Petitto 1981).

The ASL verb-agreement inflection, like the pronouns, is mastered through a prolonged and error-laden learning process, despite the relatively transparent iconicity of many agreeing verbs (Fischer 1973a; Newport and Ashbrook 1977; Hoffmeister 1978; Meier 1981, 1982). These studies have indicated that deaf children learn verb agreement as a linguistic system, in which inflected verbs have internal morphological organization. Owing to the structural complexity, verb-agreement learning begins rather late, about age 2;6, and continues past 3;0 (Fischer 1973a; Hoffmeister 1978; Meier 1981, 1982).

Moreover, for other grammatical functions, space and movement are used arbitrarily in ASL's inflectional morphology for marking aspect and distribution on verbs, pluralization on nouns (Fischer 1973a; Fischer and Gough 1978; Supalla and Newport 1978; Klima et al. 1979), and derivational morphology that distinguishes verb stems from related noun stems (Supalla and Newport 1978). Thus the spatial forms within ASL are not at all analogue in nature; rather, they are like morphologically complex forms in spoken languages (Supalla 1982; Newport 1982).

Hence in many ways modality does not play a significant role in ASL structure or in how ASL is acquired. One might wonder, then, why the structure of ASL is spatially based (rather than, for example, based more heavily on sequential order as in spoken English). This issue is especially relevant for the case of MCE and its attempt to transfer English surface structure into the visual/gestural modality. Comparing ASL structure with the structure of MCE reveals that it does share some of the same componential system; however, in regard to how its components are formed and combined, it is different in many ways.

Klima et al. (1979) argue that, unlike what is typically true in English and many other spoken languages, inflectional morphology in ASL tends not to have a sequence of morphemes, for example, root and affix. With the exception of lexical compounds, the morphological organization of ASL is strongly nonlinear in nature. That is, ASL morphemes tend to combine with one another simultaneously rather than sequentially (Newport and Meier 1986). As described by Bellugi (1980, 122), "ASL makes elaborate use of grammatical mechanisms that rely on an essentially spatial medium, simultaneous and multidimensional articulation, and on the face and body as well as the hands, all co-occurring as separable layers of structure." Thus linguists in general agree that modality has contributed to ASL's unique inflectional forms involving spatial devices.

5.2 MCE versus ASL

Manually Coded English, in contrast to ASL, does not rely on spatial devices as possible morphological markers. Though MCE uses a lexicon that borrows heavily from ASL, its inflectional morphology is strictly sequential. Consequently, the borrowed sign's spatial components do not play any grammatical role. Instead, inflections in MCE involve a nonspatial form, utilizing invented signs that map one-to-one to English morphological markers. These signed morphemes are sequentially combined with the sign stem and become bound morphemes (suffixes). Thus MCE signs occur in a spatially restricted, sequential structure along with a strict word order—subject-verb-object (SVO)—all based on English.

The striking difference between ASL and MCE centers on how their bound morphology is formed—that is, spatially versus nonspatially. This contrast in formational properties has influenced how signs are inflected, simultaneously versus sequentially. For example, the ASL verb stem IMPROVE involves a single arc path moving on the signer's arm, as illustrated in figure 5.1a. To make IMPROVE a noun, in ASL, its internal movement would be changed to a repeated and restrained circular movement, thus signaling the sign as a noun. This change in movement is illustrated in figure 5.1b. For MCE, although the sign IMPROVE is borrowed from ASL, it is considered an unanalyzable unit. That is, the sign's spatial components do not serve any grammatical purpose. To derive a noun, MCE relies instead on suffixing onto the sign IMPROVE a devised sign that represents the noun marker -MENT of English. As illustrated in figure 5.1c, the result would be two signs strung in sequence, in contrast to ASL's compacting the same information into a single sign. One possible ex-

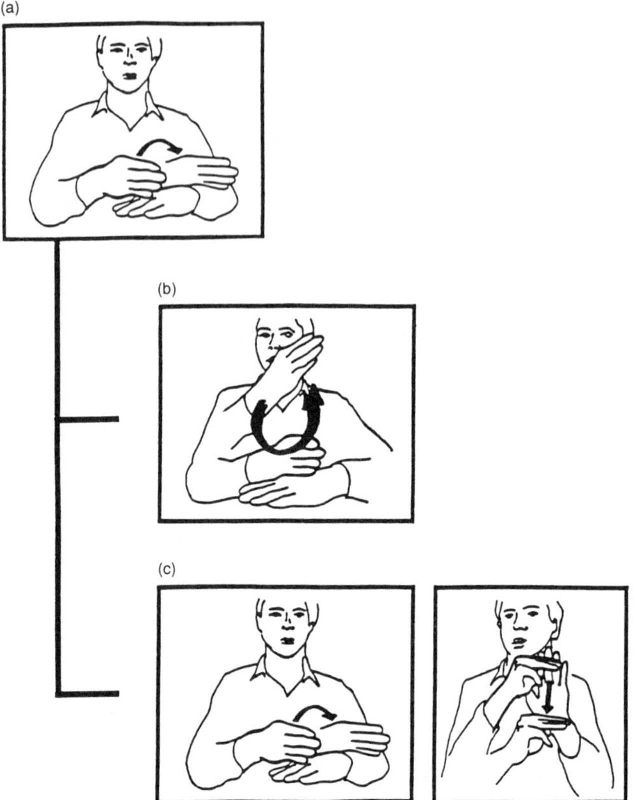

Figure 5.1. Nominal derivation, ASL versus MCE: (a) IMPROVE (citation form); (b) ASL's derived noun; (c) MCE's derived noun.

planation for ASL's compacting structure is the existence of natural neurological constraints on visual/gestural encoding and decoding of signs.

Stokes and Menyuk (1975) first raised the question of a possible violation of visual perception in MCE's morphological organization. That is, with sequential combination, MCE does not make any clear distinction between bound and free morphemes. MCE's bound morphemes might be perceived as free morphemes, and vice versa. This may result in the perceptual blurring of boundaries between bound and free morphemes, and consequently a deaf child may not correctly learn which morphemes are bound and which are free.

Temporally a sign, owing to its larger physical articulation, requires twice as much time to produce as a spoken word (Bellugi and Fischer 1972; Grosjean 1977); however, the proposition rate (the time involved in producing a sentence) is found to be equivalent in ASL and spoken English (Bellugi and Fischer 1972). MCE, on the other hand, is found to exceed the proposition rate of both ASL and spoken English by a factor of two (Bellugi, Fischer, and Newkirk 1979). This result may derive from the nature of its sequential structure, in which the number of signs in a sentence is found to be higher than in ASL. Bellugi (1980) suggests that MCE fails to meet the proposition-rate requirement imposed by the brain's central processing mechanism. This may very well overload memory, and cognitive processes coupled with the perceptual distortion of MCE's morphological organization may prevent natural language acquisition of English through MCE.

By contrast, ASL has apparently evolved a strategy for creating a structure appropriate for the visual/gestural channel, which may be vital for promoting natural language acquisition in deaf children. The strategy relies on a spatially based componential system, which enables lexical signs and inflectional indicators to be produced simultaneously. This type of structure is adapted to visual perception and also meets the general temporal demand for short-term storage and for cognitive processing.

In sum, the combination of perceptual/temporal and modality/channel constraints has been hypothesized to contribute to the difference in linguistic structure between ASL and English. From these hypotheses based on only two signing systems, however, it is still not established whether there are indeed general modality constraints on signed languages, thus distinguishing them from spoken languages in structure.

5.3 Background to the Study

A fuller understanding of the role of modality in shaping signed language development is crucial for a better understanding of natural signed languages in general. One source for such understanding could be cross-linguistic research on natural signed languages worldwide, but much of this type of research has yet to be performed. Another alternative is to investigate MCE in relation to its intended function as a language representing English in the visual/gestural mode. For this latter type of study, rich data are readily available: the deaf children in recent American deaf education. For the investigation of the role of modality in signed language development, some of these children are an ideal population. In the 1980s many deaf children have been exposed only to MCE and have received no other linguistic exposure. That is, they have received ASL-based lexical input; however, instead of ASL's spatially based grammatical structure, educators and parents have provided them with a nonspatial structure, heavily sequenced and supplemented with invented signs for the morphological markers of English. MCE is expected to function like English—that is, like a spoken language in the visual/gestural mode—and deaf children are expected to acquire it as their native language.

In my four hundred hours of classroom observation of six day-school programs, I observed signing among deaf children ranging in age from 3 to 18 years. Further, I chose Signing Exact English (SEE 2) as the target English-based sign system for my investigation, owing to its widespread popularity. The children involved had received what is claimed to be an ideal SEE 2 environment, whereby they were exposed strictly to SEE 2 and were not exposed to ASL in school or at home. The teachers (all hearing) had a minimum of five years' experience in SEE 2 and served as linguistic models for those deaf children of nonsigning parents. Only a minority of the children, under 10 percent, came from a signing home environment (their parents being competent in SEE 2) and had been exposed to SEE 2 from infancy. The ratio of deaf children in day programs coming from signing versus nonsigning homes parallels the ratio present in residential schools, where a minority of the students come from deaf families who use ASL. Analogous to the situation we see for native ASL signers at residential schools, these "native" SEE 2 signing children should theoretically become the linguistic models for the "nonnative" SEE 2 children in the classroom and playground.

The basic finding of my observation is that English competency remains a serious problem among the deaf children in these schools, and SEE 2 does not perform as a natural language should. That is, SEE 2 does not function equivalently to spoken English or ASL in how it is learned or used. When asked whether SEE 2 performs like a language, the teachers replied with a firm no.

I found that there are two common strategies among deaf children for developing an effective communication system. Children who had had even the most marginal exposure to ASL (in one case knowing someone whose sister had associated with children from a residential school) might abandon SEE 2 altogether and use ASL instead. In one day program where ASL had somehow penetrated, I noticed the deaf elementary students signing in ASL among themselves. When I asked the teacher if she noticed the difference between their signing among themselves and their signing with her, she replied, "Yes, it is two different worlds; one in this classroom and the other outside." A second copying strategy involved modifying SEE 2 so that it has a structure similar to ASL and is more appropriate for the visual/gestural mode. This second strategy seemed common among deaf children with no ASL exposure. The teachers I met also had noticed the changes their students made in SEE 2. One of them commented, "They have received SEE 2 input for at least five years, but they end up having something else."

Based on the observational data, my hypothesis was that, because of inherent problems involved in the transfer of a structure based on the spoken medium into the signed medium, deaf children in a pure SEE 2 environment may show impaired language acquisition and processing. I further hypothesized that such deaf children may readily find alternatives for becoming language competent and for communicating effectively with deaf peers. One alternative is to acquire a more natural signed language (e.g., ASL), even after surprisingly limited exposure to this language compared with everyday exposure to SEE 2. A second alternative is to change the received language so that it better fits the requirements of the modality. Such an effect was commonly found among the pure SEE 2 children who had been totally isolated from any ASL input.

I focused my research on children in this latter situation, and thus I address whether SEE 2 is indeed, as I hypothesized, modified by its child users to fit the requirements of the visual/gestural modality. Children exposed only to SEE 2 and isolated from ASL make ideal subjects for studying the effectiveness of an English-based sign system and the role modality plays in signed language development. The basic finding in my observational data is that these children spontaneously create some linguistic devices that are not used in SEE 2 but that are similar to those found in ASL or other natural signed languages (e.g., spatial devices). My claim here is that English-based sign systems have failed in their intended function to provide English competence in the visual/gestural mode and that deaf children exposed solely to such systems will resort to creating their own linguistic structures to meet the general modality constraints on signed (versus spoken) languages.

5.4 The Study

To test my hypothesis, derived from previous observations, regarding the existence of general modality constraints on signed language structures, I developed a set of questions and a specific test design. The main question focused on whether children exposed exclusively to SEE 2 produce signing with a grammatical system similar to that of SEE 2 or with a devised grammatical system more like that of a natural signed language (similar to, though not precisely like, that of ASL).

Thus my main aim was to investigate the form of devices that pure SEE 2 children used as markers of grammatical relations, asking in particular whether these children used nonspatial or spatial devices. Specifically, I chose to examine how these children marked subject (or agent) versus object (or patient) in their signing. According to my hypothesis, they would rely on spatial devices to mark these relations in their sentences. Moreover, I assumed that any such spatial devices would have been devised by the children themselves, since they completely lacked exposure to ASL or to any other signed language that marked these contrasts by spatial means. I hope that future investigation into other spontaneously created spatial devices in signing, and how they are organized linguistically, can also reveal evidence relevant to the modality question in signed language development.

Marking of subject and object relations is an ideal area of investigation, since the grammatical devices in SEE 2 and ASL contrast sharply in form— for example, nonspatial versus spatial. SEE 2, following the structure of English, involves nonspatial devices and a sequential pattern in which invented and borrowed signs are used as either bound or free morphemes. Space and movement involved in SEE 2 signing do not perform any grammatical functions. Instead, the two ways to mark subjects versus objects in SEE 2, as in English, involve *word order* and *pronominal form*. Word order in SEE 2 is usually SVO, so that the sign for the subject consistently precedes the verb and that for the object follows it. Thus the relationship is signaled through the order of the signs.

The form of pronoun signs also differs, distinguishing both subject and object cases and gender (in the third person). The contrasts in form in SEE 2 pronouns involve two formational parameters: handshape and location. For example, the sign HE (third-person masculine subject) has an E handshape and is placed at the signer's temple, a location reserved in ASL and SEE 2 for male signs, whereas the sign SHE (third-person feminine subject) has an E handshape and is placed on the chin, a location reserved in ASL and SEE 2 for female signs. The same locations are used for the objective pronoun signs: HIM and HER. However, the case distinction between HE and HIM lies in contrasting form, with the handshape E used for HE but M used for HIM. Thus the formational contrasts in these pronoun signs parallel the case, person, and gender distinctions of English.

As in English, the verb form in SEE 2 does not ordinarily play a direct role in indicating subjects versus objects; however, the verb is inflected for tense and number by adding another signed morpheme. Since in SEE 2 as in English there is number agreement between the verb and the subject, if the subject is singular and the object is plural (or vice versa), the verb can also indicate subject versus object. The regular and irregular verbs are treated similarly in SEE 2. In the present tense, the third-person singular verb is inflected sequentially with the -s sign. The sign PAST is used after the verb to indicate past tense, and so forth.

In contrast, ASL relies on a spatially based system for marking person and case; both involve distinctions in *locations* in space in front of the signer, as well as *movements* between these locations. Thus ASL uses a strikingly different type of marking than does SEE 2.

Person in ASL is signaled by marking in locations. First person (I, me) involves marking the signer's body location, while third person (she/he, it) involves marking a location in space away from the signer's own body. Deictic pointing is one spatial device used to mark these locations—that is, pointing to oneself or pointing at a location in space. It is important to note that this contrast in spatial location (body vs. space) is similar to that made in nonlinguistic gestural pointing. Person in SEE 2, on the other hand, is signaled by a difference in the shape of hand (I handshape on the body for "I" vs. E handshape on the body for "he"). In addition, distinct from nonlinguistic gestural pointing, ASL pointing is not limited to marking real-world object locations but is also used to establish abstract locations for nonpresent referents in the signing space.

The ASL verb's internal movement end points are another device used to mark the person location's through verb agreement. Moreover, ASL verb agreement also marks the person location's case; that is, the initial end point of the verb's movement may mark one person location as subject, and the final end point marks the second as object.[1] The spatial modifications within the ASL verbs for person and case marking actually fall into two basic inflectional processes, single and double verb agreement. The former involves only the final end point of the verb's movement. The latter involves both end points of the verb's movement, initial and final. ASL verbs are first subcategorized by whether or not verb agreement inflection is allowed. If it is allowed, they are further subcategorized into whether only single, or both single and double verb agreement inflections, is allowed (Padden 1983).

In short, ASL relies on contrasting locations for person marking. These person locations are marked both by the deictic pointing pronouns and by verbs through verb agreement. The case relationship between the marked person locations is marked redundantly through the SVO sign order and verb agreement inflections.

In regard to the target population of pure SEE 2 children, there are two general questions to investigate. The first asks whether these children rely on SEE 2's pronoun sign system and word order to distinguish subjects from objects and whether they inflect the verb sequentially using SEE 2's tense signs (e.g., -s).

If analysis of the pure SEE 2 children's signing shows an absence of SEE 2 features to indicate subjects and objects, then the second question is whether these children have instead devised a spatially based system to indicate these relations—specifically, whether they use some form and combination comparable to ASL's spatial devices (i.e., deictic pointing and verb agreement inflection).

To investigate these questions, I undertook a study of the performance of deaf children in a pure SEE 2 environment, comparing their elicited signing with that of their SEE 2 teacher.

5.4.1 Method

Test Materials and Procedure

To study how pure SEE 2 children mark case relations formationally, I designed a test to elicit case marking (i.e., the actor or subject of an action vs. the object of the action) from these children. The test consisted of a color film

---

1. The actual details of ASL verb agreement are more complex than presented here. For full details, see Meier (1981, 1982) and Padden (1983).

with a total length of eleven minutes, excluding the subject's response time. The film consisted of forty-five scenes: twenty-seven targets and eighteen fillers. In each target film scene two people (one male and one female) sit next to each other and perform an action with each other (for example, one gives the other a box; one yells at the other). Some of the scenes include interaction with the viewer; one of the two persons acts on the viewer or vice versa. The viewer is included in the films by having a hand of the "viewer" extended into the film from beneath the camera. The viewer must imagine that he is part of the three-person interaction, that is, the two persons in the film and himself. After subjects viewed each scene, the film projector was turned off, and two still pictures were set up on each side of the screen depicting the people in the film. The child was asked to describe the interactions between the people in the pictures and himself. To be sure the child used the desired verb in this signing, a short film of someone signing the uninflected verb was shown before each target film scene. The child was to repeat the given verb sign, showing that he comprehended the sign and its meaning. He was then instructed to use the given verb in his sentence to describe the event shown in the following scene.

The twenty-seven target items are composed of nine different action verbs (GIVE, PUT, THROW, BLOW, BITE, SPIT, YELL, TOUCH, and THANK), each presented in films involving three different case relationships. The three case relationships tested are as follows: the first type of event involves an action between the two persons in the film (for example, in English, "He gives the box to her"). The second type of event involves an action from either of the two persons in the film toward the viewer (the response in English would be, "He gives the box to me"). Finally, the third type of event involves the subject's acting on either of the two persons in the film (the response in English would be, "I give the box to him"). To make distinctions in these case relationships with the same verb, the child must rely on some case-marking system. These three case relationships were applied to each of the nine verbs to make up the total target number of twenty-seven. The twenty-seven target scenes were randomly ordered along with eighteen fillers (events involving only one person) introduced to avoid making obvious the interest in contrasting case relations.

Subjects

One group of children and one adult participated in the study. The subject group was recruited from two day programs two thousand miles apart, which had no contact with each other (via teachers or students). Recruiting of these children was based on specific criteria, which were met by five students from one day program and three students from the other. Among the factors that excluded many of their students from the study were age, multiple handicaps, and language other than English spoken at home. According to the criteria, the recruited subjects all came from families that possessed either minimal or zero signing skills. Their teachers served as the primary linguistic model, and these teachers had known and used only SEE 2 for at least five years. The rationale for excluding signing parents from this study lies in their inferior and varied signing skills compared with those of teachers. Also, ensuring that children learned SEE 2 only from their teachers meant that testing the teacher gave a reasonable indication of the children's linguistic input. In addition, children were selected from schools where only SEE 2 was used, with the children having no contact whatever with ASL or any other natural signed language. This selection criterion ensured that modifications observed in the children's signing could not have come from contact with another signed language. Any contact with ASL, even of the most indirect kind (e.g., knowing a friend whose sister associated with a friend from a residential school), was screened out by the school itself to ensure that the students were free of exposure to a natural signed language. The school also had to be one that had not admitted a deaf child from a deaf family or a residential school in its entire history. To maximize exposure to SEE 2 while still keeping the study within childhood, all subjects were about 10 years of age and profoundly and congenitally deaf.

The precise criteria for recruiting these subjects were as follows:

1. Age: 9–11
2. Grade: fourth and fifth grades
3. Language exposure
   a. Parents and siblings: nonsigning, speak English at home
   b. Signed language: exposure at school at age 5 or earlier, minimum of five years' exposure
4. Hearing loss
   a. Deaf since birth
   b. Profound hearing loss (ninety decibels or greater)

The one adult recruited for the study was a hearing teacher of the deaf whose SEE 2 experience extended eight years. In addition, this person is a native speaker of English. The purpose of including her in the study was to establish target SEE 2 structures for comparison with the responses the SEE 2 children made.

The case marking (CM) test stimuli were administered individually, in private, by an experimenter who is also deaf and a skilled signer. Before testing, the experimenter first familiarized himself with the children through frequent visits to their school in both the classroom and the playground. Though the experimenter was a native ASL signer, every precaution was taken to use

Pidgin Sign English (PSE), a diglossic English version of ASL, to avoid any possible ASL exposure for the children. The children's responses to the test were videotaped for later analysis.

Response Coding

Several coding systems were developed to allow me to examine the nine subjects (eight SEE 2 children and one SEE 2 adult model) and their responses to the CM test stimuli. First each response is coded as to the presence and type of verb and nouns. In stage 1, the subject's utterance is examined for the presence of a verb form. If the target verb is replaced with another verb, a record is made to indicate *substitution of verb,* and if no verb is found (or if the subject fails to respond at all to the stimulus), a record is also made to indicate *omission of verb.* In both cases the coding is then stopped. These trials are not included in the presentation of the data.

When a target verb is found, however, a second stage is required. A decision is made on the status of the verb, whether it has a *nonspatial* or a *spatial* form. The verb is identified as nonspatial when it is produced in its normal SEE 2 citation form. Such verbs may also be combined sequentially with one of SEE 2's tense markers. For example, the child would sign the verb GIVE, followed by the tense sign PAST after the verb, to indicate the past tense marking.

Spatial verb modification, on the other hand, is identified when the verb stem undergoes any change in its internal spatial components (i.e., movement and location). For example, if the child alters the path movement of the verb GIVE toward the location of one of the nouns in the signing space, then the verb is coded as having spatial modification.

The presence of noun forms is also examined in the subject's utterance. This examination undergoes coding steps similar to those for verbs. If no noun is found in an utterance (or if the subject fails to respond at all to the stimulus), a record is made to indicate *omission of noun,* and the coding is stopped.

When a noun is found, however, a second stage is required. This stage involves categorizing noun signs (e.g., BOY, GIRL) and pronouns (e.g., HE, HIM).

If there is a pronoun, it is identified as *nonspatial* when it consists of a SEE 2 pronoun marker (e.g., signs for HE, HIM). For example, the child would sign HE (E produced on the forehead) to indicate the person, case, and gender marking of the argument. The *spatial* pronoun, on the other hand, is identified when the signer points either to the self or to an object or person in the signing space. The test procedure involved having pictures of the people performing the actions in the film set up on the table in front of the signer, to the right and the left. Spatial pronouns typically, then, involved pointing to these pictures or to the signer's own body.

As a pilot study to determine whether the test was comprehensible to children as well as to adults and whether it was capable of eliciting grammatically contrasting forms, we gave it to six native ASL signers (four children aged 6, 8, 10, and 12 and two adults). The results show that they understood the task; they responded to the stimuli with group means of .99 for children and 1.00 for adults. In comparing their responses with expected responses, both ASL signing children and adults responded with target spatially modified verbs, as expected for ASL, at group means of .83 and .95, respectively. Deictic pointing for pronouns was used by both groups, at group means of .98 for the children and 1.00 for the adults.

5.4.2 Results

SEE 2 Devices versus Spatial Devices

The analysis first attempts to answer the main question—that is, whether the children use SEE 2 structures or whether instead they rely on a spatially based structure different from the SEE 2 input. I will first present data from the SEE 2 model, a native English-speaking teacher with eight years' SEE 2 experience, which will serve as a comparative basis for the data collected from the pure SEE 2 children.

An analysis of the data collected from the SEE 2 model confirms that SEE 2 (nonspatial) devices for case and tense marking were included consistently and uniformly in the model's signing on our test. The use of these specific markers corresponds closely with the case and tense marking rules of English. Table 5.1 shows the proportion of the model's responses that were correct according to the usage of SEE 2; verbs used in their SEE 2 citation forms (with no spatial modifications), pronouns used in the SEE 2 forms (again with no spatial modifications), and SEE 2 tense markers. As shown in table 5.1, the proportions of correct use of SEE 2 (nonspatial) verbs, pronouns, and tense, in required environments, were .89, .96, and .88, respectively.

The pure SEE 2 children's data contrast strikingly with those of the SEE 2 model. The SEE 2 devices, though vital to case marking in English, were al-

Table 5.1 Use of SEE 2 Devices by SEE 2 Model

Device	Percentage	Number
SEE 2 verbs (possible 27)	.89	24
SEE 2 pronouns (possible 27)	.96	26
SEE 2 tense signs (possible 24)	.88	21
Total responses		27

Table 5.2   Use of SEE 2 Devices by SEE 2 Children

Device	A		B		C		D		E		F		G		H		Mean
	%	No.	%	No.	%	No.	%	No.	%	No.	%	No.	%	No.	%	No.	
SEE 2 verbs (possible 27)	.32	8	.38	9	.08	2	.04	1	.27	6	.13	3	.27	7	.14	3	.20
SEE 2 pronouns (possible 27)	.00	0	.17	4	.00	0	.00	0	.00	0	.13	3	.04	1	.00	0	.04
SEE 2 tense signs (possible 24)	.00	0	.00	0	.00	0	.00	0	.00	0	.00	0	.00	0	.00	0	.00
Total responses	25		24		25		24		22		23		26		21		

Note: Letters identify SEE 2 subjects.

most entirely absent from their responses. The tense marker was completely absent. As shown in table 5.2, their proportions of correct SEE 2 (nonspatial) verbs are .20; SEE 2 (nonspatial) pronouns, .04; tense, .00. The proportions between the SEE 2 model and the SEE 2 subject group in using target verbs and SEE 2 devices are compared in figure 5.2.

Since the children's signing looked so strikingly unlike SEE 2, I reanalyzed according to the use of spatial devices. The two areas investigated were, first, whether the verbs in their responses are spatially modified in some way, and second, whether spatial locations (of the test pictures or of the signer) are established through deictic pointing (the criteria for scoring these spatial modifications are given in sec. 5.4.1). These two types of spatial indicators, though they should in theory not have been present in SEE 2 input, were nevertheless found in the SEE 2 subjects' signing. As shown in table 5.3, the use of such spatial indicators in their responses was highly consistent and uniform; their proportion was spatially modified verbs, .80; spatial locations pointed to, .86.

In contrast, the SEE 2 model's data, upon reanalysis, did not indicate any consistent use of either type of spatial indicator. As shown in table 5.4, the use of any such spatial indicators was almost entirely lacking in the SEE 2 model's responses; the proportion of their use was spatially modified verbs, .11; spatial locations pointed to, .07. A comparison of the proportions, for the SEE 2 model and the SEE 2 subject group, of using either type of spatial indicator is illustrated in figure 5.3.

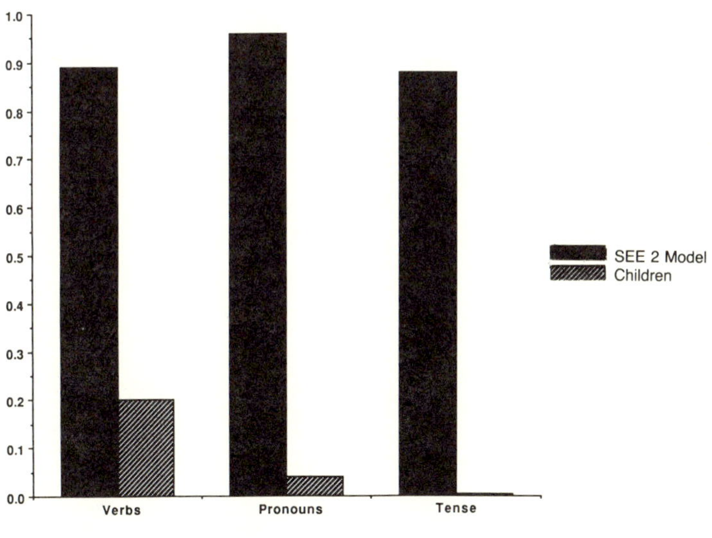

Figure 5.2. Use of SEE 2 devices: model versus children.

Table 5.3   Use of Spatial Devices by SEE 2 Children

Device	A		B		C		D		E		F		G		H		Mean
	%	No.	%	No.	%	No.	%	No.	%	No.	%	No.	%	No.	%	No.	
Spatially modified verbs	.68	17	.62	15	.92	23	.96	23	.73	16	.87	20	.73	19	.86	18	.80
Spatial pronouns	1.0	25	.92	22	.80	20	.79	19	.91	20	.96	22	.65	17	.81	17	.86
Total responses		25		24		25		24		22		23		26		21	

Note: Letters identify SEE 2 subjects.

Table 5.4   Use of Spatial Devices by SEE 2 Model

Device	Percentage	Number
Spatially modified verbs	.11	3
Spatial pronouns	.07	2
Total responses		27

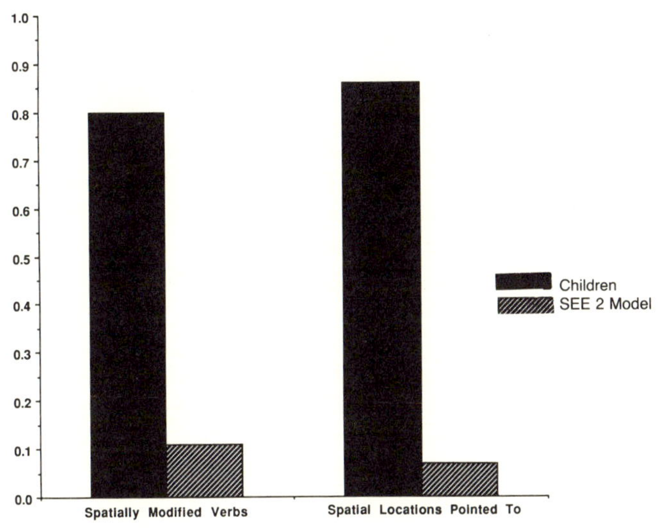

Figure 5.3. Use of spatial devices: model versus children.

In sum, as the data indicate, the children have made changes from their presumed SEE 2 input form. A striking phenomenon, these changes occur both in the form of the components and in how they are combined: SEE 2's nonspatial grammatical devices were replaced with essentially spatial ones. In short, the use of space and movement apparently was independently devised and added to their use of SEE 2.

The investigation described above has shown that the target verbs were frequently modified spatially; deictic pointing was also used. In both cases spatial locations were established either in the signing space or through the use of the signer's body itself. For example, signers would point at themselves as a location or point to a location in the signing space. Also signers would use the verb spatially, that is, moving it toward a location in the signing space or on their own bodies. More interesting, signers' bodies were consistently marked as first person, whereas the location of the test pictures was consistently marked as third person. For example, to mark first person, signers would always point at themselves or move the verb toward or away from themselves. To mark third person, signers would always point at a test picture or move the verb toward or away from it. This finding indicates that the contrasting of locations served as a person marker. That is, first- versus third-person distinctions are marked by distinctions in location, even though they are not marked in the way required by SEE 2 (e.g., using pronoun form "I" vs. "he" or "she"). Likewise, to contrast the location of one third person with that of another third person, a new location in the signing space is established (a distinction made in natural signed languages but not in English or SEE 2).

Spatial Devices and Case Marking

The next question concerns the possible grammatical structure of these spatial and location devices used by the SEE 2 children. Were space and location used consistently to indicate case relations (subject vs. object) by these SEE 2 children, as is done in natural signed languages? More generally, how is case marked in these children's signing? The full details on this issue appear in Supalla and Newport (n.d.). Below I present an overview of these findings, along with examples.

In overview, each of the SEE 2 children shows a consistent use of sign order and spatial modifications of the verb to distinguish case relations (subject vs. object). The case marking systems found in the SEE 2 children are all uniformly spatial in character; however, they are not all the same as one another or the same as the case system of ASL.

SIGN ORDER. According to Supalla and Newport (n.d.), most of the SEE 2 subjects show a strong tendency to adopt a consistent sign ordering pattern, although the pattern is not always that of English or ASL. Table 5.5 summarizes the sign order patterns for the eight children, totaled over all responses. From this table we can see that most of the children use a predominantly SVO sign order. However, the details of their individual usages are somewhat more complex. Some SEE 2 subjects use an SVO order across their sentences, while others show a different pattern when using spatially modified verbs than when using nonspatially modified verbs (Supalla and Newport, n.d.). Almost all the SEE 2 subjects also show a strong tendency to mark case as well through spatial modifications of the verb itself.

INFLECTION. With the spatially modified verbs, all the SEE 2 subjects show a strong tendency to adopt a consistent inflectional pattern, although the pattern is not always that of ASL. Moreover, these subjects also adopt inflectional patterns distinct from one another. Formationally speaking, some SEE 2 subjects use both single and double verb-agreement inflections across their sentences, while others are limited to double agreement. Table 5.6 summa-

Table 5.5 Sign Order Used by SEE 2 Children (Percentage of Stimulus Sentences Receiving a Response)

Sign Order	A		B		C		D		E		F		G		H	
	%	No.	%	No.	%	No.	%	No.	%	No.	%	No.	%	No.	%	No.
SVO[a]	1.0	25	.75	18	.80	20	.79	19	.59	13	.87	20	.42	11	.62	13
Other[b]	.00	0	.17	4	.00	0	.00	0	.32	7	.09	2	.27	7	.19	4
Verb only[c]	.00	0	.08	2	.20	5	.21	5	.09	2	.04	1	.31	8	.19	4
Total responses		25		24		25		24		22		23		26		21

Note: Letters identify SEE 2 subjects.

[a] SVO order includes sentences with SV, VO, or SVO order.

[b] Other includes sentences with VOS, VSO, OVO, OSV, VS, OV, and VSVO orders.

[c] Verb only includes sentences with only a verb, which cannot be scored for sign order.

Table 5.6   Types of Spatial Modification of the Verb by SEE 2 Children (Percentage of Stimulus Sentences with Spatial Verbs)

Modification	A		B		C		D		E		F		G		H	
	%	No.	%	No.	%	No.	%	No.	%	No.	%	No.	%	No.	%	No.
SVO[a]	.82	14	.73	13	1.0	23	.87	20	.88	14	1.0	20	.42	8	.84	16
Other[b]	.18	3	.13	2	.00	0	.13	3	.12	2	.00	0	.58	11	.16	3
Uninflected verb (number of responses)		8		9		2		1		6		3		7		2
Total responses		17		15		23		23		16		20		19		19

Note: Letters identify SEE 2 subjects.

[a] SVO modification includes verbs moving from subject to object or from signer to object.

[b] Other modification includes verbs moving from signer to subject and verbs with two stems, one of which moved from signer to subject.

rizes the inflection patterns for the eight children totaled over all responses and over both single and double verb agreement. From this table it appears that most of the children move their verbs either from subject to object or from themselves to the object. Again, however, the details of their individual usage are more complex and are presented in full in Supalla and Newport (n.d.). To illustrate the range of grammatical forms found, I will present examples from several children.

All the children, when using double verb agreement, move the verb from subject to object. However, the single verb agreement moves to the subject for some SEE 2 children, to the object for others, and to the person for yet others. In addition, the SEE 2 subjects are not limited to verb agreement for case marking; some of them rely on an auxiliary form for case marking as well. These children do a tracing movement with the index finger, from one location to another. This trace is always from subject to object. The use of this auxiliary for case marking is not found in ASL.

For example, with a specific verb stem, YELL, in the sentence, "He yells at her," two SEE 2 children's grammars are found to be distinct from that of the SEE 2 model, from each other, and from ASL. For comparison, the model SEE 2 sentence is illustrated in figure 5.4. In contrast, in the first SEE 2 child, illustrated in figure 5.5, the verb stem YELL undergoes a double verb-agreement inflection, in which its path movement starts at the location of the subject in the signing space and ends at the location of the object.

For another SEE 2 child the case marking pattern is different from the first. In the same kind of sentence, for this child the verb stem YELL undergoes a single agreement inflection in which only its final end point is modified to mark a location in the signing space. This is illustrated in figure 5.6. In this case the verb moves to the location of the subject (notice that this is different from single agreement in ASL). This verb is then followed by an auxiliary traced movement, as illustrated in figure 5.6b, which starts at the location of the subject and moves to the location of the object.

It is important to note that each child uses a pattern that is consistent across test items, although the patterns vary across children and, for some children, across subcategories of verbs. That is, these spatial modifications form grammatical systems for the children and are not merely trial-by-trial ad hoc usages. In contrast to the examples above, ASL's case marking system with the verb YELL involves only single verb-agreement inflection and is used to mark the location of the object. This differs in form from both the double agreement inflection found in the first SEE 2 child and the single agreement inflection found in the second SEE 2 child. As illustrated in figure 5.7, in ASL deictic pointing is also used along with the verb as a pronominal form. In this way, the SVO ordering of signs and the spatial agreement inflection mark the subject and object in ASL.

Figure 5.4. Model SEE 2 sentence, "He yells at her."

Figure 5.5. SEE 2 subject A's version of "He yells at her."

(a)   (b)

Figure 5.6. SEE 2 subject B's version of "He yells at her."

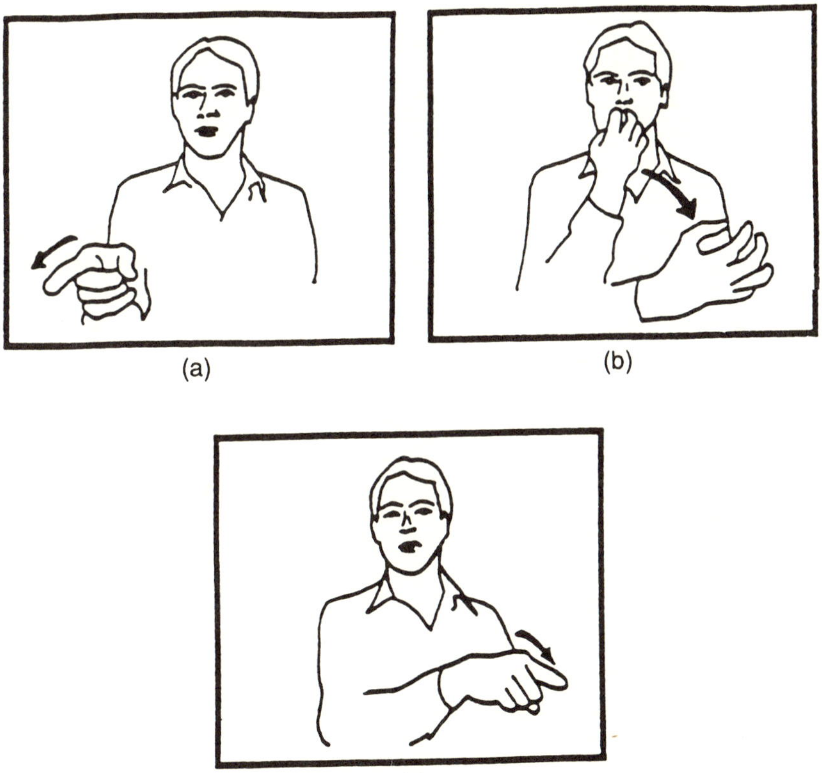

(a)   (b)

(c)

Figure 5.7. ASL version of "He yells at her."

In summary, both the SEE 2 children's signing and ASL rely on some kind of grammaticized use of space and movement for person and case marking. All the SEE 2 children used spatial devices of consistent kinds for marking both person and case, even though their input did not include such devices. These devised grammars and ASL share a common pattern in person marking. Differences between the SEE 2 children's signing and that of ASL, and among the SEE 2 children themselves, centers on how they mark case relations between the established person locations. To repeat, the full range of types of spatial grammars that appear in these devised grammars will be discussed in Supalla and Newport (n.d.).

5.5 Discussion and Conclusions

In regard to my original observational data, the findings of this study have confirmed both the teachers' and my own observations on deaf children's problems in learning and mastering SEE 2. According to my hypothesis, these problems are due to inherent difficulties involved in transfering a structure based on the spoken medium into the signed medium. In support of this hypothesis, the findings of this study confirm that deaf children exposed solely to SEE 2 resort to creating their own linguistic structures to meet the general modality constraints on signed (versus spoken) languages. All the children produced spatial modifications of the citation form of verbs and deictic pointing, even though their SEE 2 model did not do this on the same test. For person marking, these spatial devices were consistently used to mark and contrast locations in the signing space (e.g., signer's body location marked as first person as opposed to a location in the signing space marked as third person). All the SEE 2 children also devised their own sets of spatial devices and rules for case marking, consistent over the test within each individual but falling into several distinct types across the children.

The results suggest, first, a powerful tendency to symbolize deixis and semantic/syntactic case relations in signed languages in terms of spatial principles, even when there is no adult or child sign model who provides such an input. Moreover, since the children's spatial grammars differ from one another, these children apparently change the SEE 2 input independent of each other. This is probably because peer interaction is very limited in deaf day programs (there is no dormitory life), which thus may account for the lack of standardization of the language across children.

As an alternative account of the motivation behind deaf children's changing the SEE 2 input, one might argue that it is not SEE 2's inherent problems as a sign system, but rather the quality of SEE 2 input, that leads to these invented systems. This is a valid argument, since MCE input is reported to be beleaguered with deletions of vital morphological markers in both the teachers' and the parents' usage (Marmor and Petitto 1979; Kluwin 1981; Swisher 1985).

The actual input of English for some deaf children may also be Pidgin Signed English (PSE), as described by Woodward (1973a). If that is true, however, deaf children exposed to PSE or reduced MCE should undergo a creolization process in which they would "expand" and regularize their input. One would expect, on this view, that the pattern of a creolized MCE would be within the *non*spatial principles of MCE, but this nonspatial regularization of MCE clearly does not occur with my SEE 2 children. The nature of how they change the SEE 2 input may be better described as a "modalitization" process. That is, the SEE 2 input is here converted into a system more appropriate for the visual/gestural modality, with spatial principles added where none existed in the input.

To make language input via the visual mode learnable, there may be a biological predisposition for it to embody spatially based properties. This is evident in deaf children's problems in acquiring a sign system that differs radically from properties found in natural signed languages. These children have resorted to devising spatially based grammatical devices even when they have not been exposed to any. The evidence presented here suggests some constraints on learnability specific to modality, with the result that a linguistic pattern that is natural in the auditory mode may be unnatural in the visual mode.

Future research will attempt to identify some of the modality constraints in how a natural signed language should be formed and organized. I hope this work will contribute to the development of a modality-specific criterion for natural signed languages in general.

In sum, this research has provided a beginning answer to the modality question, concerning whether the structure of a spoken language (e.g., English) can be successfully incorporated into the signed medium: as hypothesized, the answer seems to be that it cannot. The problems with MCE seem to center on its learnability—that is, its structure may not be tuned to the visual perception and processing vital for natural language acquisition in deaf children. Recent literature on ASL has emphasized that modality has little effect on how deaf children acquire ASL, or on the structure of such language. This conclusion is valid in comparing ASL with natural spoken languages, since ASL is tuned to the visual/gestural modality. However, this conclusion applies solely to ASL and other natural signed languages. MCE, on the other hand, has apparently not met some of the modality-specific constraints on how a natural signed language should be formed and organized. Further research is needed to find out what modality specific constraints exist, but for the present, it is safe to conclude that the role of modality in signed language development can no longer be overlooked.

6 Conversational Interaction between Deaf Children and Their Hearing Mothers: The Role of Visual Attention

M. Virginia Swisher

6.1 Introduction

From a communicative point of view, a critical difference between vision and hearing is that visual reception requires a directional focus, whereas hearing does not. In short, while the hearing person can take in auditory input facing away from the speaker, the deaf person needs to be physically oriented toward the person who is signing.

The necessity of directional focus for visual reception of language is reflected in the convention that in a conversation between adult deaf people, the addressee maintains virtually constant visual attention to the person who is signing (Baker 1977). This implies that deaf children acquiring language in the visual mode—whether ASL or a signed code for English—also need to give visual attention to the signer. One cannot assume that such behavior is innate, however, and most deaf children are born into hearing families who have no orientation toward visual communication and its requirements. Considering that parents' lack of awareness of their children's visual needs when they are signing might lead to communication problems between parent and child as well as to limitations on the amount of language input available, it may be useful to review some of the main findings about gaze behavior in hearing people.

6.1.1 Gaze Behavior in Hearing People

Even though reception of spoken language does not require a directional focus, hearing people do not normally turn their backs to each other when they converse. For one thing, the conventions of interaction require that the

My thanks to Nancy Hatfield for sharing her insight that we needed to investigate deaf children's visual attention. Particular thanks also to Karen Christie, who had principal responsibility for coding the data and who shared her perceptions and speculations about the taped interactions as well as her comments about the drafts of the chapter, and to Delva van Roekel, who assisted with reliability and whose logical observations were particularly helpful in establishing the coding categories. As always, my thanks to Philip Dale for his typically generous feedback and to Marie Thompson for her support during the collection of the data.

addressee in a sustained conversation demonstrate that the message is received and understood. Visual attention to an interlocutor is greater when one is listening than when one is speaking oneself (Kendon 1967; Argyle et al. 1973), with reports of the difference ranging from approximately 1.5:1 (Duncan and Fiske 1977) to 3:1 (Argyle and Dean 1965).

Argyle and his associates suggest that looking at a speaker provides information from eye movements and changes in facial expression (paralinguistic information) that supplements the information received auditorily (Argyle et al. 1973). Still, the proportion of time for which a hearing person's gaze is directed toward a speaker has been reported to vary from 30 to 80 percent in a small sample (Kendon 1967), indicating that for hearing people visual attention during conversation is in some sense optional. Because gaze is not necessary for auditory linguistic input, it is free to vary in relation to factors such as sex, distance between conversation partners, status of the partners, and levels of intimacy (see Kleinke 1986 for a review).

Another important variable affecting allocation of visual attention to the interlocutor is whether conversation partners are engaged in something requiring visual attention. Levine and Sutton-Smith (1973), studying visual behavior of subjects ranging from 4-year-olds through adults, found that when the subjects were engaged in a building task, average visual attention of addressee to speaker ranged from 0.3 percent to 7 percent for the different age/sex groups. Visual attention is also affected simply by the presence of visual distractions in the environment, with attention being absorbed the most when people are discussing something they are looking at. A study by Argyle and Cook (1975, reported in Argyle and Cook 1976) found that whereas with no visual distractions the extent of gaze between conversation partners was 76.6 percent, when subjects were discussing travel plans in the presence of an outline map, their visual attention to one another dropped to 27 percent, and in the presence of a detailed map it fell to 6.4 percent. This lack of visual attention between conversation partners is possible for hearing people because they have two channels at their disposal, hearing and vision, and this raises the question of what mechanisms deaf people, with only one channel available, use to deal with the same situation.

Another aspect of the Levine and Sutton-Smith study demonstrates that the social conventions surrounding visual attention to an interlocutor are acquired gradually. Children in face-to-face conversation with peers give each other less visual attention than do adults conversing. Whereas the extent of visual attention while listening was about 70 percent for adults, 4- to 6-year-olds gave attention to the speaker approximately 40 percent of the time, and 7- to 9-year-olds attended about 55 percent of the time. For deaf children visual attention to the interlocutor is crucial for receiving information yet presumably they too must learn the behavior that is perceptually and socially appropriate for communication.

Another relevant source of experience or patterns of behavior in hearing mothers may be the typical evolution of visual interaction in hearing mother-child dyads. Research indicates that vision is extremely important for mother-child communication when the child is young but that this decreases with age. More eye contact has been found between mothers and 4-month-olds than between mothers and 6- and 8-month-olds (Friedman et al. 1976). What is happening in the interim? For one thing, from about 4 or 5 months of age, children start becoming interested in objects (and may in fact withhold gaze from the mother [Trevarthen 1979]). Because of the child's interest in toys, mother-child communication shifts from direct eye contact to joint visual attention on other things. Joint attention is achieved because the mothers tend to follow their children's gaze, fixating on the same toy the child is interested in, often pointing to it and making comments about it (Collis and Schaffer 1975). This simultaneous joint visual focus and verbal commentary provides a convenient means for the child to learn the relation between words and referents.

As children grow older, there is less reason for mothers to maintain gaze on them. Farran, Hirschbiel, and Jay (1980), for example, found that mothers of 20- and 36-month-olds gazed less at their children than mothers of 6-month-olds. It is clear that among the many changes that are happening in this period, including the child's becoming more active and independent, the child is learning to talk. Once the child has language, mother and child can communicate without joint visual focus—whether the mother is hanging wallpaper or the child is doing a puzzle: joint attention can be achieved verbally rather than visually. To highlight the obvious here, hearing mothers do not normally require the child to look at them before making a comment about the joint focus of attention.

The information above suggests that the communication situation of a deaf child growing up in a hearing family may be complicated because hearing and deaf people have different patterns of visual behavior (as well as different visual requirements), which presumably are largely unconscious. This means that the family needs not only to learn to sign to the child, but also to adapt to the requirements of communication in the visual mode, after a lifetime of being accustomed to the visual conventions of interaction among hearing people. Because such behavior is automatic, it may be difficult to unlearn or even to be aware of it. In particular, the information about gaze behavior of hearing people during discussion of objects suggests a potential conflict between the habitual communication patterns of parents and the fact that deaf children need to learn to attend visually both to the environment and to linguistic messages about the environment in one channel. In addition, that parents normally speak to the child at the same time they sign may contribute to maintaining the nonverbal behavior that accompanies their usual verbal communications.

The literature contains some hints that the difficulties hypothesized here do occur. For example, though it is logically obvious that deaf children cannot take in signs unless they are watching them, Erting (1985b) found that the hearing teacher of the deaf in her study "often began signing and talking before the children were looking at her" and frequently "neither repeated the portion of the communication that had been missed nor showed any awareness of the problem." In addition, she "usually attempted to get attention without any visual or tactile signal, even when the child's back was turned" (Erting 1985b, 119). Scroggs (1983) also reports that one of the hearing mothers she studied occasionally started talking to her deaf child when she was outside his visual range and would become annoyed when the child, not realizing he was being addressed, would fail to respond or would start to talk himself. Scroggs comments, "It is unclear to me if she realized what was annoying her" (Scroggs 1983, 129).

Another aspect of mismatching is suggested by McIntire and Groode's (1982, 318) report that "Hearing parents of deaf youngsters who have intelligible speech often complain that the youngsters demand eye contact to maintain conversations, when there are times that the parent is involved in something requiring visual monitoring and could auditorally monitor the conversation. Nevertheless, the youngster insists that the parent give undivided visual attention."

With regard to communication development for a deaf child in a hearing family, several interrelated potential problems suggest themselves. First, children do not start out as skilled conversational turn takers (Garvey 1984). Deaf children, whose linguistic and communicative needs crucially involve vision, are in the position of having to learn turn taking from parents who are not adept at communicating in a visual mode. Second, despite the importance of the children's developing visual attention for getting linguistic input and information, as well as communicating smoothly, they very likely will not see this behavior modeled in their mothers, and the mothers may or may not be aware of the need to instill this habit in the child. Third, there is the question of quantity of input: if mothers do not alert their children when they are about to sign to them, the children may miss the message or see only a fraction of it, leading to input that is even more fragmented than the incomplete signed messages often provided (Swisher 1984), and this will reduce the quantity and quality of linguistic information available to the child who is trying to acquire language. Moreover, if the child does not maintain visual attention once aware of the message, similar reduction and degrading of the input will take place. Fourth, communication from moment to moment may be disrupted by the mother's being unaware of her child's visual needs, or unskilled in managing the conversation, and this could lead to misunderstanding and frustration on both sides.

6.1.2 The Question of Input in Manually Coded English

The initial focus of this study was the amount of signed input actually received by deaf children whose mothers are using Manually Coded English (MCE) with them. The rationale for providing simultaneous signed and spoken input to deaf children is that the signs will supplement the fragmentary input provided by residual hearing and lipreading with a complete, nonambiguous form of information. The hope has been that such input would allow deaf children to acquire English naturally and successfully. However, thus far research has not shown dramatic improvements in language performance of deaf students since Total Communication was introduced (cf. Allen 1986). There are many possible reasons for this, including characteristics of the codes themselves (Cokely and Gawlik 1973; Supalla 1988), but one logical place to start investigating is with the question of whether the input being provided to the children is in fact complete. Given that input to hearing children has been found in a number of studies to be consistently grammatical (or in the words of Newport and her colleagues, "unswervingly well-formed," Newport, Gleitman, and Gleitman 1977, 121), one possible view is that deaf children learning English through a signed representation also need to see input that is complete and grammatical. Incompleteness of the input to deaf children thus stands as one of the (possibly multiple, interacting) candidate explanations for the failure of the use of manual codes to make the significant improvements in deaf children's acquisition of English that were originally hoped for. Studies have shown that in using simultaneous communication with deaf children, teachers often delete substantial amounts from the signed message (Marmor and Petitto 1979; Kluwin 1981), often resulting in fragmented and ungrammatical messages. Swisher (1984) also found that a sample of six hearing mothers using MCE with their deaf children left out between 8 percent and 26 percent of what they said, in particular the function words that are hardest for deaf children to learn.

The results above tell us only how much of the spoken message is produced in sign. This is not necessarily equivalent to what the child sees. It seemed possible that in addition to deletions in sign production by the mothers, there might be "deletions of perception" caused by the children's turning their heads or shifting their gaze. For one thing, MCE tends to be slow and cumbersome unless signers are highly skilled. For another, MCE requires the linear transmission of information in the visual mode, which may overtax visual memory. According to Bellugi (1980), deaf adults report difficulty in processing complete coded English messages. Children might be expected to have shorter attention spans than adults and less ability to integrate long strings of visual information, possibly leading to lapses in both cognitive and visual attention. These considerations suggested the need to examine the extent of the children's visual attention to their mothers' signing.

6.2 The Study

In the dyads studied, the children were between 4 and 6 years old, and their hearing losses ranged from 70 dB to no response (NR) at any frequency unaided, and from 30 dB to NR with their aids. The sample included five girls and one boy. Two of the children (labeled D and F) had cerebral palsy, but all had intelligence within the normal range. The children were the only deaf children in their families, and the mothers had not known sign language before the children were identified as deaf. The mothers had been signing for a minimum of two years, with a mean of three years. (Note: Because parents often do not become seriously concerned about the possibility of a hearing loss until the time when the child would ordinarily be starting to talk, and a positive identification of deafness and entry into an intervention program may take yet more time, a more stringent criterion was not feasible.) All the mothers used some form of MCE with their children. Four had had classes in Signing Exact English (Gustason, Pfetzing, and Zawolkow 1980) and the other two in Manual English (Washington State School for the Deaf 1972), a system that uses different signs for the different forms of the verb "to be," signs for morphological markers such as -s and -ing, and signs for articles, but does not use signs for derivational morphemes.

The mothers and children were videotaped in the home, on the third of a series of three visits in which language assessments were being performed for another study. The mothers were asked to try to interact with their children in such a way as to elicit a sample of the children's best language.

Descriptive data on the mothers and children in the sample as well as information on receptive language measures and the completeness of the mothers' signing appear in tables 6.1 and 6.2. As has been reported elsewhere (Swisher 1984; Swisher and Thompson 1985), there was considerable variation in the signing fluency of the mothers as well as in the linguistic complexity of their utterances. The mean length of the mothers' spoken utterances ranged from 3.1 to 5.75 morphemes, with a mean of 3.89. As noted earlier, the morphemes deleted ranged from 8 percent to 26 percent (mean 18 percent). The mean length of the signed utterances ranged from 2.38 to 4.93, with a mean of 3.1. The great majority of the words deleted were functors; however, these included things such as pronouns and the verb "to be," whose deletion left many sentences without subjects, main verbs, or objects.

Table 6.1   Demographic Variables by Individual Subject

| Subject | | Child | | | | | Mother | | |
	Age	Loss Unaided (dB)	Loss Aided (dB)	Age at Onset (months)	Age at Identifi- cation (months)	Years of Education	Years of Signing	Number of Sign Classes
A	4; 5	115	93	0	20	13	2	1
B	5; 9	78	30	9	10	18+	4	4
C	5; 9	NR	NR	14	15	12	4	4
D	4; 6	70	30	0	13	12	3	4
E	5; 5	99	45	0	12	17	3.5	3
F	5; 9	98	57	0	18	13	3.75	2

Note: NR = no response.

Table 6.2   Children's Language Measures and Characteristics of Maternal Input

Subject	Difference between PPVT Age Score and Chronological Age	NSST Receptive (of 40)	Mother's Spoken MLU	Mother's Signed MLU	Morphemes Deleted from Signed Message (%)
A	−1; 3	16	3.24	2.38	24.4
B	+0; 2	34	5.75	4.93	13.2
C	−2; 0	14	3.1	2.85	8.4
D	−1; 8	22	3.49	2.87	11.2
E	−1; 3	28	3.96	2.86	25.8
F	−2; 7	13	3.77	2.54	24.9

Note: PPVT = Peabody Picture Vocabulary Test; NSST = Northwestern Syntax Screening Test; MLU = mean length of utterance.

The mothers who were at the two extremes in terms of complexity of utterances as measured by mean length of utterance (MLU) were also at the extremes in terms of sign fluency. The mother with the shortest spoken MLU deleted the least but signed slowly and laboriously. Differences in utterance length as large as that from 3.1 to 5.75 are also likely to have qualitative correlates. In addition to using more complex constructions, the mother with the longest spoken MLU was the only one to use stylistic variation and idiomatic language.

Observations of the children's visual behavior were made in relation to one hundred of their mothers' utterances (except in one case [child E] where only eighty-four were obtainable that met the criteria). The utterances used were taken from the original samples from the previous study, except for utterances that the mother had not signed at all and utterances where the child had been off screen or where her face was physically obscured so that her direction of gaze could not be determined. Where necessary and possible, new utterances were added to reach the requisite one hundred.

The principal coder was herself deaf. Additional coding for reliability was done by an assistant who was the hearing daughter of deaf parents. In her case the coding was done with the sound turned off, both to create comparable conditions and to prevent interference from perceptions related to spoken communication.

For each utterance, the coder marked the signs during which children were looking, not looking, or shifting their gaze. It became apparent very early on that the eye movements were so rapid that it was difficult to determine exactly at what point in a sentence a child's gaze shifted, even with slow-motion playback. (Any notion of determining the percentage of the signed morphemes seen therefore had to be abandoned.) However, the procedure of attempting to code each sign was maintained in order to ensure close attention to the child's visual behavior. The coders were instructed to concentrate their attention on the direction of the child's gaze and to ignore subjective impressions about whether or not the child had seen a sign.

The final description of the data was limited to grosser categories: for each of the mother's utterances, the child's behavior was coded as "gaze," "no gaze," or "partial gaze." "Gaze" was defined as the child's watching the mother's face or hands throughout the utterance. "No gaze" referred to utterances where the child was not looking throughout. "Partial gaze" referred to the child's looking during some portion of the utterance. An additional category, termed "signs under nose," was used for instances when the child was not looking at the mother and the mother reached into the child's line of sight to sign something. Whole utterances in this category were classed as "gaze" in the final analysis.

The second coder categorized a minimum of 20 percent of the utterances in each sample. Interrater reliability ranged from 81 percent to one hundred percent with a mean of 91 percent (sd = 7).

6.3 Results and Discussion

The results by child are shown in table 6.3. Taken as a group, the children were seeing all the signs of an utterance an average of 62 percent of the time, some part of the signed utterance about 20 percent of the time, and none of the utterance about 18 percent of the time. In short, approximately two-thirds of the time the children were seeing their mothers' utterances in full (though this very qualified success is further weakened, one should remember, because the mothers were often signing reduced sentences).

Table 6.3   Children's Visual Attention to Mothers' Utterances and Mothers' Use of Body Taps

	Percentage of Utterances				
Subject	Seen in Full	Not Seen	Seen in Part	Partly Seen, Where First Sign Was Missed	Containing Body Taps
A	51	34	15	17	7
B	48	16	36	32	2
C	88	7	4	3	29
D	66	9	25	14	7
E	50	26	24	18	1
F	71	15	14	6	1

Note: Based on 100-utterance samples, except in the case of child E, where the sample was 84.

There were six possible interactions between completeness of the signed utterance and the child's visual attention: in cases where utterances were signed in their entirety by the mother, the child might see the whole utterance, only part of it, or none of it. Where utterances were signed only partially, vis-à-vis the spoken message, the same possibilities occurred. Examples of these categories (chosen so as to provide two utterances for each of the six mothers) are given below. The first line presents what was said, the second (in small capitals) what was signed, and the third what was seen.

I. Utterances signed completely by mother
A. Utterance seen completely
    Said: "The fire truck is allgone."
    Signed: THE FIRE TRUCK IS ALLGONE
    Seen: The fire truck is allgone.

    Said: "Do you like that book?"
    Signed: DO YOU LIKE THAT BOOK
    Seen: Do you like that book
B. Utterance seen partially
    Said: "What is the horse doing?"
    Signed: WHAT IS THE HORSE DOING
    Seen: What is the horse _____

    Said: "Do not look at the book now."
    Signed: DON'T LOOK AT THE BOOK NOW.
    Seen: Don't ___________________

C. Utterance not seen at all
    Said: "It is time for dinner, she says."
    Signed: IT IS TIME FOR DINNER SHE SAY-S
    Seen: _________________________

    Said: "Do it more carefully."
    Signed: DO IT MORE CAREFULLY.
    Seen: _____________________

II. Utterances signed partially by mother
A. All of mother's output seen
    Said: "Whose eyes?"
    Signed: WHO __ SEE SEE EYE __
    Seen: Who see see eye

    Said: "Let's make something with the clay, OK?"
    Signed: LET'S MAKE SOMETHING WITH __ CLAY
    Seen: Let's make something with __ clay.

B. Some of mother's output seen
    Said: "What's the horse doing now, hmm?"
    Signed: WHAT __ THE HORSE DO __ NOW
    Seen: What __ the horse do __ __

    Said: "That is a very very big alligator now."
    Signed: THAT IS __ VERY VERY BIG ALLIGATOR NOW
    Seen: _________ very very big alligator __

C. None of mother's output seen
    Said: "Say, look, he's gonna fall down and get hurt."
    Signed: __ LOOK __ __ __ FALL DOWN __ GET HURT
    Seen: _______________________________

    Said: "He took the chicken."
    Signed: __ TOOK __ HEN
    Seen: _______________________________

As these examples demonstrate, partial visual attention might occur because the child missed the beginning of the utterance or saw the beginning and then looked away before the utterance was finished. In most of the utterances in the "partial gaze" category the children missed the beginning of what was signed. More complex instances also occurred, particularly when the mother was trying to label something in a picture and trying to capture her child's visual attention, as in the following example:

Said: "This is a farmer—farmer."
Signed: FARM THIS THIS THIS IS A FARMER   FARMER Pt
Seen: ______________ this __________ farmer Pt.

In addition to the differences in maternal MLU, there were substantial differences among the dyads in style of interaction, which may be related to the level of hearing loss and the children's receptive and expressive language levels, as well as to individual differences in maternal style and the like. (It is interesting, however, that despite these differences the standard deviation for the "gaze" category was reasonably low [16 percent].) In a sample of this size it is difficult to obtain significant correlations and to interpret the failure of correlations to reach significance. Since we are still in the "natural history" stage of describing acquisition through simultaneous communication, however, it may be useful to treat the data from a quasi-ethnographic perspective, to identify factors that should be investigated in future research.

6.3.1 Factors Affecting Visual Attention

Mothers' Use of Attention-Getting Devices

As suggested above, because of the directional limitation of vision, deaf children's visual attention for communication depends not only on themselves but on their interlocutors' skill and sensitivity in making them aware of when they need to attend. The mothers in the present sample varied considerably in whether they used attention-getting devices to alert their children, and in which ones they used. Of the devices that are standard in the deaf community, such as waving a hand in the direction of the addressee, tapping a tabletop, and tapping the person on the shoulder, arm, or knee (Baker and Cokely 1980; Bienvenu and Colonomos 1985), the mothers used only the body tap, and only one of them used it to any extent (table 6.3).

Considering the use of this device in relation to the degree of the children's hearing losses, there is a surprising absence of consistency. Two of the children had profound hearing losses, to the extent that their hearing aids were basically nonfunctional for them. The mother of one of them, child C (who exhibited no response to sound at any frequency even when wearing her aid), was evidently well attuned to the need to give her child a physical cue before beginning to sign. She used a body tap twenty-six times before signing an utterance. Partly as a result of this cuing, therefore, the child saw 88 percent of her mother's utterances in their entirety, more than any of the other children. By contrast, the mother of child A, who also had a profound loss, used only seven body taps during the sample, and five of these were ineffective in securing visual attention in that the child would either ignore them or glance briefly at her mother's signs and then look away again.

At the other end of the spectrum were two children whose aided thresholds were 30 dB, within the range of conversational speech. Again the mothers' approaches differed dramatically. Child D's mother generally made sure of his visual attention before starting to sign, either by using body taps, by bringing her hands into initial position for a sign and waiting until he oriented, or by using his name and name sign together to secure his attention. On the other hand, child B's mother tended to start speaking and signing without warning, relying on her child to orient on her own. The child did in fact orient fairly quickly, perhaps in part because she was sitting close to her mother on a couch and may have either heard her speak or caught the motion of her hands in peripheral vision. But in terms of full attention to signs, the child inevitably missed the beginnings of sentences, particularly when she and her mother were looking at a book together. There were more than thirty utterances where she oriented late, and this is a large part of the "partial gaze" category for her.

Subjectively, both of these children seemed quite attuned to the communicative routine, being alert to what their mothers might do and for the most part orienting quickly. In particular, child B's capacity for visual attention, once she was alerted, was impressive. For example, in the course of one monologue by her mother she maintained attention for approximately sixteen seconds. Her visual skills are of interest in the light of her aided hearing loss: despite her response to sound, she was very much a "seeing child," in Samuel Supalla's term (Supalla 1986). Moreover, the absence of a physical or tactile cue from her mother led to a number of communication clashes between them, indicating that such cuing is not a trival matter, even in the case of good residual hearing. Of thirteen clashes in the one hundred-utterance sample, four involved mother and child's beginning to speak at the same time, and four involved the child's looking down at a book and beginning to talk, apparently not realizing that her mother was already signing and speaking.

In addition to using body taps or the child's name and name sign, mothers occasionally angled their faces around to gain eye contact with the child before starting to sign. One child's mother would repeat a sign until the child looked and then would start the sentence over. At times a mother would also simply wait and sign her comment when the child turned to her spontaneously. Finally, another means of securing the child's attention was the "signs under nose" approach of reaching into the child's line of sight.

There was some evidence that the mothers were selective in deciding whether to secure the child's attention, depending on the importance of the information to be conveyed. For example, mother C, who was otherwise apt to use body taps, did not do this if she was simply echoing what the child had said. As a result, the child did not see these "echoes."

From this small sample it is clear that securing the visual attention of even a profoundly deaf child is not simply a matter of "common sense" or something that can be left to a mother's natural instincts. One may wonder why the "obvious" necessity is obvious to some people but not to others. The failure of some mothers to provide visual or tactile cues indicates the need for early intervention programs to sensitize parents to the receptive requirements of the visual modality.

Communicative Context

Other factors that affected the children's visual behavior were more general aspects of the communicative situation. The most salient of these was whether the mother and child were talking about a book. In most cases the book in question was one in which the story was told entirely through pictures (Hartelius 1975). Some of the children (notably child A, so resistant to responding to her mother's taps) were very interested in the story—in which a baby alligator is raised by a chicken and grows bigger and bigger as it eats most of the things on the farm—and this claim on their attention sometimes kept them from focusing on their mothers. There was a more serious problem than simple distraction, however. As I mentioned earlier, in a conversation between hearing people the amount of visual attention to a speaker drops sharply when the people are engaged in a task, as the potentially complementary relation between the channels allows simultaneous attention to both an object and commentary on it (Argyle and Cook 1976). For the deaf child, however, to attend simultaneously to both an object and a signed comment about it is more problematic, since both are in the same channel; the child's attention may need to be given more sequentially, first to the object and then to the signed message, or the reverse. If the children are not given time to attend to both things, they may end up missing parts of their mothers' utterances.

As these considerations predict, the data showed that the visual attention of the children in this sample was less likely to be total when there was a book involved, either because the child was looking at the book initially and therefore missed part of the mother's remark, or because the mother was commenting on a picture and the child had to shift visual attention back and forth between the picture and the mother's signed comment. Communication around a book was additionally complicated by the mother's natural inclination to point to a picture to direct the child's visual attention. Because the mothers did not give the children enough time to register what they were pointing at and then to look up before they began to sign, the pointing device often backfired (Swisher and Christie 1989). Children responded to a point to a page at some times by looking at the picture, and at other times by looking immediately to their mothers' faces, then at the picture, then back to her signing. Thus, for example, child B's mother pointed to the page and signed the sentence, "That does not look like our stove," with the following result for visual attention to the signing:

Signed: PT. THAT DO ____ NOT LOOK LIKE OUR STOVE.
Seen: Pt. ____________ not look ____ our stove.

In other words, the mothers were not always sensitive to the children's need to get both environmental and linguistic information through the visual channel and seemed to be acting more in the frame of reference of hearing communication, in which the visual and auditory channels can complement one another.

For four of the children (B, C, D, and F) there were large enough segments of utterances focused on books and of utterances occurring in face-to-face interaction that it was possible to compare visual attention in the two situations. (Note: For child A nearly all of the sample involved a book-reading situation, and for child E most of the interaction was face to face.) Looking only at the percentages of utterances in each segment where the child was not attending at the beginning, we calculated the difference in the percentages for the two segments. The difference was minimal for the profoundly deaf child whose mother used physical cues (child C) but ranged between 20 and 30 percent for the other three children, a difference that was statistically significant (Test for Significance of Difference between Two Proportions, Bruning and Kintz 1977).

The Effect of the Child's Cooperation

Another important aspect of the communication situation was whether the child was inclined to cooperate with the mother's orchestration of the conversation. Some of the children had definite ideas of what they wanted to do. One of them in particular (child E) wanted to perform for the camera, by telling the story and then showing pictures, rather than talking with her mother. Since her mother had been instructed to engage the child in two-way conversation, this led in one segment to a struggle in which the mother tried to ask the child questions and the child tried to ignore her by not attending visually to the questions except in a very fleeting way. The child was clearly withholding visual attention because she did not want to go along with her mother's conversation or accept her mother's claim to the floor.

Turn Taking

Even where there was general acquiescence to conversation, problems with visual attention could occur in relation to turn taking. For example, we sometimes observed that when a mother asked her child a question, the child would glance away before responding, presumably to think and encode her answer. (This is the norm for both hearing and deaf people; Kendon 1967; Baker 1977.) At times the mother would go on to elaborate her question before the child had answered, and the child would miss part of this new utterance because of looking away. At some points in the transcript child B would look away from her mother's signed sentence prematurely, apparently because she thought her mother had finished. For example, in one utterance, "I think he looks proud to have an alligator for a friend," the child looked away on the word "for" and then looked back when she realized her mother was still signing. Of course, in these circumstances one cannot rule out that this was a random event. At times a number of reasonable explanations for the child's gaze shifting are clearly confounded. For example, in the middle of a dispute the child watched her mother sign the sentence "You are n—— forgetting to sign, and I need to have you sign to me ——," then looked away and started to protest vocally "I —— I did. . . ." Here the possible explanations include, at a minimum, looking away to process and encode; thinking her mother had finished her thought; and averting her gaze because of a negative reaction to her mother's statement (Nielsen 1964, cited in Kendon 1967).

In the two children with the shortest MLUs,[1] the child's gaze to the mother and simultaneous point sometimes served as a communicative turn. Child A, for example, after reading through a book with her mother, looked at her with

---

1. Approximate MLUs for the children (except for child D, who had cerebral palsy and whose signing was often difficult to interpret) are given below. The figures should be taken only as rough indexes of the children's expressive language for the following reasons: the children's utterances often do not look very much like English, which can make it difficult to know where one utterance ends and another begins; and young deaf children often tend to use points as part of their signed utterances, and it is not clear whether these points should be considered as adding utterance length (they were not counted for these children). These problems are exemplified in an utterance such as child A's GOOD PT. PT. GOOD EAT, or AWAY TO GO, CHICKEN TO GO PT., WORM NOT BOY, SAY-NO, which also demonstrates that one cannot infer from the child's utterance length syntactic or morphological control for English comparable to that of hearing children. Child C (the other child with a profound loss) was also problematic in this regard, producing very long utterances such as THE TURKEYS I AM MAD MAD-ING THE [mimes anger, crossing arms on chest] THE ALLIGATOR IS EAT CORN AND THE APPLE CAN EAT ALLIGATOR CORN, or I SEE CHILDREN. MANY MANYS AND VERY VERY HAPPYS HERE, where the MCE signs for inflections are used somewhat at random.

In the case of the children with more hearing, B and E, their productions are closer to English, and the MLU is based on a combination of the spoken and signed messages, as in "THE" BOY IS PLAYING IN DIRT, where "the" is spoken and the rest is signed. Child B was using mostly speech at this stage of her life, with signs added when her mother pressed her, and in her case the chief problem was to get a reliable transcription of her speech, since even her mother had trouble understanding her at times. The listener's comprehension task is more difficult at points when the child's grammar is nonstandard, as in the following example: "That is the alligator, and the fox— is going to eat the hen. . . . got very happy at the alligator, to scare the fox away." MLUs: child A, 1.74; child B, 4.17; child C, 5.7 (see reservations above); child E, 3.95; child F, 1.38.

a questioning raised brow while pointing to her father, which patently meant, "Can he read the next one with me?" Her mother responded "OK" and later said, half to herself, "Daddy helps with this one." "Gaze plus point" turns were particularly frequent in the communication between child F and her mother, though it was generally less clear what the child meant. As mother and child looked at a book together, the child would point to a picture and look up at her mother. Her mother was left to interpret what the child meant and to comment for her, for example, saying, "Is that a road?" or "The little boy's gonna *help* the horse?" This communication by gaze and point alone is reminiscent of interaction between prelinguistic children and their mothers.

Semantic Contingency of the Mothers' Utterances

Another important factor affecting the extent of the children's gaze was whether the mother was responding to a comment the child had made, as opposed to initiating something on her own. If the child had just taken a turn and looked back to the mother for response, visual attention was achieved naturally. The literature on normal acquisition emphasizes the importance of semantically contingent input, in which the mother gears her conversation to what the child has said (Cross 1977; Snow 1984). The present findings suggest that following the child's lead might be doubly important for the deaf child because of its role in synchronizing gaze.

It must be said that communication breakdowns sometimes occurred at times even when visual turn taking was superficially successful. Gaze functions not only as a channel for receiving information, but as a signal in turn taking. At times a mother would wait patiently for her turn and correctly interpret the child's look back to her as a go-ahead to speak, but then would fail to respond to what the child had said, instead introducing her own topic. In one instance where this happened, the child was so involved with what she had just said that she nodded enthusiastically through what her mother signed until she realized that her mother was talking about something else. She then nodded again, to what her mother had said, but with considerably less enthusiasm. Part of the problem seemed to be that the mothers had certain concepts they wanted to get across to the children—for example, that the alligator in the story was getting bigger and bigger, or that he was eating things he should not be eating, from apples to tractors—and their desire to make these points kept them from responding to what the child had said.

Communication breakdowns also naturally occurred when the mother did not understand what the child had signed, either because of her own limited receptive skills or because the child's language was unintelligible. If the mother did not understand or if the child was not making sense, it was difficult for the mother to respond in a "semantically contingent" way.

In addition, mothers occasionally signed something just for themselves, as when they were trying to remember or practice the proper articulation of a sign. This was most often true of the mother of child A, who was teaching a sign class in her community and who during the taping session was also showing signs to the child's father when he asked for them. This language exposure, which was not meaningful in terms of communication with the child, may have contributed to the child's not responding when her mother made a bid for her attention; the child would glance briefly at her mother's hands during these instances of practice and then look away again, as if she knew that that signing was not relevant to her. She may have drawn the general lesson that it was not always worthwhile to attend to her mother's signing.

6.3.2 Interplay of the Factors

The factors discussed here, which emerged from a description of the data, may not exhaust those relevant to visual attention in the children. In addition, these factors intersect with one another, and this logically limits their ability to be predictive of visual attention in themselves. For example, as observed above, if the mother's signed utterance is a response to something the child has just said and there is no other visual distraction, the child is likely to look back to the mother and will see what she signs. If there is a book present, however, visual attention to the mother will depend on whether the child wants or expects a response to her comment. If the child does not, and goes back to looking at the book, then visual attention to the mother's next utterance is more apt to depend on whether the mother uses an attention-getting device, even if she is responding to what the child has said. The situation is rather different if the child is not in the mood to cooperate in the interaction in the first place. That factor may affect visual attention negatively whether or not a book is present, and whether or not the mother attempts to get the child's attention.

6.3.3 The Relation of Visual Attention to Acquisition of English

Although visual attention is essential for the reception of sign language, it unfortunately does not guarantee either cognitive attention, successful language acquisition, or successful interaction from moment to moment. In this sample, child C attended more frequently to her mother than the others (partly because of the body taps mentioned earlier), and her mother also deleted less than the others (only 8 percent of the spoken morphemes). But this apparently positive situation was undercut by the fact that the child signed rapid and often unintelligible messages, sprinkled with extra -s's and -ing's, which were very difficult to follow. Her mother was often reduced to either echoing the child or asking for clarification. The mother's signing skills were also limited—she signed slowly and kept her sentences short (spoken MLU 3.1), partly because of the echoes, requests for repetition, and so forth. The dyad was thus locked in an unfortunate cycle in which the child was not getting good input but also was not making comments that her mother could elaborate on.

On the other hand, lack of consistent visual attention is not necessarily a guarantee of a negative outcome, at least if the child has functional residual hearing. Subjects B and E saw only 48 percent and 50 percent of their mothers' utterances in full, yet their language levels were the highest in the group. Among the competing explanations for this are that the mothers of these two children had substantially more education than the others (child B's mother was a Ph.D. candidate), and that the mothers had the longest spoken MLUs of the group (although this might in turn have been a response to the children's comprehension levels); because both these mothers signed rapidly and comfortably (despite deletions in their production and in the children's perception), the children may have been getting more input overall as a basis for acquisition. Perhaps even more important is that both children had comparatively good hearing with their aids, and residual hearing may well be such a powerful factor in acquisition of English that it overrides all others. There is another possibility as well: given that Manually Coded English systems use the visual medium in a way that is often not visually coherent, it may be that it is particularly important for the child learning English by this means to have residual auditory input to correlate with the signed code and its endings. That these two children had good residual hearing may have helped them make sense of the signed message and ignore the inconsistent pattern of deletions, in addition to giving them information that was not signed. Certainly we need a great deal more information about the way deaf children with different levels of hearing loss are able to process the codes and to integrate information from the two channels.

How much the children need to attend to receive input for language development is a difficult question. Concerning normally hearing children, we know only that they get enough input to acquire English successfully. We have no idea of what the limits are, or whether the child needs to see some threshold number of well-formed sentences to acquire grammatical competence. As I suggested above, the amount of complete input deaf children need to see may depend to some extent on whether they have usable residual hearing, since auditory input might be able to flesh out incomplete signed messages. As a counterargument, however, note that the elements most frequently deleted, namely functors, are also unstressed in speech; that is, they are weaker in both intensity and duration, as well as articulated less carefully, so that they are least likely to be heard.

For children whose hearing losses are effectively total, the logical situation is clearer: in that case input can consist only of what they see. This is really the test case for whether it is possible to acquire an auditorily based language through a visual representation of it. Here the evidence is not yet in and will not be obtainable unless parents and teachers of profoundly deaf children can learn to use manual codes consistently—without deletions—and unless they learn to do a better job of promoting visual reception in the children.

Another logical possibility is that children may need different amounts or types of input depending on the stage of their grammatical development. Conceivably, as their linguistic systems become more advanced, children might become less dependent on visual input and thus freer to sample the message rather than focusing continuously, because they would have the underlying grammatical competence to help them fill in the parts they missed. In this view, "looking less" might not be a bad thing across the board but would depend on the child's level. Children B and E, for example, saw fewer complete utterances than some of the others, but their language skills were higher. On the other hand, neither child was anywhere near age level in terms of expressive language. This being the case, they should therefore have been seeing ever more complex language from their mothers, which would require the maintenance of visual attention. In addition, as I mentioned at the outset, we know from Baker's (1977) work that adult deaf people maintain continuous visual attention on the person who is signing, even though they are themselves fluent in the language and though ASL presents information more rapidly and efficiently in the visual-spatial mode than coded English systems do. From that point of view, one would think that children learning signed English would need to be more attentive visually, not less.

It may be well to point out here that reduced input does not necessarily mean that parent and child are not communicating with some success, despite glitches in turn taking. Context and familiarity with communicative routines can provide support for interpretation of reduced messages, and problems of the mother's understanding the child's meaning in order to comment on it may well be more serious than those of the child's understanding the mother. At any rate, the main point here is to query how deaf children are to develop complex language based on fragments, for parent and child will need a more complex shared linguistic system in order to communicate once topics are not restricted to the here and now.

6.3.4 Limitations of the Study and Need for Further Research

Two important questions with respect to the coding decisions used in this study could affect the findings. First of all, the category of "gaze" was defined in terms of whether the child was looking at the mother's face or hands. There is the possibility, however, that deaf children might to some extent be able to read signs in peripheral vision.[2] There were times where mothers were signing fairly close to the children, so that the coders felt that the children might have been able to see the signs even though they did not appear to be watching. Because of the problems of reliability connected with subjective judgments, an early category of "peripheral gaze" was eliminated, and such utterances were categorized as "no gaze." There were a few incidents, however, in which children were apparently not looking yet gave appropriate responses to the mothers' signing. For example, child B's mother said and signed SIGN several times in the data, and the child, without looking at her, started signing again. Here the child might have been getting the message through residual hearing, peripheral vision, or both. There were also cases even with the more severely deaf children where they responded to something they had not apparently seen, sometimes nodding or signing YES with their heads down. Saying YES, of course, is not necessarily a convincingly contingent response. In a somewhat more persuasive case, a mother signed WHO THIS as the child was looking down at a picture of a fox in the book. The child responded with the appropriate handshape and movement for FOX, though in midspace.

There is also the question of how long a child needs to be looking in order to recognize a sign. Grosjean (1981) found that adults being shown increasing amounts of signs in a gating experiment needed to see only half of the sign in order to identify it (mean duration 817 msec). It is not clear how such a measure would relate to the judgments of the coders for this study. For example, if a child's gaze is judged to shift from "gaze" to "no gaze" before the end of a sentence, is it possible that in the shift to "no gaze" the child still got enough information to recognize the final sign? Among other things, we do not know whether the findings for adults can be assumed to apply to children. At any rate, it is possible that the results of the present study are conservative, for either or both of the reasons above.

In terms of the importance of visual attention for language acquisition, the case must be considered "not proven." In this sample the picture is obscured by the wide variation in hearing loss in the children as well as in the educational levels of the mothers, and these factors, in addition to introducing variability, may override the effects of how much signed input is seen. Further study is needed of a sample that is homogeneous in these respects and more

---

2. We now have evidence that deaf children between the ages of 8 and 18 are able to identify signs in isolation presented peripherally with considerable accuracy (Swisher, Christie, and Miller 1989; Swisher 1989). What is unknown at this point is how early this ability develops, and to what extent it is functional for the perception of signs that are in the process of being acquired.

heavily dependent on visual input alone. One factor that seems to suggest that visual attention is indeed important, however, is the behavior of deaf mothers with their children.

6.3.5 Input Strategies of Deaf Mothers

How do deaf adults who are accustomed to the requirements of visual communication handle conversations with their children, to prevent communication clashes and make sure the children see what they sign? The available information on deaf caregivers is sparse but tantalizing, much of it relating to very young children, at a time when parental input consists of utterances of only one or two signs. (It seems likely that maternal strategies would change over time in relation to a number of variables, including the child's mobility, attention span and other cognitive factors, and the extent to which a child has already learned to attend visually and to use appropriate turn taking behaviors.)

The mechanisms described in the few extant studies include the parents' signing directly on the child's body (e.g., Maestas y Moores 1980), signing on or near objects (e.g., Launer 1982b), signing on pictures in a book (Maxwell 1984), and bringing objects into the dyadic space and pointing to and signing about them (Kantor 1982b). Launer (1982b) reports that features of motherese such as producing a sign on its referent were found in the input until the children were nearly 2. We may note that signing on objects ensures that the child does not have to shift visual attention sequentially between a referent and a signed comment about it.

Management of the children's visual attention is also handled by touch: Maestas y Moores (1980, 5) says that parents "gently pat or tap their bodies or turn the infants' heads in the direction of the signing or fingerspelling." In addition they sometimes move their hands into the child's line of sight to sign or fingerspell.

In a longitudinal study of four deaf children of deaf parents, Harris and her colleagues (Harris et al. 1989) report that in observations when the children were 7, 10, 16, and 20 months of age the mothers' principal strategy was to sign where the children were already looking. In a sense this may be coherent with Gregory's (1985) suggestion that deaf mothers are more willing than hearing mothers of deaf children to wait for the children's attention before communicating. Active attempts to engage the child's attention before signing by tapping the child, moving an object, or adjusting the child's position were infrequent. By the 20-month session, two of the mothers studied were signing in their own signing space rather than moving into the child's visual field. The reason given is that the two children at 20 months both made use of an "attentional switching strategy" in which they periodically looked at the mother in the middle of an activity, giving her a chance to comment. The authors also report that by 20 months about 70 percent of the four mothers' utterances had a "salient context"—they related to the child's prior focus of attention or to an activity that was about to happen.

In terms of acquisition of the conventions of conversational interaction, McIntire (personal communication) reports that in her study of the development of discourse in a 13-month-old deaf child of deaf parents, the child had not yet learned the mechanisms of turn taking and attention getting used by adults (as described in Baker 1977). However, the child did not miss information because her mother "worked very hard at accommodating her inability to 'converse'—using a virtually endless repertoire of devices, including tickling, banging on the floor, etc., to gain and keep her daughter's attention."

The strategies mentioned here do not fully answer the question of how language is learned when the eyes must do "double duty," taking in both linguistic and nonlinguistic information: for example, in addition to the parents' bringing objects close to the child before signing, logically they must also allow the child enough time to distribute attention between object and sign. Most important in relation to the present study, we as yet have no information about how deaf children of deaf parents share visual and cognitive attention between linguistic and extralinguistic information once signed utterances start becoming longer. However, it is at least clear from what is reported in these studies that deaf parents are aware of their children's visual and communicative needs and that the multiple demands on visual attention do not impede acquisition of a natural sign language such as ASL.

Unfortunately, there is very little information on deaf parents using MCE with their children. However, the one subject for whom we have data (Swisher and Christie 1989), a hard-of-hearing mother who is a native signer, is notable for her close monitoring of her child's visual attention, often morpheme by morpheme, as evidenced by her repetitions of signs the child missed, waiting for the child to orient before signing, or drawing out signs until the child looked. She also stands out in her insistence that the child watch questions until the end before responding. This mother, at least, evidently considers it very important for the child to see everything that is signed.

6.4 Summary and Conclusions

The data presented here confirm the suspicion that deaf children of hearing parents miss part of the input signed to them because of the directional nature of vision and because the children do not focus consistently on the parents' signing. This is particularly a problem when there is something else in the environment (e.g., a book) to which they must also give visual attention. In such a situation the children are more dependent on their conversation partners to alert them when they are beginning to sign or to allow them time to look at a picture before the parent begins to sign about it, and the mothers in this sample often did not display this kind of helpful behavior. I speculate that this may result in part because the mothers continue to be influenced by communication behavior they have learned as hearing people and because they are speaking as they sign, which also makes it difficult for them to focus on the information the children are getting in the visual channel.

One might suppose that the fact that these children were frequently missing parts of signed utterances poses a particular problem for acquiring a visual mapping of English, which is sequential in its morphology and syntax. We normally assume that acquisition of a language depends on the child's having complete input, and a sizable body of research indicates that the input to young hearing children is consistently grammatical. Studies involving simultaneous communication (Marmor and Petitto 1979; Swisher 1984) have shown that deaf children often do not have complete input signed to them, and the present findings demonstrate that the children's inconsistent visual attention makes the available data yet more fragmented. Although these studies do not assert that adults cannot sign more completely or that hearing parents cannot learn to handle their children's visual attention more successfully, they do indicate some of the potential pitfalls of the systems. Fragmented input may help explain why the English competence of deaf students, as reflected through the indirect measure of reading achievement, has not increased dramatically since the advent of Total Communication.

We can look to deaf parents for help and models in developing awareness of deaf children's visual needs. On the other hand, we also need to remember the caveat that reception of ASL is one thing and reception of MCE is another. It is apparent that ASL is adapted to visual reception, and it may even be that it is adapted to being seen in peripheral vision at the grammatical level as well as at the lexical level, as Siple (1978b) has described. For one thing, morphological information in ASL involves characteristic patterns of motion, which vary in temporal and spatial organization, and the periphery of the eye is adept at perceiving motion. In addition, the grammatical mechanisms of ASL allow information to be transmitted quickly and compactly that in signed forms of English must be strung out in time. YOU-GIVE-ME BOOK can be signed more rapidly than the signed English version GIVE ME THE BOOK, to take a simple example. Slobin (1977) has suggested that one pressure languages respond to is the demand that they be "quick and easy," so that people can make their points quickly and retain their interlocutors' interest as well as the floor. This suggests that if language form is too cumbersome, nonessentials are likely to drop away. For the most part we concentrate on meaning, not form; this may play a role in deletions in the mothers' signing of MCE (though in some cases even the gist of the message is lost), as well as in the children's visual attention (we attend perceptually and cognitively until we feel we have gotten the point). Where grammatical realization and rapid transmission of information are in competition, as in the case of MCE, language form is likely to be endangered. This suggests that the codes may have some inherent limitations as means for providing input for acquisition of English, or at least that they are at risk for disposing toward reduced input in practice.

In addition, even if all utterances were signed and seen completely, it may be that signed codes for English present a more difficult receptive task than ASL, in terms of both visual perception and cognitive integration of messages, which in MCE must perforce be longer. It seems likely that deletion of grammatical information because of performance factors on the part of both parent and child would add to the complexity of the child's task in acquiring an auditorily based language through the visual mode.

On a practical level, the data show us that deaf children need the assistance of their interlocutors if they are to see everything that is signed to them, because people do not get visual cues to attend if their heads are turned. It is worrying that the mothers are only imperfectly tuned in to this fact and to the signed information their children are getting through visual reception. As we have seen, severity of the child's loss is no guarantee that the mother will develop this sensitivity. It is clear that at least some mothers are in need of consciousness raising about the visual signal, and it may be that a period of practice signing without voice would help them to become more aware of what the children are or are not seeing and to share the experience of the visual world they live in.

7 The Effects of Bimodal Communication on the Intelligibility of Sign and Speech

Susan D. Fischer, Dale Evan Metz, Paula M. Brown, and Frank Caccamise

7.1 Introduction: Simultaneous Communication

Simultaneous communication—speaking and signing at the same time, hereafter abbreviated SC—has both educational and theoretical implications. It is an important and timely issue, since many schools serving deaf students have adopted SC as their major, if not sole, communication method. One constraint on speaking and signing at the same time is that one must sign in some form of English, since the grammatical rules of ASL, not to mention human beings' cognitive and linguistic capacities, do not permit one to speak English while signing ASL. Exactly what form of English is represented on the hands has been an issue in a number of studies. For example, Marmor and Petitto (1979) argue that teachers of the deaf who use simultaneous communication are inconsistent in their manual representation of English; many spoken items are not represented in signing, particularly function words. The teachers' communication is supposed to serve as a model of English to their pupils and indeed is often their primary linguistic input.

Baker (1980) performed a similar study using four dyads, two of hearing people and two of deaf people. She found little difference between what was expressed in the two modalities by the deaf people, but a large difference in what was expressed by the hearing people, with many items (again usually function words) deleted in signing but not in speech. Baker uses this evidence to argue against the use of SC in classrooms serving deaf children, since the use of speech, she suggests, makes the signing deteriorate. By the same token, advocates of oral/aural approaches to the teaching of English (Geers, Moog, and Schick 1984) have argued that signing is detrimental to the use or acquisition of speech.

In looking at SC, we must make three important distinctions: the first is between *learning* a skill and *utilizing* that skill once it is mastered. The second distinction is between learning to perform two tasks *separately* and learning to

This research was supported under an agreement between the United States Dept. of Education and the National Technical Institute for the Deaf at Rochester Institute of Technology.

135

perform them *together.* The third important distinction is between *production* and *perception.*

Ling (1976) makes the important distinction between learning a skill and utilizing an already mastered skill. He speculates on the possible influence of signing on speech*reading,* and in particular on the *learning* of speechreading, as opposed to the *processing* of speechreading once the skills of speechreading and signing have been mastered. He suggests:

> There has been no direct research bearing on the matter [of the possible effects of signing on speech development], and . . . the evidence as to whether teaching by sign detracts from speech development is at best equivocal. If the child is totally deaf and no tactile cues are provided, then he must observe both the lips and the hands and be capable of processing both modes—which involve different coding processes—at one and the same time in short-term memory. One suspects that certain persons with well established skills in both speechreading and signing might be able to keep pace with the task if rate of presentation were favorable, but that it would be beyond the capability of a child whose performance in either mode was yet unskilled. (Ling 1976, 60–61)

Ling also addresses the second issue of learning two skills separately versus simultaneously. It might indeed be that learning to attend to the two signals in SC is more difficult than learning to attend to either one in isolation, if the signals are competing. It might equally be the case that once the skills of signing and speechreading are well established, the redundancy provided by two reinforcing signals outweighs the difficulty posed by attentional problems. On the production side, it is also important to consider the differences among learning to sign, learning to speak, and learning to put the two skills together. One might well argue that SC is a good strategy for communicating while recognizing that it may not always be the best strategy for modeling English for children. Indeed, one of the explicit tenets of responsible advocates of the Total Communication approach is that SC has its place, but that at times the child's needs may necessitate unimodal communication (UC) in either speech or sign.

The third issue of perception versus production also needs to be addressed. It is possible, for example, that simultaneous production is relatively more difficult than simultaneous perception of sign and speech. This could, theoretically, interact with other variables such as how well each skill has been mastered. Ling was concerned with the *perception* of speech in the presence of sign. In this chapter we are focusing on *production.* Before doing so, however, we should perhaps examine more closely some of the assumptions in

Ling's discussion. Implicit in it are a number of issues concerning the problem of simultaneity that have occupied cognitive psychologists for some time.

7.2 Simultaneous Tasks in Perception and Production

In the case of perception, there is some evidence that the same message conveyed in two modalities is more easily grasped. Erber (1979a, 1979b) summarizes work showing that for both deaf and hearing people the task of perceiving speech in two modes (listening and speechreading) can be coordinated; the tasks are not competing but reinforcing, to the extent that with visual or auditory distortions or reduced signal-to-noise ratios, accuracy of perception of the visual and auditory signals together exceeds accuracy of perception in either modality alone. This point is also made by Caccamise (1973), who found that some speech elements that were not identifiable under condtions of either speechreading alone or listening alone could be detected if speechreading and listening were combined. Carol DeFilippo (personal communication) provides a useful elaboration of Erber's ideas. She suggests that one signal can *complement* another (providing information that the other does not), *supplement* another (adding information that may not be so necessary), or be *redundant* with the other signal (repeating information already stated).

In the cognitive psychology literature, the effects of simultaneous tasks have been discussed extensively. In the areas of both perception and production, discussion centers on *attention*. Some have argued, for example, that performance on a secondary task reflects the amount of attention required for a primary task. Norman (1976, following James 1890) suggests that if a skill is automatized, it will by definition *not* interfere with the performance of a secondary task; in the case of perception, for example, it will not increase reaction time. Here again, the distinction between learning a skill and using that skill once it is automatized or mastered is important.

Klein (1976) discusses a number of studies that compared performance on a primary task alone with results from the same task performed simultaneously with a difficult secondary task. He reports that though simultaneity tends to adversely affect performance on the primary task, that adverse effect is greatly lessened if the task is well practiced (more automatized) or if it is redundant. Spelke, Hirst, and Neisser (1976) performed a study that also directly addresses the importance of practice on simultaneous tasks. They chose two tasks, reading for comprehension and either writing to dictation or shadowing material totally distinct from what the subject was reading, which at first glance seems virtually impossible. Although the skills described were probably equally automatized, putting them together initially wreaked havoc with their performance. Subjects initially performed abysmally on the simultaneous task compared with the single tasks in isolation. After three months of practice, however, they were able to perform the simultaneous task with virtually no decrement in performance as measured by both speed of reading and accuracy of both comprehension and dication or shadowing. A follow-up showed that this skill was not lost with disuse.

Several studies in the cognitive psychology literature and the field of deafness have shown that simultaneous performance of two tasks may either be easier or, in the case of communication, provide more information than either modality alone. McNeill (1985) summarizes a number of studies he and his colleagues performed that collectively suggest that signing and speaking at the same time might not necessarily adversely affect production of either modality. McNeill and his colleagues are interested in the coordination of gesture with speech, whereas here we are considering gesture as nonlinguistic in character (in contrast to signing, which though nonoral is still linguistic). They have found that there is complementarity between gesture and speech. For example, McNeill and Levy (1982) analyzed a videotaped story where the narrator was talking about someone chasing someone else with an umbrella. The narrator used the general verb "chase" and simultaneously gestured to show exactly what was being used as a weapon and how (swinging it from side to side). The gesture channel was thus providing information that was lacking in the speech channel, and vice versa.

Further support for the notion that speech and gesture do not necessarily interfere with each other comes from a study by Levelt, Richardson, and La Heij (1985). They found that gesture and speech are closely timed together and that fully or partially preventing someone from gesturing while speaking impedes the fluency of speech.

The two studies just cited are concerned with the coordination of gesture with speech where the gesture, though certainly conveying information, is not, properly speaking, *linguistic* in nature. What happens when the speech and the gesture *are* both linguistic? In particular, what happens to speech and signing when the two tasks are performed simultaneously? Are they necessarily competing, as argued by Marmor and Petitto or Baker, or can they too be reinforcing? Are they redundant enough in DeFilippo's sense to ease the task of production?

There is some evidence that, at least perceptually, many profoundly deaf people perceive more of a message from SC than from speech alone (Caccamise, Brewer, and Meath-Lang 1983). Further, some important recent studies by Maxwell and her colleagues (Bernstein, Maxwell, and Matthews 1985; Maxwell and Bernstein 1985; Maxwell, Bernstein, and Mear, this volume) suggest that if one focuses on how much English is being conveyed in the entire signal rather than just on the hands, the picture changes dramatically. Maxwell and her colleagues replicated Marmor and Petitto's 1979 study but used a different scoring system. In results somewhat reminiscent of McNeill's, Maxwell has found that what is not on the hands may well be easily caught from other aspects of the signal or from the syntactic and pragmatic context. For example, Maxwell and Bernstein (1985) discuss a case where the *-ing* in "losing" is present in the speech but not in the sign. However, Maxwell and Bernstein point out that the progressive aspect can be interpreted from this utterance owing to the context in which it is uttered. While most of the mismatches they find are where the speech contains something the sign does not, they also found cases where in the same sentence one aspect of the structure will be represented only on the hands, while another aspect of that structure will be represented only in speech. This is an example of where the sign and speech can indeed be complementary rather than competing.

Although the studies cited have focused on what happens to English when it is represented on the hands in SC, the issue of the effects of SC on speech or sign communication has not been directly addressed, despite its importance for both practical and theoretical reasons. This report is an attempt to address that issue. We shall discuss the results of a study that compared speech and sign intelligibility under conditions of speaking alone, signing alone, and speaking and signing together.

Does SC *entail* lower speech or sign intelligibility than unimodal communication? We wanted to test that question under the most optimal conditions: among deaf persons who are highly skilled speakers and signers and whose English would not interfere with intelligibility. The rationale here is that these highly skilled, highly practiced persons will be the subjects for whom SC is most likely to be automatized and who therefore will be least affected by the attentional demands of SC.

7.3 Method

This study occurred in three phases: Collection of speech/sign samples from deaf subjects; ratings of speech intelligibility; and ratings of sign intelligibility. We shall describe each of these phases in turn.

7.3.1 Phase 1: Sample Collection: Deaf Signers/Speakers

Subjects

Subjects were deaf students from the National Technical Institute for the Deaf (NTID). Seven deaf students were selected so that they met the following communication criteria, as measured by a battery of tests given all entering NTID students:

1. Primary criteria
    a. Their speech intelligibility as measured by the Spontaneous Message Intelligibility Test (Card, Spector, and Walter 1980) exceeded 4.5 on a scale of 5.

    b. Their score on the CID Everyday Sentence Manual Reception Test (Caccamise 1979) was at least 80 percent.

    c. Their English reading and writing skills were sufficient to produce an E-score (Crandall 1978a) of 29 or above, considered proficient at NTID.

2. Additional criteria

    a. They had been rated to be proficient sign communicators based on the Sign Communication Proficiency Interview (Newell et al. 1983).

    b. They had learned to sign by age 12 (Fischer 1985).

    c. Age of onset of deafness was no later than age 3.

The first two primary criteria were intended to ensure that the subjects were highly skilled in both speech and signing. The third primary criterion was chosen to ensure that the subjects had sufficient English skills that grammatical intelligibility would not be confused with speech intelligibility. The additional criteria were chosen to ensure that the subjects were in fact prelingually deaf and further ensured that subjects were skilled signers. Out of about five hundred NTID students on whom we had data, only fifteen met these strict criteria; of the fifteen, seven[1] agreed to participate. The average PTA loss was 80.3 dB HL in the better ear. Table 7.1 summarizes relevant data on our seven subjects.

Procedure

The deaf subjects were asked to perform three tasks:

1. Read a list of words from the Fisher-Logemann Test (Fisher 1966);
2. Summarize an animated nonverbal story presented on videotape.
3. Tell a personal anecdote about the funniest or scariest experience that had ever happened to them.

All three tasks were performed under three conditions: speaking alone (unimodal communication with voice (speech, UCV)), signing alone (UCS), and speaking and signing simultaneously (simultaneous communication, SC).

For the UCV condition, subjects performed the three speaking tasks to an audience of one hearing person with no knowledge of sign language. Subjects were informed only that the person had normal hearing and did not know sign language. Similarly, for the UCS condition, the signing was performed for an audience of a deaf native signer who did not use speech during the course of the experiment. Subjects were informed that the audience was deaf. For this

---

1. Actually eight; technical difficulties prevented us from using one subject.

Table 7.1   Communication Characteristics of the Seven Subjects

Subject	Speech	MRT	E-Score	Onset	PTA (dB)	Parental Hearing Status	Elementary School	High School	Age of Learning to Sign
TW	5.0	96	30.5	0	67	HI	PD	RD	0
DS	4.8	96	33.5	0	75	HI	PD	PD	1
SC	5.0	86	30.5	0	62	H	DD	RD	3–4
HS	5.0	90	29.8	3	82	H	PR	P	9
RM	4.5	88	31.3	0	86	H	PD	PD	12
PM	4.7	94	29.8	0	70	H	PD/PR	RD	12
ME	5.0	96	32.0	0	120	H	DD/P	RD	12

Speech: NTID speech intelligibility profile.
MRT: Manual Reception Test (Caccamise 1979).
E-score: English composite score (Crandall 1978a).
Onset: Age of onset of deafness.
PTA: Pure tone average, in decibels.
Parental hearing status: H = hearing, HI = hearing impaired.
Elementary school: Type of school attended (PD = public school with classrooms for deaf children; PR = mixture of public and residential school; DD = day classes for deaf children; RD = residential school for the deaf; P = regular public school).
High school: Type of high school attended (see explanations above).
Age of learning to sign: Age at which subject learned to sign.

condition, subjects were asked to sign "in English" rather than in ASL, in order to reduce possible confounding of distinctions in intelligibility with distinctions in language or grammar. They were not given explicit instructions about lip movements, but if they asked, they were told that lip movement was permitted. For the SC condition, the subjects performed the three communication tasks for an audience of two persons: one normally hearing person with no knowledge of sign language, and one deaf person whose primary mode of communication was sign language. Subjects were informed of the composition of this audience. As in the UCS condition, in the SC condition subjects were instructed to perform the SC tasks "in English." Since it appears to be impossible to produce two languages simultaneously, we did not ask subjects to sign in ASL and speak in English, although the signing they did produce contained many ASL grammatical mechanisms consistent with English syntax.[2]

2. Generally one could characterize the subjects' English signing as Deaf PSE, that is, Pidgin Sign English that incorporates many aspects of ASL grammar consistent with English word order. Our subjects, although they may use a few initialized signs borrowed from such artificial systems as Signing Exact English, do not borrow grammatical devices from such systems.

The purpose of providing different audiences for the three conditions was to place communication demands on the subjects that were appropriate for the particular experimental condition. The subjects were instructed to communicate as effectively as possible for the particular audience. This aspect of the design is crucial, since sociolinguistic research has shown that people will adjust their communication style to fit the audience (Ervin-Tripp 1973). It was therefore important to encourage subjects to pay equal attention to both the signed and spoken modalities in the simultaneous condition.

All three tasks (word list, film summary, anecdote) under the experimental conditions involving speech (UCV and SC) were audiotaped. Similarly, in the two conditions involving signing (USC and SC), all tasks were videotaped. The three signing and speaking conditions were counterbalanced across subjects, but within each condition the three tasks were in the fixed order of word list, film summary, and anecdote, in increasing order of naturalness. Labov (1972a) has shown in his work on the social stratification of English among hearing people in New York City that using this type of order maximizes the chance of obtaining a valid sample of unmonitored, naturalistic language data. In his research he found that on a word list people monitor their pronunciation carefully, paying more attention to form than to content, whereas in telling a story about the scariest experience of their lives, people become so absorbed in the content of what they are saying that they pay little attention to the form. The film summary task permitted us to control for content while allowing form to be free and also provided a midpoint between more and less monitored communication.

Three rating tapes were made from the original audiotape recordings. The first tape consisted of the fourteen readings of the word lists, the second consisted of the first minute of each of the fourteen summaries, and the third consisted of the first minute of the fourteen anecdotes. The order of subjects and conditions on each tape was randomly assigned. Analogously, three stimulus videotapes were made from the original videotape recordings. The first contained the fourteen word lists, the second contained the first minute of each of the fourteen summaries, and the third contained the first minute of each of the fourteen anecdotes. A different random order of subjects and conditions was assigned.

7.3.2 Phase 2: Listening Task (UCV and SC: Hearing Raters)

Raters

The listeners were thirteen undergraduate speech pathology and audiology students at SUNY Geneseo. All listeners passed a 20 dB HL hearing screening at 500, 1,000, 2,000, and 4,000 Hz; spoke English as their first language; and reported no significant prior experience listening to the speech of hearing-impaired persons.

Procedure

Listeners were divided into three groups. Seated in these groups, they heard the deaf subjects' recordings via a calibrated playback device. Each listener was asked to scale the intelligibility of each speaker on all three speaking tasks. The order in which these tasks were presented to the listeners was counterbalanced across the listening groups.

The listeners were instructed to rate the intelligiblity[3] of each speaker on all speaking tasks and under both conditions, using the Direct Magnitude Estimation (DME) task. The instructions given to the listeners were based on those suggested by Engen (1971). A speaker (the eighth subject, whose sign-alone data had been lost and whom we therefore could not otherwise use) was selected from the low-to-middle range of speech intelligibility of the deaf subjects, and samples of that person's speech were played to the listeners at the beginning of each task. Listeners were told to rate the standard speaker with a modulus value of 10 and to scale the intelligibility of the other speakers relative to that standard. The task was illustrated by showing a picture of seven parallel horizontal lines ranging from 0.32 to 25 centimeters long, including a 2.5-centimeter standard assigned a modulus value of 10, and by demonstrating that the length of the lines could be scaled relative to the standard with DME (e.g., the 25 cm line would be given a scaled value of 100, while the 1.25 cm line would be given a scaled value of 5).

7.3.3 Phase 3: Viewing Task (UCS and SC: Native Signer Raters)

Raters

Viewers were ten NTID employees who are bilingual in ASL and English. All had deaf parents who had signed to them from infancy. They reported their visual acuity as normal or corrected to within normal tolerances.

Procedure

Viewers were again divided into three groups. Seated in these groups in a classroom, they watched the video recordings of the signing parts of the tasks. As in the listening task, each viewer was asked to scale the intelligibility of each signer on all three signing tasks under both conditions, using DME. As in the speech-rating task, raters were trained in the use of DME, and a modulus was given to the raters first; this modulus was a signer (a volunteer native signing staff member) taken from the mid to high range of sign and speech intelligibility. Order of presentation of the three videotapes was counterbalanced across the viewer groups.

---

3. The instructions used the words (or signs) "clear" and "understandable."

7.4 Results and Analysis

7.4.1 Speech

Geometric means were computed for each of the thirteen listeners' DMEs of each subject's speech intelligibility on each speaking task and under both conditions. Table 7.2 shows each subject's average rated speech intelligibility for each task under both conditions of UCV and SC.

Geometric means rather than arithmetic means were used for two reasons; first, magnitude estimates for a single stimulus are log normal—that is, the log of the range of estimates approximates a normal curve. Using geometric means gives us a more normal distribution. Second, the distribution of magnitude estimations, because they are open ended, tends to have a few scattered, aberrantly high scores at the high end. Using geometric means reduces the undue influence such scores would otherwise have and generally normalizes the distribution while preserving the average ratio of estimates (Marks 1974). In particular, Schiavetti, Metz, and Sitler (1981) demonstrated that the continuum of speech intelligibility has properties that are more appropriately examined using DME procedures rather than interval or category scaling. We should also point out that magnitude estimates are dimensionless values and *should not* be interpreted as having a linear relationship with more standard estimates of intelligibility such as percentage correct scores. For this reason, the choice of low-end or high-end moduli is basically irrelevant.

The geometric means were then submitted to a 3 (task) $\times$ 2 (condition) analysis of variance. The results indicated that neither the main effect for task ($F = 0.37$; df $= 2, 5$; $p = .7$) nor the main effect for condition ($F = 1.0$; df $= 1, 6$; $p = .36$) was significant, suggesting that the context of speech and the mode of communication had no influence on the relative judgments of speech intelligibility. The task by condition interaction ($F = 4.2$; df $= 2, 5$; $p = .08$) also failed to reach significance.

Table 7.2   Geometric Means of DME Ratings for Speech Samples

Subject	Word Lists		Film Retelling		Scary Experience	
	UCV	SC	UCV	SC	UCV	SC
TW	18.79	16.26	22.54	23.59	28.28	28.45
DS	11.63	11.32	17.28	10.91	18.47	15.48
SC	19.38	23.01	10.31	16.32	10.16	15.66
HS	9.73	10.67	11.48	8.12	10.54	10.41
RM	13.27	6.76	12.56	7.47	9.25	6.58
PM	20.32	17.72	13.98	10.28	13.86	12.00
ME	20.12	18.85	23.98	18.74	17.83	19.26

UCV: Unimodal communication with voice only.
SC: Simultaneous communication (only voice portion evaluated here).

Table 7.3   Geometric Means of DME Ratings for Sign Samples

Subject	Word Lists		Film Retelling		Scary Experience	
	UCS	SC	UCS	SC	UCS	SC
TW	9.0	10.7	9.7	11.3	13.0	14.7
DS	18.9	18.7	25.8	18.5	23.9	23.2
SC	10.5	13.3	17.1	15.3	14.9	15.6
HS	6.9	5.8	6.3	6.7	4.6	8.9
RM	7.3	8.4	5.9	11.3	8.0	9.0
PM	10.8	10.7	14.4	10.1	12.4	9.4
ME	8.6	7.4	11.6	7.9	7.6	5.4

UCS: Unimodal communication with sign only.
SC: Simultaneous communication (only sign portion evaluated here).

7.4.2 Sign

Analogously to the speech rating task, we computed geometric means for each of the ten viewers' DMEs of each subject's sign intelligibility on each signing task and under both conditions (UCS and SC). Table 7.3 shows each subject's average rated sign intelligibility for each task under both conditions. These geometric means were then submitted to a 3 (task) $\times$ 2 (condition) analysis of variance.

As in the speech intelligibility data, neither the main effect for task ($F = 4.09$, df = 2, 5; $p = .09$) nor condition ($F = 0.08$, df = 1, 6; $p = .79$) attained significance, suggesting again that neither the content of what was signed nor the presence of speech while signing had an effect on overall judgments of intelligibility. The interaction also failed to achieve significance ($F = 0.75$, df = 2, 5; $p = .52$).

7.5 Discussion

Our results show that deaf adults who are highly skilled in speech, sign, and English reading and writing can sign and speak at the same time without any significant decrement or improvement in speech or sign intelligibility. These results therefore support the notion that speaking and signing can be supplementary or complementary rather than necessarily interfering. There was a noticeable trend toward an interaction between task and condition in the speech-rating part of the experiment; in particular, most subjects showed a difference of at least 3 between the UCV and SC conditions on the retelling of the film. It is possible that the memory load entailed by the retelling of the film, in contrast to the other two tasks, was sufficient to cause some breakdown in processing. It is important, however, to keep in mind that even with geometric means, these differences are not strictly linear.

Interestingly, the least difference between conditions in the speech tasks occurred on the most spontaneous (and least monitored; Labov 1972a) task—telling the personal anecdote. Since everyday communication is closer to this last task than it is to reading word lists or summarizing stories of nonverbal videotapes, these results suggest that for the purposes of normal communication by deaf people with good speech and sign skills, simultaneous communication will be as intelligible as single-mode communication.

It has long been part of the folklore of deaf education that learning to sign inhibits the development of speech. The claim that learning sign language interferes with the development of speech skills is virtually untestable, given the myriad variables that can affect the development of speech. And in fact it has never really been tested, though it has been bruited about for years.[4] What *can* be tested in a controlled study is what happens to speech in the presence of sign and to sign in the presence of speech. Given our data, the claim that signing will necessarily interfere with speech or that speech will necessarily interefere with sign appears to be unwarranted.

Keeping in mind Ling's distinction between learning a skill and utilizing it, one must still allow for the possibility that while a deaf person is *learning* to sign, there might be a temporary decrement in speech intelligibility, owing to allocation of scarce linguistic, attentional, or motor resources to the new skill until that skill becomes more automatic. It is also possible that for those whose speech or sign skills are not as fully developed as the skills of our carefully screened subjects, signing might affect speech (or speech, sign) more severely than in good speakers, since more attention would presumably have to be devoted to the effort to communicate clearly in the mode that is not yet automatic. This conjecture is supported by the results of Spelke, Hirst, and Neisser (1976), who found that even automatized tasks were adversely affected by being performed simultaneously but that with practice it was possible to perform tasks as well simultaneously as singly.

We mentioned earlier that the modalities of speech and sign might be adversely affected in a differential manner: that is, that there could be an asymmetry in the effects of speaking on signing versus the effects of signing on speaking. Although this speculation is not borne out by the group data, in individual cases it may well be. Clearly, some subjects' speech or sign was not affected at all by SC; some, however, had depressed speech in the presence of SC, and some (not always the same ones), had depressed sign in the presence of SC. For at least one of our subjects, SC was consistently *better* than UC. Interestingly, those subjects for whom there was the least difference between

4. It is probably true that if someone does not speak, speech intelligibility will deteriorate. One thing that happens when oral students start to sign is that by becoming part of the Deaf community, they do not talk as much as they used to; if they continue to practice their speech, with or without the presence of signing, probably very little will happen to their speech.

SC and UC were those who learned to sign earliest. Perhaps by being more completely bilingual and bimodal, these subjects in fact have the most automatized language processing systems and are therefore least affected by the additional load.

The idea that there might be differential effects in different subjects is borne out in a different realm by data of Stewart, Akamatsu, and Bonkowski (1990). They suggest a notion of "speech-driven" versus "sign-driven" simultaneous communication. Their idea is that in certain situations SC is controlled, in a sense, by what the person is signing (or speaking) and that the speech (or sign) in some sense follows along. Although Stewart, Akamatsu, and Bonkowski look at speech-driven versus sign-driven SC from the point of view of the same subjects in different situations, their hypothesis can, it seems to us, be extended quite naturally to different persons as well. Clearly, for most hearing persons just learning to sign, their sign is speech driven (sometimes even if the speech is not present); this is analogous to using the grammar of one's first language in speaking a second, or the notion of noncompound bilingualism where one language is dominant. There are also clearly some deaf signers whose speech is clearly sign driven. For a subject whose SC is speech driven, then, one would predict that SC might be worse than speech alone, while sign alone might not be so affected, and vice versa for someone whose SC is sign driven. Perhaps what a good simultaneous communicator does is to not let either system get the upper hand, analogous to a balanced bilingual.

Many unanswered questions remain, in particular those we alluded to above about the differences between learning and processing, or between production and perception, the effects of different skill levels on the processing of SC, and the general issue of individual differences in experience and learning. Further work with a larger number of subjects might reveal significant differences that we did not find in our small sample. These are questions that deserve to be explored in the future.

8 The Manual Representation of Speech by Deaf Children, Their Mothers, and Their Teachers

RHONDA WODLINGER-COHEN

8.1 Introduction

Methods in deaf education have changed radically in the past fifteen years. Classrooms advocating a Total Communication philosophy have replaced oral programs as the norm in this country. As a result, most deaf children are now learning language via some form of Manually Coded English that has been incorporated into the curriculum. These English sign systems, Seeing Essential English (Anthony 1971), Signing Exact English (Gustason, Pfetzing, and Zawolkow 1972), and Signed English (Bornstein 1974), were designed to be used simultaneously with speech, so that the deaf child exposed to one of these systems would have the opportunity to see spoken English in much the same way a hearing child hears it. The hope is that given this opportunity, the deaf child might learn language in a more natural and effortless fashion, which in turn might improve the poor reading ability that has historically gone hand in hand with deafness. As a result, teachers of the deaf are in theory required to represent all of their speech exactly and simultaneously in sign. Hearing parents of deaf children are trained and encouraged to do the same, as are the deaf children themselves.

Although the literature on Manually Coded English (MCE) is not extensive, the body of research that does exist has answered some of the early and basic questions that arose when classrooms adopted this method, in addition to pointing out new avenues that need exploring. At this time, three different questions have been posed:

1. What does language development look like in a deaf child exposed to an English sign system?
2. How, if at all, is the child's language affected by his adult model?
3. What is the relation between speech and sign in this bimodally produced language?

The use of sign with very young deaf children does not appear to impede the development of speech as was originally feared. In fact, various case studies that trace the acquisition of simultaneous spoken and signed language suggest that early access to sign might actually promote development of oral language. A common developmental pattern in children who are exposed to early and consistent sign and speech is that the child initially communicates in sign alone, gradually adds speech to the sign, and slowly drops out the sign to the point of using speech alone, except in the presence of other signers or deaf individuals (Schlesinger and Meadow 1972; Gardner and Zorfass 1983). Furthermore, deaf children exposed to English sign systems appear to follow language acquisition patterns similar to those demonstrated by hearing children learning spoken English (Schlesinger and Meadow 1972). Though the patterns are similar and deaf children do progress steadily over time (Raffin, Davis, and Gilman 1978), their development is slow compared with that of their normally hearing peers, and their expressive language abilities lag well behind their receptive knowledge (Bornstein, Saulnier, and Hamilton 1980).

That a child's language development is influenced by adult models is indisputable. Children universally learn the specific language provided by their environment. However, it is also clear that children bring their own innate language-learning capabilities to the task of language acquisition, since they do not merely imitate utterances provided by their environment but continually create novel utterances that have not been provided by another speaker. Therefore the question that arises in studying language development, whether a spoken or a signed language, is which specific aspects of a child's language are influenced by the adult model and to what degree. The enormous variability that exists in the deaf population and their normally hearing family members in terms of the type of sign language used (ASL vs. MCE), and the consistency or frequency of use makes this question difficult to answer.

Crandall's (1978b) analysis of the use of inflectional morphemes by deaf children and their mothers (some hearing and some deaf) yielded an interesting finding. A mother's use of inflectional morphemes was found to be a good predictor of her child's use of the same morphemes. Erting (1985a) studied deaf preschool children in an attempt to discover if the way they communicated varied as a function of their communication partners' hearing status. The communication partners in the study were the major language models in the children's environment; their normally hearing teachers and their parents (some deaf and some hearing). Erting's results suggest that role, rather than hearing status, accounted for the linguistic variation the children exhibited. The children used ASL features frequently with their parents, but practically never with their teachers. In addition, a high percentage of the signs the children produced in conversation with their teachers were marked with MCE features. The same was not true of their conversations with their parents.

MCE, as used by teachers and most hearing parents, is a bimodally produced language. In theory, the relation between speech and sign in MCE should be a direct one-to-one correspondence, but the literature suggests that in actual practice it is not so simple. Upon analyzing the simultaneous communication of two hearing teachers of deaf children, Marmor and Petitto (1979) found that the teachers' signed utterances (when considered separately from their concurrent spoken utterances) were highly ungrammatical because many spoken items were not represented in the signed portions of their utterances. In a similar study of hearing mothers of deaf children, Swisher (1985) found a wide range of variability. Some of the mothers performed like Marmor and Petitto's (1979) teachers, while others did a fairly respectable job of signing their spoken utterances in a simultaneous fashion. Maxwell and Bernstein (1985) chose a different perspective for their investigation of the relation between speech and sign, as demonstrated by users of simultaneous communication. Rather than looking for a morpheme-to-morpheme match, they analyzed the match between speech and sign at a semantic or "message" level of analysis. Their results indicated that though a direct morpheme-to-morpheme match was often absent, meaning was preserved in 86 percent of the utterances. In other words, no major propositional differences were conveyed between the two channels in the vast majority of cases (see also Maxwell, Bernstein, and Mear, this volume).

The study presented here addresses two questions that arise from this unique language-learning situation. First, are teachers and parents capable of representing their speech simultaneously in sign and, if not completely, then to what degree? Second, given the input from their teachers and parents, what patterns of speech and sign production are the children using?

8.2 Method

8.2.1 Subjects

Three groups of subjects participated in the study: deaf children; their mothers; and their classroom teachers. The first group comprised six deaf children. Criteria for participation in the study were:

1. The child must have a severe to profound hearing loss that had occurred prelingually.
2. The child must be enrolled in a special education classroom for the deaf utilizing a signed English system of communication throughout his educational career.
3. The child's parents and other family members must be normally hearing.
4. The child must have no additional handicaps.

The children were paired by chronological age: The first pair consisted of two 5-year-old girls; the second pair consisted of two 10-year-old girls; and the third pair consisted of two 14-year-olds (one boy and one girl). The children in each pair were in the same classroom and therefore had the same teacher. In addition, each pair of children had been in that classroom, with the same teacher, for a minimum of two years.

The special education program the six children were enrolled in was part of a suburban public school system that had adopted a Total Communication philosophy for its deaf students. Each child had been in this particular program since age 3 and had participated in a hospital-sponsored parent-infant program before that. Thus each child's exposure to the simultaneous production of speech and manual communication (signed English) began before age 3 in this parent-infant program, when their parents began learning and using signed English to accompany their speech at home. The signed English system utilized by this school district was Signing Exact English (Gustason, Pfetzing, and Zawolkow 1972).

Also included as subjects in the study were nine adults; the three classroom teachers and the six mothers of the six children. Teachers had between five and ten years of teaching experience in their particular special education programs and therefore had at least five to ten years of signing experience. Because the children had each begun signing before age 3 and were now between the ages of 5 and 14, the six mothers varied in the number of years they had been signing. According to the school administrator and educational records, the mothers of the 5-year-olds had been signing for approximately three years; the mothers of the 10-year-olds had been signing for approximately eight years; and the mothers of the 14-year-olds had been signing for approximately twelve years. However, each mother was regarded by the program administrator as a proficient and conscientious signer.

8.2.2 Procedure

To obtain samples of spontaneous language that represented the individual's usual communication style, we videotaped each subject in a familiar setting with a familiar communication partner. The three teachers were videotaped in their classrooms for a thirty-minute period in which each taught a typical language or reading lesson.

The children were videotaped on two separate occasions in two different settings. On the first occasion, each child was taped at school interacting with his or her same-age partner. That is, the two 5-year-olds were taped together, as were the two 10-ten-years and the two 14-year-olds. In an effort to stimulate conversation, each pair was given age-appropriate toys, games, or activities to share. The 5-year-olds were given dolls, clay, and assorted wind-up toys and were instructed to play together and share all the toys. The 10-year-olds were given a card game that required them to ask each other questions as well as a bowling game and a more structured game in which they interviewed each other. The 14-year-olds were given a board game with no instructions besides those printed on the box and were instructed to figure out how to play the game and to play it together. Like the card game, the board game required the 14-year-olds to answer questions from each other. Each videotaped session at school for each pair of children lasted approximately thirty minutes. In each case the children played at a table in their classroom while the experimenter videotaped them.

Each child was videotaped a second time at home, interacting with their mother. Not only did this session provide another sample of each child's language, but a sample of the mothers' language was obtained as well. At the start of each home session, the children were shown an action-packed nonverbal cartoon and then told to tell their mothers the story of the cartoon. The mothers were told they could ask questions if the child had difficulty remembering the cartoon. Upon completing the cartoon activity, the mother-child pair engaged in an age-appropriate activity that they frequently performed together. The mothers of the 5-year-olds were given a large bag of assorted toys (dolls, wind-up toys, and picture books) and instructed to play with their children as they normally did. The mothers of the 10-year-olds cooked with their children, and the mothers of the 14-year-olds looked through magazines with their children. All the mother-child pairs also looked through their family photo albums together at the end of the session to stimulate more conversation. The home sessions lasted approximately forty minutes.

Each videotape was then transcribed. A verbatim transcript was made of each speaker's speech and sign. The verbal mode was always transcribed on one line and the manual mode on the line directly beneath it, so that the simultaneity of the two modes could be examined. More specifically, the transcripts were analyzed to determine for each subject what aspects of language were represented in sign alone, in speech alone, and in sign and speech simultaneously. In addition, the transcripts were analyzed to determine which, if any, obligatory morphemes were omitted.

8.3 Results

8.3.1 Teachers

Before analyzing the representation of specific language properties by mode, I examined the types of utterances each teacher used. Every spoken utterance for each teacher was classified as either complete, incomplete, ungrammatical, one-word, or unintelligible. Clearly, complete sentences are not the only acceptable types of utterances in a conversation. Incomplete and one-word utterances are perfectly appropriate at certain points in a conversational situation. The rationale for separating out the ungrammatical utterances was that it made little sense to analyze the signed portion of a teacher's communication if in fact the spoken portion turned out to be highly ungrammatical. Upon completing this analysis, I found that the opposite was true. That is, the three teachers had an extremely low percentage of ungrammatical utterances in their language corpus. For each teacher, the percentage of ungrammatical utterances accounted for 1 percent or less of the total utterances. Furthermore, all three teachers followed the same pattern of distribution, in terms of this utterance-type classification. In all three cases, complete sentences accounted for the highest percentage of utterances, followed by one-word utterances, incomplete sentences, and ungrammatical utterances.

The next step was to look at the transcripts in detail, to determine how precisely these teachers were representing their speech in the manual mode. This was done by examining every lexical and syntactic unit in each utterance and determining whether the teacher used speech alone, sign alone, or speech and sign simultaneously to represent that particular unit in that particular instance.

The overall findings were as follows: First, these three teachers were highly accurate in representing their speech exactly and simultaneously in their signing ("accuracy" being defined here as the overall percentage of spoken morphemes accompanied simultaneously by their signed morpheme equivalents). Second, degree of overall accuracy decreased as the age of the students increased. Third, degree of accuracy in representing the specific morpheme types followed a consistent pattern across teachers. And fourth, degree of accuracy in representing two particular morpheme types decreased as the age of the students increased.

Figure 8.1 illustrates that when both speech and sign are taken into account, the teachers do not omit any obligatory morphemes. The first finding, that all three teachers exhibited a high degree of accuracy, demonstrates that teachers are capable of representing their speech exactly and simultaneously in the manual mode. When the data on all three teachers were combined, an overall accuracy rate of 88 percent was found. That is, 88 percent of all the morphemes found in speech were also present simultaneously in sign. Looking at each teacher individually, we do find some variation. The teacher of the 5-year-olds had an overall accuracy rate of 95 percent; the teacher of the 10-year-olds had an overall accuracy rate of 91 percent; and the teacher of the 14-year-olds had an overall accuracy rate of 81 percent. For this small group of teachers, the data yielded a pattern of accuracy decreasing as student age increased. However, a larger sample of teachers would be needed to determine if this pattern occurs for teachers of the deaf as a whole. In addition, the use of sign alone was very rare for all three of the teachers. If a simultaneous presentation was not used, speech alone seemed to be the preferred alternative.

The next step was to examine the manual representation of speech in terms of its grammatical or syntactic function. I examined three categories of lexical and syntactic properties of language: open-class morphemes, closed-class morphemes, and bound morphemes. The open-class morphemes were all the nouns, main verbs, adjectives, and adverbs that the teachers used in speech

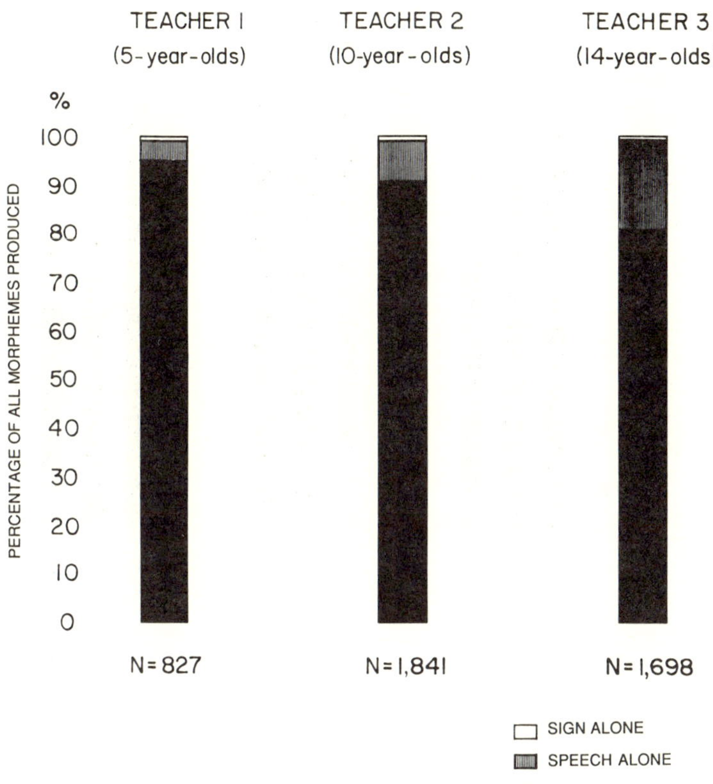

Figure 8.1. Teachers' representation of all morphemes as percentage
of all morphemes produced.

and sign. The closed-class morphemes were all the copulas, auxiliary verbs, question words, pronouns, prepositions, articles, negatives, and conjunctions they used. Finally, the bound morphemes were the *-ing,* plural *-s,* third person *-s,* regular past, irregular past, possessive *-s,* third-person irregular, agentive (in sign), comparative, and superlative markers the teachers used. This list accounts for all the bound morphemes that were present in the teachers' speech or sign.

As can be seen in figure 8.2, none of the teachers were uniformly accurate across morpheme types. The percentage of open-class, closed-class and bound morphemes represented in the simultaneous mode varied across teachers. If speech and sign were not used simultaneously to represent a particular morpheme, it was most likely that the teacher would delete the signed portion and use speech alone. For each teacher, the incidence of representing any of the morpheme classes in sign alone never amounted to more than 1 percent of

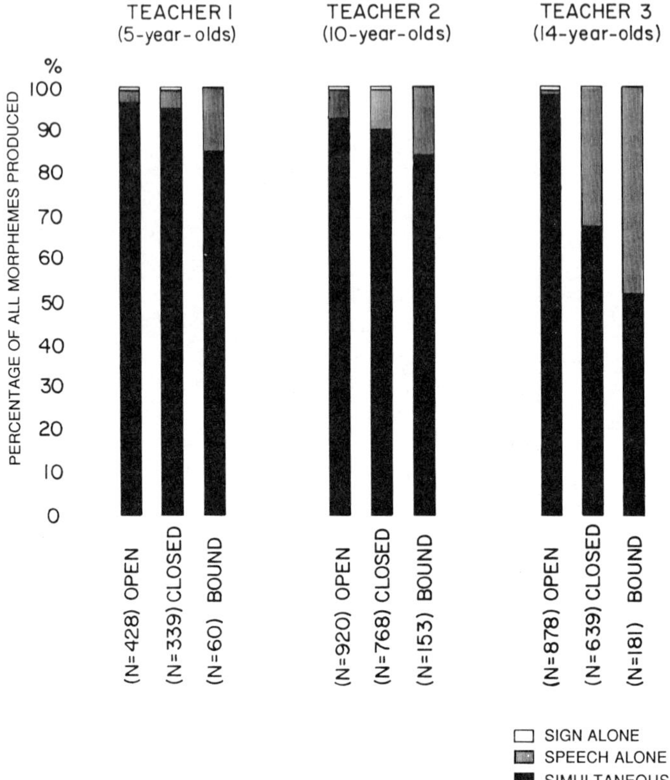

Figure 8.2. Teachers' representation of morphemes by class as percentage
of all morphemes produced.

the total. However, the interesting pattern here is that each of the three teachers followed the same distributional pattern of accuracy by morpheme class.
Open-class items had the highest percentage of simultaneous representation,
followed in order by closed-class and bound morphemes.

Upon looking at the specific morpheme types across the three teachers, I
discovered another trend. The percentage of simultaneous representation of
closed-class and bound morphemes decreased as student age increased. The
percentage of closed-class morphemes present in sign as well as speech was
highest for the teacher of the 5-year-olds and lowest for the teacher of the
14-year-olds. Similarly, the percentage of bound morphemes present in both
modes was greatest for the teacher of the 5-year-olds and lowest (only 48 percent) for the teacher of the 14-year-olds. Here again more teachers need to be
observed to confirm that student age rather than individual differences is the
determining factor.

Finally, the possibility existed that the teacher of the 14-year-olds had the highest percentage of deletions in the signed portions of her utterances because her utterances were more complex, owing to the relative language sophistication of her older students. Assuming that longer utterances tend to be more complex and therefore more difficult to sign accurately than shorter utterances, I checked the frequency of deletions in the signed portions of all the various utterances and discovered that utterance length had no effect on the number of deletions. In other words, shorter (simple) sentences were just as likely to contain deletions in the signed portions as were the longer (more complex) utterances.

8.3.2 Mothers

Because 74 percent of deaf children live at home with their families and the vast majority have hearing parents, it is important to know if these parents are exposing their children to a complete model of signed English and, if not, what their pattern of production looks like. The following results are based on five, rather than six, mothers. The data from the mother of the 14-year-old girl are not included here. Because of technical problems, the audio portion of that session was not recorded and therefore could not be analyzed in the same fashion as the other tapes. Like the teachers, the mothers' spoken utterances were classified as either complete, incomplete, one-word, or ungrammatical. Every one of the mothers exhibited the same pattern as the teachers; that is, most of their spoken utterances were complete sentences, followed in order by one-word sentences, incomplete sentences, and ungrammatical sentences. As a group, ungrammatical sentences accounted for approximately 1 percent of the mothers' total utterances.

In general, the mothers were not as homogeneous as the teachers. There was a great deal of variability in terms of representing their speech and sign simultaneously (fig. 8.3). Although the mothers were not as highly accurate as the teachers were, the same pattern of representation of morpheme class was found within each mother. Open-class morphemes were expressed simultaneously in speech and sign, most often followed in order by closed-class and bound morphemes. As a result of not using a simultaneous mode as often as the teachers, the mothers tended to use speech alone much more often than the teachers did. Only 35 percent of the mothers' spoken morphemes were simultaneously represented in sign, contrasted with 88 percent for the teachers. However, the mothers resembled the teachers in that they almost never used sign alone to produce morphemes, irrespective of class.

The mothers of the 5-year-olds were fairly similar to each other in their communication styles. The only real difference between them was that one mother used speech and sign simultaneously to a greater degree than the other. Otherwise their patterns of representation by mode and morpheme class were

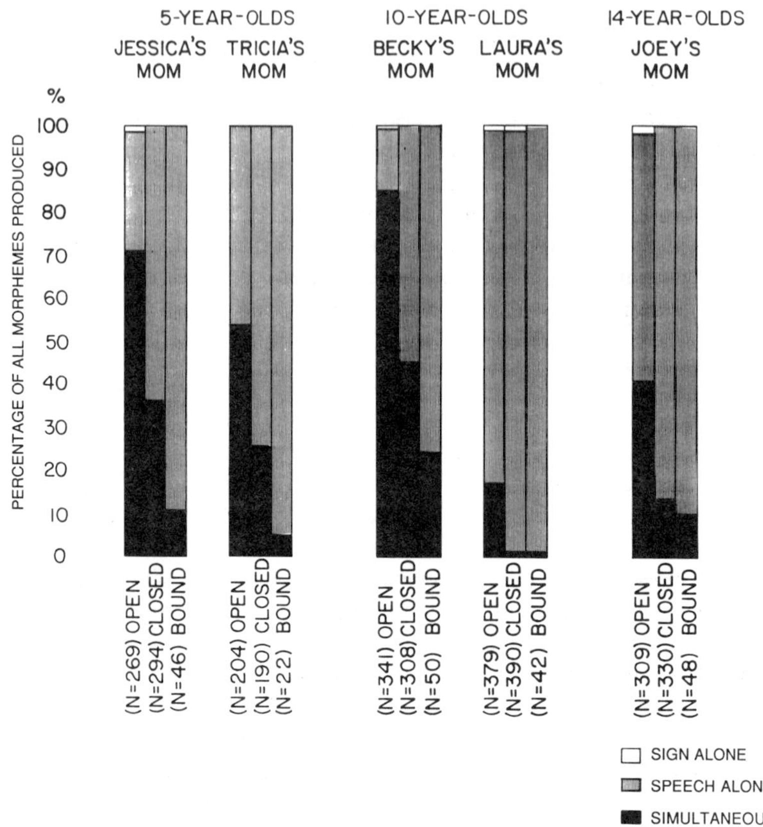

Figure 8.3. Mothers' representation of morphemes by class as percentage
of all morphemes produced.

identical. Jessica's mother represented 70 percent of her open-class morphemes in speech and sign simultaneously, 36 percent of the closed-class
morphemes in both speech and sign, and 11 percent of the bound morphemes
in both modes. Tricia's mother represented 54 percent of the open-class morphemes that she used in speech and sign simultaneously, 26 percent of the
closed-class morphemes, and only 5 percent of the bound morphemes.

The mothers of the 10-year-olds approached the task of communicating
with their daughters very differently from one another. Becky's mother used
speech and sign simultaneously to a greater degree than all the other mothers.
She followed the typical pattern of representing open-class morphemes most
faithfully wand bound morphemes least faithfully. Laura's mother also appeared
to follow the pattern, but she rarely signed anything that she said. Becky's
mother bimodally produced 85 percent of her open-class morphemes, 45 percent of her closed-class morphemes, and 24 percent of her bound morphemes

in the simultaneous mode. Laura's mother used speech and sign simultaneously to represent 17 percent of her open-class morphemes, 2 percent of her closed-class morphemes, and 2 percent of her bound morphemes. When all three morpheme types are collapsed into one group, the difference between these two mothers is striking: Becky's mother represented 63 percent of the morphemes she used in speech and sign simultaneously, while Laura's mother produced a mere 9 percent bimodally.

Like Laura's mother, the mother of the 14-year-old primarily used speech alone to converse with her child. When speech and sign were used simultaneously, however, a similar pattern of representation by morpheme class was found: she represented 41 percent of open-class morphemes, 14 percent of closed-class morphemes, and 14 percent of bound morphemes.

8.3.3 Children

Keeping in mind the language models that the teachers and mothers are providing, we can now move on to the second question this study attempted to address: Are children capable of learning this sign system, and how are they representing their language in terms of speech and sign? Let us first examine the language the children use when they are in school with their same-age peers.

By looking at the 10-year-olds, we can see that the children are learning the system. Although they never omit an obligatory open-class morpheme from both their speech and sign and rarely omit an obligatory closed-class morpheme, bound morphemes are entirely omitted in a good many instances, as can be seen in figure 8.4. Like their teachers, they rarely use sign alone, and they are most likely to use both sign and speech for open-class morphemes. There is no clear preference for closed-class morphemes, but when bound morphemes are produced it is almost always in speech alone. Furthermore, the two children are not that different from one another in this analysis. These 10-year-olds appear to have come close to mastering this system. Thus the next step is to examine the productions of some beginners and then some even more experienced children.

The 5-year-olds appear to be at the beginning stages of language development. In general, they can be described as being at the one-word stage. Because practically all their utterances had an overall mean length of utterance close to one, it was not possible to determine obligatory omissions. In addition, given their level of language sophistication, it is not surprising that neither child produced any bound morphemes. This low level of language development is surprising, given the type and amount of parent/teacher input. It is possible that the taping sessions were not representative of one of the subject groups. Either the children are usually more prolific in their conversations, or the adults are not always as conscientious as the tapes indicate.

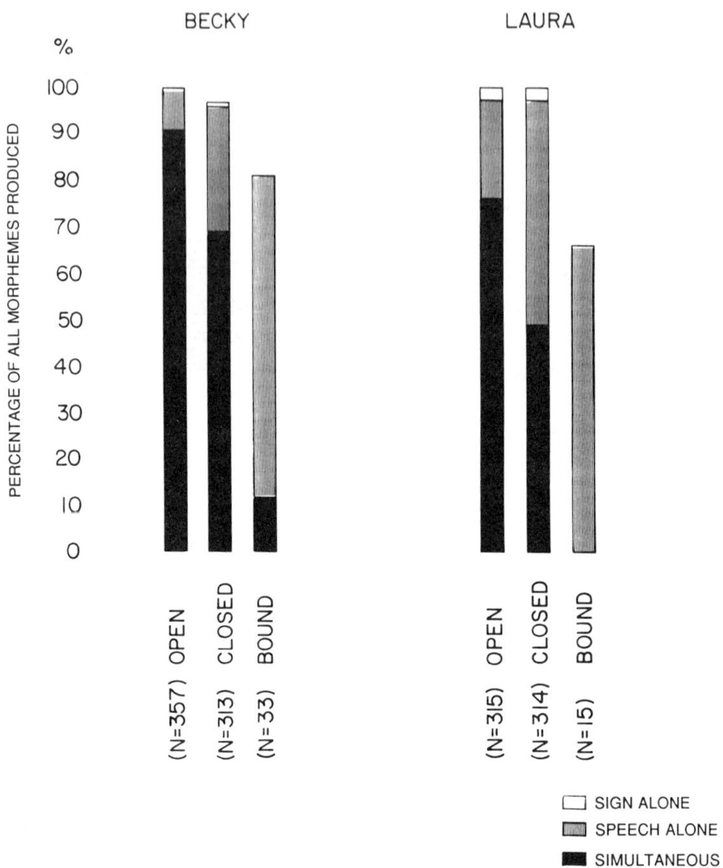

Figure 8.4. Ten-year-olds: child-with-child situation representation of morphemes by class. In this and the following figures, omissions are indicated by the difference from 100 percent.

Figure 8.5 illustrates that the 5-year-olds look very different from both the 10-year-olds and the hearing adults in this study but do look very much like each other. For these young children, sign alone appears to be the preferred mode of communication. Speech is rarely used alone, while the simultaneous mode is used somewhat for open-class morphemes and about half the time for closed-class morphemes.

The 14-year-olds are at the other end of the continuum. They have been using this system for a very long time, and one might expect that by now they would have not only mastered the system but begun to adapt it in a manner that best suits their needs. This appears to be the case. In some ways they look like their teachers and the 10-year-olds, and in other ways they have made some subtle changes (fig. 8.6).

As in the other groups, open-class and closed-class morphemes are not

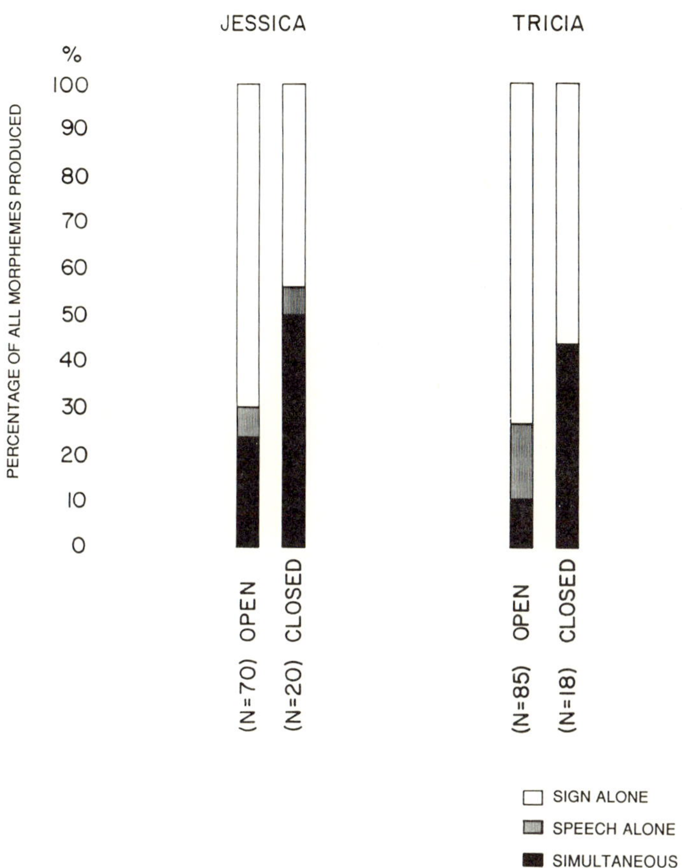

Figure 8.5. Five-year-olds: child-with-child situation representation of morphemes by class.

often omitted from both the spoken and signed portions of the 14-year-olds' productions. However, both children use a very small number of bound morphemes in their utterances, and for one child a significant number of obligatory ones are omitted in both modes. Again, they are like the other groups in that in most cases, open-class and closed-class items are produced in a simultaneous mode. But when we look at their preferred alternative to the simultaneous mode, we find that, unlike the adults and 10-year-olds, these children are most likely to use sign alone. The exception to this rule is bound morphemes. Once again, if a bound morpheme is produced at all, it is most likely to be represented in speech alone. The question one might ask now is what determines mode preference. Upon comparing the children's productions with their peers to their productions with their mothers, we see that communication partner seems to play a vital role in this preference.

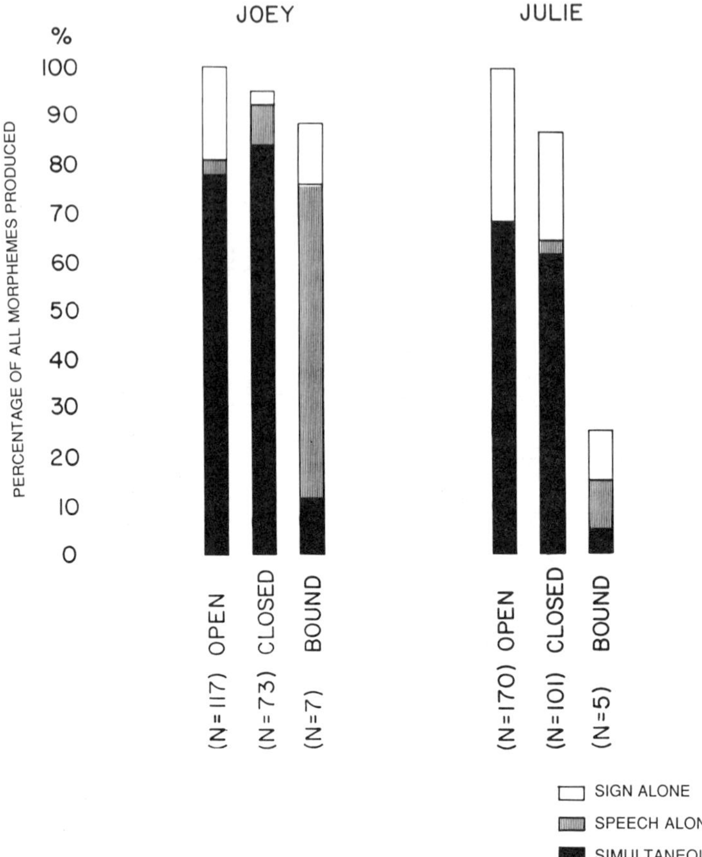

Figure 8.6. Fourteen-year-olds: child-with-child situation representation
of morphemes by class.

The second time the children were videotaped, they were at home with their
mothers. This session had two purposes when it was originally planned: first,
it was to provide a sample of the mothers' spontaneous language; second, it
was to provide more child language. Recall that the mothers in this study primarily used speech alone in communicating with their children. Now, one
could entertain a number of hypotheses as to what a deaf child's spoken and
signed language might look like when conversing with a deaf peer, as opposed
to what it might be like when conversing with a hearing mother. The two most
obvious possibilities are that the children are exactly the same with their peers
and their mothers or that they all alter their communication style in some way
when they go to the mother situation. A third possibility is that the particular
way mothers represent their language in speech and sign affects the way their

children represent their own language. The results appear to support this third hypothesis.

The analysis of the children's language when they are communicating with their mothers indicates that these children have also achieved a certain level of conversational competence. That is, they appear to make modality decisions based on their communication partner's spoken and signed language abilities. By looking at the way the children represent their language in speech and sign in the two different situations, we can see the effect the communciation partner has on modality use.

Starting with the oldest child, Joey, we can see a striking difference between his use of mode in the peer and mother situations (fig. 8.7). When con-

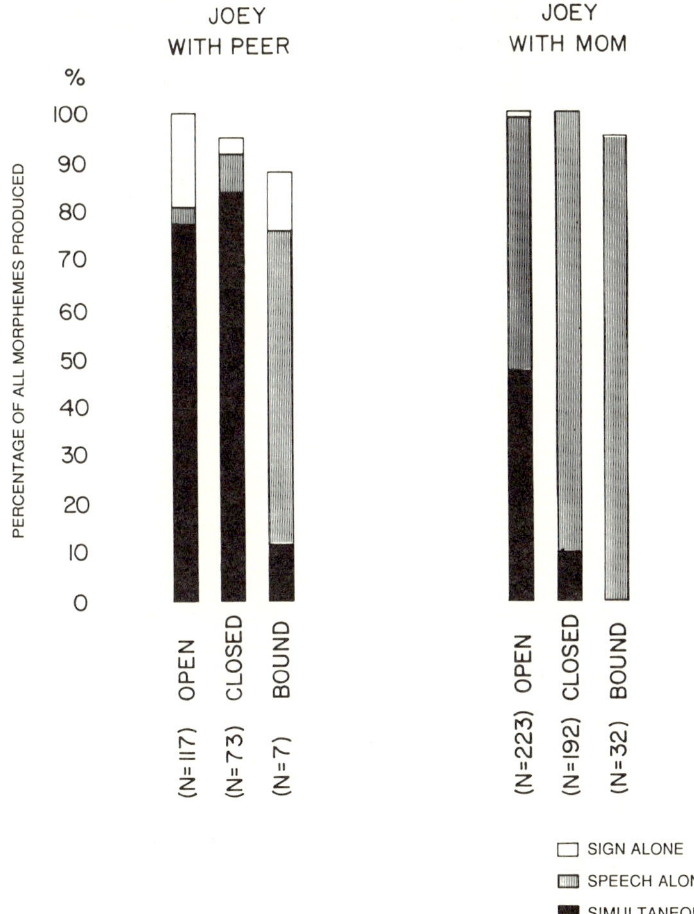

Figure 8.7. Effect of communication partner: Joey.

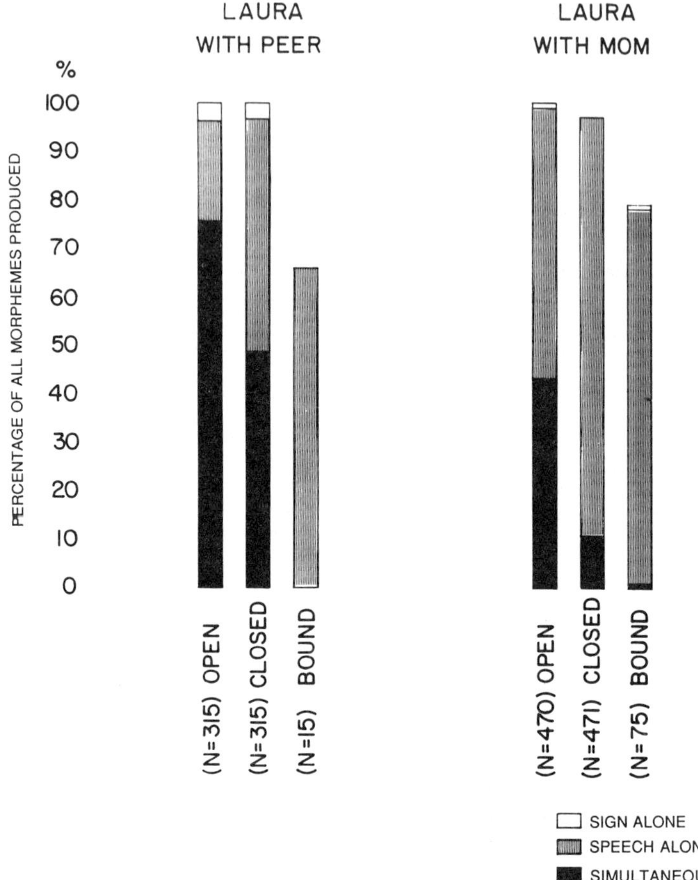

Figure 8.8. Effect of communication partner: Laura.

versing with his mother, Joey decreases the amount of simultaneous speech
and sign, virtually eliminates the use of sign alone, and tremendously increases the amount of speech alone that he uses. Looking at Laura, a 10-year-
old (fig. 8.8), we see the same alternations in mode use: less simultaneous
speech and sign, almost no sign alone, and a lot of speech alone when communicating with her mother. Even children as young as 5 appear to be making
the same distinctions between the two communication partners. Tricia (fig.
8.9) goes from using mostly sign with her peer to using speech almost exclusively with her mother. Jessica (fig. 8.10) also uses less sign alone in the
mother situation, but she does not make quite the dramatic change in speech

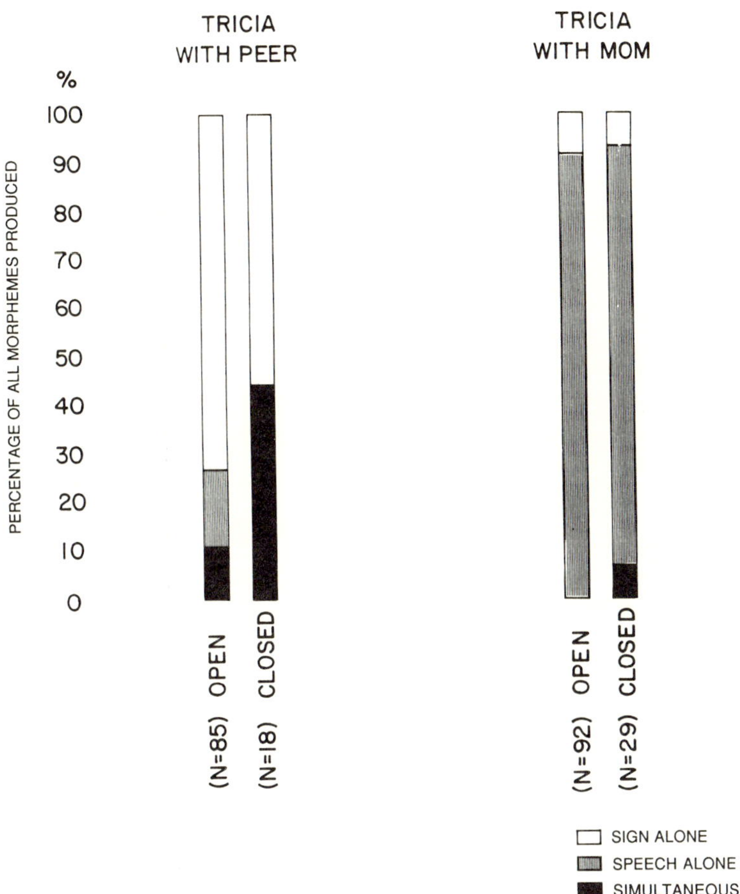

Figure 8.9. Effect of communication partner: Tricia.

alone that Tricia did. This may be because Jessica's mother uses slightly more simultaneous speech and sign than Tricia's mother does.

One child in this study, Becky (a 10-year-old), does not change noticeably from the peer situation to the mother situation (fig. 8.11). Recall that the mothers previously discussed primarily used speech alone with varying, but still proportionately small, amounts of simultaneous speech and sign. Becky's mother, on the other hand, produced more open-class, closed-class, and bound morphemes in speech and sign simultaneously than all the other mothers, thereby also using less speech alone. In fact Becky's mother uses speech and sign in practically the same way that Becky's peer Laura does in the peer

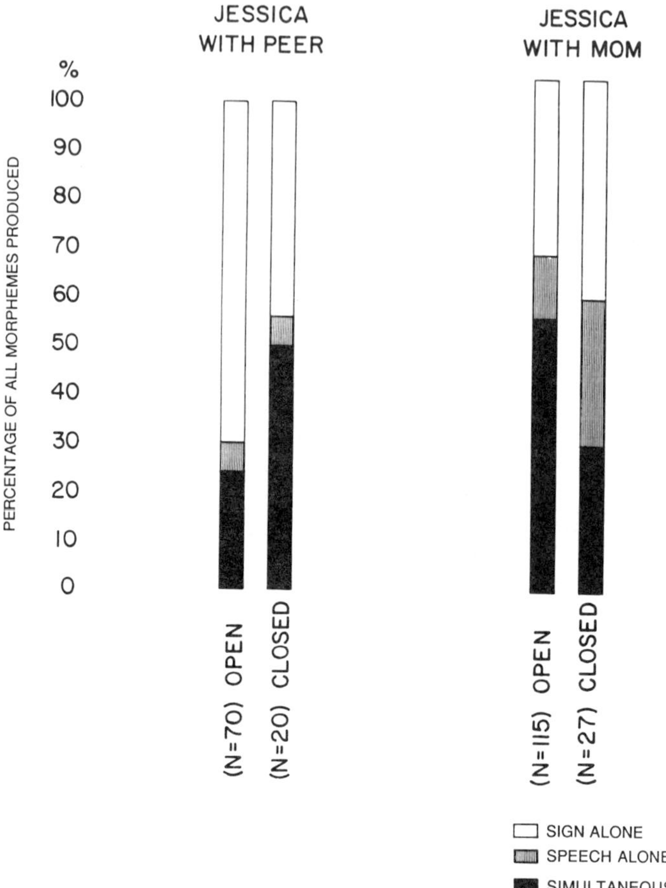

Figure 8.10. Effect of communication partner: Jessica.

situation. Therefore, if the way a child's communication partner uses speech and sign determines the child's productions, it is not surprising that Becky did not alter her mode use, inasmuch as there was no change in the way her partner was communicating from one situation to another.

8.4 Discussion

Many of the criticisms that have been leveled against the use of signed English have had as their bottom line that these systems, because of their artificial nature and the temporal constraints of sign in general, are impossible to produce. The argument that follows has been that if teachers and mothers

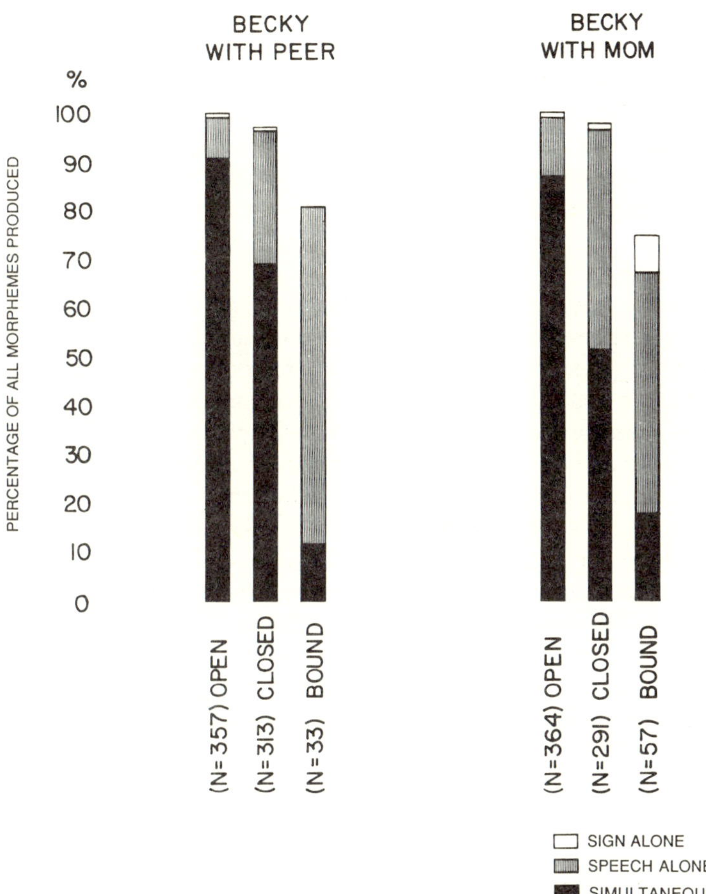

Figure 8.11. Effect of communication partner: Becky.

can provide only a very impoverished model of signed English, then surely we cannot expect deaf children to learn it. The findings presented here suggest that such criticisms and arguments are not entirely well founded.

These results demonstrate that it is possible to put the theory behind using signed English systems into practice in classrooms. Teachers are capable of providing complete language models, in both speech and sign, for their deaf students. In addition, the data suggest that the way these three teachers construct this model may be influenced by the language ability of the students they teach. The three teachers in this study clearly understood that they were in a Total Communication program and were skilled enough to practice this philosophy in their classrooms. However, these data do not allow us to assume that we need not look at teachers if deaf children are not developing language at an acceptable rate. As previous studies have shown (Marmor and Petitto 1979), it is possible that individual teachers will have great difficulty in carrying out the Total Communications philosophy in actual day-to-day teaching. Furthermore, the same point can be made with respect to mothers. If we remain committed to this method, then a good deal of our effort should be concentrated on training teachers and mothers in a much more rigorous fashion. Specifically, more emphasis must be placed on developing proficiency in signed English.

That these teachers showed a decrease in overall accuracy, as well as in accuracy of representing closed-class and bound morphemes, as their students got older suggests that teachers may be aware of the language capabilities of their students and adjust their own communication accordingly. Whether the teachers' decision to represent open-class morphemes most faithfully and bound morphemes least faithfully is conscious or unconscious, it is certainly a logical one. The youngest children need to be provided with a complete and precise model of spoken language, inasmuch as they have little or no language skill at this point in their development. The older children, however, do have some language competency. If they are given most of the open-class morphemes but only some of the closed-class or bound morphemes, which are the glue that hold the open-class items together in a meaningful fashion, they are able to perform a type of visual-lingual closure to fill in the missing parts and complete the message. They should be able to do this if they too were provided with the more complete and precise model of English when they were beginning language learners. However, these interpretations must be viewed as mere speculation until a similar study is done with a much larger number of subjects.

These data also indicate that children are capable of learning signed English, even though it is not a language that has developed naturally like ASL and even though their mothers might not be the best language models. The children also appear to be quite sophisticated in the art of conversation, with respect to their use of modality. In general they use very little speech alone when communicating with another deaf individual, indicating their awareness of their communication partner's receptive capabilities. In contrast, when conversing with a hearing adult who demonstrates limited signing capabilities, they turn to speech or speech combined with sign and eliminate the use of sign alone, to communicate in the most effective manner possible. If hearing adults are proficient signers, however, the children will treat them as such and not alter their use of speech and sign.

The results presented here also suggest that bound morphemes are an odd class of morphemes. Of the three morpheme classes, only bound morphemes were omitted from speech or sign, or both, in the children's language corpora, when they were obligatory, a large percentage of the time. The dropout rate for bound morphemes, when they were obligatory, ranged from 5 percent to 75 percent for the children in this study. This information, along with the fact that both the children and mothers produced most of their bound morphemes in speech alone, suggests that this group of morphemes may be subject to the temporal constraints of sign production.

Bellugi and Fischer (1972) found that it takes approximately twice as long, on average, to produce an ASL sign as it does to say an English word in connected discourse. Findings like these have led to the criticism that signed English requires the signer to produce too many signs in too little time. If one considers all the closed-class and bound morphemes required to produce grammatical English signing, one would assume that some economizing must take place. The possibilities are that either speech must be considerably slower than normal or signs must be omitted. The latter appears to be the case for bound morphemes. That is, users of signed English seem to have discovered that if bound morphemes are to be produced at all, they are often more economically produced in speech alone, rather than in sign alone or in speech and sign simultaneously. The teachers in this study appear to be the exception to this rule. It is possible that if we looked at their videotapes more carefully, we would find that their speech is slowed to accommodate the simultaneous production of these markers.

In summation, there are three major findings in this study. First, these three teachers are capable of producing grammatical signed English, and their pattern of simultaneity suggests that they adjust the language model they provide to the capabilities of their students. Second, mothers were found to be less bimodal and more heterogeneous than teachers in their speech and sign communication. Finally, the children are able to learn the system and, furthermore, to adjust their use of modality based on the speech and sign language abilities or preferences of their communication partners.

9 Bimodal Language Production

Madeline Maxwell, Mark E. Bernstein, and Kimberly Matthews Mear

As far back as l'Epée, sign codes have been invented to accompany spoken language. Linguistic investigations, as distinct from prescriptive descriptions, of this unique bimodal simultaneous form of communication have appeared only recently. Even so, they have been based solely on the sign component of the communication, stressing that it is ungrammatical qua ASL and English both. For example, Marmor and Petitto (1979), Kluwin (1981), and Strong and Charlson (1988), studying the classroom communication of hearing teachers of the deaf, have concluded that "simultaneous communication" (henceforth SC) is a deficient and impossible code: that SC utterances are not grammatical English and may in fact be unsatisfactory for communication. They went further and raised serious questions about the appropriateness of the use of SC in the education of deaf children. Swisher (1985), in a similar study of hearing parents of young deaf children, has raised questions similar to ours about the natural processing pressures that may bear on SC.

From another angle, others (e.g., Woodward 1973a; Fischer 1978) have compared sign used in deaf-hearing interaction to spoken pidgins, noting the many structural similarities bewteen pidgin languages and this form of signing. Again, though, the focus has been on the nature of the sign channel alone. In an earlier paper (Maxwell and Bernstein 1985), we discussed the pidgin similarity issue at some length, questioning whether the analyses put forth by advocates of the pidgin view apply to *all* cases of deaf-hearing sign. What we have been questioning is the idea that all cases of SC are either pidgins or simply sign codes for speech; other alternatives are worthy of exploration.

We have been engaged in a series of studies that we think represent an advance in this line of inquiry by focusing on the *interaction* between the vocal and visual channels during simultaneous production in order to understand the uniqueness of SC. Based on others' work on this topic, one could easily conclude that SC is so deficient as to preclude communicativeness; a "receiver" of SC would be provided such ungrammatical structure in the signing that it might almost be incoherent. Such a view, we maintain, is seriously short-sighted and stems from the way SC studies have been carried out. Only the sign channel has been looked at. The issue of completeness of representation of English is of course a serious one, but mainly from a pedagogical perspective in relation to the development of English in deaf children: If children were to be exposed solely to the sign component of SC and were expected to acquire English from that input alone, *and* if the sign presented a "poor" or incomplete model of English, then there might indeed be a serious problem. The pedagogical issue, though, is only one rather limited aspect of the study of SC and does not really get at the point of how SC *works*. In any case, no one really knows much about the process of *comprehending* SC utterances; whether children (or anyone else, for that matter) fully understand SC utterances is deserving of careful research. Hence conclusions regarding pedagogy and language acquisition are apt to be premature.

A major issue in SC studies concerns the standard by which SC utterances are judged: implicit in some research is a presupposition that the only appropriate "standard" is grammatical English. The evaluation of the English abilities of deaf children or of the English input provided by hearing teachers is an important aspect of the study of SC, but that is only one way to look at it. English grammar is not the issue in our studies; our questions revolve around the semantic match between the sign and speech channels and on the linguistic feature match between the channels, not around how "good" SC is as a representation of "standard" English. The fact of the matter is that SC is used daily by many, many people, both hearing and deaf, who communicate fluently in this manner. And of course the use of SC does involve the *simultaneous* production of speech and sign. Further, judgments regarding the ungrammaticality or "deficiency" of the sign channel are slippery in themselves—this question requires careful descriptions of the structure of the sign channel, not merely gross counts of omissions of spoken morphemes. These points led us to consider a more descriptive analysis of SC, to assess the nature of the relationship between the two channels in an attempt to better understand (without a pedagogical agenda) the structural and semantic phenomena with SC. This research captures SC as it is used by both deaf and hearing persons in natural conversations as well as instructional discourse.

9.1 Method

9.1.1 Consultants

This chapter presents a description of the SC of a number of persons in separate videotaped informal conversations: two deaf adults, two deaf adolescents, and four hearing adults. All the adult consultants are teachers of the deaf at a state residential school; the two adolescents (both age 19) were students at the school. One deaf adult was a native signer, the other learned to sign in college at age 16. Both adolescents learned to sign when they came to the school, one at age 6, the other at age 14. The hearing consultants all learned to sign as young adults as part of their professional training. Their signing experience ranged from five to ten years. They were selected as skilled signers for the study by their supervisors. Two were elementary teachers and two were secondary teachers. All the consultants were female. We make no claims about the typicality of our consultants; this chapter is limited to describing the SC of a particular sample of individuals who use SC regularly and fluently for informal communication and for classroom discourse.

9.1.2 Procedures

The deaf consultants were videotaped separately in conversations with hearing signers (two of the authors). The hearing consultants were videotaped separately in conversations with a deaf signer. The interlocutors used SC with the consultants, who had been told we were interested in conversing in the kind of English sign that deaf and hearing people use with each other every day. Topics of the conversations ranged from early experiences in school to preparations for upcoming holiday family visits, a wide and comfortable set of conversational subjects for all involved. The hearing consultants were also videotaped conducting instruction in their classrooms; in this case they were asked to use their normal mode of communicating in the classroom.

9.1.3 Transcription

Each videotaped conversation or classroom session was examined and single-mode utterances, completely unintelligible or nonvisible utterances, and repetition interrogatives were eliminated from analysis. From each conversation one hundred consecutive utterances were transcribed and analyzed. In all, the deaf consultants provided four hundred utterances and the hearing teachers eight hundred, for a total corpus of twelve hundred utterances for analysis.

Each channel was transcribed in parallel, with the speech written in standard orthography and the sign recorded as English glosses in small capital letters, following standard practice. Approximate relative timing was indicated by the positions of the words and sign glosses in the transcript. Additionally, instances of ASL features were transcribed, and each letter of a fingerspelled word was underlined. Transcription difficulties were discussed and resolved by consensus among the three coder-authors. A native bilingual who had not been present for any of the taping sessions also watched segments of the videotapes without any sound and spoke into an audiotape recorder to provide a check on overinterpretation.

9.1.4 Coding

The utterances were coded twice: at the level of the message and at the morphological level. The degree of message equivalence between the spoken and signed channels was determined by the judgment of the three coders, based on the following categories:

Exactly equivalent: Each channel clearly represented the same propositional content.
Essentially equivalent: The previous discourse precluded erroneous interpretation despite some differences between the channels.
Nonequivalent: One or more constituents differed between the two channels to such a degree that the messages were not identical; that is, some propositional content was either missing or different.

Differences in the channels that did not affect the propositional content of the message(s) were ignored in this first aspect of coding. At this point the question was not whether the subjects were saying and signing the same elements, but whether the propositional content they were saying and signing was the same.

Each utterance was then evaluated to determine correspondence and difference between the actual morphemes presented in the two channels. At the level of morpheme comparison, specific differences in the speech and sign channel were noted through the use of seven categories of mismatch:

Semantic mismatches
1. *Sign and speech not identical.* For example, signing TO while saying "and."
2. *Several possible glosses for a sign.* Included here would be the use of a sign such as TRUE, which might also be glossed as "real," "really," etc.
3. *No equivalent sign gloss available.* For example, the use of a complex sign expression roughly translated as GROUP-COME-TOGETHER (using classifier handshapes), for which there is no single English lexical equivalent.

Structural mismatches
4. *Presence of a free morpheme in only one channel.* This is a large category of omissions of an element in one or the other channel, such as saying the word "the" but not producing any sign.
5. *Presence of tense, aspect, or adverbial markers in only one channel.* For example, saying "playing" while signing unmodulated PLAY.
6. *Presence of personal pronouns in only one channel.* An example would be saying the pronoun "I" but not signing it.

7. *Presence of markers of number (on nouns) in only one channel.* For example, saying "books" but signing unmodulated BOOK.

9.2 Results

9.2.1 Characteristics of the Utterances

The frequency and conditions of occurrence of seven categories of semantic and structural morpheme mismatch were recorded, and the relation between morpheme mismatches and message equivalence was statistically analyzed in several ways. The analyses we carried out resulted in (1) comparison of the message/propositional content in the sign and speech channels; (2) morpheme-by-morpheme comparison of the semantic and structural content of each channel; and (3) assessment of the relation between the morpheme comparison and message equivalence.

The statistical results are presented in detail in other forums, for the deaf consultants (Maxwell and Bernstein 1985) and for the hearing consultants (Mear, Maxwell, and Bernstein 1991). The data on frequency and distribution of morphemes are presented here in tabular form for easy reference. Table 9.1 displays the frequency of each degree of message equivalence for the deaf and hearing consultants. Table 9.2 lists the distribution of each type of semantic and structural mismatch.

In these data we found a high incidence of morpheme mismatches (more than 90 percent of the utterances contained at least one), yet the overall effect of mismatch on message equivalence was virtually nil. Details of the statistical analysis of the relation of the frequency of different mismatch types and of the density of mismatches per utterance to message equivalence are available in separate publications for the deaf (Maxwell and Bernstein 1985) and hearing (Mear, Maxwell, and Bernstein 1991) consultants. A brief summary of some of the major points is included here for background. This chapter, though, focuses on qualitative aspects of the bimodal relationship.

Remarkably few of the utterances were judged to be nonequivalent at the

Table 9.1   Degree of Message Equivalence

Utterance Classification	Deaf		Hearing		Total	
	Number	Percentage	Number	Percentage	Number	Percentage
Exactly equivalent	249	62.3	572	71.5	821	68.4
Essentially equivalent	95	23.7	167	20.9	262	21.8
Nonequivalent	56	14.0	61	7.6	117	9.8
Totals	400	100	800	100	1,200	100

Table 9.2   Distribution of Morpheme Mismatches

Morpheme Mismatch Type	Deaf		Hearing		Total	
	Number	Percentage	Number	Percentage	Number	Percentage
Semantic						
1	25	1.8	56	2.0	81	1.9
2	256	18.6	748	26.4	1,004	23.8
3	22	1.6	36	1.3	58	1.4
Structural						
4	600	43.5	1,239	43.7	1,839	43.6
5	195	14.1	269	9.5	464	11.0
6	223	16.2	359	12.7	582	13.8
7	58	4.2	125	4.4	183	4.4
Totals	1,379	100[a]	2,832	100[a]	4,211	100[a]

[a]After rounding.

message level (and most of those only technically nonequivalent, rather than truly incompatible at the message level, as will be discussed below). Further, density (number per utterance) of morpheme mismatches did not lead inevitably to nonequivalence of meaning. Perhaps the most striking finding in the statistical analyses is that the numbers do not tell the whole story. In one sense our statistical analyses represent the last step in this particular direction—they may very well close the issue. The numerical differences (frequency, distribution, density) do not explain or even relate closely to message quality. Some descriptive analysis of the coding categories and morpheme mismatch types will illuminate this point.

Although the number of consultants is not adequate for statistical comparisons between groups (deaf/hearing) or contexts (adult informal conversation/classroom discourse), there are apparent individual differences between the classroom discourse and the adult informal conversation and especially between instruction in elementary and in secondary classrooms. The role of context will be discussed below, as well as specific differences between the deaf and hearing consultants.

There was a high degree of systematicity in the *pattern* of morpheme mismatches across consultants. Although the actual numbers (frequencies) varied with the consultant, the *relative proportions* of each type of morpheme mismatch, and the nature of these, was highly consistent and predictable. We think this result has more to do with the nature of English and the constraints of bimodal production than with the skills of the consultants. The focus of this chapter is on the qualitative results of the studies and what they may tell us about bimodally produced communication in English.

9.2.2 Message Equivalence

First, we found very high compatibility between the messages of the two channels with all consultants. With rare exceptions, the message in the sign channel was at least essentially the same as that conveyed in speech. That is, our consultants did not seem to be saying one thing and signing another (or to be signing something wholly incoherent). This point is underscored when we consider the nature of the nonequivalent classification. The criterion used for this category was strict and often revolved around a highly specific mismatch of one particular morpheme. The numbers reveal that the sheer density of mismatches *was* statistically related to utterance classification, but density of morpheme mismatches in an utterance, per se, was never the primary reason for categorizing that utterance as exactly equivalent, essentially equivalent, or nonequivalent. There was no a priori criterion that directly linked density of mismatches to equivalence category; judgments of messages were holistic and preceded the feature analysis. At no time was a message judgment consistent with simply counting numbers of mismatches and assigning an equivalence level to an utterance solely on the basis of exceeding some density threshold. On the contrary, message equivalence judgments most often hinged on the omission or mismatch of a single critical element or two, rather than on the total number of mismatches present.

Consider the following example, which was coded as nonequivalent:

(9.1)   I refuse that   trip because I don't want to take my
       REFUSE THAT TRIP BECAUSE NOT   TAKE

       daughter   in the car for one thing.
       DAUGHTER IN   CAR FOR ONE THING

Although ten mismatches do occur in this example (omissions and other kinds of morpheme mismatches), this utterance was judged nonequivalent solely owing to the discrepancy between the spoken verb "want" and the sign channel. The difference alters the meaning of the sign channel message compared with that in the speech channel. That there were as many as ten mismatches in the utterance was irrelevant to that judgment. If the consultant had included the verb in the sign channel of SC, this utterance would have been categorized as exactly equivalent even though it had a high density rate.

Similarly, consider the following:

(9.2)   Since you're going to argue with me about it
       SINCE   ARGUE   ME ABOUT IT

The utterance is heavily loaded with mismatches (a high density), but it was coded as essentially equivalent solely on the basis of the discrepancy between the two channels involving the pronoun "you." Although the sign channel message does not specify who is arguing, the missing referent is easily recoverable from the conversational context—which accounts for the essentially equivalent, rather than nonequivalent, classification. There were scores of utterances that were coded in a fashion similar to these examples; simply counting numbers of mismatches per utterance reveals little about SC.

Nonequivalence was so specific that the potential for misunderstanding (for incompatible or confusing message equivalence) was also very specific. When nonequivalence of sign and speech messages was noted, it was rarely tied to *specific* linguistic features (there is no one type of mismatch that *always* led to nonequivalence). Examining aspects of the specific morpheme mismatch types will illustrate how this works and will reveal a synergistic relation between the channels in this bimodal form of language production.

9.2.3 Morpheme Mismatches and the Synergy of Bimodal Production

What appears to occur in the SC used by our consultants, both deaf and hearing, is that their utterances are English based, coded and expressed bimodally. To fully understand how this SC works, we must take into account that there are two channels operating at the same time. Much of what appears to be happening in the sign channel alone can be understood only with reference to the peculiar synergy that occurs when an English utterance is bimodally coded and produced simultaneously. The sign and speech are supportive and complementary in the language production of our consultants. Usually, in their SC production, the speech (whether audibly spoken or just silently mouthed) presents the English sentence with complete morphology, while the sign channel presents a characteristically altered version with highly systematic omissions or substitutes of morphemes from the full version. These were consistent across our consultants despite their differing backgrounds and variation in skill, and they do not at all seem to be random performance errors.

It is important to note here that the processes of *comprehension* of SC are as yet poorly understood. Although our data suggest much about the importance of the concept of bimodal synergy between the two channels for descriptions of SC production, we have not studied the extent to which *receivers* of SC attend to and make use of the bimodal nature of the utterances for comprehension. We do not wish to minimize this issue. It is conceivable that a receiver might pay attention to the speech only, or to the signs only, or to some combination of the two. We think the latter possibility is most likely, but this aspect of SC communication has not been systematically studied. Certainly receiver variables (English competence, speechreading skill, receptive sign skill, and others) will play a large role in the process, just as, surely, such variables must affect the nature of SC produced by different individuals.

The SC our consultants produced usually consisted of a relatively well-formed and full English utterance in the speech channel, with a somewhat skeletal version of the same thing appearing in the sign. Major constituents or content words were rarely discrepant; on the other hand, function words and affix morphemes of English were largely present in the speech but not in the sign. The major exception involved pronouns (as sentential subjects or objects). In general, pronoun discrepancies and other sentence-by-sentence discrepancies are accounted for by the synergy notion and by a consideration of the psycholinguistic processing of SC in *context,* as will be discussed below. Consider the different types of morpheme mismatches we examined.

9.2.4 Type 1: Sign and Speech Not Identical

Type 1 mismatches were exceedingly rare in our data and highlight both some differences between the deaf and hearing consultants and the synergy within SC production. In our analysis of deaf consultants' type 1 mismatches (Maxwell and Bernstein 1985), we suggested that they did not often lead to serious incompatibility between the messages of the speech and sign and could possibly be explained by reference to an "omission plus timing" error on the part of the consultant, a psycholinguistic effect. In short, what seems to be happening is that the consultant omits a morpheme of the utterance from the speech channel and omits a different but neighboring morpheme from the sign channel. An error in timing results in an overlap of the remaining morphemes in both channels, which gives the appearance of a localized mismatch of the overlapped morphemes. Three-quarters of the deaf consultants' type 1 mismatches could be explained this way, but only one of the hearing consultants' type 1 mismatches fit this pattern.

Consider the following example from a hearing consultant:
The underlying form was:

(9.3) *But I thought it was Massachusetts.*

The utterance produced was timed:

(9.4) I thought it was Massachusetts.
       BUT THINK   MASSACHUSETTS   [sign]

As it was, only 28 percent of the utterances that contained a type 1 mismatch were classified as nonequivalent, and in only slightly more than half of

those cases was the type 1 mismatch directly responsible for the nonequivalence judgment, as in the following:

(9.5)   What happens if the jar is loose?
         WHAT HAPPENS IF   JAR IS TIGHT?

In the next example, however, despite the type 1 mismatch, the meaning of
the sign channel is not discrepant from that of the speech:

(9.6)   Because I think we are gonna get a bicycle.
         BECAUSE   THINK   BUY BICYCLE

"Get and "buy" are semantically related in that the concept of "get" is entailed in (i.e., part of the meaning of) "buy." Lexical retrieval of the sign for
the word may result in such a substitution. Another alternative is that the consultant translated the sign in order to communicate a more exact meaning. For
example, "get" in English is a general word; in ASL, however, GET has the
more restricted meaning of physically seizing something. The consultant may
have used the sign BUY to indicate the specific meaning of the spoken message.

The type of mismatch shown in the example above may be explained by
Laver's (1970) description of how communicators retrieve information from
their story memory. An addressing system is needed to retrieve stored information. In recalling this information, the addressing system activates more
items than it finally selects to communicate. These items are all semantically
related because the addressing system is semantically directed. At times a
communicator may make an error and retrieve the wrong item from stored
memory, but this "error" will usually be a semantically related word. This
process may be responsible for most the type 1 mismatches made by the hearing teachers; 61.5 percent of this mismatch category involved substitutions of
semantically related signs.

The semantic similarity of mismatches was not always evident when looking at the words in isolation:

(9.7)   There are many plants like that.
         MANY PLANT SAME THING

In the example above, "that" and "thing" are not semantically related in isolation. However, the utterance was coded as equivalent at the message level
because saying "like that" and signing SAME THING convey the same meaning
in context. The remaining cases of utterances containing type 1 mismatches
that were still judged to be equivalent were either instances of the consultant's
substituting a sign for a phonetically similar word—for example, saying

"thing" and signing THINK—or cases of simply signing a meaning different from the spoken one. But in both of these types, at times enough information was included in the sign and speech channels so that the propositional content of the utterance was still essentially intact and not incompatible in the two channels, for example:

(9.8)   I   saw some really cute stories about Thanksgiving.
         THAT SEE SOME REAL CUTE STORY ABOUT THANKSGIVING

In the example above, even though the consultant signed THAT and said "I," the basic meaning equivalence of the utterance is not greatly affected because the rest of the message is intact and because by convention omitting the sign "I" would not affect the message of an utterance.

It may be that the differences between the deaf and hearing consultants' type 1 mismatches are related to their different processing strategies. The nature of the deaf consultants' type 1 mismatches suggests that they may process and code their language for output in large units—similar to the notion of a tone group (Laver 1970). Laver has described the tone group as the unit in which speakers code their language for output. It may consist of up to seven or eight syllables with one prominent syllable on which a change of intonation occurs. Pauses and syntactic chunking also determine the boundaries of tone groups. The omission-plus-timing effect would be consistent with the idea that at some preliminary stage of output, processing a large structured unit of elements is represented in a "buffer" of some sort. The "mismatched" morphemes are each essential elements of a single underlying structure. By contrast, the lack of omission-plus-timing errors in the SC of the hearing consultants suggests that their units for output programming are perhaps only one word in size rather than the larger-scale chunking apparent in the deaf consultants.

Aspects of the hearing consultants' SC style and the specific errors they made support the possibility of processing differences; in certain situations the hearing consultants might not code their language in tone group–size units as the deaf consultants seem to do. In many of these utterances, it seemed that the hearing consultants were able to adequately code a spoken English message; however, in assembling the *signed* counterpart of the spoken message for output, a breakdown in processing the information occurred because the individual could not remember a certain sign or call it up immediately. This situation might require more internal processing time to search one's lexicon for the correct sign. This would subsequently disrupt the timing of the utterance and the coding unit of the message, resulting in a slower and more labored speech message, in addition to certain mismatches in the speech and sign channels. This was observed in the videotapes, especially during episodes in which type 1 mismatches occurred. The breakdown in the coding process may result in a word-by-word or sign-by-sign coding unit. This explanation (applicable to over half of the hearing consultants' type 1 mismatches) may account for the difference in the kind of type 1 errors made by the hearing and deaf consultants.

Why the difference in processing style? These two groups may be coding signed output in different ways owing to different degrees of familiarity with the fluency in the language and with bimodal coding. It is conceivable that this is a factor related to experience; the deaf consultants would be more used to coding signed output and therefore may use psycholinguistic strategies more similar to those used for speech output than do the hearing individuals we studied. While most of the deaf consultants have signed for most of their lives and at present rely daily on a visual representation of language to communicate for all purposes, the hearing teachers have used SC for at most ten years. None of them use it with their families. The deaf consultants' SC did look "smoother" to the judges than did that of several of the hearing signers. Perhaps the two channels are better integrated for the deaf than for the hearing; for the latter, signs may be organized as subordinate or supplemental to spoken words.

9.2.5 Type 2: Several Glosses Possible

There were numerous instances of type 2 morpheme mismatches. These never resulted in a message equivalence problem. In considering these ubiquitous mismatches, a number of possibilities arise. One is that they may be primarily a translation and coding artifact. That is, there are often multiple English glosses for the same sign, and these are often semantically quite similar. There really is no basis for selecting the "right" sign in production or the "right" word in transcription. To code an English morpheme with a particular sign during SC output presents a problem to the signer if several choices are equally available, and what results may be a matter of the range and depth of the signer's lexicon or the flexibility and speech of a person's bimodal production processing strategy. The introduction of fingerspelled handshapes to supplant the original ASL handshapes of certain signs was an attempt to differentiate English synonyms and near synonyms, such as *team, family, group, tribe, class*. The practice is limited in scope, however, and is little used, especially in our data. Our consultants used few initialized signs that have not already entered the general lexicon of ASL (Battison 1978).

It should come as no surprise, of course, that a type 2 mismatch does little violence to message equivalence of the channels; translation is rarely exact, and the various glosses for a sign are usually very similar in meaning. When the "exact" English word is spoken and the "multiple gloss" translation for it is simultaneously presented, the synergy between the two channels generally affords more than sufficient clarity to avoid nonequivalence or incompatibility. We are currently examining the type 2 morpheme mismatches in the SC of interpreters and have noted one interesting point in an interpreting context—the interpreters frequently use a general type 2 sign and then immediately follow up with a fingerspelled version of the spoken Enlgish word, all without missing a beat. Presumably this strategy helps ensure the accurate conveyance of all nuances of meaning expressed by the English speaker who is being interpreted. It seems likely that the looseness of fit inherent in matching signs and spoken words has consequences for processing time, if not for the likelihood of semantic confusion. Such a semantic comparison of ASL and English is a separate line of study. Our analysis in the SC studies was not subtle enough to reveal such issues, if indeed they are a problem.

9.2.6 Type 3: No Equivalent Gloss or Sign Available

Type 3 mismatches occurred very rarely in the data. Most often these involved uses of complex ASL sign expressions that required several English morphemes to translate, or mime gestures that could not readily be translated by a single English word. For both groups of consultants these occurred less than 2 percent of the time. The deaf consultants tended to eliminate spoken words while performing a type 3 sign (although there were characteristic ASL facial gestures or mouth movements accompanying the signs); the hearing consultants in all but one case did use speech to accompany such a sign. The appearance of type 3 mismatches may reflect code switching involving translation occurring in the midst of SC discourse. It is likely that the frequency of occurrence of this process will vary with different signers and situations—a possibility that deserves further study.

9.2.7 Type 4: Presence of a Free Morpheme in
Only One Channel

Omissions of signs for spoken morphemes were by far the most common type of mismatch in these data (about 50 percent of all mismatches). What is so interesting about this mismatch type is how rarely it was the apparent basis for an equivalence classification. A closer look at the type 4 subtypes provides some clarification. Table 9.3 displays a breakdown of the distribution of grammatical categories within type 4.

As we suggested earlier, most discrepancies between sign and speech in the SC we studied were omissions in sign of noncontentive morphemes that were spoken. Verbs were the largest subcategory of type 4 omissions (28.8 percent for the deaf consultants, about 50 percent for the hearing), which seems to contradict this generalization. Further, the omissions of verbs seem to be critical in terms of message equivalence. But it is essential to note that only a

Table 9.3   Distribution of Type 4 Morpheme Mismatches

Subtype	Number	Percentage
Verbs	511	27.8
Main verb	58	11.0
Copula	247	48.3
Auxiliary	206	40.3
Other form classes	1,328	72.2
Subject nominals	110	6.0
Articles	440	23.9
Prepositions	154	8.4
Conjunctions	202	11.0
Possessives	55	3.0
Infinitives	110	6.0
Miscellaneous (includes nominal objects, adverbs, contractions, etc.)	257	14.0

relatively small proportion of the verb omissions were omissions of *main verbs* (18.5 percent for the deaf, 8 percent for the hearing). In relation to the overall pool of omissions, these numbers shrink considerably in their significance—we found that only a minuscule proportion of all omissions of spoken words were of main verbs. Overwhelmingly, the omissions were of copulas and auxiliary verbs, with very little effect on message equivalence. This is not surprising considering that these same structures are not used as obligatory morphemes in many languages, including ASL. There is a general convention that the copula is "understood" if omitted in certain syntactic contexts (see Klima and Bellugi 1979). Furthermore, auxiliaries in English carry very little semantic information; they serve primarily to "fine tune" or to perform syntactic functions.

Nouns were virtually never omitted. Indeed, rarely were the main content-bearing morphemes of an utterance omitted from a channel. Thus the phrase structure of the utterance was carried fully in both channels in almost all instances.

9.2.8 Type 5: Presence of Tense, Aspect, or Adverbial Markers in Only One Channel
Type 7: Presence of Markers of Number (on Nouns) in Only One Channel

Type 5 and type 7 will be discussed together, since they present a similar manifestation of the synergistic relation between the channels and the resulting message equivalence. Both of these mismatch types were statistically related to message equivalence. A type 5 mismatch, however, only rarely was directly responsible for a judgment of essential equivalence or nonequivalence. Type 7 mismatches were, at times, but then only in a technical sense; they rarely seemed to lead to serious incompatibility or incoherence. What seemed to be going on was a particular kind of synergy between the channels, in that redundancy within the utterance played a large role in determining the effect of a mismatch or omission of these morphemes. For example, a type 5 mismatch (almost always an omission of the sign marker for the spoken affix, rather than the signing of a "wrong" affix, and only occasionally the signing of an unspoken affix) rarely affected equivalence because the information that might be conveyed by that affix was easily recoverable from the rest of the utterance itself.

Consider the following example of a type 5 mismatch:

(9.9)   I think   maybe she's ready   now   because   last   August   for   her
      THINK MAYBE   READY NOW BECAUSE LAST AUGUST FOR HER

(9.9)   birthday   we thought about   it . . . .
      BIRTHDAY WE THINK   ABOUT IT . . .

Although the past tense is not marked on the sign verb THINK, the utterance as a whole is marked by the signs LAST AUGUST.

Type 7 morpheme mismatches, discrepancies in the marking of plurality on nouns, sometimes involved displacements because of the different structural properties of ASL and English; for example:

(9.10)   M made a cheesecake   with   cherries on top.
      M MAKE   CHEESECAKE WITH CHERRY ON TOP

      + DISTRIBUTION-CLASSIFIER

CHERRY is signed with no plural marker, but the ASL distribution marker is signed at the end of the utterance.

In other cases a plural marker may have been omitted completely from one channel, but the plural meaning was represented by a numeral or other modifier; for example:

(9.11)   So it was 3 or 4 teachers with 100 kids.
      SO   3–4 TEACHER WITH 100 KID

In this example, the correspondence of the meaning of the two channels is evident because of the signed numerals. Semantically, there is no need to redundantly denote plurality on the nouns because the numerals have already done the work.

The following is a different, but related, example of an omission of a plural marker that does not affect message equivalence:

(9.12)   I've heard   many different   variety of stories . . .
         HEAR   MANY DIFFERENT VARIETY OF STORY

This mismatch also does not affect message equivalence because the consultant signed and said MANY and VARIETY, which makes it obvious that more than one story was heard. Although the type 7 category accounted for only 6.2 percent of the total number of mismatches for the hearing consultants and only 4.2 percent for the deaf consultants, the coding on certain omissions of plural markers was so strict that there was a statistically significant relation to message equivalence.

9.2.9   Type 6: Presence of Personal Pronouns in Only One Channel

The last mismatch type to be examined presents an interesting SC feature. Although the consultants did at times make use of various manual English initialized signs to denote personal pronouns, they seemed to omit them fairly often from the sign channel; this category was the third largest mismatch type (16.4 percent of all mismatches). Of all type 6 mismatches, 40.2 percent were omission of the pronoun "I" in the sign channel. A type 6 omission rarely affected the message equivalence of an utterance because, as we mentioned earlier, in sign communication it is generally understood that if a subject is not designated it is the signer. That 59.8 percent of the type 6 omissions were personal pronouns other than "I" most likely accounts for the statistical relation of this mismatch category to the essential equivalence category. This is because deleting a pronoun other than first person requires one to use the local conversational context to identify the referent of the utterance. As we indicated above, the use of context to disambiguate a message in our coding scheme requires that the utterance be coded essentially equivalent. This is another demonstration of the complex nature of SC. Simply counting omitted morphemes would lead to an erroneous conclusion about the interpretability and message congruence of the channels of utterances that contain type 6 mismatches. Given the context of conversations and the utterances themselves, the omission of personal pronouns presented few problems in our data. Nevertheless, this is an area of ambiguity that might indeed place an increased load on processing, and as such it deserves further study.

9.2.10 The Role of Content

Many of the features of SC described above make reference to conversational or local utterance context. This appears to be a critical element in the analysis of SC. In fact, we coded on the basis of single utterances, *without* context, in order to arrive at judgments of message equivalence. That is, given a particular utterance containing one or more mismatches, we asked whether the context *might* function to reveal equivalence. If the answer was yes, then the utterance was coded essentially equivalent. In actual conversations, both parties *do* have access to the immediate context and history of the discourse. This would only serve to further reduce the possibility of apparent incompatibility or outright misunderstanding that might otherwise seem likely. In a sense, our judgments of message equivalence were a good deal stricter than would be the case in an actual conversation.

We did discover a degree of variation in the use of SC in different situations. The hearing consultants were videotaped in both informal adult conversation and classroom instruction. Both the elementary- and secondary-level hearing teachers had a higher proportion of exactly equivalent utterances in their classroom discourse than in informal adult conversation. In addition, although the relative distribution was similar, they made more mismatches generally in the informal settings. It is possible that the teachers have (or at least attempt) a degree of control over their SC characteristics. It may be that they are trying to present a more "complete" signed utterance to correspond to their speech when in the classroom. The systematicity of the morpheme mismatches still holds, however.

The elementary teachers in both data collection settings tended to produce more exactly equivalent utterances than did the secondary teachers, as well as a smaller total number of mismatches. Although it is not known why teachers use SC as they do, it is possible to speculate that elementary teachers may include more of the morphemes of English in their signed messages because of their focus on teaching English to young students. The elementary-school child is considered to be at a crucial stage for language learning, so teachers may concentrate on including more of the morphemic structure of English in their signs, as they are instructed to do by many advocates of simultaneous speaking and signing (e.g., Bornstein and Saulnier 1984). Another possible explanation for this apparent difference in the use of SC by teachers at different levels may be that the supervisors who selected them had different criteria for what constitutes a "good signer" at different levels. Further research is needed to determine if the use of SC by elementary and secondary teachers in this study is representative of hearing teachers, as well to determine the effects of different communicative situations on the production of SC.

We suspect there is more variability than many previous studies suggest. For example, one segment of sign communication involving an 8-year-old deaf child revealed very different sign styles. She began a session with language very similar to that of these elementary teachers, switched to ASL, and then used SC more like our other consultants, with English phrase structure and many mismatches of morphology (Maxwell, n.d.).

9.3 Conclusions

Clearly, we are dealing with a complex language behavior in fluent SC. We think our data and analyses demonstrate three important findings that advance research and understanding in this area:

1. The kind of SC we are looking at is produced *bi*modally.
2. The two modes do not simply repeat each other.
3. The relation between message coherence and linguistic features is not a mechanical one.

As its detractors have told us, the sign in SC does not fully represent all the grammatical/morphological elements of spoken English. Bound morphemes invented by educators to provide for such "full representation" are absent in wholesale numbers from our fluent users' communication, especially in informal adult conversation. Furthermore, the fit between the ASL lexicon and the English lexicon is of course uneven. The lexicons of no two languages have an exact fit between them. Even if our consultants had not also known at least some ASL, though, it is clear from our type 2 multiple-gloss analysis that the relation between the sign lexemes and speech lexemes is a complicated one. Its implications should be further explored, but our analysis did not reveal any major consequences for message congruence.

The systematicity we uncovered in the relation between the modes has implications for how we think about SC as a language form. The elements that do not appear are highly predictable, nonstressed, redundant grammatical elements. We are not saying that such omission is unimportant or that it has no implications for pedagogy; we are saying it is predictable and, further, that it has little effect on the communication of messages. The lack of fit between channels in unstressed morphological redundancies and the looseness of fit in the lexicon create additional potential for lapses in communication and certainly introduce translation issues for those who know ASL, as well as raising possible processing-time issues. What is astonishing is how rarely this potential seems to be realized in our data. Obviously we need careful comprehension studies, but at least in the kinds of discourse we studied, utterances were appropriate and contingent and repairs were no more common than in single-mode discourse.

The predictable elements that were "expendable" were not the contentives that carry heavy information loads; almost all of the "missing" and mismatched elements came from the closed class of morphemes. These are elements that are generally unstressed, redundant, and used over and over in a multitude of contexts, carrying little or no semantic content of their own. Slobin (1977) referred to this class of morphemes as "fragile" because of their treatment in running speech. To provide for efficiency in language use, certain elements are foregrounded while others are backgrounded, certain elements are stressed while others are destressed to provide focus in sentences and produce all components at a relatively steady rate within tone units. Speakers strive for efficiency in production; consequently, what they produce is subject to "phonological squeezing." In Slobin's words, such squeezing is the "inevitable concomitant of rapid, fluid communication among linguistic experts." Some elements are dropped from speech, others are devocalized; probably the most common process is elision. It is the "fragile" elements of this closed class that are most vulnerable to phonological squeezing. What is the "inevitable concomitant of rapid, fluid communication among linguistic experts" using SC? When an utterance must be produced bimodally, there is an extra difficulty standing in the way of efficiency. In our discourse, the consultants spoke in normal conversational cadences and did not overarticulate; thus their speech displayed such squeezing. And so did their sign. The question to address to the sign channel is, What is the result of such normal squeezing in fluent production of SC by experts? The answer seems to be a great deal of omission of closed-class signs. Perhaps the difficulty of bimodal production leads inevitably to omission/mismatch. (This may have something to do with the tendency of some SC users to mouth but not to vocalize.) Hence the simplification of the sign channel in English-based SC. To make matters even more difficult for an SC signer, "invented" sign morphemes for English affixes and functors are rarely phonologically suitable to be easily elided, deemphasized, and "squeezed" (Maxwell 1987).

We noted above that there appears to be a difference in the size of the language chunks processed by our deaf and hearing consultants—the tone unit seems to be of normal size for the deaf consultants but perhaps smaller for the hearing teachers we studied, even though they are fluent. Further investigation of tone unit structure and other aspects of prosody may increase our understanding of how SC production works and may relate to comprehension as well.

The third advance we offer concerns the relation between message coherence and linguistic feature matches. Our data provide overwhelming evidence that there is no quid pro quo between comprehensibility and specific types of mismatches or even density of mismatches. Mismatches in linguistic features make it more likely that there will be a mismatch in message content, but they do not lead directly to such message mismatch. Instead, message nonequivalence is locally determined by a mismatch of a *critical* element—critical to that particular utterance. Another way of saying this is that every message problem has its own story, its own source of the problem. This finding should lead to research on a number of questions. For example, experiments could probe the consequences of such critical mismatches. If aspect and qualification are primarily restricted to the speech channel, does that mean SC is restricted in its ability to exploit and convey linguistic nuances? How do users of

SC play, argue, wax poetic, and how often are they having enough trouble just getting the message across? These are interesting sociolinguistic questions. We may be ready now to deal more perceptively with the issue of mismatches of interlocutors; that is, we cannot always assume a language conflict or language contact situation (pidginization) when deaf and hearing people sign to each other. Nevertheless, there are differences in language knowledge and skill, and these should be investigated more systematically to provide an understanding of SC that may not be English based, as in our studies. We were, in fact, surprised at how little code switching and how few features of ASL we found. Studies of individual adaptation to different communicative situations might reveal a greater variety of language ability than previous models have suggested. Our data remind us that the sign language used in the United States is not a single homogeneous language code and that it is worthwhile to open our minds and direct our attention to the varieties of sign language and the combinations of speech and sign modes that we can see around us.

Finally, we wish to make a few remarks about the topic we have avoided, the education of deaf children. SC has been studied before primarily as an educational code. We are sensitive to the decisions that educators are trying to make in deciding on language and language modes to be used to help children acquire language—English in particular—at home with hearing parents or in schools of various kinds. Although educators do not have the luxury of waiting on research before they communicate with deaf children and their parents, we still think that the kind of work we are doing is necessary background to any decent evaluation of the pedagogical issues. There is no question that we need research on the input offered to deaf children and on what the children derive from that. Maybe a little child does receive only the sign channel, maybe the teachers are all incompetent; on the other hand, maybe the children receive something from the speech/mouthing channel at some point, and maybe some teachers are competent. What we are trying to do in our studies is to explore how fluent communication in SC works; we do not see how we can either advocate or condemn behavior in teaching children without this understanding. In other words, we have what may be a foolish dream, that we can separate the political issues of education from the linguistic ones. For all we know, this system may be terrible as language input for acquisition or terrible for interlocutors who do not use the speech channel receptively. That does not make it intrinsically terrible. Like other linguistic varieties throughout the world, it exists. Some people use it and some do not.

10 The Acquisition of Fingerspelling by Deaf Children

CAROL A. PADDEN

10.1 Introduction

This chapter examines the emergence of fingerspelling in young deaf children whose first language is American Sign Language (ASL). Fingerspelling consists of positioning one hand to the side of the body and delivering a rapid sequence of hand configurations, each corresponding to a letter of the alphabet. The conventional wisdom is that young deaf children use fingerspelling to represent alphabetic characters. As I will demonstrate, however, the discovery that hand configurations correspond to alphabetic characters comes relatively late for deaf children.

Fingerspelling is particularly interesting because of its unusual properties as a language system. Fingerspelling is not an independent language system; instead, like writing, it is a representation of some other system, in this case English orthography. Yet it occupies a peculiar and constrained position in the larger system of ASL. Fingerspelled vocabulary does not appear freely but seems to be limited to a small set of grammatical categories. These and other types of constraints are among the knowledge young deaf children acquire as they become competent spellers.

That fingerspelling attempts appear long before young deaf children are able to read and write supports the general observation that fingerspelling has a prominent role in the language environment of deaf children in deaf families, but little has been reported on how they go about learning to use this unusual system—what types of productions they make and how learning it compares to learning a natural language. I present first a description of fingerspelling as a language system, then an account of the emergence of fingerspelling in young deaf children from age 2;1 to 4;9.

This chapter is a revised version of a presentation given at the Conference on Theoretical Issues in Sign Language Research, Rochester, New York, in 1986. Suggestions from Tane Akamatsu, Vicki Hanson, and an anonymous reviewer of an earlier draft have been gratefully incorporated in this version. I also thank Anne Dyson, Peg Griffin, Tom Humphries, David Perlmutter, Laura Petitto, Mark Seidenberg, and Ted Supalla for fruitful discussions on various aspects. Merrie Davidson generously assisted with the data collection and analysis.

10.2 The System of Fingerspelling

In terms of its distribution in language communities, fingerspelling resembles written language. Comparatively few oral languages have accompanying written systems; likewise, comparatively few signing communities use a manual system for representing the oral language of the surrounding society. Furthermore, in communities where a manual system exists, the system tends to be used minimally, in far fewer categories than in the North American deaf community (in the United States and English-speaking parts of Canada). Deaf foreigners who meet American signers complain that they fingerspell "too much" and "too quickly."

Fingerspelling is only one system in a larger category of "manual systems" used in signing communities. It is not clear how such systems become adopted and widely used by a community of signers, since there are many signing communities that do not use a manual system at all. The American system of alphabetic hand configurations can be traced to an alphabetic system invented in the seventeenth century by a hearing priest, Juan Pablo Bonet, who developed it for the education of a young deaf boy. The system was subsequently adopted by a French educator, Abbé Sicard, who founded a number of public schools for deaf children in France. The system was later transported to Ireland and the United States. Great Britain's educational system for deaf children developed independently of the French system; its signed language is unrelated to ASL, and its alphabetic system is not one handed but two handed. Deaf people in Denmark use a "mouth-hand" system that coordinates lipreading and hand configurations. Deaf Thai signers have an extraordinarily complex manual system for Thai script, including its diacritics for tone. In Taiwan and Hong Kong, deaf signers trace ideographs in the air. (A collection of different manual systems can be found in Carmel 1975.)

The inventories of fingerspelled hand configurations and ASL hand configurations do not entirely coincide. Those fingerspelled hand configurations that also appear in ASL are A (also appears in PATIENT), B (also appears in HELLO), C (SEARCH), E (only in a regional sign, CUTE), F (INDIAN), G/Q (HOMOSEXUAL), H/U (NAME), I/J (THIN), L (FAST), O (ZERO-ON PAGE), R (BRAIDS), S (WORK), V (LOOK-AT), X (DOLL), Y (PLANE), Z (TRUE).[1] The remainder of hand configurations appear only in "initialized signs," a special subset of ASL signs considered "borrowed" from English: the hand configuration is the same as the fingerspelled first letter of its English translation. D appears

---

1. Signs are represented by glosses in small capitals—for example, TAKE, "to take." For a sign that requires more than one word to translate it, the glosses are joined by hyphens. Fingerspelled letters and words are represented by small capitals; in words, the letters are joined by hyphens; for example, C-A-R-O-L ("Carol"). Glosses for fingerspelled loan signs are preceded by the symbol #: #OK ("Okay"). The symbol + represents a morphological boundary.

in DEVELOP, K (KITCHEN), M (MISSIONARY), N (NOBLE), P (PRINCIPLE), T (TOILET), and W (WATER). In contrast, there are many hand configurations in ASL that have no counterpart in fingerspelling: the outstretched 5 hand (FATHER, MOTHER), the clawed 5 hand (MAD, YELL), the bent 2 hand (STRICT, SNAKE), the baby O shape (PICK-ON).

But what is often overlooked about fingerspelling is that there are other aspects to the task that are rarely made explicit: the construction of movement units that make up the fingerspelled item. For example, double letters may appear with a characteristic bouncing segment as in H-E-L-L-O, or with a movement internal to the handshape, as in T-R-E-E. The letters *J* and *Z* have tracing movements that are assimilated by segments preceding and following it. The G handshape has a number of different orientations depending on neighboring letters. In addition, there are conventional transitions between certain sequences and within common morphological segments—for example, I-O-N (the derivational morpheme *-ion*). These and other movement rules are among the conventions about fingerspelling that young children learn.

10.3 Subjects and Their Families

The data that form the basis for this chapter were taken from a larger home study with eleven deaf children ranging from age 2;1 to 8;5. This chapter focuses on the six younger children, ranging from age 2;1 to 4;9. The parents are also deaf except for one family where the parents are hearing but are native signers of ASL, having learned the language from their deaf parents. A primary language used in the home is ASL. Videotaped interviews and play sessions involving spelling, writing, and signing, ranging in length from about a half hour to an hour per visit, were carried out with each child. Table 10.1 below summarizes videotaped records for each child by age. In addition, field notes from an earlier study of child SS (Padden and LeMaster 1984) at age 2;9 were included, and in some cases the data collected in this study are supplemented by other colleagues' video records.

The parents of the children included in this study are white, middle class, and nearly all college educated. Except for those of one child, VV, one or both parents are employed at a local school for deaf children. In interviews they report that they consider learning to read and write an important goal, more important than learning to speak and lipread English.

All parents use ASL, but some use a more stylized language with their children, including "manual English" signs developed for pedagogical purposes. All parents in this study, however, agree that fingerspelling is an ideal way of representing English to their children and will use it to instruct their children

Table 10.1   Ages When Videotaped Records Were Made of Six Deaf Children

CC	TT	MM	KK	BB	VV
2; 1	2; 9	3; 11	4; 3	4; 6	4; 7
2; 3		4; 1		4; 8	4; 8
		4; 2			4; 9

in "what the English words are" even if they are using pedagogical signs in the home. Note that fingerspelling is probably more prominent in these particular families because of the parents' professional and personal interest in teaching their children about English. In other deaf families it may be used less. Maxwell (1983b, 1984) describes some deaf families where fingerspelling is used to a much lesser extent than in the families in this study. In such families the children may not learn fingerspelling until they arrive at school.

The parents said they actively tried to encourage print-fingerspelling associations when they felt children were ready, sometimes as young as 2 years of age. All had a large assortment of educational toys for introducing print to their children. One child had a playroom where the parents attempted to replicate the environment of the school, along with school-issue chairs and desks, play blackboards, books, paper, and pencils. The children in this family were encouraged to sit at their desks while writing and drawing. Children as young as 2 years were encouraged to play with plastic letters, and at about 3 years the parents urged them to begin making sequences of letters for spelling their names and those of their siblings. With children they felt were "ready," the parents played games matching plastic letters with fingerspelled characters, usually for spelling out the child's name.

Despite the parents' early efforts to associate fingerspelling with print, very young children seem unaware of the connection between a hand configuration and an alphabetic character until about 3 years of age. Even then, their associations between fingerspelling and print remain tenuous and uncertain.

10.4 Fingerspelling among Deaf Adults

Before exploring how deaf children acquire fingerspelling, it seems sensible to ask how the system is used by adult signers. Unfortunately, fingerspelling has received little of the attention directed to signed languages. It has been well documented that ASL, the primary language of the American deaf community, is not dependent on or derived from English (for a recent summary, see Padden 1988). Fingerspelling, in contrast, is typically identified as an example of a manual activity that is not signed language. It is described as a code, a system used for representing the alphabetic characters of English orthography.

In one of the few published analyses of adult uses of fingerspelling, Battison (1978) observed that many fingerspelled items enter the sign lexicon in the form of "loan signs." In such cases of "unstable fingerspelling," the resulting loan form loses much of its original structure and absorbs structural properties of signs. Newly borrowed items typically have a reduced number of hand configurations, from the full number of configurations for each letter in the word in fingerspelled words to only two in their loan sign counterparts. In these reduced forms, loan signs are phonologically consistent with the class of signs in ASL that may have at most two hand configurations per segment (Perlmutter 1990). Many loan signs are verbs—for example, #NO ("to say no to"), #BACK ("to go back to")—incorporating inflectional movement.

But basic questions about the category of fingerspelled items, not loan signs, and how signers use fingerspelling have not been investigated. As a preliminary way to answer questions about adult use of fingerspelling, four segments of an adult's conversation with another adult were transcribed. Segments roughly identical in length were taken, one from each of four topics: how to bake a meat dish, a personal experience with the police, a description of a television movie, and a description of how to buy a house. A total of 2,123 manual lexical items (an item is equivalent to a "word") across all segments were recorded, excluding morphology marked by facial or body position. A sign with complex morphology such as a classifier sign was counted as one item. Out of 2,123 manual items, 105 were fingerspelled and 32 were loan signs. The proportion of fingerspelled items among manual items, words and loan signs combined, across the three segments was approximately 6 percent. Some topics had a higher proportion of fingerspelled items: how to bake a meat dish had 12 percent (27 fingerspelled items out of 231 items) compared with 4 percent (17 out of 432) for a personal experience with the police. (Table 10.2 summarizes these figures.)

From an inventory of all the fingerspelled items (table 10.3), at least one striking difference emerged between fingerspelled words and signs: there were almost no fingerspelled verbs. When verbs are followed by prepositions, fingerspelling is restricted to the prepositions, for example, TAKE O-V-E-R. From

Table 10.2   Number of Fingerspelled Words and Loan Signs in Four Excerpts from an Adult's Signed Conversation with Another Adult

Activity	Number of Total Items in Segment	Number of Fingerspelled Items	Number of Loan Signs	Percentage of Fingerspelled Items
Watching television	824	20	19	5
Buying a house	636	48	6	8
Baking a meat dish	231	24	3	12
Experience with the police	432	13	4	4

Table 10.3   The Different Fingerspelled Items Produced by an Adult in a Conversation with Another Adult across Four Videotaped Segments

English terminology	Proper names	Phrases
C-H-A-N-N-E-L	T-O-Y-O-T-A	ON S-A-L-E
T-V D-I-N-N-E-R	J-O-H-N	TAKE O-V-E-R
G-A-S-O-L-I-N-E	J-A-N	MOVE O-U-T
J-U-R-Y	A-L-B-A-N-Y	CLEAN O-U-T
C-A-S-E	L-A-N-E-Y	FORGET I-T
D-U-P-L-E-X	S-L ("San Leandro")	STOP S-I-G-N
D-O-W-N ("payment")		COOKIE S-H-E-E-T
U-N-C-L-A-I-M-E-D	*To identify members*	GREEN P-E-P-P-E-R
T-A-X	*of a descriptive class*	L-E-A-N MEAT
N-O-T-E-S ("trust deeds")	H-O-L-E	O-R E-L-S-E
F-E-E	T-R-A-Y	
E-S-C-R-O-W	S-L-I-C-E	*Replicating print*
D-U-O	C-A-R-R-O-T	F-O-R S-A-L-E
C-O-M-M-I-S-S-I-O-N	B-A-C-K-S-E-A-T	T-H-E O-W-N-E-R
O-W-N-E-R	G-A-R-A-G-E	("For Sale by Owner")
D-E-A-L	S-H-E-E-T	T-H-E BURN B-E-D
M-P-H ("miles per hour")	G-R-O-U-N-D B-E-E-F	("The Burning Bed")
L-B-S ("pounds")	D-O-O-R	
F-O-I-L		*Function words/pronouns*
C-E-L-E-R-Y	*Verbs and adjectives*	I-F
P-A-R-S-L-E-Y	S-E-X-Y	O-R
P-L-A-S-T-I-C	S-I-C-K	T-H-E-N
R-E-N-T ("rental unit")	Q-U-I-L-T-Y ("guilty")	U-N-L-E-S-S
R-E ("realtor")		H-E
A-D-U-L-T		
O-I-L		
R-E-P-A-I-R		
F-L-A-T		
O-W-N-E-D B-Y		
O-R E-L-S-E		

observations of fingerspelling in nonvideotaped conversations among adults, some verbs do appear, but they are relatively rare. Over 50 percent of all fingerspelled items were English nouns or proper names. Fingerspelled loan signs, in contrast to fingerspelled words, can be verbs. Fingerspelling and signing appear to differ not only in structural organization but also in the grammatical categories represented. When fingerspelled items are borrowed into the sign lexicon, the resulting forms are no longer constrained in grammatical category.

Of those fingerspelled words that appeared in the sample, nearly all can be placed into one of a small set of categories. The first category is made up of items that represent or translate English terminology or abbreviations of English terminology (including proper names). Within this category are fingerspelled phrases to represent common English phrases. A second category, equally common, is made up of items that identify a specific member of a descriptive class. These include sequences of classifiers followed by a finger-spelled word identifying the specific member of the classifier inventory. The third category involves use of fingerspelling to represent print, as in titles and on signs. A final category is made up of items that are themselves gram-matical markers.

Some items listed under "English terminology" have roughly equivalent sign translations—for example, "fee," can be translated as CHARGE, "pounds" (WEIGH), "duplex" (TWO-ENTITIES-NEXT-TO-EACH-OTHER), "re-pair" (FIX), "adult" (ADULT). Fingerspelling seems to function in these con-texts as a means of directly translating key English terminology, needed in situations when signers discuss events involving these terms.

Other fingerspelled items are not translations but independent lexical items. The sign RENT/MONTHLY (verb) means "to pay a monthly fee." There is also a loan sign, #RENT, which means "to rent," as in "to rent a car." The finger-spelled words R-E-N-T, as used by the adult in these segments, has yet another meaning: "a rental unit." Battison (1978) notes that loan signs typically have meanings that do not coincide with the range of meanings for the original En-glish word, but the same seems to be true of some fingerspelled items. The fingerspelled function words appear also to have meanings unlike their closest sign translations. ASL has a number of complementizers, including IF, WHICH/WHETHER, FINISH, BUT, and others, but these have slightly different meanings than the fingerspelled items. These examples suggest that finger-spelling is used not only for representing English terms but, like loan signs, for creating lexical items that need to be distinguished from existing sign vocabulary.

A prominent class of fingerspelled items includes those that identify a spe-cific member of a descriptive class. For example, the descriptive classifier HORIZONTAL-FLAT-OBJECT is used for a wide range of objects, including the shape of a bed, countertops, and floors. In one segment the signer uses HORI-ZONTAL-FLAT-OBJECT, then follows it with the fingerspelled word "sheet." The signer has identified a specific item, a baking sheet, from among several possible flat objects. In another example, the fingerspelled word "garage" follows the sign TWO-VEHICLES-LOCATED-SIDE-BY-SIDE. The classifier does not mean "garage," but rather refers to two vehicles parked together in a par-ticular location. The signer uses the fingerspelled word to disambiguate be-tween several alternative meanings—for example, "two cars next to each other in a parking lot," or "two cars next to each other in a garage." Simi-larly, the fingerspelled C-A-R-R-O-T is used following the signer's use of a re-gional sign CARROT, not likely to be known by many other signers.

The latter uses of fingerspelling do not coincide with the commonly held view that fingerspelling is used solely for representing English words; instead, at least in limited cases such as these, fingerspelled words have meanings independent of English words and ASL signs. But what is surprising about fingerspelling is the almost total absence of verbs in the transcribed sets. In the case of fingerspelled words that follow classifiers, the examples suggest signs and fingerspelled items appear in certain constrained structures. The system of fingerspelling is not entirely marginal or supplementary but occupies a peculiar niche for deaf signers and, it would be reasonable to expect, for deaf children as well.

10.5 Parents' Fingerspelling with Children

From our videotaped records of parents interacting with their children, the parents seem to fingerspell less with young children. MM's mother, in one exchange of stories with her daughter, used 5 fingerspelled items, 4 fingerspelled signs (#OR, #OK, #OK, and #WHAT), which appeared in a total of 284 manual items (3.9 percent). TT and KK's father used 11 items in his exchange, 10 fingerspelled words plus an 11th item, a fingerspelled sign, #ALL. Of the 207 manual items that appeared in his story, 5 percent were fingerspelled items. An inventory of the different fingerspelled words appears below in table 10.4.

Since the adult data show a higher percentage of fingerspelled items in a signed exchange, those data suggest that parents modify the amount of fingerspelling they use with their children—at least their younger ones. However, the range of items used by parents falls into the same categories found in adult fingerspelling.

As replacements for items they would normally fingerspell, parents said they substituted signs. One parent described how the family had gone along with his child's invented signs for the different cereals he ate: MONSTER CEREAL, "Count Chocula," TIGER CEREAL, "Frosted Flakes," although he and his wife fingerspelled the names of the cereals to each other. Another parent invented special signs for the different types of juices, for example, Hawaiian

Table 10.4   Different Fingerspelled Items Produced by Parents during Conversations with Their Children

English Terminology	Proper Names	Function Words/Pronouns
Y-A-R-D	B-A-R-B-I-E	A
Y-A-R-D-S	K-E-N	O-F
D-O-G	B——[name of child's playmate]	O-R
B-L-O-C-K-S		S-O

Punch. However, the parents say they try to fingerspell more to their children as their perceptions about their "readiness" change.

10.6 The Emergence of Fingerspelling

The earliest fingerspelled attempt by a young child is very often the child's own name. Middle-class deaf parents believe that being able to fingerspell one's own name and others' names at an early age is a good sign of precociousness and language skill. In one videotape, a deaf mother is shown prompting her deaf child at age 2;7 in how to fingerspell his name. MM at 3;11 can successfully fingerspell her own name. But CC at 2;3 can only use his "name sign." Deaf parents usually, but not always, give name signs to their children. Sometimes in the case of very short names, the parents may opt to only fingerspell the name. Name signs commonly use the alphabetic hand-shape of the first letter of the child's first name with one of a small set of possible movement and location structures (Supalla 1990). CC at 2;3 can correctly use the name signs for himself and his brother. He can also correctly identify himself and his brother when shown their name signs. As a test to see how well the child could recognize his own name sign, the experimenter invented a name sign with movement and location similar to the child's own but with a different hand configuration. CC was confused and then pointed to a place outside the room, showing that he could recognize hand configurations in name signs and make correct judgments. At ages younger than 4, however, children can usually fingerspell only their own names and occasionally that of a sibling.

From an early age, deaf children start to theorize about the differences between signing and fingerspelling. In field notes with SS at age 2;9, we see an example of a deaf child's early functional differentiation between signing and fingerspelling/spelling. When SS was asked what something was, she provided a sign, but when asked the name of an item, she reverted to fingerspelling. MM at age 4;2 explained to her mother in one videotape that the ELEPHANT+'S NAME was too long and she liked the CAT+'S name better because it was easier to fingerspell. The girls' functional differentiation between fingerspelling and signing resembles early differentiation between drawn and written representations in hearing children (Ferreiro 1984). Ferreiro describes how young children identify the picture of an object as "what something is" but its written word as "its name." As an indication of the "nameness" of a written word, Ferreiro observes that the children in her studies label their picture of a doll as "*a* doll" but label its written representation as simply "doll." The omission of the article signals the child's awareness of the object's "name."

MM at age 4;2, and likewise SS at 2;9, understands that fingerspelling and signing differ in distribution. While playing with the video camera, MM's older sister tells MM to "say something into the camera." MM begins to introduce herself, then mimics fingerspelling to give names of people around her. Her "fingerspelling" involves no clear sequence of hand configurations; instead, she blurs the handshapes and bounces her hand up and down in the characteristic fingerspelling style. She has not yet learned how to spell names, but she knows in what form and context they are to be produced.

The conventional wisdom about fingerspelling is that learning to fingerspell, and consequently learning to spell, involves learning to create the right sequence of hand configurations. From her studies of hearing children of deaf parents from age 3;8 to 5;3 learning to fingerspell, Akamatsu (1982) describes how her children learn to mimic the "movement shape" of the target fingerspelled word. In such attempts, individual hand configurations are often substituted or deleted altogether. She argues that, contrary to popular expectation, children are not merely learning to create a sequence of hand configurations but are learning the characteristic grosser movements involved in constructing the fingerspelled word. These movements include distinctive transitions between hand configurations and the movements within the handshapes themselves as they learn to "fingerspell." Her work makes clear that the distinctive units of fingerspelling are not solely the hand configurations themselves, but also movement units that combine to construct the movement sequence of the whole word.

Padden and LeMaster (1985) report videotaped records of similar examples in deaf children of deaf families as young as age 2;7. As DD tries to spell the name of a relative, D——, he makes the first hand configuration corresponding to the alphabetic letter *L*, then changes to the hand configuration for the remaining two letters, which are doubled. For the doubled letters, he bounces his hand to the side in an exaggerated form of the normal doubled handshape sequence. The mother corrects the child and fingerspells the three hand configurations distinctively, including the correct initial handshape D. Following Akamatsu's analysis of early fingerspelling attempts, DD correctly analyzes the feature [+extension] in the target production of the hand configuration D and substitutes another hand configuration marked [+extension]: L. Then the child moves into position for the hand configuration corresponding to the next letter and exaggerates the characteristic bounce for doubled handshapes, indicating again that the salient features of fingerspelling to the young child are not exclusively features of hand configuration.[2]

SS's mother reported that SS at age 2;6 had made several fingerspelling attempts, including an attempt at I-C-E that involved a repeated movement clos-

---

2. I thank Ursula Bellugi for making this videotaped segment available to me.

ing the hand between the open "clawed" hand configuration and the configuration for the letter *E*. SS replaced the closed, fingers-bent hand of the hand configuration C with an open, clawed shape and followed it by the enclosed shape of the letter *E*. She then produced repetitions of the sequence. Another example of SS's early productions was her approximation of O-K, "Okay." In the adult form, the transition from O to K is produced with a wrist flick downward. SS's production involved the same wrist flick downward, but with only one handshape, K.

This activity of generating a movement unit, or a sequence of movement units, I shall call "fingerspelling," and I shall distinguish it from another activity called "spelling." By about 4 years old, deaf children know how to position the hand correctly for fingerspelling, but they are faced with a more difficult problem. On what basis do they select the sequence of hand configurations that make up a fingerspelled word?

10.7 Differences between Fingerspelling and Spelling

At the same time SS was mimicking the shape of fingerspelling, she was also doing a different activity. At age 2;9 SS was asked what the name of her dog was; she produced a sequence of three clearly articulated segments: U-B-A. (The dog's name was Sasha.) She was then asked to name other objects in the room. For the table, she produced: E-B-A. When asked what her name was, she replied with the name sign assigned to her by her family. When asked to FINGERSPELL, she hesitated and looked at her mother. She then produced E-U-B. (None of these letters appear in her name.) Her mother reported later that SS had just started to learn how to spell her name but had not yet succeeded. Later, at her mother's prompt for the first letter, SS tried her name again, choosing three letters that were correctly drawn from the letters in her name. Although this sequence of configurations was not correct, they were in the correct order. But not all such attempts, as shown in the earlier examples of U-B-A, E-U-B, E-B-A, coincide with the target fingerspelled item. The activity of consciously constructing a sequence of hand configurations I shall call "spelling."

At age 2;9 SS had a perplexing task ahead of her: to select the "correct" sequence of hand configurations when spelling, to learn to spell her dog's name as S-A-S-H-A, rather than U-B-A. Akamatsu (1982) reports that by the time the hearing children in her study had reached school age, they had begun forming correspondences between sound and hand configurations. Early attempts at these sound-configuration correspondences closely resemble Read's examples of creative print spellings in young children (1971, 1975), for example, L-I-E-N ("lion"), T-R-D-L ("turtle"), and M-U-C-E ("mouse"). But for deaf children, forming an association between fingerspelling and English words requires strategies different from the ones hearing children use, for at least one obvious reason—they do not yet know the sound structure of English.

When she was asked to "name" objects around her, SS at age 2;9 was unperturbed. She was willing to provide an attempt when asked. "Spelling" to SS merely involved executing a sequence of hand configurations. At older ages—MM at 3;11 and 4;1, BB at 4;8, and VV at age 4;7—children begin to suspect there is more to the task of "spelling" than creating any sequence of hand configurations. VV at 4;7 was willing to comply with requests, but she was easily distracted. She spelled C-N-I-T in response to a request to name a computer keyboard. A picture of an airplane elicited Y-O-B and a coat, R-I-B. These selections are not entirely random; in the next section, some strategies for selection are outlined. By age 4;11, VV was clearly uncomfortable with such requests and squirmed whenever she was persuaded to try. She finally understands that there is a fixed sequence for every English word, and she does not yet know them. Along with this awareness comes discomfort and embarrassment at not being able to produce the sequences.

At these ages, however, children's ability to recognize spelled sequences outstrips their ability to spell the words themselves. KK at age 4;3 could recognize fingerspelled color words. When asked to select correct colored pens upon being shown their fingerspelled names, KK confused only "black" and "blue," most likely because the initial two letters are identical. MM at 4;2 could correctly distinguish all fingerspelled colors including black and blue. MM could also recognize a small fingerspelled vocabulary including cat, dog, pig, boy, girl, boat, elephant.

At age 2;6, TT could use several fingerspelled loan signs, but the forms were reduced: #TV ("television"), but instead of the initial T handshape, she substituted the formationally similar S shape. TT also used #OFF ("take off"), but did not articulate the initial O handshape and instead selected F, using the characteristic sweeping movement of the loan sign.

What do early spelling attempts by deaf children look like? TT could fingerspell, laboriously and carefully, only her name and that of her brother, KK. She offered only one handshape, R, when asked by a parent to fingerspell "radio." She was later prompted by the parent into spelling the remainder of the word, but she could not produce the same word a few minutes later. It is not until the children are into the middle or late part of their third year that they show attempts at sequences of hand configurations.

As stated earlier, the spelling attempts of deaf children in this study do not resemble those of Akamatsu's children, indicating that some other strategy for selecting hand configurations is in place. From the spelling attempts collected, at least three basic strategies can be detected. As will be seen from the examples below, some strategies are system internal, based on generalizations about fingerspelling itself; others are system external, based on theories about the correspondence of fingerspelling to other language systems in their environment.

10.8 System-Internal Strategies for Spelling

One strategy involves executing the first handshape of the fingerspelled word in its correct initial position. Examples of the different attempts from KK, MM, VV, and BB using this strategy appear in table 10.5.

For some attempts, other letters in the word are correctly selected, including the final position letter—for example, D-A-G ("dog") and A-R-I-L-E ("apple")—but in other cases the remainder of the word bears no resemblance to the original: B-A-T for "bird," and O-W-Y for "orange."

A second strategy involves replicating other salient features of the fingerspelled word. A common feature is the characteristic movement that accompanies double letters. For both "green" and "tree," many children correctly replicated the E-E sequence. In some cases the children repeated the characteristic movement but incorrectly selected the letters to be doubled. For example, instead of L-L in "ball" and "doll," two children doubled the preceding letter. Certain other sequences seem to be especially salient, for example the O-W- sequence in words like "yellow" and "brown."

Finally, there are spelling attempts that seem to be theories about comparisons across words, those that recognize that words can have similar sequences. The O-W sequence appears in both Y-E-L-L-O-W and B-R-O-W-N. One child spelled G-E-E-N for both G-R-E-E-N and T-R-E-E. The sequence B-L-U-K-E for B-L-U-E indicates a comparison between B-L-U-E and B-L-A-C-K.

Table 10.5   Deaf Children's Spelling Attempts Using First
Letter of Word

Target	Spelling Attempts
Black	B-A-K-L-K, B-L-A-K
Blue	B-A-K, B-U, B-L-U-K-E
Pink	P-I-K
Red	R-I-E, R-A-P, R-L-E
Orange	O-W-Y, O-S
Yellow	Y-P-E-W, Y-O-W-N
Green	G-E-E-N, G-S-E-E
Purple	P-U-P-L-E
Cat	C-T-F, C-D-T
Ball	B-O-O-L
Dog	D-A-G
Apple	A-R-I-L-E
Bird	B-A-T

These system-internal strategies point to attempts by deaf children to generalize about sequences of letters based on the small inventory of fingerspelled words they recognize and can themselves spell.

10.9 System-External Strategies for Spelling

The two strategies described above draw from within the system of fingerspelling and children's new, but limited, knowledge of English orthography. There is another strategy that, unlike the other two, draws from outside the system of fingerspelling—from the natural language ASL. In this strategy children use the hand configuration of the sign as the first letter of the fingerspelled word. For most signs in ASL, there is no direct correspondence between the hand configuration of the sign and its nearest English translation. But for a small set of ASL signs, including vocabulary young children are likely to use—color words—the hand configuration corresponds to the first hand configuration of its fingerspelled translation. For example, the sign BLUE has a hand configuration that is also the fingerspelled handshape for the letter *B*. This set of signs are called "initialized signs."

A large subset of initialized signs used in the deaf community are name signs. Name signs use the first letter of the person's first, middle, or last name. At age 2;6, TT identified herself using her name sign. She identified her brother by his name sign, which coincides with the first letter of his name. TT began spelling her brother's name, correctly choosing the first hand configuration, but she was unable to finish it. VV at age 4;7, when asked to fingerspell the name for a list of signs, demonstrated that she exploited initialized signs as a good source of information about at least the first letter of its fingerspelled translation. When asked to name an individual whose name sign used the letter *C*, VV mimicked a fingerspelled word with only the first letter, *C*, clearly identifiable.

The problem facing these young children is that they do not yet know which signs are initialized and which are not. The same B handshape that is used for BLUE is also used in a great many other signs in which the first letter of their English translations is not *B*—for example, WINDOW, DOOR, SOCCER, and WOOD. When shown a picture of a racket, VV gave the correct sign, then proceeded to produce the first letter of the word using the same hand configuration for the sign, S. The hand configuration for AIRPLANE is Y; VV produced a Y-O-B sequence in response to a picture of an airplane. Neither RACKET nor AIRPLANE is an initialized sign. KK was shown a picture of a chicken and given the correct sign, which involves a G hand configuration. Then he spelled its name as G-I. For TREE, with an outstretched 5 hand configuration, KK offered the 5 handshape as the first letter of its fingerspelled word, but he was unable to finish the word. Younger children are willing to try spelling not only those hand configurations that coincide with the small inventory of alphabetic hand configurations, but even shapes outside this inventory. Older children, about age 5, understand that the outstretched 5 handshape is not in the inventory of possible fingerspelled characters and will simply say that they do not know how to spell the word (Padden, n.d.).

Children as young as 3 to 4 years already display rudimentary awareness of English orthography. They are beginning to understand which letters are likely to appear word-initially. Beginning at about age 5 and 6, deaf children's spelling attempts begin to resemble the target words more closely in length and sequence. By age 8 or 9, deaf children begin to make errors more similar to errors made by deaf adults, including many that involve omissions or additions of syllables and reordering of letters—for example, *replite* for "reptile" and *mirgate* for "migrate" (Hanson 1982b; Hanson, Shankweiler, and Fischer 1983; Padden, n.d.).

As a summary of the spelling data collected from six deaf children at age 2;1 to 4;9, the following progression can be outlined.

1. *A minimal sequence of hand configurations.* TT at age 2;9 produces only a single hand configuration whenever asked to spell, except for her name and that of her brother. SS at 2;9 begins to produce sequences, but usually no longer than three letters: U-B-A, E-U-B, E-B-A. What seems to matter most is the production of a minimal sequence of hand configurations rather than attending to which hand configurations should be chosen.

2. *Selection of hand configurations.* The older children begin to attend to choices of configurations, but not their sequence. VV, at age 4;9, spells "cat" with the initial *C,* but the sequence is realized variously as: C-R-I and C-N-I. From field notes with AA, SS's older sister, at age 4;11, AA was playing with her father and was purposely distracted while the father removed a piece of candy she had left on the table. When AA returned to playing with her father, she quickly noticed that her candy was gone and demanded to know where it was. The father, in mock seriousness, explained that E-T ("the Extraterrestrial") had taken the candy away. AA laughed and said it could not have been him, spelling the name as T-E. MM at age 4;2 accepted either P-I-G or G-P-I for a picture of a pig.

From analysis of older children, starting from about the end of their fourth year, it seems their spelling attempts reflects awareness of both selection and sequence. During an outing with her family, VV at age 6;6 could spell many words correctly but had difficulty remembering how to spell "Coke." When her father asked her at a restaurant what she wanted to drink, VV began to spell: C-A-O, then stopped herself and tried again C-O-K. . . . The father prompted E, and VV nodded her head impatiently: C-O-K-E.

10.10 Interaction of Fingerspelling and Writing

From their work with hearing children learning to write, Ferreiro (1984) and Dyson (1986) find that early written attempts are not isolated but often interact with children's understanding of other systems in their symbolic world, notably drawing. In some early writing attempts by hearing children, a written character can be represented as both a figure and a letter, as in the case of one young child who used the same line element to represent both "a nose" and "a letter." Later they make the transition to identifying the naming properties of writing.

Not surprisingly, early fingerspelling attempts show interaction with writing as deaf children explore the ways fingerspelling can be connected with making print. Almost always, when the 4-year-olds were asked to write, they fingerspelled to themselves, producing a hand configuration for the letter before beginning to write it. VV, at age 4;8, had interesting ideas about how fingerspelling and print are related. Like hearing children who attend to properties of speech, VV attended to the physical properties of fingerspelling as she attempted to write characters for the individual hand configurations.

VV was asked to write the names for stickers representing objects on a piece of paper. She insisted she did not know which letters to put on the page and wanted them spelled out for her. The experimenter then proceeded to fingerspell the word, at which point VV interrupted and asked the experimenter to deliver only one hand configuration at a time. For example, she would look at the first hand configuration, P, write a character, look up again and wait for the next configuration, write the character, and so on until informed by the experimenter that "there are no more." VV made no comments about length of the fingerspelled word or its appropriateness to the sticker; instead she devoted her efforts to writing the character. Figure 10.1 shows that several of her characters were ideographic attempts to represent the features of the hand configuration.[3] The character λ, which she used to represent the first letter in "purse," mimics the two outstanding features of the handshape P: the higher extension of the index finger, and the lower extension of the middle finger (see fig. 10.2).

The following month, at age 4;9, VV performed the same task with a different set of stickers (fig. 10.3). Some of the same ideographic representations she used the previous month appear in this sample as well. She used her invented representation for P for a formationally related hand configuration, K. The handshape K is minimally distinct from P; in P the hand is oriented upward, but in K, it is oriented downward. VV also used a small set of written

---

3. The background is dark because the writing was done on dark red construction paper.

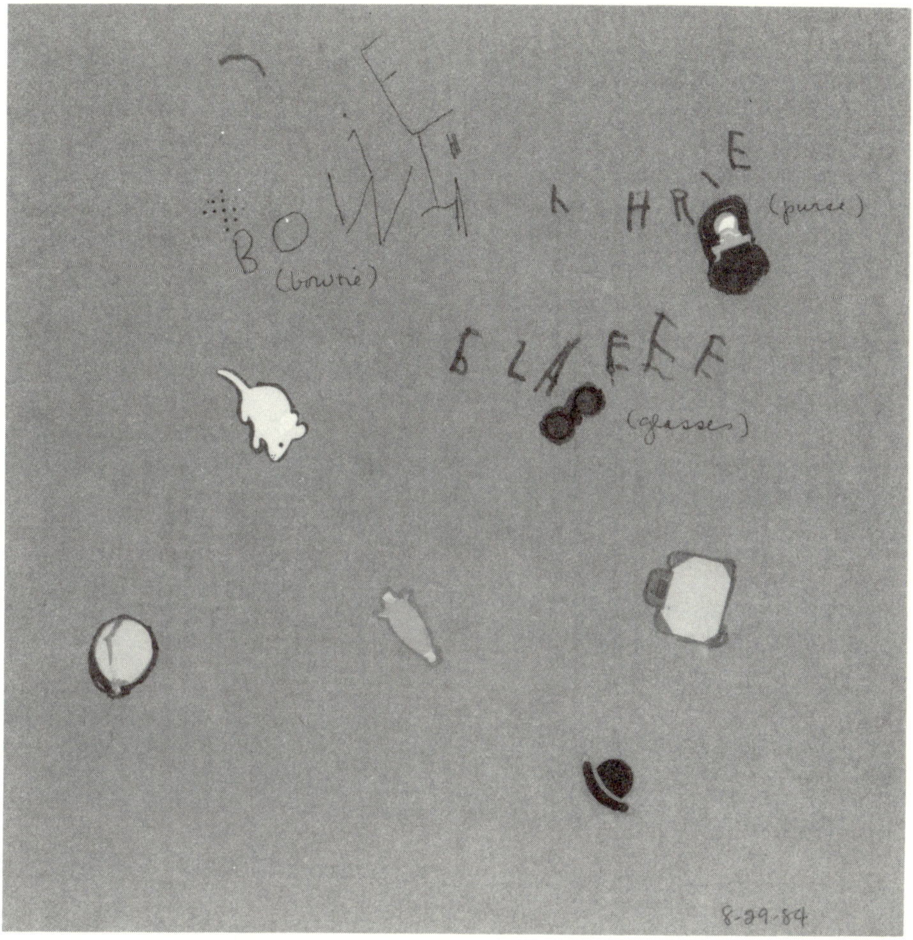

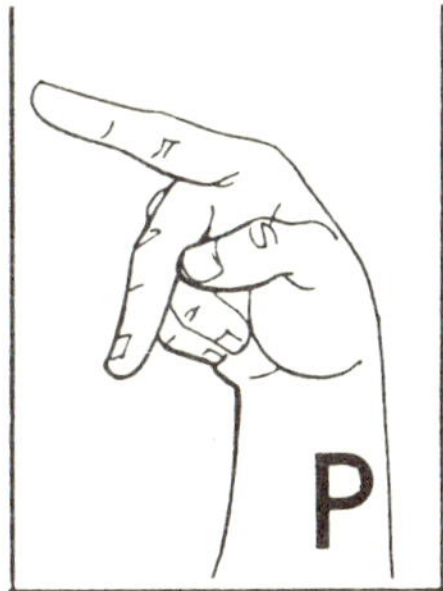

Figure 10.1. VV's attempts to write at age 4;8.

Figure 10.2. Fingerspelled hand configuration for *P*. From Tom Humphries and Carol Padden, *A Basic Course in American Sign Language* (Silver Spring, Md.: T. J. Publishers, 1980).

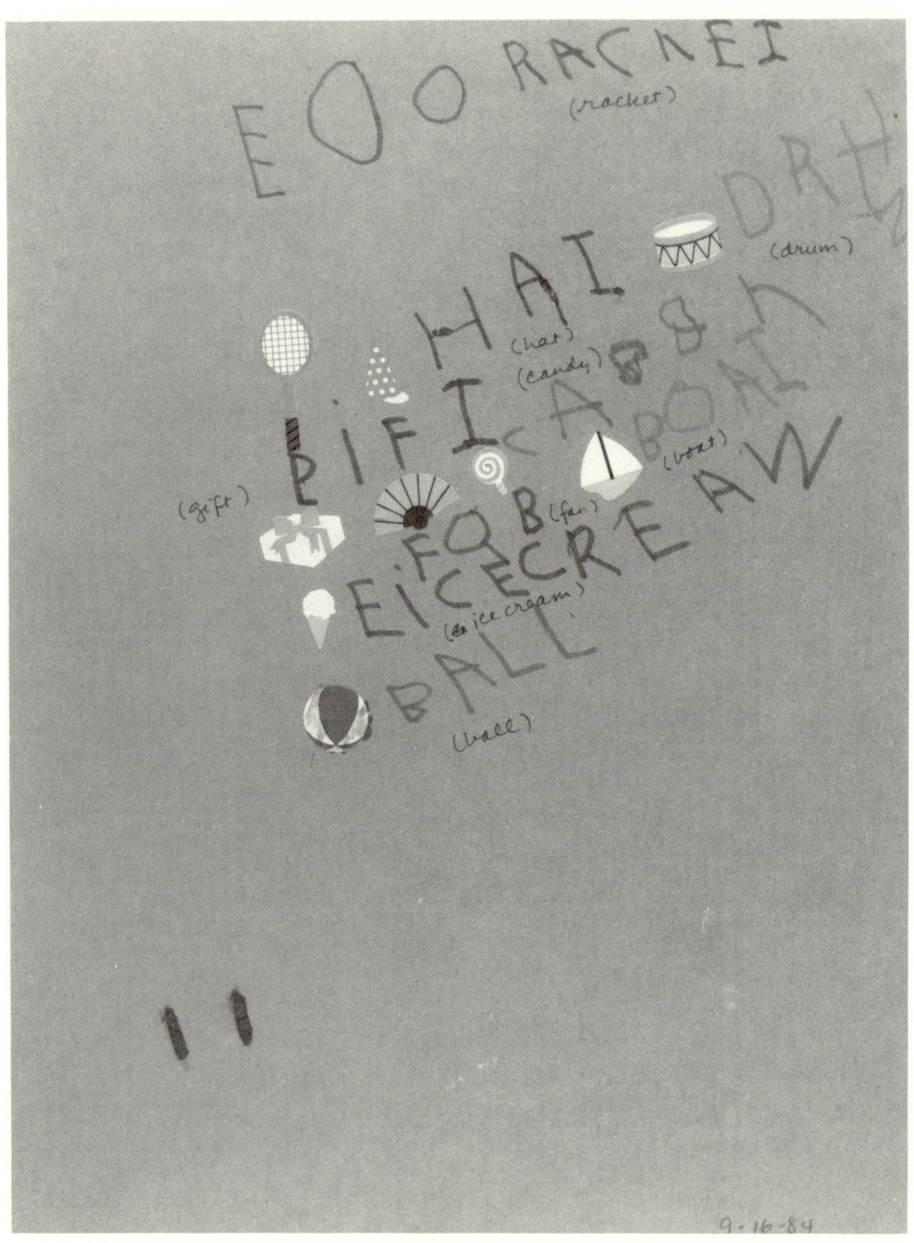

Figure 10.3. VV's attempts to write at age 4;9.

characters repeatedly to represent several configurations that share key features. She used the written *E* to represent *S* as well (in her written attempt for glasses), but the *E* used for the letter *s* has a small mark, or "diacritic," underneath it, perhaps to distinguish it from the following *e* letter. VV used *I* for *T* (as in "gift," "hat," and "racket") and for *S* ("purse"). All three handshapes involve closed fingers. She also used the letter *H* for *U,* as in "drum" and "purse."

Like hearing children learning to write, VV used the same written character for graphically similar letters, for example, *I* is used for both *i* and *t,* and *W* is used for both *w* and *m.* Her attempts at writing show that she draws from several different sources in constructing written language, including features of the hand configurations used in fingerspelling.

10.11 The Special Case of Fingerspelling

All the children in this study are highly verbal, capable of producing grammatically complex ASL sentences and participating in highly structured signed discourse. Their fingerspelled vocabulary is small, however, even though, like signed language, it is a manual system. Their ability to read fingerspelling outstrips their ability to produce fingerspelled words, but both vocabularies are far smaller than their sign vocabulary. Why are there such dramatic differences in competence between the two systems, given that both are present in the language repertoire of their parents and the other adults around them?

There are at least two possible explanations for the special difficulties of fingerspelling. First, the children have comparatively less exposure to fingerspelling than to signed material. The distribution of fingerspelled compared with signed items in adult discourse is low. As table 10.1 shows, fingerspelling accounts for as much as 12 percent or as little as 6 percent of all items manually produced. Adults fingerspell much less with children. Furthermore, table 10.2 shows that fingerspelled items are not equally represented across grammatical categories. Fingerspelling is made up disproportionately of nouns, and verbs rarely appear. Perhaps children have difficulty learning the system because so little of it is available to them.

Another possible explanation for these differences between fingerspelling and signing may lie in the structural properties of fingerspelling. The structure of fingerspelling—its units and how the units are constructed syntagmatically—is such that it is not a natural language, but instead is connected crucially to rules external to the system. Although, as this chapter demonstrates, children attempt to discover rules about fingerspelling by generalizing from the items they already know, for the most part deaf children cannot figure out from fingerspelling itself how to spell. Instead they must begin to learn about written English in order to increase their fingerspelled vocabulary. Although they are able to produce the elements basic to fingerspelling, the selection of letters cannot be hypothesized from within the system but instead must be retrieved from without, that is, from English orthography.

10.12. Summary and Conclusions

This investigation into how deaf children learn to fingerspell has yielded a number of interesting observations. First, contrary to popular descriptions of fingerspelling, the system is not compartmentalized but interacts in specific ways with other language systems—not only with writing, but also with signing. Some of these interactions are popularly and informally known: initialized signs borrow from the system of fingerspelling and some alphabetic characters, for example, *C, I, J, L, M, N, O* are manually similar to their graphic representations. Battison's descriptions of fingerspelled signs have shown how fingerspelled items can lose their original stability and enter the sign lexicon in changed forms. However, a few other intriguing interactions have emerged from this study. Notably, with respect to nouns and verbs, fingerspelling is overwhelmingly composed of nouns, and verbs are very infrequent. Furthermore, fingerspelled items seem to fall into a limited set of possible categories. These newer observations suggest that fingerspelling and signed languages, both manual systems used by the signing community, co-exist in an unusual structural distribution that has yet to be explained.

A second key observation has been that learning to fingerspell does not merely involve learning to associate manual alphabetic configurations with print characters but entails learning the special interactions between fingerspelling and other language systems. This observation is not unexpected, given similar observations elsewhere about the relation between speaking and writing (e.g., Read 1975) or drawing and writing (e.g., Dyson 1986). Young deaf children's early efforts to fingerspell reflect attempts to generalize from within the system as well as outside it. System-internal attempts include those that try to coordinate knowledge about fingerspelling movement units and spelling, as in the case of children who remembered that there were doubled letters in the fingerspelled word but chose the wrong letter to double. System-external attempts are those that try to bring knowledge about signed language and English orthography into learning how to spell. Finally, deaf children's early attempts to spell show that, like hearing children, they form connections between spelling and other language systems; but unlike hearing children's, their connections appear to be much more orthographically based than speech based. These findings suggest that much of what takes place in language learning is not merely learning the primary language, but learning its interactions with other language systems in the environment.

11 Children's Memory for Sign and Fingerspelling in Relation to Production Rate and Sign Language Input

Rachel I. Mayberry and Gloria S. Waters

11.1 Introduction

How signed words are remembered in contrast to spoken words is not well understood. Some facts are known about adult memory for signed words, but how the skill develops is largely unknown. In this chapter we examine how children recall two different kinds of words in sign language—signs and fingerspelling—in order to answer two questions. First, does the model of working memory for spoken words proposed by Baddeley, Thomson, and Buchanan (1975) also explain how signed and fingerspelled words are remembered? Second, does the sign language input available to children who are learning sign language affect their development of memory for signed and fingerspelled words? The answers to these questions are complex. We find, first, that the sign language input available to children affects the rate at which they develop memory for both signed and fingerspelled words. Memory for fingerspelled words looks like memory for spoken words, but how signed words are remembered is unclear. Before describing our study, we discuss three issues that underlie its design: research findings about adult sign memory, the Baddeley, Thomson, and Buchanan (1975) model of working memory, and the heterogeneous language backgrounds of deaf children who sign.

For adults, some parallels have been found between memory for spoken words and signed words—that is, the signs of American Sign Language, or ASL. For example, when remembering spoken words, some of the intrusion errors speakers make are related to the phonology of the stimuli they are trying to recall. This shows that speakers use a phonological code in recall. Similarly, when remembering signs, some of the intrusion errors signers make are related to the phonology (or formational parameters) of the stimuli they are trying to recall. This suggests that signers, like speakers, also use a "pho-

The research reported here was supported in part by a grant from the National Institutes of Health to Rachel Mayberry (NS20142) and the University of Chicago (where the work was carried out) through funds provided by the Spencer Foundation. We thank Rhonda Wodlinger-Cohen for her invaluable assistance in testing subjects and Beth Belenski and Drucilla Ronchen for their meticulous transcriptions. We are especially indebted to the children who made this research possible by participating in our studies with much good humor. Last, we thank three reviewers who shared thoughtful comments on an earlier version of this chapter.

211

nological" code in recall even though the phonology is gestured rather than spoken (Bellugi, Klima, and Siple, 1975; Hanson 1982a; Krakow and Hanson 1985; Poizner, Bellugi, and Tweney 1981; Shand 1982; Siple, Caccamise, and Brewer 1982). Speakers tend to remember best the spoken words they hear last and signers, the signs they see last (Bonvillian et al. 1987; Krakow and Hanson 1985). These similarities suggest that memory processes for spoken and signed words are similar even though the perception and production modes are not.

There are some unexplained differences between memory for the two kinds of word forms, however. One salient characteristic is that memory span for signs has been consistently reported to be less than that for spoken words (Bellugi, Klima, and Siple 1975; Bonvillian et al. 1987; Hanson 1982a; Krakow and Hanson 1985). Several alternative hypotheses may explain the discrepancy, but here we consider two.

The first hypothesis is that memory for words that are gestured and watched is related to the rate at which they are produced. In fact, a current model of working memory proposes that the rate at which spoken words are produced is causally related to how many words can be remembered. Baddeley, Thomson, and Buchanan (1975) posit that working memory consists of a central store, finite in capacity and temporally limited, with two rehearsal loops that help retain items. One rehearsal loop is based on motor production and the other on sense perception. Within this framework, memory processes for gestured words would be the same as those for spoken ones in terms of basic functions—a central store with two rehearsal loops—but the way spoken and gestured words are rehearsed would be different. The rehearsal loops for gestured words would be linked to manual production and visual perception, whereas the rehearsal loops for spoken words would be linked to oral production and auditory perception.

Evidence in support of Baddeley's model comes from both developmental and cross-linguistic studies. Developmentally, English-speaking children's memory span for words increases from about two or three items at 3 years of age to about seven or eight items in adulthood (Huttenlocher 1984). One puzzling question has been exactly what causes this increase (Huttenlocher and Burke 1976). One candidate is rate of word production. For adults, rate of word production is highly correlated with memory span in terms of word length. More short words than long ones can be remembered when syllabic structure is held constant. Word production rate also accounts for individual differences in word memory (Baddeley, Thomson, and Buchanan 1975). Similarly, as children age, their rate of word production increases. Nicholson (1979) found a linear relation between English-speaking children's memory span and the rate at which they could read words aloud between the ages of 8 and 12 years. Hulme et al. (1984) found similar results.

From a cross-linguistic perspective, rate of word production also explains quantitative memory differences among speakers of different languages. Ellis and Hennelly (1980) found that regardless of dominant language, adult Welsh-English bilinguals showed longer memory spans for English digits than Welsh digits. Welsh digits take more time to produce than do English digits. Likewise, Stigler, Lee, and Stevenson (1986) found that Chinese children between the ages of 5 and 10 had significantly longer memory spans for Chinese digits than age-matched American children had for English digits. Chinese digits have a shorter temporal duration, or faster production rate, than do English digits. Thus, ample developmental and cross-linguistic evidence supports the Baddeley, Thomson, and Buchanan (1975) model of working memory. Rate of word production predicts memory span for speech. Is the same true for sign language?

One possible consequence of covert word rehearsal in the manual modality might be a reduced memory span. The sign-production data currently available suggest that the production rate of individual signs is significantly slower than that of spoken words. Bellugi and Fischer (1972) found sign production to take twice as long as production of spoken words. Correspondingly, several researchers have found memory span for signs to be half or less that of spoken words (Bellugi, Klima, and Siple 1975; Bonvillian et al. 1987; Krakow and Hanson 1985).

The second reason memory span for signed words is less than that for spoken words may relate to the language background of signers. Typically, language acquisition is much more heterogeneous for signers than for speakers. The circumstances in which deaf children learn sign language vary widely. Only a small proportion of deaf children learn sign language at home, because most (over 90 percent) have hearing families who do not know sign language (Schein and Delk 1974). Thus an important source of variation among signers is the circumstances in which they learn to sign, both the amount and kind of sign language input they receive as children and also the age at which they first learn to sign.

Acquiring language under atypical conditions may affect the development of word memory. For example, Mayberry and Fischer (1989) have found a linear relation between the number of years signers had used sign language (from two to twenty years) and their ability both to remember and to comprehend narration and isolated sentences given in sign language. Developmentally, Newport (1984) has found that signers who first learned to sign after childhood showed decreased accuracy in producing ASL morphology compared with early-childhood learners despite considerable experience. Similarly, Mayberry (1991) found that age of sign language acquisition (as well as spoken language acquisition) has a lifelong effect on signers' ability to remember complex sentences in ASL. Thus, differences in memory span for signed and for spoken words may reflect the varying degrees of sign language knowledge signers possess instead of, or in addition to, the rate at which signed words are produced.

The purpose of the study we present here was to determine whether children's memory for the words of sign language is related to, first, the rate at which these words are produced, and second, their acquisitional experience with sign language. To achieve this goal, we examined children's memory for two kinds of words in sign language: signs and fingerspelling.

Although both signed and fingerspelled words are gestured, each might show a unique developmental pattern because they are structured differently. The most common type of word in sign language is the sign. Signs are articulated by a combination of handshape, movement, orientation, and location units. The formational parameters (or phonology) of signs are organized spatially to a greater degree than is the case for fingerspelling, although there is a sequential element in sign structure too (Bellugi 1980; Liddell 1984; Liddell and Johnson 1989).

Fingerspelled words are less frequent than signed ones and are a means by which sign language borrows words from spoken language (Battison 1978). Fingerspelled words are articulated by a series of hand gestures (handshapes), each representing a letter of the English word as it should be written. Although fingerspelling is derived from English orthography, deaf children learning ASL from their parents learn these kinds of words at the same time as they learn signs, long before they can read (Akamatsu 1985; Maxwell 1983a; Padden, this volume; Padden and LeMaster 1985). Because the articulatory units (or letters) of fingerspelled words are gestured in series, their sublexical organization is more sequential in nature than that of signs, although there is clearly a spatial component in fingerspelling also. Thus, if the organization of sublexical structure inflences how words are remembered, then signed and fingerspelled words may show varying relations to word production in memory development.

Thus we examined the effect of two factors on children's memory for signed and fingerspelled words. The first was chronological age. The age range we studied was 7 through 15 years. The second was sign language input, by which we mean the amount and kind of sign language experience the children had had while learning to sign throughout early childhood.

We controlled sign language input by including children who lived in two types of households. Half the children lived in households headed by deaf adults who use sign language as their primary means of communication. As a consequence, these children communicated in sign language with most of the important people in their lives, both at home and at school. The remaining children lived in households headed by normally hearing adults, many of whom neither knew nor used any sign with these deaf children. Consequently their sign language input was more restricted because their opportunity to use sign language in interpersonal communication occurred primarily during school hours. All the children we studied began to acquire sign by the age of 3 (4 for one child), so that the major difference between the two groups, unlike previous studies, is not their age of sign language acquisition per se, but the overall amount and kind of sign language input that was available to them during early childhood.

The study addressed several related questions. First, what is the developmental course of memory for signed and fingerspelled words? If memory for the two types of gestured words develops like that for spoken words, then we would expect children to remember increasingly more words across the age range. Second, how does sign language input during childhood affect the development of memory for signed and fingerspelled words? If the amount of sign language input children receive determines their familiarity with signed and fingerspelled words, then children who see and use sign language all the time should remember both kinds of words better than children whose sign language input is more limited.

Third, what is the developmental course of production rate for signed and fingerspelled words? And fourth, how is this affected by sign language input? If word production skills in sign language develop similarly to those in spoken language, then the children should show increased rates of word production throughout the age range 7 to 15 years. If, however, sign language input determines children's motor familiarity with signed and fingerspelled words, then the children with unrestricted input should show faster word production rates than those whose input is more restricted.

Finally, is there a relation between deaf children's memory for sign and fingerspelling and the rate at which they can produce the two kinds of words? Is this relation affected by childhood sign language input? If covert manual production plays a role in memory rehearsal for gestured words, then the children's memory for signed and fingerspelled words should parallel their production rates for sign and fingerspelling throughout development. Such a finding would provide evidence that the Baddeley, Thomson, and Buchanan (1975) model of working memory explains how gestured words are rehearsed in memory as well as how spoken words are rehearsed. Such a finding would mean that gestured and spoken words are remembered in the same fashion despite the sensory and motor differences between them.

11.2 Method

11.2.1 Subjects

Forty-three children participated, ranging in age from 7 to 15 years. All were severely or profoundly deaf from birth. Half lived in deaf households and half in hearing households.

Twenty-two children lived in households where their deaf parents communicated with them in sign language all the time, generally using ASL, but not always. A few deaf parents primarily used Pidgin Sign English (PSE) accompanied by speech with their children.[1] In two families the deaf parents used the sign language of their native countries, Mexico and Spain. In addition, several of these children also had deaf siblings with whom they communicated in sign.

Twenty-one children lived in households with normally hearing parents and siblings. The mode of communication in the hearing households varied considerably. According to the reports of the children, in approximately one-third of the households both hearing parents used some signed English with speech.[2] In another third, only the hearing mother used signed English with speech, and in another third no adult in the household used any signs with the child. In addition, several of these children reported that their normally hearing siblings used some signed English with them independent of whether or not the hearing parents did (for a more detailed desription of the children and their language skills, see Mayberry and Wodlinger-Cohen 1987).

All the children began special education before the age of 3 (4 for one child), regardless of household hearing status. Both groups attended the same day classes and schools, where the teachers communicated to the students through simultaneous speech and signed English. The students were encouraged to do likewise, but ASL and no speech was also accepted by the teachers.

Because all the children had always lived at home with their families, a major difference between the two groups is the amount of sign language input they have received during childhood—that is, the opportunity provided by their home environment to communicate in sign language, including both ASL and the signed English of simultaneous speech and signed communication. Most of the children living in hearing households, as previously described, received the bulk of their sign input primarily during school hours in the form of signed English from teachers and classmates, with some additional ASL input from classmates who knew and used it. In contrast, the children living in deaf households communicated in sign nearly all the time—both at school and at home—although the linguistic structure of the sign language they saw varied considerably across the two situations, generally signed English structure at school and mainly ASL structure at home.

1. Pidgin Sign English (PSE) is a dialect of ASL in which the ASL lexicon is signed in English word order. ASL lexical items are typically signed without the spatial morphology of ASL. Instead, English closed-class morphology is sometimes fingerspelled. See Woodward (1973a) and Wilbur (1987) for detailed descriptions.

2. Signed English is an educational sign system specifically invented as a tool to teach deaf children English. PSE lexical items (see above) are signed in English word order. English closed-class morphology is signed with a series of invented gestures. See Mayberry and Wodlinger-Cohen (1987) and Wilbur (1987) for detailed descriptions.

Table 11.1   The Children's Background Characteristics

Sign Language Input	Sex		Mean Age	Mean Hearing Loss[a]	Mean Block Design[b]	Mean Picture Arrangement[b]
	F	M				
Hearing households	3	4	8; 8	98 dB	11.7	11.4
Deaf households	2	4	8; 4	93 dB	11.0	11.8
Hearing households	3	4	11; 11	94 dB	12.1	11.3
Deaf households	4	3	11; 5	91 dB	12.8	12.1
Hearing households	4	4	14; 6	81 dB	12.3	12.1
Deaf households	4	4	14; 5	91 dB	12.5	12.4

[a] Pure tone average for 500, 1K, 2K Hz for the better ear.
[b] Nonverbal subtest of the WISC (Wechsler 1974); performance is given in scaled scores.

The two groups were divided into three age levels: 7 to 9 years, 10 to 12 years, and 13 to 15 years. There was a similar number of boys and girls at each age level across the two groups. Each age level (across the two input groups) had similar hearing losses as well as similar performance on two nonverbal subtests of the Wechsler Intelligence Scale for Children (WISC)— Block Design and Picture Arrangement.

Table 11.1 shows the background characteristics of the groups. Note that the mean performance of both groups on the WISC subtests is higher than that reported for the hearing school-aged population (mean scaled score is 10; Wechsler 1974). Also note that the children's mean performance is higher than that reported for the deaf school-aged population (Sisco and Anderson 1980). This indicates that the deaf children who participated in the present study, regardless of home environment, are brighter than average and thus are a biased sample. Importantly, however, this also means that the children living in hearing households were highly unlikely to suffer from other undiagnosed problems (such as physical or cognitive handicaps) that may be associated with hearing loss of either exogenous or unknown etiology (Brown 1986). This assumption is further supported by the fact that none of the children were reported to have any problems other than corrected vision.

11.2.2 Stimuli and Procedure

Sign Short-Term Memory

The stimuli for the short-term memory sign task were 105 ASL signs that are used similarly in both ASL and signed English—that is, both the phonological form and the lexical meaning of the sign are identical in ASL and signed English usage, such as the signs WORLD, SCHOOL, and TRAIN (according to Stokoe, Casterline, and Croneberg 1965; and Gustason, Pfetzing, and

Zawolkow 1972). The sign stimuli were organized into seven lists ranging in length from two to seven words, with three trials at each word length. The signs within each trial were dissimilar in both sign formation and meaning. Also, within each trial the English translations of the signs were all mono-syllabic, were dissimilar in phonological and orthographic form, and had a similar frequency of occurrence in print (according to Carroll, Davies, and Richmond 1971).

The children were tested individually. They were instructed in either ASL or simultaneous signed English and speech to watch each of the signs the ex-aminer produced and then to reproduce the same signs immediately afterward in the same serial order. The examiner produced the signs at the rate of one sign per second without speech or lip movement and with a neutral facial ex-pression. Testing always began with the two sign trials and proceeded until the child failed to correctly recall the signs of three consecutive trials at a given word length, without regard to sign order.

Fingerspelling Short-Term Memory

The stimuli for the fingerspelling memory task were eighty-one monosyl-labic English words ranging in length from three to five letters. Each English word did *not* have a common, single ASL sign translation as determined by a deaf native ASL informant, such as for the words "air, mud," and "map." The fingerspelling stimuli were organized into six lists ranging from two to seven words, with three trials at each word length. Within each trial the words were dissimilar in phonological and orthographic form and in lexical mean-ing, but all had the same frequency of occurrence in print (Carroll, Davies, and Richmond 1971).

Testing procedure for fingerspelling word memory was the same as for the sign word memory task except that the children were instructed to fingerspell the stimuli immediately afterward in the same serial order as the examiner did. Testing began with the two-word trials and proceeded until the child in-correctly recalled the words of three consecutive trials at a given word length regardless of order.

Sign Production Task

The word production tasks were the same as those used in previous speech studies with children (for example, see Hulme et al. 1984). There were three trials for the sign production task. For the first, the child was shown one sign taken from the memory task and asked to repeat it as quickly and clearly as possible until told to stop. The examiner recorded with a stopwatch the time it took the child to repeat the sign ten times. The second trial consisted of a series of two different signs (also taken from the memory task) repeated ten times. Production time for the two-sign series was measured the same way as for the single sign. The third trial consisted of a three-sign series with three different signs also taken from the memory task. Production time was measured the same way as for the first two trials. The children were given no instructions on how they should repeat the signs other than to repeat them as "quickly" as possible while still being "clear." The children were not required to return to neutral sign position at any time during their repetitions, and none did so.

Fingerspelling Production Task

There were also three trials of the fingerspelling production task. For the first, the child was shown a three-letter word taken from the memory task and asked to fingerspell it repeatedly as quickly and clearly as possible until told to stop. As for sign production, the examiner recorded with a stopwatch the time the child required to fingerspell the word ten times. The second trial consisted of a four-letter fingerspelled word, and the third a five-letter fingerspelled word. The production rate for each word was measured the same way. As in the sign production task, the children were given no specific instructions on how they should repeat the fingerspelled words other than that they should be "clear."

11.2.3 Transcription and Reliability

The children's performance on the two memory tasks and two production tasks was videotaped and later transcribed. For the memory tasks, the transcribers (two experienced teachers of deaf children and two native ASL signers) noted the children's word recall and order of recall. For the production tasks, the transcribers retimed the subjects' word repetitions. Agreement among the transcribers for the transcription of memory performance was high, ranging from 1.00 to 0.94 across all trials. Agreement for measurement of the word production tasks was also high, with an average of 0.03-second variation for sign production and 0.04-second variation for fingerspelling production.

11.3 Results

The children's performance on the memory and production tasks was analyzed with analysis of variance and correlation. For the memory task, the dependent measure was the number of words (signed or fingerspelled) the child accurately recalled in correct serial order summed across all trials.[3] For

---

3. Memory span was not used as a dependent measure because it was characterized by scant variability compared with the sum of words recalled (in serial order across all trials). Mean span for sign memory ranged from 3.00 for the youngest children (7 to 9 years) to 4.50 for the oldest

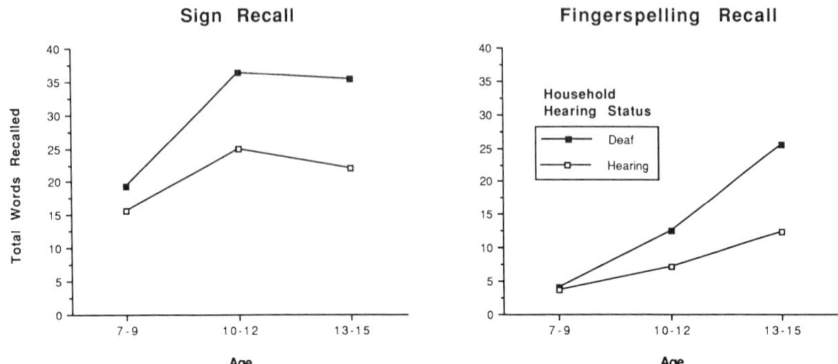

Figure 11.1. Sum of words recalled by children grouped by age and
sign language environment.

the production task, the dependent measure was the time the child required to
produce ten repetitions of the target word or words (signed or fingerspelled).
The dependent measures, total words recalled in order and word production
rate, were analyzed in relation to one another and as a function of two factors:
chronological age and sign language input. As described above, the children
were grouped into three age categories, 7 to 9 years, 10 to 12 years, and 13 to
15 years, and lived in two kinds of sign language environments: deaf households and hearing households.

Figure 11.1 shows the children's recall of signed and fingerspelled words as
a function of age and sign language input. As expected, the results of the sign
analysis (two-way analysis of variance for the effects of age and sign language
environment) showed that the children remembered more signs as they grew
older (F [2,37] = 5.24, $p < .01$). Surprisingly, however, the increase was not
constant throughout the age range. Rather, the oldest children, 13 to 15 years,
and the mid-aged children, 10 to 12 years, remembered more signs than the
youngest children, 7 to 9 years ($p < .05$, Tukey HSD statistic with a harmonic
mean for n). The oldest children, however, did not remember significantly
more signs than the mid-aged group, as shown in the first panel of figure 11.1.
This asymptotic performance beginning in adolescence characterized the sign
memory of the children from both deaf and hearing households. In addition,
the children living in deaf households remembered more signs overall than did
those living in hearing households regardless of age (*F* [1,37] = 7.48, *p* <
.01). These results indicate that the amount of sign language input children
receive in early childhood affects their ability to remember single signs.

---

children (13 to 15 years) living in deaf households, and from 3.00 to 3.38 for children from hearing households. Mean span for fingerspelling memory ranged from 1.50 to 3.25 for the children
living in deaf households and from 1.50 to 2.63 for those from hearing households.

The children's memory for fingerspelled words showed a different developmental pattern. As was the case for sign memory, the children's fingerspelling memory increased as they grew older (F [2,37] = 24.46, p < .01). In contrast to sign memory, however, fingerspelling memory increased throughout the age span of 7 to 15 years without an adolescent asymptote (p < .05 for each comparison). Children from both deaf and hearing households showed a similar memory increase as they grew older. The children from deaf households remembered more fingerspelled words than those from hearing households regardless of age (F [1,37] = 11.48, p < .01), however, as shown in the second panel of figure 11.1. This means that increased sign language input during childhood promotes the development of memory for gestured words regardless of whether the words are fingerspelled or signed.

To give a general picture of children's rate of sign production, figure 11.2 shows the groups' production rate in seconds per *single* sign regardless of stimulus set (one, two, or three signs). The data, however, were analyzed in terms of the total amount of time required to repeat each set ten times. This procedure determined whether the ability to repeat sequences of signs changes with age in addition to the rate at which single signs are produced. In fact, the results of the three-way analysis of variance (for the effects of age, sign language input, and stimulus set) showed that the primary developmental change in children's sign production is in the rate at which they can repeat sign sequences rather than single signs.

The oldest children's production rate of the one-, two-, and three-sign sets did not differ significantly; that is, they produced thirty signs (the three-sign set ten times) in the same amount of time as they produced twenty signs (the two-sign set ten times) as well as ten signs (the one sign set ten times). The mid-aged children, by contrast, produced the three-sign set significantly more slowly than the two- and one-sign sets (which they produced in similar

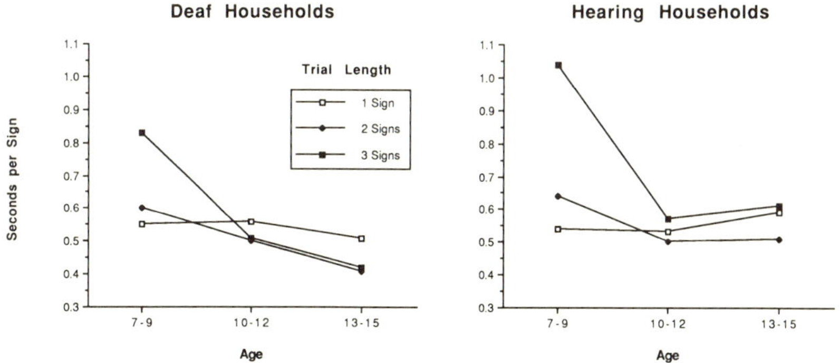

Figure 11.2. Sign production rate of children grouped by age and sign language environment.

amounts of time). Completing this developmental pattern, then, the youngest children produced the three-sign set significantly more slowly than the two-sign set and, in turn, produced the two-sign set more slowly than the one-sign set. Across the age groups, the children's production rate of the three-sign set increased significantly with age, but this was not the case for the two- and one-sign sets (F [2,58] = 6.35, $p < .01$; $p < .05$ for each comparison). These findings indicate that, like spoken word production, rate of sign production increases with age. But unlike spoken word production, a developmental increase is apparent only for production of sign sequences, not single signs.

The children's sign language input also influenced their production of sign sequences but not single signs. The children from deaf and hearing households did not differ in the rate at which they repeated the one- and two-sign sets. However, those from deaf households repeated the three-sign set significantly faster than those from hearing households regardless of age (F [2,58] = 6.35, $p < .01$; $p < .01$ for the comparison).

Figure 11.3 shows the children's fingerspelling production rate in units of seconds per fingerspelled word. As was the case for the sign analysis, the dependent variable for the fingerspelling analysis was how much time it took the children to repeat each stimulus ten times (a three-, four-, and five-letter word). The results of the three-way analysis of variance (for the factors of age, sign language input, and word length) showed that the children fingerspelled words faster as they grew older, but the development varied as a function of word length.

The children's development of fingerspelling production showed the same increased speed of sequence production as did their development of sign production. The rate at which the oldest children fingerspelled the three stimulus words did not differ significantly even though the words were of increasing

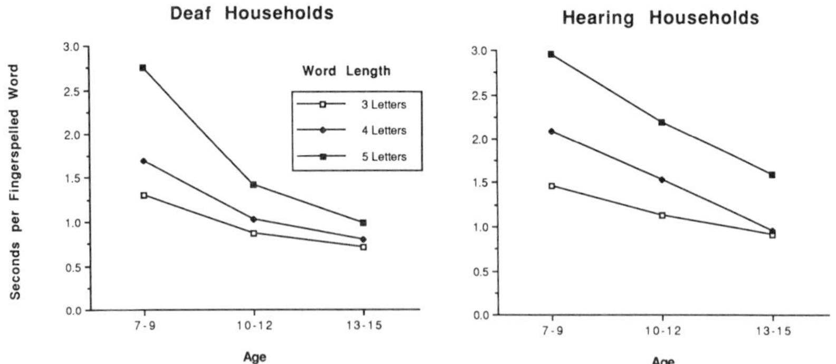

Figure 11.3. Fingerspelling production rate of children grouped by age and sign language environment.

Table 11.2   Correlation between Fingerspelled Words Recalled and
Fingerspelling Production Rate

	Fingerspelled Words Recalled	
Production Rate	Deaf Households	Hearing Households
Three-letter word	−.69**	−.63**
Four-letter word	−.65**	−.60**
Five-letter word	−.64**	−.69**

**$p < .01$.

length (three to five letters). The mid-aged children fingerspelled the five-letter word significantly more slowly than the four- and three-letter words (on which they did not differ). Completing the pattern, then, the youngest children needed significantly more time to repeat the words of each length. Likewise, across the age groups, production of the five-letter word increased significantly with age. The two older groups' production of the four-letter word did not differ, but both were significantly faster than the youngest group. The groups' production of the three-letter word did not change with age (F [4,70] = 4.78, $p < .01$; p $< .05$ for each comparison).

As was the case for sign production, sign language input influenced the children's fingerspelling production. The children living in deaf households were significantly faster than those from hearing households regardless of age or word length (F [1,35] = 4.72, $p < .05$).

The relation between fingerspelling memory and production rate was examined with separate correlations for the children living in deaf and hearing households, as shown in table 11.2. There were significant and high correlations between the total number of fingerspelled words the children recalled and the rate at which they could fingerspell. The relationship characterized the fingerspelling skills of the children from both hearing and deaf households. The development of memory for fingerspelled words shows a strong relation to the rate at which words can be fingerspelled. This means that the developmental relation between word memory and production rate previously found for speech is *not* modality specific. The relation characterizes fingerspelled words that are watched and gestured as well as words that are spoken and listened to.

The relation between word memory and production rate was much less clear for signs than for fingerspelling, as shown in table 11.3. For the children living in hearing households, no correlation reached significance. For the children living in deaf households, only one correlation reached significance—production rate of the three-sign set and sign memory (the correlations for the

Table 11.3   Correlation between Signs Recalled and
Sign Production Rate

	Signs Recalled	
Production Rate	Deaf Households	Hearing Households
One sign	−.05	−.07
Two signs	−.26	−.23
Three signs	−.48*	−.33

*$p < .05$.

children from deaf and hearing households did not differ significantly). Thus the relation between word memory and word production is very clear and robust in the case of fingerspelling but unclear and weak in the case of sign.

11.4 Discussion

The results of this study suggest that not all gestured words are remembered alike. In addition, they shed light on two related questions. First, what does the development of word recall and production rate in sign and fingerspelling look like? Second, how does the sign language environment influence the development of these word skills?

First, the fingerspelling results fit well the model of working memory proposed by Baddeley, Thomson, and Buchanan (1975). Children's memory for fingerspelled words significantly correlates with the rate at which they can produce these words. The result holds regardless of word length and sign language input. This finding suggests that children rehearse fingerspelled and spoken words in a similar fashion—that they covertly reproduce them. Furthermore, the finding demonstrates that sensory and motor modality is not the critical factor that determines how words are remembered or rehearsed. Fingerspelled words are gestured. Nonetheless, recall of fingerspelled words shows the same relation to production rate as does recall of spoken words.

In contrast to the fingerspelling results, the sign results do not fit Baddeley's model of working memory. The link between word memory and production rate is weak for signed words. A relationship exists, but only sometimes— only when the production task involves repetition of a sequence of three different signs. This outcome may be due to three interrelated contrasts between sign and fingerspelling, differences in the experimental tasks of the present study, differences in how the two types of gestured words are rehearsed, and differences in the lexical structure of the two word types.

First, the production tasks in fingerspelling and sign were not strictly comparable. The stimuli for the fingerspelling task, always single words, varied in length. However, the stimuli for the sign task varied in the number of words to be repeated (one, two, or three signs). Possibly the sign production task constituted a memory task, especially at the three-word length for the younger children. This would explain why the correlation coefficient between sign memory and production rate increases concurrently with the number of signs in the production task for both groups of children (see table 11.3). But when we recomputed the correlations while omitting the data from the youngest children (pooling across groups), the same pattern of results occurred. Memory and production rate for signs are not significantly correlated, and the correlation coefficient increases with the number of items in the stimulus set. The results for signed words are quite different from those for fingerspelled words, where memory and production rate are significantly correlated regardless of word length. This finding argues against the interpretation that the sign results were spurious because the production task was actually a memory task.

Note that there is no correlation between the children's production rate for the single sign and their sign memory. Usually when word memory and production rate are related, the relationship holds for repetition of single words as well as word sequences. This is the case for children and adults across several languages, including English, Welsh, and Chinese (Baddeley, Thomson, and Buchanan 1975; Ellis and Hennelly 1980; Hulme et al. 1984; Stigler, Lee and Stevenson 1986). In the present study we find parallel results for fingerspelling memory and production (repetition rate for a single word is correlated with word memory), but not for sign memory and production.

Why would word memory and production rate be related for fingerspelling but not for sign? One possibility is that the children rehearsed the fingerspelled words but not the signed words. However, there is no a priori reason to believe that all the children, from both deaf and hearing households, would adopt selective rehearsal strategies for the two kinds of gestured words unless there was some compelling reason to do so. The reason might be related to the fact that the lexical organization of fingerspelled and signed words is not the same. Most likely the children rehearsed the signed words just as they did the fingerspelled ones but did so in a different manner.

The sublexical organization of fingerspelled and signed words is not the same, although similarities exist. Both kinds of words are spatial—the shape and orientation of the hand is important to lexical formation and identification. In fingerspelling, however, handshapes are sequenced one after the other to form words. In sign, handshapes co-occur with hand and arm movements, all of which are crucial to lexical identification and formation (Clark and Grosjean 1982). At the level of the isolated word, fingerspelled words may share with spoken words a greater degree of sequentiality than is characteristic of signed words. The implication is that the organization of lexical structure may play a critical role in determining how words are rehearsed in memory.

Sequentially formed words, whether fingerspelled or spoken, may evoke covert production as a means of rehearsal. Simultaneously formed words, such as signs, may evoke some other means of rehearsal such as covert visualization.

If the sign production task was not a memory task but simply a production task as intended, then the fact remains that memory and production rate are related only for sequences of signs, not for single signs. This suggests that the rehearsal mechanisms for fingerspelled and signed words may differ in some way. Comparing tables 11.2 and 11.3, we see that the correlation coefficient between memory and production rate for signed words approximates that for fingerspelled words only when the sign task entails a sequence of three signs. Coincidentally, the shortest fingerspelled word was a sequence of three letters. The similarity here is that both production tasks require ordering three distinct handshapes (three letters for fingerspelling and three words for sign). This supports our hypothesis that sequentiality may play an important role in determining how words are rehearsed in memory.

At this point we can only speculate on exactly what the rehearsal mechanisms of signs look like, because scant data specifically address the question. Siple and Brewer (1985) postulate that signs are rehearsed in a mixed fashion depending upon the skill and predisposition of the signer. In examining whether visual or motor tasks interfered with sign memory, they found multiple patterns among signers, suggesting that sign rehearsal is especially characterized by individual differences. Some signers appeared to use a speech-based code, others a manual-sign mode of rehearsal, and still others a visual sign rehearsal strategy. Siple and Brewer postulate that the individual differences they observed were due in part to the heterogeneous language backgrounds of signers.

The data of the present study clarify the question. The children have homogeneous language backgrounds (especially those from deaf households). Despite this homogeneity, they show word memory and production relationships for sign unlike those they show for fingerspelling (and unlike those reported for speech). Thus the possibility exists that some aspect of the sign rehearsal mechanism is unique. Sign rehearsal may depend on both manual and visual mechanisms, for example, according to what kind of words and how many are being recalled. Isolated words may be covertly visualized. Groups of words may be covertly reproduced. Clearly much more work is needed to discover how signed words are rehearsed in memory.

Our second major finding is that the development of memory for fingerspelling looks different from that for sign across varying sign language environments. The children's memory for signed words did not increase after age 10 to 12. In contrast, their memory for fingerspelled words continued to increase through age 13 to 15. Another important element in the pattern is that the children's memory for fingerspelled words lagged behind their memory for signed words but increased faster. Between the ages of 7 and 15, the children's sign memory increased 50 percent, whereas their fingerspelling memory doubled, by 103 percent.

The gap between the youngest children's memory for sign and for fingerspelling may have been accentuated because the fingerspelling stimuli did not have common sign translations—that is, they were not signable. Consequently these fingerspelled words were probably less familiar to the children than were the signed words. (Even though both kinds of words were equated for frequency of occurrence in print, they may not occur with equal frequency in sign language, either ASL or signed English.) The developmental pattern for fingerspelling memory we find here reflects the children's ability to remember words purely in fingerspelling form without the support of sign. Presumably there would be less gap between memory for the two kinds of words if the fingerspelled words had been signable. Eventually, though, memory for fingerspelled words may approximate that for signed words. In a college-aged sample, Krakow and Hanson (1985) found no quantitative differences between memory for signed and fingerspelled words, nor did they find any effect of signability on memory for fingerspelled words.

Our third finding is that children's rate of sign and fingerspelling production increases as they grow older, just as does the rate of speech production. However, increased word production rate in sign is accomplished differently from speech. Hulme et al. (1984) report that hearing children, regardless of age, take longer to repeat words nested in sequences than isolated words. We find the opposite pattern here. The deaf children require less time to repeat signs nested in sequences than isolated signs. This difference may reflect the contrasting mechanisms by which production rate is varied in speech and sign. Grosjean (1979) found that speech is speeded by shortening interword intervals, whereas sign is speeded by shortening intrasign movement (although Hulme et al. found that word duration, not pause time, changed with age in speech).

The data of the present study also replicate earlier work showing that signed words take longer to articulate than spoken ones. Yet the magnitude of the difference we find here is not as great as that reported by Bellugi and Fischer (1972), who found that signed words are produced twice as slowly as spoken ones. Comparing our sign production data with that of Hulme et al. (1984), whose word production tasks are similar to ours, we find that 7- to 9-year-old deaf children produce sign triads roughly 70 percent more slowly than 8-year-old hearing children produce speech triads. The deaf children's sign production rate shows a greater increase with age than does the hearing children's speech production, however. Between the ages of 7 and 12, the deaf children increased their production rate of sign triads by 49 percent, whereas the hearing children increased production of speech triads by only 11 percent. By 10 to 12 years, the deaf children produced sign triads only 20 percent more slowly than 10-year-old hearing children produce speech triads. Bonvillian et al. (1987) reported anecdotally that deaf college students repeat signs even more quickly than hearing students are reported to repeat speech (on a task of overt word rehearsal). Taken together, these results show that sign production rate can be nearly as fast as that of speech under some conditions.

The results of this study further extend our understanding of how children develop word production skills in fingerspelling. Previously, Akamatsu (1985) and Padden and LeMaster (1985) described the first stage of fingerspelling acquisition as consisting of the child's production of word "envelopes" that share certain visual and temporal features with actual fingerspelling but are not real fingerspelling. At the second stage of development, the child discovers that fingerspelled words consist of individual letters and consequently fingerspells each letter of these words separately. Our data uncover yet a third stage of fingerspelling development that we call *fingerspelling synthesis*. At the third stage, the child reconstructs the fingerspelled word as a whole entity rather than as a string of separate elements.

This synthesis is best illustrated by the contrastive patterns of fingerspelling production rate the children exhibit as they grow older (shown in fig. 11.2). The oldest children (13 to 15 years) produced all the fingerspelled words in the same amount of time regardless of the number of letters in each word (five, four, or three letters). By contrast, the youngest children (7 to 9 years) had not yet developed word production skill in fingerspelling to this level of internal organization. Still at the second stage of fingerspelling development, they needed concomitantly more time to fingerspell each word as the number of letters in the word increased.

Finally, the results of this study demonstrate that variation in sign language input during childhood can affect sign language development at the level of word memory and production for both sign and fingerspelling. The children from deaf households recalled more words in both sign and fingerspelling than did their peers from hearing households. They also produced fingerspelled words and sign triads more quickly than their peers from hearing households.

The pattern of results suggests that the effect of sign language input on the development of word memory and production is quantitative in nature rather than qualitative. The effect manifests itself primarily as slowed, but not atypical, development. The children living in hearing households showed the same overall trend in word memory and production with respect to age for both sign and fingerspelling as did those living in deaf households. Likewise, the relation between memory and production rate in fingerspelling and sign was essentially the same for the two groups of children.

Do children living in hearing households eventually catch up with those living in deaf households in terms of word memory and production skills? Some studies suggest that the answer is yes. For college students, Krakow and Hanson (1985) report no significant differences between the two groups on measures of word memory given in sign and fingerspelling. Likewise, Bonvillian et al. (1987) report no word memory differences with respect to home environment (but as they note, the small number of subjects from deaf households precluded making any generalizations). Inferences based on comparisons between college students and schoolchildren need to be made with caution because college students are a biased sample; colleges select deaf students on the basis of language skill. As we previously noted, however, the children who participated in the present study were also a biased sample in terms of nonverbal intelligence.

Recent studies showing that age of sign language acquisition has a lifelong effect on sign language production and comprehension (for example, Mayberry 1991) examine an effect different from the one we explore here. The children in the present study all began to acquire sign during early childhood. Their language experience varies primarily in terms of how much opportunity they have had to converse in sign. The adult subjects of the age-of-acquisition studies, by contrast, were not exposed to sign language at all during early childhood. However, the results of the present study in conjunction with the age-of-acquisition studies show that sign language development is highly sensitive to the circumstances of language acquisition.

In summary then, we find that children's word memory and production skills in sign and fingerspelling increase rapidly between the ages of 7 and 15 years. Children's memory for fingerspelled words is related to the rate at which they can fingerspell, suggesting that fingerspelling rehearsal in memory is carried out via covert reproduction. Children's memory for signed words is weakly related to the rate at which they can sign. Exactly how signs are rehearsed in memory remains a puzzle in need of further exploration. Last, the sign language input children receive during childhood affects the rate at which they develop word memory and production skills in both sign and fingerspelling, but not the relationship between the two word skills.

12 Boundary Conditions on Language Emergence: Contributions from Atypical Learners and Input

ADELE ABRAHAMSEN, MAUREEN LAMB,
JACQUELINE BROWN-WILLIAMS, AND SUSAN MCCARTHY

12.1 The Crucial Role of Data from Atypical Learners and Input

Language emerges from the interaction between at least two individuals: a learner, who has certain capacities but does not yet know the target language, and a model, who displays the language in the course of various kinds of interaction with the learner. Though the process is highly interactive, it is often useful to abstract two sets of conditions: characteristics of the learner, and the nature of the input the learner is exposed to.

Our distinctive approach to understanding language emergence is to observe *unusual learners* over long periods of exposure to *unusual input*. Specifically, young learners with mental retardation or other developmental delays (chronological age $1\frac{1}{2}$ to 5 years) are provided with bimodal language input (spoken English with selected words augmented by simultaneous manual signs borrowed from ASL), and their achievements in the two modalities are traced across the crucial developmental age range of 1 to $2\frac{1}{2}$ years. This is not

Toddler Sign Program 1 was aided by Social and Behavioral Sciences Research grant 12-47 from the March of Dimes Birth Defects Foundation. We thank Kathryn LeLaurin, director of the cooperating program in New York City. Marie Cavallo and Allison McCluer played a major role in carrying out this study, and Lia Di Bello, Randall Nolan, Tom Rosamilia, and Fred Sciascia coded videotapes. Grant NICHD-19265 from the National Institute of Child Health and Human Development supported Toddler Sign Program 2, as well as the preparation of this chapter. We appreciate the support of John D. Baird (executive director) and Fran McCall (educational coordinator) of the cooperating program at the Cerebral Palsy Center of Atlanta/the Children's Rehabilitation Center. Cecilia Myrick, Judy Fiocco, Lorie Delk, and John Mungo made valuable contributions to the research. We thank Duane Rumbaugh for the numerous forms of support he has generously and steadfastly provided over several years. Also we thank Mary Ann Romski, Lauren Adamson, Roger Bakeman, and James Pate for collegial contributions that included making various resources available and commenting on aspects of the research.

For both programs, we gratefully acknowledge the many contributions of the children who participated, as well as their parents, teachers, and other staff, without whom the programs could not have been carried out. Special thanks here go to Gina and David Ferguson and to Paula Harger. Finally, we thank John Bonvillian, Patricia Siple, and William Bechtel for carefully reading the manuscript and making suggestions we incorporated; however, the positions explicated are our own and should not be attributed to those individuals.

to deny the importance of studying the usual learners and input conditions. But, any account of a domain of competence that is based only on data from typical conditions is incomplete and is more limited in its applicability than is usually appreciated.

What is lacking is the ability to specify how generally the various phenomena of the domain apply. We need to know the boundary conditions for learner and input characteristics beyond which a phenomenon or generalization is lost but within which it applies. By carrying out comparative analyses of data obtained from a broad range of learners and types of input within the language domain, the proper level of generalization is set for central claims about language and its acquisition. Some phenomena will be found to have very broad applicability even across unusual conditions; these are referred to as *robust* phenomena (in the spirit of Wimsatt's 1981 discussion of robustness analysis and Goldin-Meadow's 1982 distinction between resilient and fragile properties of language). For phenomena that are less general, the conditions that require special accounts will be clearly identified, and working out those accounts should enhance understanding of the overall domain.

For the language domain, one way of broadening the range is to observe the acquisition and use of various sign languages, such as American Sign Language, Chinese Sign Language, and Italian Sign Language. These are fully evolved, complex languages that can be studied individually, as examples of language in general, but are particularly rewarding to study comparatively and particularly in comparison with spoken languages. In this way one can determine which linguistic and psycholinguistic phenomena have boundary conditions that are subject to modality (owing to causative factors that must then be determined) and which are more general, applying across different language modalities. This particular comparative strategy requires that modality serve as the primary point of comparison, with other factors held as constant as possible. Researchers using this strategy, therefore, study learners with intact human brains (hearing-impaired or not), who are acquiring or using fully evolved languages under input conditions that are typical except for modality (e.g., Klima and Bellugi 1979; Orlansky and Bonvillian 1985).

Once the role of modality as such has been investigated, more remote boundary conditions can be considered by examining language in either modality in a variety of circumstances. These investigations address questions other than the role of modality, even when the language under study is a sign language or some other manual system. However, including both modalities can create certain opportunities and ensure the continued generalizability of the findings. In what follows, we illustrate the advantages of examining atypical conditions by considering certain findings on the development of syntactic structure within the manual modality. Broadening the data base beyond typical input and learner conditions makes it possible to set boundary conditions such as critical periods for input. We then apply the same strategy to an earlier phase of language acquisition: the use of single words and signs before syntax. Specifically, we present comparative data on the acquisition of signs and words under atypical input conditions (speech-dominant bimodal input) for both typical and atypical learners and show how the data have guided us to reconstrue the claim that signs are acquired earlier then words. That claim becomes subsumed as a particular case under the broader generalization that signs are acquired more robustly than words—that is, under a timetable that is stable across a variety of learners.

12.1.1 An Illustration of the Role of Atypical Conditions: Acquisition of Syntactic Structure in Signed versus Spoken Language

Comparing Language Modalities under Otherwise Typical Conditions

It is typical for a primary language to be acquired under certain conditions in which (1) exposure to the language has already begun at birth and becomes integrated into the developing social interaction between the infant and other family members and (2) the language is one that is readily learnable on a developmental timetable that has been fairly well established empirically and that depends upon a suitable match between the language's characteristics and the learner's emerging capacities. These conditions are met routinely for hearing children of hearing parents and for the minority of deaf children who have at least one deaf, signing parent. Thanks to the work of investigators such as Fischer (1974b), we know that children acquiring ASL as a first language make the transition from single-sign utterances to two-sign combinations that are syntactically and semantically similar to the early word combinations of children learning various spoken languages. With further development, more language-specific aspects of syntactic structure are added. In parallel with acquisition of spoken languages, some of these are complex and late to emerge—for example, the use of space for pronominal and discourse functions and flexible command of the agglutinative morphology of ASL (Supalla 1982). In general, syntax acquisition follows a similar course in signed and spoken languages, but consideration of sign helps to set the proper level of generalization and also presents the opportunity to observe certain modality-tailored syntactic devices (see also Reilly, McIntire, and Bellugi, this volume, and Newport and Meier 1986).

The Contributions of Data from Less Typical Learners and Input

There is a long-standing debate over the extent to which the typical developmental sequence reflects a biological predisposition for language as well as biological constraints on the optimal structure and timing of language input.

Traditionally, data from atypical learners acquiring spoken languages have been brought to bear on these issues (e.g., Lenneberg 1967). In recent years, sign language researchers have taken advantage of opportunities uniquely presented by deaf individuals' acquisition of sign languges. More varied circumstances of input structure and timing have occurred for deaf individuals than for hearing individuals, and the variation can be used to draw general conclusions about biological factors in language acquisition.

In particular, Goldin-Meadow and her colleagues (e.g., Goldin-Meadow 1982; Mylander and Goldin-Meadow, this volume) have analyzed the sign languages deaf toddlers invent under the extreme condition of no sign input in the early years. (During this period, speech input exists but is fairly inaccessible, resulting in little functional input in either modality.) Though syntax is somewhat delayed in these circumstances, to an impressive extent the children replicate the major early advances that are familiar from observing acquisition under more typical conditions (that is, provision of well-formed speech or sign input to hearing or deaf children). Hence the boundary conditions for emergence of stage 1 syntactic structures, as well as some later advances such as recursion, are seen to be quite broad. Goldin-Meadow (1982) argues that these are resilient properties of language; in the related terminology we are using here, their emergence is a robust phenomenon of language acquisition.

However, all languages have numerous devices that are language-specific in their detail and will not be acquired without sufficient input (Goldin-Meadow's fragile properties). Evidence from children suffering brain damage at different ages has suggested that to be fully acquired these devices do require exposure during a critical period. However, it would be useful to have confirming evidence that does not involve brain damage, and data on sign acquisition by deaf individuals provide this opportunity. Some deaf children are exposed to sign language from birth, others not until middle childhood or even later. Newport (1990) has examined age of exposure as a boundary condition on the nature of the language that is ultimately acquired by adulthood. She has found that late exposure results in a structurally more limited sign language than when exposure begins during infancy. This would be attributed primarily to a learner condition (maturational level at the time input is provided, relative to the biological critical period).

That sign input is often delayed beyond the typical age of first-language acquisition is not the only atypical circumstance deaf children face. The nature of the input itself also shows considerable variation. In addition to an essentially unimodal sign language such as ASL, deaf children may also be exposed to systems of simultaneous manual-vocal communication designed to satisfy the pedagogical aim of promoting English (though satisfactory evidence of success has not yet been obtained). Wodlinger-Cohen (this volume) has examined one such non-ASL system, signed English, in which signs accompany and manually reflect the structure of spoken English sentences. In particular, grammatical distinctions such as plurality and tense are signed as separate morphemes appended sequentially to open-class (noun or verb) morphemes, in contrast to the use of simultaneous morphemes that is characteristic of unimodal sign languages such as ASL. Wodlinger-Cohen measured the extent to which these morphemes are preserved both by adults who learn the system in order to serve as language models to deaf children and by the children who are exposed to the adult models as their primary bimodal input. Although this may appear to be a study only of input characteristics as a boundary condition on what is acquired, in fact the results suggest that biologically based learner characteristics play a role as well. Sequentially signed grammatical morphemes are not well incorporated by either adults or children, suggesting that learner characteristics are responsible for the selection for simultaneous morphemes in the evolution of natural sign languages such as ASL.

The work on syntax acquisition has tended to emphasize that the fundamental phenomena are similar regardless of modality. When attention has been focused on the early phases of vocabulary acquisition, in contrast, investigators have been struck by an apparent difference between the modalities. In the next section we describe the initial claim, discuss limitations on its generality, and point out the advantages of consulting atypical data to achieve a higher level of generalization. The rest of the chapter summarizes the empirical work and analyses we have carried out to this end.

12.1.2 A Controversy: Acquisition Timetables for Manual Signs versus Spoken Words

Comparing Language Modalities under Otherwise Typical Conditions: The Claim That Signs Are Acquired Earlier Than Words

When investigators have compared the acquisition of ASL (by deaf or hearing toddlers) with the acquisition of English (by hearing toddlers), it has appeared that signs are acquired earlier than words; that is, the developmental timetable for vocabulary acquisition appears accelerated, or at least displaced to an earlier starting point, for sign compared with speech. The data are not in question; the early observations on small numbers of children acquiring sign alone (Schlesinger and Meadow 1972) or sign and speech together (Prinz and Prinz 1979) have recently been replicated on a larger sample (Bonvillian et al. 1983; Orlansky and Bonvillian 1985). Caution is advisable in interpreting these data, however. Abrahamsen, Cavallo, and McCluer (1985) have argued that the sign advantage may apply to form but not to function. Manual movements are easy for young children to imitate and acquire, but decontextualized referential use and the attainment of a structured language system may rely on other factors for which signs show little advantage (see Volterra and Caselli 1985 and Petitto 1986 for related arguments).

There is indirect evidence for the importance of function in Pettito's (1985a) investigation of sign pronouns and pointing, but the issue has been most explicitly addressed in more recent work from Bonvillian's laboratory. Specifically, in a study of nine children of deaf parents, Bonvillian and Folven (1990) found the following mean ages of attainment of early language milestones: first sign, 8.2 months; first referential sign (used nonimitatively to name an object or person), 12.6 months; ten-sign vocabulary, 13.1 months; first two-sign combination, 16.1 months. The only one of these milestones that involves functional criteria is the first referential sign, and this is the only one of the four milestones for which the mean age of attainment is similar to that for spoken words (it has not yet been determined whether there is a small sign advantage or no difference). The remaining milestones involve criteria of form but not of function, and each of these shows a sign advantage of two months or more.

Hence, when the usual amount and quality of native-language input is provided, children learning signs progress faster than children learning speech in mastering early vocabulary and the simplest combinations; most or all of this sign advantage may be lost when criteria of function are applied. Further research is needed to determine the impact of functional criteria for milestones other than the first word and to determine whether any sign advantage extends into the period of rapid linguistic progress that begins at about 2 years of age.

The Contribution of Data from Less Typical Learners
and Input: Differences in Robustness between Modalities
as the Most General Phenomenon

We have seen that an acquisition advantage for signs does exist, but that its generality is limited by which functional criteria are applied, and possibly by developmental level. The sign advantage is a genuine phenomenon but is limited in ways that restrict the implications it holds for theoretical accounts of language onset. Bearing in mind that the sign advantage may hold for learning of form but not of function, further probing at the generality of this phenomenon can be achieved by considering outcomes from less typical learners and less typical input; the more general the phenomenon, the more extreme should be the boundary conditions that delimit its applicability. For example, it would be rather impressive if the advantage for the acquisition of sign forms over word forms were to survive even when speech input was of considerably higher quantity and quality than sign input, if the size of the advantage were even greater for certain kinds of learners, or if there were circumstances in which the advantage held for function as well as form.

In fact, there exists at least one set of circumstances within which these three suppositions have been jointly realized (although in what follows we will extract a different theoretical lesson than has been offered by other investigators). Individuals with mental retardation and autism are at high risk for delayed speech; often the delays in speech are greater than the delays in other developmental domains. In the 1970s, programs of *augmentative sign* were developed to make the manual modality available as an alternative vehicle for vocabulary acquisition in such individuals (Bonvillian, Nelson, and Rhyne 1981; Fristoe and Lloyd 1978). In this approach spoken English is the primary input, but some words are accompanied by manual signs (usually borrowed from ASL citation forms). Examples include: "EAT your COOKIE, Alice!" "DO YOU WANT to have MORE?" "GOOD, YOU'RE SWINGing the BABY." Because grammatical morphemes usually are not signed in this type of system, English-speaking adults find it relatively easy to learn. When adults have provided augmentative sign as input to language-delayed children, many participants have learned signs more easily than the accompanying spoken words (e.g., Kahn 1981), although some have not (Bonvillian and Blackburn, this volume).

As a practical matter, augmentative sign was developed to suit the (perceived) communicative needs of certain learners with mental retardation, just as signed English was developed to suit the (perceived) educational needs of certain hearing-impaired learners. Hence, augmentative sign (an atypical input) will most often be made available to children with mental retardation or autism (atypical learners). The input is atypical, as are the learners, but a certain match of input to learners is intended, and the resulting data are within the range that should be considered in constructing accounts of language emergence.

Initially our interest was attracted by the fact that some children acquire signs more easily than words, even when there are massive input advantages for speech in the learner's total environment. This appears to buttress the argument that there is a general advantage for signs over words in early vocabulary acquisition. However, the programs that had been designed for primarily therapeutic purposes lacked certain characteristics that we felt were needed in order to properly evaluate the sign-advantage claim and to carry out other analyses of general theoretical interest. We ensured those characteristics by designing and carrying out our own augmentative sign program, Toddler Sign Program 1 (followed later by Toddler Sign Program 2).

As will be shown in the account of those studies that follows, it turned out that a sign advantage is not really the most general phenomenon at all. A different phenomenon—the relative *robustness* of timing for sign compared with speech—emerged instead as most salient for both theory and application (Abrahamsen 1985; Abrahamsen, Cavallo, and McCluer 1985). Briefly, the manual signs are acquired according to the same developmental timetable across a variety of learners, but the timetable for spoken words varies dramatically according to the type of learner. Some learners even show a word advantage rather than a sign advantage (under input conditions that favor words). The sign advantage is best regarded as a particular pattern of modality ordering, which occurs under certain combinations of input conditions, language function, and type and age of learner. Many combinations of conditions generate a sign advantage, but others generate equal performance in the two modalities, and a few (more extreme) conditions even generate a word advantage. All three of these patterns, and an understanding of what conditions generate each item, have a role to play in arriving at a complete account of language emergence. However, the fact that each such relationship is contingent on specific conditions makes it appealing to have access to a higher-level generalization that spans those various conditions. Sign *robustness,* which has to do with the degree of variability in acquisition timetable across a variety of learners, was discoverable only by making input in two modalities available to atypical as well as typical learners. Two studies we designed and carried out to this end are next described.

12.2 Evidence That Signs Emerge More Robustly, but Not Always Earlier, Than Words: Toddler Sign Program 1

Toddler Sign Program 1 (TSP-1) is a program of augmentative sign that was designed specifically to address developmental questions, including the generality and proper interpretation of a developmental advantage for manual signs. The range of learners who participated, as well as the input and procedures, differed in some respects from programs designed to satisfy therapeutic goals alone. A summary of the method and results follows; see Abrahamsen, Cavallo, and McCluer (1985) for a more complete account.

12.2.1 Participants: Three Groups of Atypical and Typical Learners

Three distinct groups of toddlers participated in the program.

1. Toddlers with Down syndrome, who exhibit mental retardation in connection with a genetic anomaly (trisomy 21). Children with Down syndrome are known to be at particularly high risk for delayed speech (e.g., Blanchard 1964; Cunningham, Glenn, and Wilkinson 1985), but they have a relative developmental strength in the manual encoding of information (Bilovsky and Share 1965). They are frequently selected for participation in therapeutic programs of augmentative sign.
2. Toddlers with developmental delays due to other disabilities. This was a heterogeneous group of children who had in common only that their mental or physical disabilities had resulted in developmental delay. There were no further specific reasons to expect them to show particular difficulty in acquiring speech. Therefore it could be expected that this group would include some children who would not, when older, be selected as good candidates for an augmentative sign program. It is impor-

tant to see what happens when such children are exposed to sign input anyway, building a data base that is not restricted to those children with mental retardation who have particularly delayed speech.

3. A group of normally developing, nondelayed children, who would not ordinarily be provided with augmentative sign input. The purpose was to achieve a relatively controlled comparison; it is hard to evaluate the results of using atypical input with *atypical* learners if you do not know what happens when the same atypical input is provided to *typical* learners. Augmentative sign input was designed for use with delayed children, but using it with typical nondelayed children provides data that are just as relevant for developing a theoretical account of language emergence. Typical children do not "need" to learn signs along with words, but we need to watch them do so; mainstreaming provides a reason for them to learn and an opportunity for us to watch.

The participants lived in an urban area and were all enrolled in the same cooperating program: a grant-funded demonstration project in which developmentally delayed children aged 0–3 years were mainstreamed in a full-day program of nonresidential educare with normally developing children in the same age range. The children were heterogeneous in race/ethnicity (Caucasian, Hispanic, black) and in socioeconomic status (lower to middle class). For data analysis they were divided into three groups based on diagnostic status and further described in terms of the range across children in developmental age (DA) and chronological age (CA) at the time of the first vocabulary posttest. The groups were: DS (four Down syndrome toddlers, DA 8–19 months, CA 21–34 months); DD (eight toddlers with developmental delays, DA 9–20 months, CA 15–30 months); ND (twelve normally developing, nondelayed toddlers, DA 12–34 months, CA 13–33 months). A variety of developmental disabilities were present in the DD group; most prominent were prematurity, hydrocephalus, porencephalus, and sensory-motor problems ranging from nystagmus and high myopia to spina bifida. No hearing deficits had been diagnosed as of the beginning of the study, but one DS child (Dana) later was found to have a mild to moderate bilateral hearing impairment, probably an effect of persistent otitis media. Data from an additional ND child who received bimodal input at home were included in some analyses.

12.2.2 Procedure: A Method for Providing Speech-Dominant Bimodal Input and Assessing the Outcome

Because our emphasis is on comparing the manual and vocal modalities, we often refer to augmentative sign as *speech-dominant bimodal input*, or more generally as *unbalanced bimodal input*. This terminology highlights the fact that the total input to each child strongly favors speech both in quantity and in quality. Using naturally occurring languages as a standard (whether signed or spoken), speech-dominant bimodal input is clearly atypical. The speech modality carries a naturally occurring language, but the manual modality is composed of ASL signs that have been removed from their natural context and piggybacked onto the very different fabric of English. The signs constitute a limited vocabulary and display some of the morphological structure of ASL—and in those respects they are a fragment of a conventional language—but they have no independently generated syntax. In fact, the bimodal input might better be viewed as a single system in which certain vocabulary items are specified not only by phonological features (the elementary constituents that specify word forms; e.g., voiced, labial) but also by cheremic features (the analogous constituents that specify sign forms; e.g., flat handshape, midface location). The greater number and variety of features would make these vocabulary items particularly distinct. The morphophonology of such a system would be of special interest in that it would combine aspects of both English and ASL morphology, but no connections to other aspects of ASL grammar would be expected.

Our primary theoretical aims could have been carried out using balanced bimodal input instead. (No simultaneous system is truly balanced, since the structure of one language will predominate. However, it is possible to achieve a rough parity in the amount of information carried in each modality by ensuring that every English morpheme has a counterpart in the manual modality, or the converse.) What was critical was that several types of toddlers receive input in two modalities during the developmental period appropriate to early vocabulary acquisition. Relevant results would be obtained whether the input was balanced or unbalanced across modalities; ideally, data would eventually be obtained for both types of input, providing the broadest possible database for comparative analysis.

If only one system is to be studied, however, unbalanced bimodal input does offer certain advantages. First, the focus of study was vocabulary acquisition, especially during the single-word period of development. More balanced systems such as Signing Exact English (SEE) and Signed English, in which grammatical morphemes are separately signed, could conceivably be so complex that children would find it harder to acquire open-class morphemes such as nouns and verbs. Second, adults can learn fairly quickly to provide unbalanced bimodal input, making it possible to have several teachers and research assistants provide input to different groups of children at different times. In contrast, fluency in a system such as SEE, Signed English, or signed English is difficult to attain, limiting the number of potential language models and making it more difficult to ensure continuity of input across a year-long project. Third, the results from unbalanced bimodal input are more readily applied to improving the design of therapeutic programs. Balanced and unbalanced input are equally relevant from a strictly theoretical standpoint, but only unbalanced bimodal input offers the close interplay between theory and application that is one of the most attractive features of this research area.

The input was provided in fairly intensive group sessions led by the children's teachers or by an investigator using pictures, objects, play activities, and stories. Sessions lasted 15–30 minutes a day, at least two but usually four days per week, and focused on structured elicitation of individual word/sign pairs. In addition, functional and combinatorial use of bimodal vocabulary was modeled sporadically in appropriate contexts during the day, especially at mealtimes. Parents were supplied with sign illustrations and "Total Communication Picture Books." The overall objective was to provide bimodal input not just when adults needed to communicate, but as a project in itself; the bimodal input was viewed as a kind of nourishment needed to encourage growth in each modality. As a result, the amount of sign input was probably greater than for some therapeutic uses of augmentative sign directed to children with mental retardation (those for whom the focus is limited to communicative needs), but certainly much less than the amount in the best therapeutic programs or especially in a typical signing deaf family.

Approximately once every six weeks over the nine-month duration of the program, old vocabulary was posttested and new vocabulary was pretested in formula elicitation sessions that were videotaped for later coding by two independent coders (with disagreements resolved by a third coder). On each trial the investigator attempted to elicit production of a target word/sign pair by displaying a picture and asking "What's that?" or "What's she (he) doing?" Unless both labels were produced, she attempted to elicit imitation by providing a bimodal model (e.g., "It's a CUP!"). Follow-up queries specifically requesting the word and sign individually were also used under specified conditions. The data of interest here are the percentages of correct responses on the posttests for word production, sign production, word production/imitation, and sign production/imitation. (Production/imitation was credited if the target item was produced or imitated or both.)

12.2.3 Results: The Robustness of the Manual Modality

Figure 12.1 summarizes the results that are most salient to the relative timing of the manual and vocal modalities as vehicles for early vocabulary. For each group of children, data from the 12–19 month DA range were used to obtain mean percentages correct on production (the hatched portion of each bar) and on production/imitation (the entire length of each bar). (Data from TSP-2 are also shown at the far right of each graph and will be discussed in a later section.) It is clear from this figure that it was essential to expose

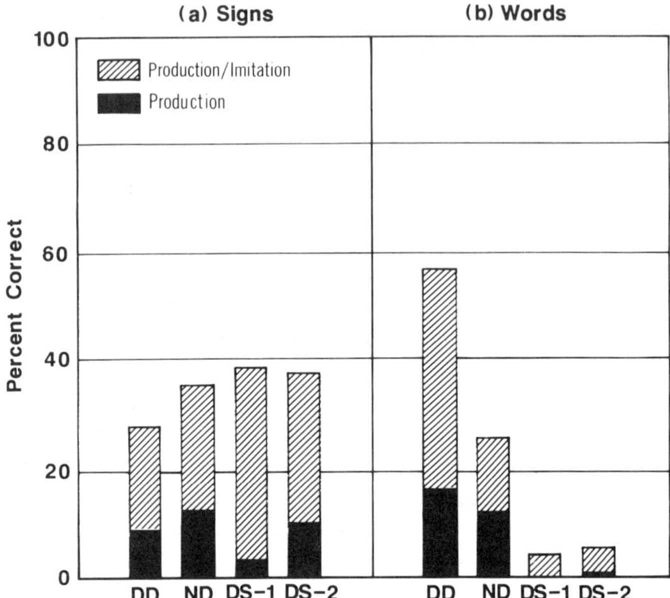

Figure 12.1. Mean percentage correct on signs versus words in the developmental age range 12–19 months for each group of children.

both typical and atypical learners to the same type of bimodal input in order to draw the most appropriate generalizations about the relation between modalities.

Looking first only at the data from the typical learners (group ND), we can see that toddlers do have an affinity for the manual modality. Considering that most of the bimodal input was limited to a single fifteen- to thirty-minute period, two to four days per week, it is impressive that they performed as well on signs as they did. Specifically, throughout the 12–19-month age range, signs were produced and imitated as well as words. (At 20–26 months, not shown here, there is a word advantage for production but not for imitation.) We are inclined to attribute the excellent performance on signs to the relative ease of matching adult models in the manual modality. If the analysis was carried out using criteria that deemphasized form and emphasized function, we would expect to see signs do relatively less well, consistent with Bonvillian and Folven's (1990) findings for toddlers receiving typical ASL input.

Affinity for the manual modality in typical learners does *not* ensure the robustness of the acquisition timetable. Robustness is established by extending one's investigation to atypical learners; what is necessary is that the timetable of vocabulary learning relative to DA, whether early or late, be the same across a variety of learners. In fact, the results in figure 12.1 from the two groups of delayed (atypical) learners tell us that toddlers' affinity for the manual modality is no greater, and no less, across a variety of handicapping conditions that result in delayed development. If groups of toddlers are equated for developmental age, their ability to acquire signs is fairly equal as well. The DS toddlers are not better at acquiring signs than typical toddlers, but neither are they worse. The same can be said of the DD toddlers (whose slightly lower mean score does not even approach statistical significance in comparisons by ANOVA and t). This similarity of performance across groups is maintained at DA 20–26 months.

The situation is quite different in the vocal modality. As expected, the DS toddlers are clearly delayed in their ability to acquire words. More interesting, because not specifically predicted, the DD toddlers actually perform *better* on word production/imitation than the typical (ND) toddlers in the same developmental age range. The result is due entirely to a relative developmental strength for word imitation; when imitation is excluded to arrive at a measure of word production, or when data are examined from the next DA range (20–26 months), the DD group performs similarly to the ND group. This suggests that their precocious word imitation is a somewhat isolated skill. It is of interest nonetheless, because when combined with their merely average skill at sign imitation, the result is a word advantage. This contrasts with the balanced performance of the ND toddlers on the imitation/production measure and the sign advantage shown by the DS toddlers (at DA 20–26 months as well).

Hence, under the conditions of this study, there is no overall finding of a sign or word advantage. All children develop similarly in the manual modality, and it is the steadiness of progress in that modality across a broad range of learners that leads us to speak of its robustness. The same timetable is found, relative to overall development, for both typical and atypical learners. The vocal modality, in contrast, develops by a different timetable for each of the three groups, a difference that is statistically significant for the production/imitation measure ($p < .01$). Differences in *word* performance are solely responsible for the derivative findings of a sign advantage, word advantage, or no advantage that characterize the separate groups. A sign advantage, when it occurs, depends on particular combinations of input conditions and learner characteristics. It is a phenomenon that is conditional; it is subject to boundary conditions that, while broader than the conditions that yield a word advantage, must be specified and utilized in drawing implications. The more general phenomenon is the robustness of the developmental timetable for manual signs (for a given quantity and quality of sign input). It is likely that exceptions to that timetable would involve only a few specialized circumstances of obvious relevance, such as missing or disabled upper extremities.

There remain some empirical gaps that it would be desirable to fill. First, it would be of interest to observe the effects of different degrees of sign exposure. For example, *balanced* bimodal input should produce better performance on signs, but how much better would it be? And would the greatest benefit occur early (e.g., DA about 12 months) or later (e.g., DA about 18 months)? Would the benefit be equal across the three groups of participants, as it should if the robustness of the manual modality is maintained at all degrees of exposure?

Second, exactly what kinds of delayed children perform especially well in the vocal modality? Our DD group included several with hydrocephalus, immobilized lower limbs, or both. Swisher and Pinsker (1971) found that older children with hydrocephalus and spina bifida cystica had a relative strength on tasks of auditory-vocal processing, but their speech lacked appropriateness and referentiality. Our results may be capturing the earliest stages of development that lead toward this pattern. Presumably, other unselected samples of delayed children would include some who would look more like the Down syndrome group in their use of modality and others who would resemble the present sample. We have not pursued either of these roads of investigation.

The third empirical gap is one we have recently addressed. The distinctive relation between modalities for the Down syndrome toddlers (signs on schedule, words behind schedule) is itself an interesting developmental pattern that would be rewarding to study in more detail. The number of children in the DS group was small (four children, of whom only two provided any substantial quantity of data), so an initial question would be whether the pattern would be replicated on a larger sample of children with Down syndrome. If so, the pattern could be said to be characteristic of the syndrome. Detailed study of the pattern would then be informative not only as a special case of modality relations, but also as a study of the syndrome. We designed Toddler Sign Program 2 to pursue these goals. The study is ongoing, but some of the early results from four children are summarized in the section that follows. For a later report that includes data from two additional children, see Abrahamsen, Lamb, and Myrick (1988).

12.3 Pursuit of the Distinctive Relation between Modalities for Down Syndrome Toddlers: Toddler Sign Program 2

12.3.1 Participants

The participants in Toddler Sign Program 2 (TSP-2) were eight children with Down syndrome (DA 8–20 months and CA 22–53 months at onset). All attended the same early-intervention center for developmentally delayed children under age 5. They were homogeneous in race/ethnicity (black) and heterogeneous in socioeconomic status (lower to middle class). In both TSP-1 and TSP-2, all Down syndrome children in the target range for DA and CA were accepted for participation in the study. Hence the sample was representative rather than selected. Some children had no major medical complications, whereas others had characteristic conditions such as congenital heart disease and persistent otitis media or premature birth and neonatal complications. In this preliminary report, initial data are presented from two children who began their participation at approximately DA 12 months, and two who began at approximately DA 18 months. They are referred to by the following pseudonyms: Cece (DA 12 months, CA 27 months); Dean (DA 13 months, CA 21 months); Eric (DA 17 months, CA 42 months); and Hoyt (DA 20 months, CA 47 months). Within the total group of eight participants, Dean and Cece had the fewest medical complications. Eric and Hoyt had moderate medical complications including persistent otitis media, which affected their hearing during some periods.

12.3.2 Procedure

In TSP-2, the use of individual rather than group sessions made it possible to provide intensive input to each child and to collect data continuously. Each child was seen for fifteen to forty-five minutes a day, four to five days a week for four to twenty-six months. The first four to six months focused on a core vocabulary of thirty word/sign pairs (ten mealtime pairs such as "CUP" and "EAT"; ten object pairs such as "CAR" and "BABY"; and ten functional pairs such as "POTTY" and "ALLGONE"). Additional sets were introduced during the remaining months of participation. Those who participated longest (a total of 112 weeks) worked with four additional sets: ten actions and vehicles; twenty-three initial animals; thirty other animals; and twenty other actions. In this report, results are reported only for the thirty core vocabulary pairs (fig. 12.1) and the core plus the ten actions and vehicles (table 12.2). For Dean, results are limited to the core vocabulary, because he moved to another city after his fourth month of participation.

Two days a week, a formal elicitation of production and imitation was carried out using procedures similar to the TSP-1 posttests. On each trial, a researcher displayed a referent (an object or a picture, determined by a schedule that counterbalanced the order of sets and the type of referent within each week). She attempted to elicit production by asking "WHAT'S THAT?" "WHAT'S she (he) DOING?" or "WHAT'S HAPPENING?" and then provided two opportunities for imitation by modeling the word/sign pair. The child was then allowed to play with the toy (or picture) unless the responses were well below the child's ability. Occasionally a sign was molded or a word was exaggerated at the end of the trial to help improve the child's form. A second (and sometimes also a third) researcher recorded the primary sequence of events within each trial using a portable computer that had been modified for use as an event recorder by S & K, Inc. (Toronto). There were primary codes for sign production, word production, sign imitation, and word imitation, and for whether the form of the sign or word was good, approximate, or only an attempt. Additional codes included nontarget sign, nontarget word, vocalization, gesture, spontaneous communication, adult-child interaction, play, and attention. The time of each key press was recorded, so that simultaneous events could be identified during analysis.

On the remaining two to three days a week, informal sessions focused on pragmatics and bimodal combinatorial language, a type of interaction that was much less frequent in TSP-1. For the core vocabulary and the action/vehicle set, these informal sessions were carried out by providing subsets of toys to play with and using bimodal utterances to comment, question, command, name, and socially interact with the child. A second researcher recorded selected events on a form designed for the purpose. Beginning in the third month, all sessions (formal and informal) were also videotaped for further analysis.

Additional data were collected on each child's developmental progress, symbolic play, comprehension of target pairs, performance on sign-only versus word-only input, spontaneous usage, and generalization to other referents. However, this report is limited to preliminary results from the formal elicitation sessions for four participants within the first four to thirteen months.

12.3.3 Preliminary Results on the Developmental Timetable in Each Modality

Percentage Correct on the Production and Production/Imitation Measures

Summary measures of performance in each modality were obtained by computing each child's percentage correct on the mealtime and object sets during the formal elicitation sessions, averaged across the first four months of participation. As in the case of TSP-1, two measures were used: percentage correct on production, and percentage correct on production or imitation or both. The mean percentages for the three youngest children are shown in figure 12.1 (bars labeled DS-2) and are quite consistent with the data previously obtained in TSP-1. The fourth child, Hoyt, was beyond the 12–19 months DA range used for figure 12.1. His scores (27 percent sign production, 16 percent word production, 70 percent sign production/imitation, 31 percent word production/imitation) were consistent with the results for DA 20–26 months obtained in TSP-1 (see Abrahamsen, Cavallo, and McCluer 1985).

Hence the two Down syndrome groups both exhibit a sign-first pattern: word acquisition is delayed but sign acquisition is not, with the result that signs are learned first. This contrasts with the typical toddlers in the ND group, for whom words and signs are learned equally well in the DA range 12–19 months. The TSP-2 data therefore provide additional evidence that an acquisition pattern in which signs precede words is characteristic of toddlers with Down syndrome, but not of typical toddlers, when speech-dominant bimodal input is provided beginning about DA 12 months or later.

Cumulative Vocabularies

Because formal elicitation sessions occurred so frequently in TSP-2, it is possible to examine progress across time on each individual vocabulary pair. A word or sign is regarded as acquired (in imitation or in production, computed separately) when a correct or approximately correct response has been observed on seven different dates by one observer and confirmed by a second observer on two of those dates or on two other dates. The date when this criterion is met is defined as the date of acquisition. As an example, table 12.1 displays the cumulative sign and word vocabularies of one child (Eric) across the first six months. Each month's schedule includes six formal sessions, so the criterion of seven elicitations can first be met during the first formal session of month 2.

Eric's vocabulary growth is shown by day of acquisition for month 2, and by week of acquisition for months 3–6, for imitation and production separately. At any given point in time (column labeled with session numbers), the cumulative vocabulary consists of all items within and to the left of that column. We can see that Eric's cumulative vocabulary was larger for signs than for words throughout. For example, by the end of month 4 he could imitate all thirty signs but only ten words and could produce ten signs but only one word. The other three children also had higher cumulative vocabularies for signs than for words, though the differences were not always so large. Specifically, by the end of month 3, Hoyt could imitate all thirty signs and twelve words and could produce twelve signs and six words. The two younger children could imitate several signs (thirteen for Cece and three for Dean) and one word each and had not yet met any production criterion.

Relative Order of Acquisition within Bimodal Pairs

From the dates of acquisition in the cumulative vocabularies, each word/ sign pair can be classified by its acquisition status: (1) neither modality acquired; (2) simultaneously acquired (same session or adjacent sessions); (3) sign only acquired; (4) sign acquired first; (5) word only acquired; (6) word acquired first. Table 12.2 shows the result of this classification for each of the four children, including the ten vehicle/action pairs as well as the thirty core vocabulary pairs (except that Dean is limited to the thirty core pairs). Few vocabulary pairs were simultaneously acquired in both modalities (and these tended to meet criterion early, suggesting that the child knew many of these words, and possibly the corresponding signs, before the program began). In

Table 12.1   Cumulative Vocabulary across the First Thirty-six Sessions for Eric (TSP-2)

Month 2						Month 3			Month 4			Month 5			Month 6		
7	8	9	10	11	12	13–14	15–16	17–18	19–20	21–22	23–24	25–26	27–28	29–30	31–32	33–34	35–36
Vocabulary items meeting the imitation criterion at each session: signs (total = 30) and words (total = 16)																	
APPLE	COOKIE	TELEPHONE	POTTY	DUCK	MUSIC	SHOES	JUICE	HI	ALLGONE	ALLDONE							
EAT	BRUSH	AIRPLANE	SLEEP	BOOK	SPOON	PLATE	WANT		BYEBYE								
HAT	BABY	DRINK	BALL		BOWL	MORE			LOVE								
		MILK	CAR			CUP											
							Baby	Hi	Bowl	Byebye	Spoon	Apple	Hat	Allgone	Alldone		Brush
							Ball		Car	Duck	Potty			Cup			
										Book							
Vocabulary items meeting the production criterion at each session: signs (total = 13) and words (total = 5)																	
						TELEPHONE	AIRPLANE	COOKIE	APPLE	BALL	SLEEP		SPOON		DUCK		
						BRUSH		CAR			MUSIC				BOOK		
						HAT											
										Car							
															Apple		Baby
															Hat		Book

Note: Signs are shown in small capitals, words in upper- and lowercase letters.

Table 12.2 What Was Acquired, and in What Order, for the First Forty Word/Sign Pairs: Number of Pairs Showing Each Acquisition Pattern Based on TSP-2 Imitation Data

Child	None	Sign = Word	Sign Only		Sign Then Word		Word Only		Word Then Sign		Total
			High	Low	High	Low	High	Low	High	Low	
Cece	0	2	22	0	6	9	0	0	1	0	40
Dean	21	0	2	5	0	1	0	0	0	1	30
Eric	0	1	13	0	17	9	0	0	0	0	40
Hoyt	0	6	12	0	13	9	0	0	0	0	40

Note: Each numerical entry is the number of word/sign items that showed a particular relative order of acquisition for a particular child. "High" indicates items that meet a strong criterion of successful elicitation on at least seven dates according to one observer, with confirmation on at least two dates by a different observer. "Low" indicates emerging items that meet a weaker criterion of being successfully elicited on at least three dates according to one observer.

only one instance was a word clearly acquired before the corresponding sign. Rather, the great majority of pairs were acquired sign first or sign only. The order-of-acquisition data are therefore consistent with the percentage-correct data in figure 12.1. That is, at the level of types as well as tokens, word performance lags behind sign performance for toddlers with Down syndrome.

12.3.4 Other Robust Phenomena in Bimodal Acquisition

Confirmation of the distinctive sign-first acquisition pattern for Down syndrome toddlers was only one aim of the second study. The atypical pattern of DA-appropriate sign acquisition followed by delayed word acquisition presents interesting research opportunities for examining language onset at the boundaries. That is, we can examine language onset under learner and input conditions that lie at the periphery of what is usual, rather than at the center, but that are crucial for achieving an overall understanding of that process.

Specifically, the following question presents itself. If a particular child acquires vocabulary faster in one modality than the other, is the earlier modality used as a base for the acquisition of the second modality? If so, base utilization would be claimed to characterize language acquisition in two modalities (consistent with Goldin-Meadow and Morford's 1985 findings on the relation between gesture and speech in so-called unimodal acquisition). The alternative possibilities are that the modalities develop independently or even that there is a dependence in a negative direction (the absence of any overlap in vocabulary across modalities, for example). Because the answer to the question could be different depending upon which modality is first, or for different types of learners, the data from Down syndrome toddlers are especially crucial. The children can be expected to acquire signs first and then words. Compared with toddlers who acquire words first and then signs (e.g., typical toddlers who receive bimodal input after speech acquisition has begun), Down syndrome toddlers can help answer the question of base utilization in its most general, modality-neutral form.

We are currently exploiting these possibilities by carrying out two kinds of analysis on the TSP-2 data, in comparison with the TSP-1 data. First, one can ask whether there is a statistical dependence between signs and words, at least during certain periods of acquisition. For TSP-1 it has already been shown that the proportion of words correct multiplied by the proportion of signs correct underpredicts the proportion of items for which both the word and sign are correct; that is, there is dependence rather than independence. This could have causes other than base utilization, however, and the analyses have not yet been performed for TSP-2. A second kind of analysis examines individual test trials, seeking sequences in which the ontogenetically earlier modality also occurs earlier within the microstructure of the trial. If, for example, the sign is elicited first alone and then simultaneously with the corresponding word, the sign would appear to be functioning as a base to which the word is appended. Evidence that such sequences predominate over the converse (word first) type of sequence for Down syndrome toddlers has recently been provided by Abrahamsen and Lamb (1987). Further, it is the word-first sequences that predominate for other groups of toddlers, indicating that the base-utilization phenomenon is robust enough to be modality neutral. Data from both sign-first and word-first learners were needed to demonstrate this phenomenon at the proper level of generalization.

Finally, it would be appropriate to return to the question of form versus function in comparing modalities. We have presented data from two important but limited contexts: elicited imitation and elicited production. How would it affect the results if other, nonelicited utterances were examined with respect to functional criteria to trace the emergence of spontaneous naming, requesting, and other functional uses of words and signs? We have detailed records of the toddlers' spontaneous utterances across time (including some instances of two-sign combinations) and plan to carry out analyses that incorporate functional criteria. Together with the results on elicited imitation and production, these investigations of base utilization and spontaneous utterances will yield a more complete, and doubtless more complex, account of language emergence in two modalities than is currently available.

12.4 Recapitulation: A New Perspective on Language Emergence in Two Modalities

At the root of our inquiry is the question, What role does modality play in language emergence? If there are *differences* between the manual and vocal modalities—for example, as vehicles for early vocabulary—what are the differences and what is their significance? Just as important, what are the *similarities* and their significance? We believe that no single research strategy is sufficient in isolation. If various investigators each cast their nets somewhat differently, we will obtain an array of findings that can be put together to yield understanding. From this perspective it is fortunate that modality research has clustered around three different research strategies but unfortunate that the findings thus obtained have not been sufficiently integrated to arrive at an overall account of the role of modality.

One of these research clusters focuses on the role of manual gestures in the typical course of language development, a role that is constrained by the fact that caretakers tend to provide only a small inventory of gestural models to their young auditors but that is nonetheless not trivial (see, e.g., Bates et al. 1979). The other two research clusters have in common a focus on circumstances in which manual input is considerably richer, but they differ in the richness of the input and in the characteristics of the learners. Specifically, the researchers in the second cluster study the acquisition of independent, fully formed sign languages such as ASL by deaf or hearing children of normal intelligence. Researchers in the third cluster study the consequences of making unbalanced bimodal input (augmentative sign) available to children with developmental delays due to mental retardation, autism, or other conditions. Our own research lies primarily within this third cluster but incorporates some of the major elements of the second cluster as well (by including nondelayed children as one type of participant and by studying language onset during the earliest possible developmental period). Our concern in this chapter has been to present our own findings and to consider them in juxtaposition with findings from the second research cluster. The goal is to achieve a broader account than has been possible within any one research cluster. We have also incorporated findings from the first research cluster in our thinking, but we cannot detail those contributions in this space (see Abrahamsen 1985; Abrahamsen, Cavallo, and McCluer 1985).

The following picture of the role of modality in the emergence of early vocabulary can be extracted from our findings in conjunction with those of other investigators.

1. *Redundancy.* Redundancy is built into the phylogenetic program for human language emergence, in that both the manual and vocal modalities develop in ways that make them available to serve as vehicles for symbolization and communication. The degree to which this potential is actualized in each modality depends in large measure upon the type of input learners are exposed to.

2. *The sign advantage.* Although relevant development occurs in both modalities, young toddlers are more successful in matching the form of adult models in the manual modality than in the vocal modality. Hence, if manual signs and spoken words are equally available in adult input, toddlers will show a sign advantage in their acquisition of those forms. Even under the limited manual input that was offered in Toddler Sign Program 1, signs were acquired as well as words. Under more favorable conditions of native-language input, Bonvillian and his colleagues found a clear advantage for sign forms relative to comparison data on acquisition of word forms, at least through an age level of $1\frac{1}{2}$ years. Younger toddlers do have an affinity for the manual modality and enjoy the competence they can display in that modality. It is not yet well understood what consequences that affinity may bring, but we know that the affinity and its consequences have limits, as follows.

3. *Limitations on the sign advantage.* Acquisition of language forms is a necessary but not a sufficient condition for the recruitment of those forms as vehicles for particular symbolic and communicative functions. The child must be developmentally ready to carry out those functions, and readiness will de-

pend upon other strands of development. Bonvillian and Folven's findings (1990) illustrate this point with respect to the function of referential naming. The sign advantage may be limited to language form, as instantiated in a small number of very limited functional contexts (e.g., interactive routines). Other functions critical to language acquisition, from referential naming onward to describing and questioning, may show no sign advantage or a much reduced advantage; research is needed to identify these. Finally, additional limitations are imposed by type of learner and input, acquisition criterion, and developmental level (e.g., under the speech-advantaged input of Toddler Sign Program 1, the developmentally delayed group had a word advantage for imitation, and the normally developing toddlers above DA 20 months had a word advantage for production). These various limitations suggest that the sign advantage is a conditional phenomenon, for which *boundary conditions* must be specified to appropriately delimit its range of generalization. Determining those conditions and interpreting their significance is an important and unfinished task.

4. *High variability in the vocal modality.* The vocal modality shows high variability in its availability as a vehicle, at least when that availability is assessed across different groups with normal and delayed development, and perhaps within those groups as well. In our studies, children with Down syndrome in particular have been identified as showing a modality-specific *delay* in speech. During the developmental period in which they could be expected to be acquiring a variety of language functions, based on their overall level of development, they are prevented from fully realizing that capacity by their difficulty in acquiring speech forms. The variability is also instantiated, however, by the unexpected finding of a relative *strength* for imitating speech forms in the DD group.

5. *Low variability in the manual modality.* If the redundancy offered by two modalities is exploited by making unbalanced bimodal language models available to learners, much less variability is observed in the manual modality than in the vocal modality. Toddlers with Down syndrome as well as other delayed toddlers acquire sign forms on the *appropriate developmental schedule,* as determined from normally developing comparison children matched for DA. This result applies at least to sign forms in contexts of elicited production and imitation; we plan to address questions of sign function in forthcoming analyses. It is likely, but we have no plans to demonstrate, that the same low variability for acquisition of sign forms would be obtained under *balanced* bimodal input and (in a between-subjects design) under unimodal input as well.

6. *The robustness difference in favor of signs.* The findings in (4) and (5) can be summarized by stating that manual sign forms emerge *robustly,* that is, by a similar developmental timetable across a variety of learners, whereas

spoken words show a relative *lack of robustness* in their timetable of emergence. This is a finding that depended upon making bimodal input available to typical as well as atypical learners in the same study, a design feature that is perhaps unique to the Toddler Sign Program.

7. *Sign robustness as a higher-order generalization.* The sign advantage in (2) and the robustness difference in (6) are two different phenomena at different levels of generalization: the robustness difference *requires* a comparison across groups of learners, whereas the sign advantage can be demonstrated within a single group or even within an individual learner. The two phenomena are not in competition, and the genuineness of one neither excludes nor implies the genuineness of the other. It has been empirically demonstrated, however, that the sign advantage is contingent on various conditions. While it is true that the advantage for sign forms is lost only under rather extreme conditions such as highly speech-advantaged input, the point is simply that the sign advantage *is* conditional, and the conditions delimiting its applicability must be appreciated. Under those same extreme conditions sign robustness is maintained. This relative independence from contingency is an appealing property of the sign robustness phenomenon.

8. *Modality-neutral generalizations.* The instability of the speech timetable, placed against the stability of the sign timetable, *generates different relations* between words and signs for different groups of learners exposed to the same input conditions. The variety of acquisition patterns that result can be used to explore language emergence and arrive at *modality-neutral* generalizations. An example is our own recent evidence that the earlier-learned modality is used as a base for acquiring vocabulary in a second modality, regardless of which modality is the earlier one.

These eight conclusions corroborate our claim that knowledge of certain phenomena of language emergence simply cannot be obtained if study is limited to typical, unimodal input and typical, normally developing learners. Atypical learners often are provided with atypical input for pedagogical reasons, but the resulting developmental events have singular importance for the construction of a general account of language emergence. The phenomenon of sign robustness contributes a new perspective in the ongoing construction of this account and creates a broader context within which to study sign-first and word-first patterns of acquisition.

13 Manual Communication and Autism: Factors Relating to Sign Language Acquisition

JOHN D. BONVILLIAN AND DEBORAH WEBB BLACKBURN

13.1 Introduction

In many of the early accounts of autistic children, the syndrome of childhood autism was characterized as largely a social and emotional disorder. As more investigations of childhood autism were conducted in subsequent years, however, there was a gradual change in perspective as to the underlying nature of the disorder and the proper focus for intervention programs. Today most investigators consider the cause of childhood autism to be some form of organic brain dysfunction, and much more emphasis is placed on the serious cognitive and language deficits autistic children exhibit (Rutter 1978). The language disturbances in autistic children have been found to extend from mutism, echolalia (immediate or delayed repetition of words or phrases), and severely delayed onset of speech to the use of highly metaphorical language employed with little apparent intent to communicate. Because alleviating such deficits probably would do much to enhance the development and adjustment of autistic children, increased efforts are being made to teach or foster language and communication skills in programs for these children. Moreover, many current investigators are especially interested in the myriad problems of autistic children who fail to acquire any useful speech. The prognosis for these children historically is very bleak (Eisenberg 1956), as many of them remain unable to communicate even basic needs after years of speech training.

Since the early 1960s, two major innovations in language training for autistic children have emerged (Bonvillian and Nelson 1982). The first innovation, speech training using behavior modification techniques, has proved particularly helpful in fostering spoken language skills in autistic children who either are echolalic or have some useful speech. The results of operant

This research was supported by Social and Behavioral Sciences Research grant 12-126 from the March of Dimes Birth Defects Foundation to John Bonvillian. We thank the children and staff members of the DeJarnette Center of Staunton, Virginia, and the Grafton School of Berryville, Virginia, for their participation and assistance in this study. We are especially grateful for the assistance of Lee Blackburn, Raymond J. Folven, Patricia Jacobson, Gail Mayfield, and Melissa Wyer in the data collection and interpretation. Mary W. Riser made many helpful comments on an earlier version of the chapter.

speech training have been much less encouraging, however, for most mute autistic children. These children frequently have failed to progress beyond imitating a few words within the training setting. Moreover, although most autistic children score within the retarded range on IQ tests (Rutter 1978), autistic children who failed to acquire speech usually had the lowest IQ scores. The second and more recent approach to language training has been the use of sign language, either alone or in combination with speech therapy, with low-functioning autistic children.

The initial studies of sign language acquisition in nonspeaking autistic children revealed that manual language training can be a remarkably effective means of establishing a first avenue of communication for many such language-deficient children (e.g., Bonvillian and Nelson 1976; Creedon 1973; see also Offir 1976; Miller and Miller 1973; Webster et al. 1973). Subjects in these studies often were able to acquire a vocabulary of signs and later to combine signs to convey more complex semantic and syntactic relationships. Their enhanced communication skills were often accompanied by marked improvements in their social and personal behavior. Subsequent studies (e.g., Carr et al. 1978; Konstantareas, Oxman, and Webster 1977; Schaeffer et al. 1977) have continued to highlight the efficacy of manual communication with these children.

Thus there is at present a considerable research literature that underlies the potential effectiveness of manual communication training with low-functioning autistic children. Before their participation in sign language training programs, many of the subjects in these studies spent long periods, sometimes several years, in speech-oriented language therapy programs without making noticeable progress. It should be noted, however, that though most subjects in the sign language programs showed improvement, the range in individual outcomes has been wide. For many children sign language has proved to be their first effective means of communication. Others have made virtually no progress in attaining even rudimentary signing skills, suggesting that certain autistic children do not benefit from sign language training. Such diversity in training outcomes, however, has received little attention from investigators.

Despite the growing number of reports on the efficacy of manual communication training with autistic children, it has proved difficult to determine what influence subject characteristics and treatment procedures have on sign language mastery. One reason for this situation is that most previous investigations involved only a small number of children, and the records of their performance were often incomplete. A second reason is that the ability levels of subjects frequently were reported in descriptive terms and anecdotal accounts rather than through more objective measures. Over the past several years it has become apparent that until these very basic limitations in research are rectified, progress will not be attained either in understanding the sign acquisition process or in determining which subject-selection and training approaches will be most beneficial.

There are important practical as well as theoretical reasons for undertaking a systematic analysis of factors related to success in sign learning. Until such analyses are conducted, it will not be possible to design maximally effective programs for autistic children, nor will the resources available for their training be utilized in the most efficient manner. Indeed, this point is highlighted by the finding (Kiernan, Reid, and Jones 1982) that the choice of a particular communication program was influenced primarily by the personal preferences of the participating speech therapists rather than by specific characteristics of the children. Moreover, for those autistic children who are shown to be poor candidates for success in a sign program, alternative approaches that do not entail the memory and motor demands of manual communication may be more appropriate. Such systematic analyses may also help determine whether differentiating various subgroups of nonspeaking autistic children would be useful.

In addition to the possible practical consequences of these empirically based assessments, such analyses promise to shed light on important theoretical issues in the field of language acquisition. Previous investigations have identified various factors presumed to be involved in language acquisition in general, as well as subject and treatment characteristics related to sign language development in autistic children in particular. Investigators of children's early language acquisition often have argued that language develops out of a framework of communicative gestures, symbolic play, and caregiver-child interaction (Bruner 1978). In this approach, such nonverbal gestures as showing, pointing, and giving are viewed as indicating the infants' capacity to interact effectively with others and to refer to objects and events before the onset of language (Bates et al. 1979). Symbolic play (e.g., pretend play with objects), on the other hand, has been linked with young children's language acquisition because the same mental representational capacities supposedly mediate both language usage and symbolic play (McCune-Nicolich 1981). Language thus is seen as rooted in both turn taking and gestural exchange, with the cognitive basis of language exhibited in the representational capacities involved in symbolic play. If this model of language growth holds for autistic children as well, one would expect that those children who used gestures to communicate and who demonstrated higher levels of play and social skills would likely be more successful in language training programs. Correspondingly, if development of these capacities is unrelated to the acquisition of communicative competence in autistic children, that raises concern about the adequacy of this model of developmental precursors for theories of language acquisition in general.

With regard to language development in autistic children in particular, examination of subjects' background characteristics and language outcome levels in previous studies of sign language acquisition has revealed various trends in the data (Bonvillian and Nelson 1982; Layton 1987). Even within the restricted IQ range of autistic children participating in sign language training programs, IQ measures have been strongly related to outcome levels, with higher-functioning children typically acquiring greater fluency. In contrast, severity of autistic symptoms has been reported (Miller and Miller 1973) as inversely related to sign language mastery. Thus, autistic children with more severe symptoms would be expected to acquire fewer signs. Investigators also have reported an increase in the number of signs acquired over time by subjects in training programs (Layton 1987). Perusal of individual case reports, however, has shown wide individual differences in acquisition rates, and this variability might be expected to influence the generally positive relationships expected between program duration and sign language development. Miller and Miller (1973) also observed that their younger autistic subjects acquired more signs than their older subjects. It should be noted, though, that their subject groups were not equivalent on several dimensions and that older children may be more capable on a number of dimensions of language learning even if the optimal time for sign intervention is earlier. Fine motor skill development often has been noted in the clinical literature as a prerequisite for signing success. Indeed, physical or motor disability was one of the most frequently cited reasons why autistic children did not learn to sign (Kiernan, Reid, and Jones 1982). Thus one would hypothesize a positive relation between fine motor skills and sign language development. Finally, a number of investigators have reported that children who initially displayed greater speech or language competence were more likely to succeed in sign language training programs than those who showed lower levels of language skills (Carr and Dores 1981; Layton 1987).

Until the present study, no investigation had undertaken as its primary focus the systematic examination of these hypothesized relationships in autistic children. The factors or characteristics examined in this research include cognitive skills or development, age at program admission, severity of autistic symptoms, length of participation in sign training, language skills, quality and type of play, fine motor skills, use of communicative gestures, and social development or skills. In addition, we rely primarily on objective measures or indices rather than on descriptive reports or anecdotal accounts of the ability levels of the autistic subjects.

To summarize, the study was undertaken to investigate factors believed to be related to sign language acquisition in autistic children. We hoped that such information would help in the design of appropriate training programs as well as provide a greater understanding both of the syndrome of autism and of language development in general. With these two goals in mind, we began a longitudinal investigation of sign language acquisition in two training programs for autistic children.

13.2 Method

13.2.1 Subjects

Subjects were recruited from two residential programs for autistic children: DeJarnette, a state hospital, and Grafton School, a private nonprofit facility. Three criteria were employed in selecting the subjects. The first was that the children's behavior and developmental histories conform to the diagnosis of infantile autism. The five essential diagnostic features of infantile autism recognized by the National Society for Autistic Children (Ritvo and Freeman 1977) guided the selection. These features included social and language problems before the age of 30 months; problems affecting language and communication; disturbed developmental rates and sequences; unusual or abnormal responses to sensory stimuli; and abnormal ways of relating to people, objects, and events. We evaluated children from the two residential programs according to these features by perusing their background records. These records frequently included diagnostic formulations by physicians, psychologists, and educators. In the few cases where the diagnosis of autism was unclear from the records, the assessments of the residential staff members were used to make the final subject designations.

The second selection criterion was that the children be participating in manual communication training programs. Both residential facilities employed a communication approach of simultaneous speech and sign within the context of a behavioral analysis model. The subjects typically participated in daily sign language training sessions. In these sessions the children were shown how to form signs both through the teachers' modeling of the signs and through the teachers' molding the children's hands into the correct sign configurations and guiding them through the appropriate sign movements. In addition, various behavioral techniques, including prompting, fading, and reinforcement, were used to shape appropriate responses. This formal training was supplemented by the spontaneous signing of the teachers, staff members, and children in their interaction outside the classroom. Although the sign language training programs at Grafton and DeJarnette shared a number of features, factors such as staff characteristics and the extent of subject record keeping were not controlled.

The third criterion was that the children have relatively complete background information files and up-to-date records of sign and spoken language acquisition. However, as we noted above, there were some differences in the amount and quality of the information or data recorded on the subjects from the two residential programs. For example, it was possible to trace the learning of an individual sign to a 90 percent accuracy criterion for each of the Grafton subjects, but comparable data on percent accuracy were not available for the DeJarnette subjects.

By employing these selection criteria, we chose fourteen Grafton residents and eight DeJarnette residents for the study. The total sample consisted of seventeen males and five females. Eighteen subjects were Caucasian, including one with a Hispanic background, and four were black. Although all twenty-two children met the three criteria for inclusion, they differed on a number of dimensions, including level of functioning, age, length of time in a residential program, and additional handicapping conditions. For example, whereas most children required close supervision for basic toileting, eating, and dressing, two subjects had been promoted to sheltered work settings. Length of stay varied widely as well, ranging from six months up to seven years and six months. Also, two autistic subjects were profoundly hearing impaired as well.

13.2.2 Measures

The measures used consisted of nine scales of the subjects' performance levels at the time they entered their residential treatment programs (pretreatment measures) and three scales of the subjects' subsequent language performance levels (outcome measures).

Pretreatment Measures

Many of the subjects' pretreatment scores were based on standardized test instruments. Of these, the Early Learning Accomplishment Profile or Early-LAP (Glover, Preminger, and Sanford 1981) was by far the most widely used. The wide range of ages and abilities at the time of admission precluded the use of identical tests for each subject. Thus it was often necessary to use a variety of test scores for each pretreatment measure. Age-equivalent scores were derived from the various tests or measures used, and the subjects' performance was analyzed based on these scores. (Because age-equivalent scores derived from different test instruments are not strictly comparable, one should exercise caution in interpreting these scores.)

Cognitive skills. Cognitive skills were assessed using the Early-LAP, the Brigance Diagnostic Inventory of Early Development (Brigance 1978), and the Hiskey-Nebraska Test of Learning Aptitude (Hiskey 1966). A mental age score was computed for each child.

Language skills. The background information files were used to determine whether an individual child was mute, using single words, or echolalic on entering the residential program. Measures of receptive language skills included the Early-LAP (Glover, Preminger, and Sanford 1981), the Peabody Picture Vocabulary Test—Revised (Dunn and Dunn 1981), and the Denver Developmental Screening test (Frankenburg et al. 1975). A receptive language age score was computed for each subject.

Age at admission. Age in years and months was computed for the date each child entered the residential program.

Severity of symptoms. A nine-point diagnostic tool developed by Creak (1964) was used as an index of the severity of autistic symptoms. Using the background information files, the symptom constellations each child displayed on entering the residential program were added up to compute a total symptom score. Examples of the diagnostic behaviors Creak included were "gross and sustained impairment of emotional relations with people" and "pathological preoccupation with particular objects or certain characteristics of them, without regard to their accepted functions." Although this instrument was not initially designed as a scale of symptom severity, scores derived from it have been used as a measure of severity of autism in the past (e.g., Miller and Miller 1973).

Length of participation in training program. Duration in the training program was computed from the time each child entered the program at each residential facility to the date when outcome measures of sign acquisition were obtained.

Fine motor skills. Fine motor age equivalent scores were obtained using the Early-LAP (Glover, Preminger, and Sanford 1981), the Brigance (Brigance 1978), the Denver (Frankenburg et al. 1975), the Bender Visual Motor Gestalt Test (Bender 1938), and the Developmental Test of Visual-Motor Integration (Beery and Buktenica 1967).

Social skills. Measures of social skills included the Early-LAP (Glover, Preminger, and Sanford 1981), the Vineland Social Maturity Scale (Doll 1953), and the Denver (Frankenburg et al. 1975). Social age equivalent scores were derived from these scales for each child.

Quality of play. Two categories of behavior were used to assess quality of play: stereotyped, nonimaginative play, and inappropriate or bizarre use of objects or toys. Through perusal of the background records and discussion with the children's language teachers, we scored each child as displaying one, neither, or both of these behaviors. Thus a higher score indicated more deviant play behavior.

Gestural communication. Instances of pointing, showing, or other gesturing were noted in the background records and in discussion with each child's language teacher to determine whether a child used gestures (1 = yes, 2 = no) to communicate before or on entering the manual communication training program.

Outcome Measures

Several widely used indices of sign and spoken language development were used as the outcome measures. The measures were obtained by interviewing each child's language therapist regarding the child's current level of speech and sign language development. Specific elicitation procedures were not used. Rather, scores on the outcome measures depended both on current observations of the child by the therapist and on detailed recordings of language sessions available in each child's language notebook.

Sign vocabulary. Each child's language therapist was asked to list all the signs the child could currently produce without directly imitating the signs of another person. Thus, signs produced spontaneously or with prompting were counted. For example, a child who was asked, "What is this?" and correctly signed the name of the indicated object was credited with producing that sign.

Longest sign combination. The language therapist also listed the longest sign utterance each child ever produced. This information was readily available from the language notebooks of each child.

Expressive speech. The language therapists noted whether a child had ever used expressive speech while at the residential program. Speech was defined as the utterance of recognizable words rather than nonword vocalizations or sound production.

13.2.3 Procedure

The study proceeded in several steps. First, we obtained the scores on the nine pretreatment measures from the background records of each child. We developed a twenty-five page coding device for extracting the pertinent information. This coding device included spaces for demographic information, developmental history and observations, a behavioral checklist, and assessment data and was used in calculating the measures of all pretreatment variables. Standardized assessments of cognitive, receptive language, fine motor, and social skills were administered by the residential teaching and support staff, and those measures given closest to each child's entrance to the residential program were selected as the pretreatment variables. The pretreatment measures of severity of symptoms, quality of play, and use of gestures to communicate were coded by the investigators from the behavioral checklist section of the coding devices and from discussions with the children's language teachers and were not standardized assessment measures.

Second, after the pretreatment scores had been obtained, the investigators interviewed each child's language therapist to determine the child's level of sign and spoken language development for the three outcome measures. This information was supplemented by observing the children and examining their language notebooks.

Finally, the hypothesized relationships between the pretreatment measures and level of language acquisition were assessed using both correlational and regression analysis techniques. Data from the Grafton and DeJarnette subjects were analyzed as a group and separately to control for possible differences between sign training programs at the two institutions.

13.3 Results and Discussion

The results supported certain of the hypothesized relationships between pretreatment measures and subsequent levels of language acquisition and failed to support others. As expected, expressive sign vocabulary size and length of longest sign utterance were significantly correlated with higher scores on cognitive, receptive language, fine motor, and social skills. Sign language acquisition also was positively correlated with age at admission and length of participation in a training program, although the interpretation of these last two findings is problematic because of design limitations.

The measures of language acquisition revealed a wide range of outcome levels among the subjects (see table 13.1). Several of the children acquired extensive sign language lexicons (estimated vocabulary size = 450) and combined these signs in utterances up to five signs in length. More common were subjects who acquired a small spontaneous, expressive sign vocabulary of three or four signs and rarely or never combined these signs. Most of these children, however, had been credited with mastering many more signs in their behaviorally oriented sign training sessions. In between these two groups were a handful of subjects who acquired a working sign language vocabulary of a dozen or more signs and who combined these signs in utterances ranging from two to six signs. The children's progress in spoken language development was more limited than their sign language growth, as only seven subjects produced any recognizable words. Two of these subjects, however, showed greater progress in speech than in sign.

The language outcome measures also revealed that the two indices of sign language progress were significantly related ($r = .69, p < .001$). Neither index of sign language acquisition, however, was related to progress in spoken language development, as the correlations were small and statistically nonsignificant ($r = -.17$ for speech and sign vocabulary; $r = .02$ for speech and length of longest sign utterance). Interpreting these latter two correlations, though, is more difficult because so few subjects made any progress in speech skills.

Several approaches were used in analyzing the data. Pearson product-moment (see table 13.2) correlation coefficients were computed between each of the nine pretreatment and three language outcome measures. (Spearman rank-order correlations were calculated as well, because such a statistic requires only that the variables be measured on an ordinal scale and does not

Table 13.1   Subjects' Pretreatment Scores and Language Outcome Measures

	Pretreatment Scores[a]									Outcome Measures		
Subjects	Mental Age	Language	Age	Creak	Length	Fine Motor	Social	Play	Gesture	Signs	Combination	Speech
1	11	8	56	6	43	21	24	3	1	3	0	0
2	24	0	73	8	42	27	24	3	2	3	0	0
3	24	24	—	7	16	32	33	1	1	4	0	0
4	16	12	65	9	53	24	15	3	2	4	0	0
5	17	8	60	5	42	21	20	3	1	3	2	0
6	16	0	63	5	15	16	18	2	2	3	2	0
7	10	5	63	7	58	9	15	2	2	4	0	0
8	—	33	123	8	77	—	92	2	2	450	5	0
9	81	61	133	5	67	86	77	4	1	450	5	0
10	39	55	105	7	91	36	68	1	2	450	5	0
11	16	8	42	9	9	23	24	1	1	8	0	5
12	48	24	103	4	22	72	61	1	1	75	6	0
13	16	12	86	5	9	24	18	1	1	26	2	0
14	18	15	79	4	8	30	22	1	1	45	2	10
15	22	18	74	5	38	32	32	4	1	34	5	30
16	6	8	50	4	13	20	8	3	2	0	0	0
17	54	30	150	4	3	42	—	4	1	12	3	5
18	32	18	156	6	19	24	35	3	1	2	0	0
19	0	—	92	6	38	36	28	4	1	4	0	13
20	5	3	79	3	22	—	6	3	2	0	0	—
21	18	10	70	7	6	22	12	3	1	4	0	11
22	—	—	130	8	40	—	—	4	1	30	0	30

[a]Cognitive, language, admission age, participation length, fine motor, and social scores in months; dashes indicate missing data.

Table 13.2   Pearson Correlation Coefficients between Pretreatment Scores and Language Outcome Measures

	Mental Age	Language	Age	Creak	Length	Fine Motor	Social	Play	Gesture
Signs	.69	.85	.43	.06	.73	.63	.89	−.11	.21
n	(20)	(20)	(21)	(22)	(22)	(19)	(20)	(22)	(22)
	$p < .001$	$p < .001$	$p < .05$	n.s.	$p < .001$	$p < .005$	$p < .001$	n.s.	n.s.
Combination	.70	.70	.38	−.42	.38	.71	.78	−.14	−.06
n	(20)	(20)	(21)	(22)	(22)	(19)	(20)	(22)	(22)
	$p < .001$	$p < .001$	$p < .10$	$p < .10$	$p < .10$	$p < .001$	$p < .001$	n.s.	n.s.
Speech	−.13	−.04	.11	.01	−.09	−.01	−.11	.43	−.40
n	(20)	(20)	(21)	(22)	(22)	(19)	(20)	(22)	(22)
	n.s.	n.s.	n.s.	n.s.	n.s.	n.s.	n.s.	$p < .05$	$p < .10$

rest on the assumptions of linearity, homoscedasticity, and normality of data as in the Pearson product-moment correlation. Both correlational approaches produced very similar patterns of results. Only the Pearson product-moment correlations are reported here, since this approach was the one consistent with the subsequent statistical analyses described below.) An overall intercorrelation table also was computed for the nine pretreatment, and three outcome measures. In addition, correlations were computed between the pretreatment and language outcome measures for the subjects in the two training programs and again when the three most fluent signers (two of whom were hearing impaired)—who might be considered outliers—were removed from the sample. Finally, a regression analysis was performed to determine which measures best predicted sign language acquisition.

13.3.1 Relation between Pretreatment Measures and Sign Language Acquisition

Cognitive Skills

The mental age scores at the time the subjects were admitted to their residential training programs ranged widely, extending from lows of "untestable" and from 5 months up to 81 months. In general, the children with the higher scores evinced greater success in sign language acquisition. As predicted, a significant correlation was found between mental age and number of expressive, spontaneous signs mastered ($r = .69$, $p < .001$). Similarly, mental age was significantly correlated with length of the subjects' longest sign combinations ($r = .70$, $p < .001$). These correlations remained statistically significant even when the three most fluent signing subjects were excluded and when the Grafton population data were examined alone. When the DeJarnette data alone were used, the correlations, based on eight subjects, were positive but were not statistically significant.

Thus a strong positive relationship between cognitive skills and sign mastery was obtained, as subjects with higher IQs acquired more signs and combined them into longer utterances. This finding is in accord with earlier reports that demonstrated the value of initial IQ scores in predicting future levels of intelligence and social adjustment in autistic children (Lockyer and Rutter 1970).

More detailed perusal of individual IQ and sign language acquisition data reveals additional facets of the relation between the two measures. One observation is that the more fluent subjects typically scored at 18 months or above on mental age, whereas the less fluent signers tended to score below this level. A certain minimal level of functioning on measures of cognitive skills therefore may be necessary to make substantial progress in sign training.

Language Skills

Because all the subjects were mute at the commencement of their manual communication training, the measures of their language skills consisted only of their receptive spoken language scores. The children's scores varied widely on this dimension as well, though in most cases their receptive language age equivalents were below their mental age equivalents. Regardless, receptive language skills at time of admission were highly predictive of later expressive sign vocabulary ($r = .85$, $p < .001$) and length of longest sign utterance ($r = .70$, $p < .001$). When the data from the three highly fluent "outlying" subjects were excluded, the correlations between receptive language scores and the two measures of sign language acquisition remained statistically significant. When the data from the two training programs were analyzed separately, the receptive language age scores continued to be highly significantly related to signing success in the Grafton pupils ($r = .90$, $p < .01$ for vocabulary; $r = .73$, $p < .01$ for utterance length), but not in the smaller DeJarnette sample ($r = .44$, $p > .10$ for vocabulary; $r = .62$, $p = .10$ for utterance length).

These findings are consistent with those of previous research, which had shown that children with greater initial competence in speech or speech comprehension tend to make greater progress in sign training programs (Howlin 1981; Layton 1987). Furthermore, our results suggest that a certain minimal level of language comprehension or competence may be necessary for successful progress in sign training. Whereas the receptive language skills of the more fluent children tended to be at the preschool level, most of the subjects who acquired only a minimal number of signs demonstrated receptive language skills below the one-year level.

Age at Admission

The children who were older when admitted to their sign training program tended to be somewhat more successful in acquiring sign language skills. This finding is seen in the significant positive correlation between age at admission and expressive sign vocabulary ($r = .43$, $p < .05$). (The correlation between age at admission and length of longest sign utterance also was positive, $r = .38$, $p < .10$, but did not reach generally accepted levels of statistical significance.) The impact of this finding is considerably lessened, however, when we excluded the data from the three most fluent signers, two of whom were hearing impaired; neither of the correlations was statistically significant.

The finding that the older subjects tended to learn more signs and to combine signs into longer utterances ran counter to expectations. However, as was often the case in previous research, these results are seriously confounded by the comparison of older, more highly functioning subjects with younger, very low functioning subjects. One reason for this recurring problem in research design is that autistic children who are adapting more successfully often remain in their homes or in local facilities for longer periods. Thus the effect obtained for age may result primarily from other differences that covaried with age among the subjects. To examine more clearly the relation between age and sign mastery, it will be necessary in future research to control for other relevant variables, especially levels of cognitive, language, fine motor, and social skills, as well as previous training.

Severity of Symptoms

The scores on the diagnostic scale developed by Creak (1964) extended from 4 to 9, spread relatively evenly across this range. The correlation between Creak scale scores and expressive sign vocabulary, for all the subjects, was not significant ($r - .06$, $p > .10$). This finding was contrary to expectations, because the children with higher Creak scale scores (more symptoms of autism) were predicted to be much poorer candidates for sign learning. At the same time, the correlation between length of longest sign utterance and Creak scale score approached statistical significance ($r = -.42$, $p < .06$) and was negative, as predicted. When the three highly fluent outliers were excluded from the analysis both the correlations were negative ($r = -.42$, $p < .10$ for vocabulary size; $r = -.65$, $p < .01$ for utterance length), although only the correlation for the length of longest sign utterance measure reached generally accepted levels of statistical significance. When the subject populations were split into the two training program groups, the resulting correlations were not significant.

The correlational results between the number of diagnostic symptoms of autism as measured by the Creak scale (Creak 1964) and the two indices of sign language acquisition are thus difficult to explain. The absence of a relationship between Creak scores and number of expressive signs acquired runs counter to a finding reported earlier by Miller and Miller (1973). At the same time, the significant correlation between length of longest sign combination and number of autistic symptoms might be viewed as indicating that the Creak scale was measuring a dimension related to success in signing.

In viewing this unexpected pattern of results, one should keep in mind that certain investigators have pointed out that the Creak scale was not designed as a measure of autistic symptomatology (Kiernan, Reid, and Jones 1982). Rather, it was meant to be used primarily to identify children with the particular syndrome of infantile autism. Thus the Creak scale probably provides only a partial quantitative index of severity. For example, a child who is consistently aloof with people and has difficulty in reciprocal relations would be rated as showing "gross and sustained impairment of emotional relation-ships," just as would a child who does not even appear to recognize people as anything other than objects. Indeed, to compare the autistic subjects on sever-ity of autistic symptomatology, a different and more sensitive measure of the nature of the symptoms may be needed. One such index that appears to merit careful future examination in this regard is the Childhood Autism Rating Scale (Schopler et al. 1980), as it contains rating scales of the relative severity of the different defining characteristics of autism. Regardless, examination of other measures of symptom severity as well as further consideration of the interrela-tions between sign combination and Creak scores is merited.

Length of Participation in Training Program

The individual subjects attended the Grafton and DeJarnette programs from 3 months to over $7\frac{1}{2}$ years, with the large majority ($n = 17$) of the children involved in sign training for more than one year. As expected, length of par-ticipation was correlated with number of spontaneous, expressive signs ac-quired ($r = .73, p < .001$). The correlation between length of participation and length of longest sign utterance, however, did not reach generally ac-cepted levels of statistical significance ($r = .38, p < .10$).

Although the overall finding that children who had participated in the train-ing programs for longer periods learned the most signs is in accord with previ-ous research, there are real problems with this finding. One problem is that this result is accounted for almost entirely by the lengthy involvement of the three most highly functioning subjects, two of whom were profoundly deaf. When these subjects are excluded, the analysis results in negative correlations of small magnitude between length of participation and both measures of sign mastery. A second problem is that length of participation is confounded in part by severity of symptoms, as some of the children who were youngest at admission, and thus the longest participating, were among the lowest-functioning subjects. In general, however, the size of each child's vocabulary tended to increase with time, so that individually there was a clear positive relation between sign lexicon and length of participation. Still, it is important to note that some of the subjects learned more signs in their first six months of participation than their cohorts did in a couple of years of training.

Fine Motor Skills

The subjects' fine motor skill scores extended from a low of an age equiva-lent of 9 months to a high of 86 months. As in previous studies of autistic children (DeMyer, Hingtgen, and Jackson 1971), the subjects' motor develop-ment scores were consistently below their chronological age level. The scores on this measure were highly predictive of success in sign training. This is evident in the significant correlations between fine motor ability and expressive sign vocabulary size ($r = .63$, $p < .005$) and between fine motor ability and length of longest sign utterance ($r = .71$, $p < .001$). These relations were robust ones as well, as they remained statistically significant when the three highly fluent outliers were excluded ($r = .77$, $p < .001$ for sign vocabulary size; $r = .69$, $p < .01$ for length of longest sign utterance). Moreover, when the data for the two training programs were analyzed separately, fine motor skill scores predicted vocabulary size ($r = .65$, $p < .02$) and sign utterance length ($r = .77$, $p < .01$) among the Grafton subjects. In the smaller DeJarnette sample, however, the correlations ($r = .41$ and $r = .54$, respectively) were not statistically significant, although they were in the predicted direction.

These findings of a positive relation between motor skills and signing are in accord with various anecdotal reports of language therapists. The signs learned by the less fluent signers tended to involve mostly gross motor movement, whereas the more fluent signers typically acquired a variety of signs requiring both gross and fine motor skills. None of the current language therapists, however, specifically reported physical disability or impairment as a primary reason for the lack of sign language success among the children in the present study. Nevertheless, these results suggest that a minimal or threshold level of fine motor control is necessary to learn some signs, and that recent efforts (e.g., Bornstein and Jordan 1984) to modify certain signs to make them easier to produce motorically while retaining the signs' recognizability may be beneficial for many autistic children.

Social Skills

As with most of the other pretreatment measures, there was a wide range of scores among the subjects on social skills. The age-equivalent scores extended from a low of 6 months to a high of 92 months, with about half the subjects scoring at age 2 years or under. As expected, there was a significant correlation between social skills and number of spontaneous, expressive signs acquired ($r = .89$, $p < .001$) and between social skills and length of longest combination ($r = .78$, $p < .001$). What we did not anticipate, however, was that the social skills scores would be the best predictor of signing success, as these two correlations were slightly higher than several other significant predictors. When the three most fluent, outlying subjects were excluded from the analysis, moreover, the correlations between social skills and sign vocabulary size ($r = .68$, $p < .01$) and social skills and longest sign utterance ($r = .63$, $p < .01$) remained statistically significant. Finally, when the correlations between social skills and the two measures of sign mastery were run separately for the two training group samples, the correlations were highly significant in the Grafton sample ($r = .91$, $p < .001$ for number of signs; $r = .84$, $p < .001$ for sign combination length), but not in the smaller DeJarnette sample ($r = .48$ and $r = .45$, respectively), although in the anticipated direction.

It is not clear why social skills are such an effective predictor of success in sign training. Although the social abnormalities of autistic children have been probed less frequently in recent years than the other features of autism (Rutter 1983), it is likely that the children's difficulties in attending to and interacting with others are important component skills that adversely affect their learning to communicate. Also, when autistic children have severe social behavior deficits, such as failing either to attend to others or to engage in self-stimulation, they are likely to fail to make even rudimentary progress in sign training.

Quality of Play

The quality-of-play scores were unrelated to either measure of sign language development for the subject population as a whole, for the Grafton subjects analyzed alone, or when the three most fluent signers were excluded from the analysis. Somewhat surprisingly, then, the correlation between play quality and sign vocabulary size was statistically significant ($r = .71$, $p < .05$) among the small number of DeJarnette subjects, and in the direction opposite from that predicted. That is, the few subjects who exhibited more bizarre, stereotyped play behavior tended to learn more signs. The correlation between quality of play and length of longest sign utterance in this group was in the same unexpected direction ($r = .55$, $p > .05$) but was not statistically significant.

Thus the relationship between the subjects' play behavior and sign language skills turned out to be a complex and perplexing one. Whereas stereotypic or inappropriate play was related to sign production among the DeJarnette children, the correlations generally were negative and of small magnitude among the Grafton participants. It is possible that the two population groups differed on various play-related behaviors. However, a more likely explanation for the wide variation in correlations between the schools may have been that our requests for information were interpreted differently by the staff members in the two schools. Another problem with this measure was its limited range, though this was dictated in part by the subjects' very limited levels of play. A larger, standardized scale of play behaviors, perhaps including a range of symbolic and functional (e.g., conventional use of toys) play behaviors, might more fully and reliably capture the children's play skills in future studies. Consideration also should be given to observing the children's play directly and systematically rather than relying on interview data and background records. Support for this approach is provided by the findings of a recent study (Mundy et al. 1987) that employed an observational measure of autistic children's spontaneous play behaviors; these children's functional and symbolic play skills were found to be significantly related to their expressive and receptive language skills.

Gestural Communication

Slightly more than half of the present subjects used gestures to communicate their desires when they entered the training programs. Contrary to expectations, there were no significant correlations between gestural communication and either of the sign language acquisition measures. This held for the subject population as a whole, when the three most fluent signers were excluded from the overall sample, and when the analyses were conducted on the two training groups separately. This finding runs counter to certain models of language acquisition as well as to previous informal observations of autistic children in manual communication training programs. In one model of language acquisition, various communicative gestures, such as showing, giving, or pointing, are viewed as necessary precursors to language, as they indicate a capacity for shared reference and conventionalized communication (Bates, Camaioni, and Volterra 1975). Similarly, other theorists (e.g., Bruner 1978) have emphasized that prelinguistic, often gestural, communicative exchanges and routines between caregiver and child provide the framework out of which language develops. Investigators of sign language acquisition in autistic children also occasionally have voiced the belief, based on informal observation, that children who signify their pretreatment desires by gestures are good candidates for sign language training (Bonvillian, Nelson, and Rhyne 1981).

Several reasons may account for the absence of the expected relation between communicative gestures and language development in the present study. One reason is that background records and teachers' recollections may not be a fully accurate index of the subjects' gestural usage upon admission. A related explanation is that the limited range of the scale and the behaviors sampled may have severely constrained any possible findings. Relevant to this point is the finding by Mundy et al. (1987) that only certain types of nonverbal communication, primarily the use of gestures to coordinate visual attention with others, were related to language development in autistic children. A third reason is that it is not at all clear whether the autistic children's gestures should be considered equivalent to those of normal infants first learning to communicate. The initial steps of autistic children's language may differ from that of normal infants in their gestural as well as cognitive and social concomitants. In fact, contrary to expectations based on theories of normal language development, Mundy et al. (1987) reported no relation between such nonverbal social behaviors as engaging in turn taking or combining eye contact with reaching out to another person and measures of language development.

A fourth possible explanation rests on the fact that the previous models of language acquisition and communicative gestures have been based on studies of young children learning to speak. When young children learning to sign have been observed systematically, the full pattern of interrelation between language usage and gestural production was not replicated (Folven, Bonvillian, and Orlansky 1984–85). Thus, communicative gestural production and sign language learning may differ in the normal acquisition process from the acquisition of gesture and speech.

13.3.2 Expressive Speech Acquisition

In light of the limited progress made on speech skills by the large majority of the subjects, it was not surprising that most of the correlations between the number of spoken words learned and the subjects' pretreatment scores were of small magnitude and statistically nonsignificant. The pretreatment use of communicative gestures, however, was marginally related to speech acquisition ($r = -.40$, $p < .10$), since children who used communicative gestures tended to make greater progress in speech. In addition, the correlation between the children's quality of play behavior and words learned was significant ($r = .43$, $p < .05$), although in the direction opposite from that hypothesized.

13.3.3 Intercorrelation and Regression Analyses

Table 13.3 reveals that the subjects' scores on a number of the pretreatment measures were highly intercorrelated. This was especially true for the measures of cognitive, receptive language, fine motor, and social skills, where the intercorrelations among these indices were all .75 or above. Apparently these standardized measures are tapping highly related underlying skills among the subjects.

Multiple regression analyses were performed separately for the three language outcome measures. For expressive sign vocabulary size, the score on the measure of social skills was the best predictor (loaded on first in the regression equation), accounting for 79 percent of the total variance. Additionally, age at admission and fine motor skill scores were significant predictors, since together they accounted for 14 percent of the remaining variance. The strength of the measures of social skills in predicting signing success was not anticipated, because IQ level consistently has been reported as the single best predictor of treatment outcomes for autistic children (Lotter 1978). Let us point out, however, that this population of low-functioning autistic children represents a restricted range of abilities and that three other measures (cognitive skills, receptive language ability, and length of participation in training program) did not emerge as predictors in this model because they were so highly correlated with social ability. That is, the variance ac-

Table 13.3   Intercorrelation Matrix for Pretreatment and Outcome Scores

	Mental Age	Language	Age	Creak	Length	Fine Motor	Social	Play	Gesture	Signs	Combination
Language	.84										
Age	.72	.67									
Creak	−.31	−.15	−.15								
Length	.24	.53	.16	.34							
Fine motor	.84	.75	.57	−.34	.21						
Social	.88	.84	.70	−.02	.64	.85					
Play	.11	.02	.28	−.04	.10	.13	−.12				
Gesture	−.28	−.16	−.26	.36	.41	−.35	−.03	−.12			
Signs	.69	.85	.42	.06	.73	.63	.89	−.11	.21		
Combination	.70	.70	.38	−.42	.38	.71	.78	.14	−.06	.69	
Speech	−.13	−.04	.11	.01	−.09	−.01	−.11	.43	−.40	−.17	.02

counted for by cognitive skills, receptive language ability, and length of participation in training program is essentially the same variance explained by the social ability factor.

In the second multiple regression analysis—that for length of longest sign combination—social ability also emerged as the strongest predictor. Social ability accounted for 61 percent of the total variance. The next three predictive factors, in order of relative contribution, were Creak scores, age at admission, and fine motor skill. These three measures explained an additional 26 percent of the variance. Again, as in the first regression model, cognitive skills and receptive language ability did not emerge as separate predictors because of intercorrelation with the social ability factor. Finally, the multiple regression analyses performed on speech skills confirmed the general findings of our correlational analyses, as no significant factor emerged.

13.4 General Discussion

Overall, the study achieved its primary goal of identifying those pretraining factors that are related to sign language acquisition in low-functioning autistic children. The outcome data also revealed a wide range in the individual achievement levels of the subjects. The most successful children became adept at sign communication, other children learned to use a small vocabulary effectively, and the least successful children made only minimal progress. Regardless, it should be noted that all but one of the subjects acquired at least one expressive sign, and that progress in spoken language development generally was small and trailed sign language acquisition.

The study indicates that pretreatment assessment of autistic children provides valuable prognostic information. Children who eventually acquired an extensive sign vocabulary and who spontaneously combined signs demonstrated greater cognitive, receptive language, fine motor, and social skills than children who acquired only small working sign vocabularies. The significance of these findings is that they provide evidence that it may be possible to identify beforehand through standardized assessment tools those children who will benefit maximally from sign communication training. Such findings also run counter to recent reviews (e.g., Peck and Schuler 1987) critical of the usefulness of standardized tests in assessing autistic children. Moreover, the present findings appear to be robust, as they held up despite the procedural shortcoming of using different standardized assessment tools because of the wide range in ages and background characteristics among the subjects at admission. Of course, additional systematic analyses of subject characteristics and training outcomes will be needed before a fully adequate prognostic model can be developed.

An additional important finding was the high degree of intercorrelation between various pretreatment measures. Although the measures of social ability accounted for slightly more of the variance in predicting sign training success than did cognitive, receptive language, and fine motor skills, all four measures were highly predictive. In the future it will be interesting to determine whether there are characteristics in common across these scales that result in such high interrelationships.

In light of the present finding that autistic children who perform very poorly on measures of cognitive skills, receptive language, social ability, and fine motor skills are relatively poor candidates for sign language training programs, there appear to be at least several possible approaches for these children. One approach would be to try various other augmentative communication programs, systematically testing whether any of them improves communication skills in these children. A second approach would be to try to enhance these lower-functioning autistic children's performance on these measures, with the hope that improved performance in cognitive, language, social, and fine motor skills would bring more substantial progress in manual communication. The third approach would be to focus on new ways of teaching signs. Such an approach would need to foster the spontaneous communicative aspects of signing, as this dimension appears to be a particular area of difficulty for the less fluent children.

One unanticipated finding was the relatively weak relationship between the number of signs learned in training sessions by many of the less fluent subjects and the likelihood that these same signs later would be used spontaneously. For example, in the training sessions at Grafton, a subject needed to attain a 90 percent accuracy criterion before being credited with learning a particular sign. Despite this stringent learning criterion, only a small proportion—about a third—of the signs acquired in the training sessions were observed being used by these subjects spontaneously outside the training sessions. Often only basic vocabulary items, such as "eat/food," "drink," or "toilet," were used and retained by these children, while the signs for clothing, foods, furniture, or people seemed to disappear. There are several implications from this finding. One is that statements in the literature about the sign vocabulary sizes of autistic children based solely on the number of signs trained to criterion may considerably overrepresent their real working vocabularies. A second implication is that although some low-functioning autistic children are able to learn a number of signs in training sessions, those gains may be lost when the particular signs are no longer taught or reinforced. For these children, knowledge of the signs appears to exist only within the confines of the training session or location and does not readily generalize to useful communication. A third implication is that institutional staff members probably need to make much more effort to teach and use signs outside the training sessions to promote generalization of signing skills. Demonstration of the functional or pragmatic aspects of spontaneous sign usage, moreover, appears to be particularly important for fostering useful language in autistic children. Indeed, there is a growing recognition in the field that only when discrete-trial behavioral training procedures (e.g., prompting, fading, differential reinforcement) are combined with language instruction that focuses on the autistic child's interests in a natural context will maximal gains in communication be attained (Carr, Kologinsky, and Leff-Simon 1987).

Our findings underline the importance of individual children's characteristics in their relative success in manual communication training. Clearly, the lowest-performing children on several pretreatment measures made only the most limited strides in learning to sign. The findings also raise concern about the frequent use of various typologies in describing autistic children. In our investigation all the subjects were initially classified as mute, low-functioning autistic children, yet the range in their training outcomes was very wide. Nevertheless, it is important to recognize that many of the lowest-functioning autistic children will probably make only minimal progress in learning to communicate in sign language training programs as they are currently conducted. One reason this recognition is important is that investigators need to search for alternative communication systems or ways to teach signs that may be more effective. A second reason is that programs for autistic children need to be accurate in representing to the children's families the progress that can be expected for their children. And last, it is important that the teachers' expectations for the children's language and communication progress not be raised to a level where they cannot typically be fulfilled, or the outcome is likely to be frustrated and disappointed teachers and staff members (Konstantareas 1985).

Finally, although some of the autistic children in the present study made only minimal progress in acquiring manual communication skills, for other subjects the product of their sign training was their first relatively effective means of communication. Moreover, for many of these children, progress in sign training came only after years of failure to produce recognizable speech. Thus, when autistic or other developmentally disabled youngsters fail to achieve communication skills in one language mode, it may be possible to make far greater progress in another.

References

Abrahamsen, A. A. 1985. Robustness, redundancy, and cross-domain relations in development: An afterword. *Merrill-Palmer Quarterly* 31:223–28.

Abrahamsen, A. A., M. M. Cavallo, and J. A. McCluer. 1985. Is the sign advantage a robust phenomenon? From gesture to language in two modalities. *Merrill-Palmer Quarterly* 31:177–209.

Abrahamsen, A. A., and M. Lamb. 1987. Modality relations in toddlers with and without Down syndrome. Paper presented at the Fourth International Symposium on Sign Language Research, Lappeenranta, Finland.

Abrahamsen, A. A., M. Lamb, and C. Myrick. 1988. Evidence against a delay in language emergence for toddlers with Down syndrome: The role of modality. Paper presented at the Twenty-first Annual Gatlinburg Conference on Research and Theory in Mental Retardation and Developmental Disabilities, Gatlinburg, Tennessee.

Akamatsu, C. T. 1982. The acquisition of fingerspelling in pre-school children. Ph.D. diss., Department of Psychology, University of Rochester.

———. 1985. Fingerspelling formulae: A word is more or less the sum of its letters. In *SLR '83: Proceedings of the Third International Symposium on Sign Language Research,* ed. W. Stokoe and V. Volterra, 126–32. Silver Spring, Md.: Linstok Press.

Allen, T. E. 1986. Patterns of academic achievement among hearing impaired students: 1974 and 1983. In *Deaf children in America,* ed. A. N. Schildroth and M. A. Karchmer, 161–206. San Diego, Calif.: College-Hill Press.

American National Standards Institute. 1969. *Specifications for audiometers.* ANSI 53.6-1969. New York: ANSI.

Andersen, R. 1983a. A language acquisition interpretation of pidginization and creolization. In *Pidginization and creolization as language acquisition,* ed. R. Andersen, 1–56. Rowley, Mass.: Newbury House.

———, ed. 1983b. *Pidginization and creolization as language acquisition.* Rowley, Mass.: Newbury House.

Anthony, D. 1971. *Seeing Essential English manual.* Anaheim, Calif.: Educational Services Division.

Argyle, M., and M. Cook. 1976. *Gaze and mutual gaze.* Cambridge: Cambridge University Press.

Argyle, M., and J. Dean. 1965. Eye-contact, distance and affiliation. *Sociometry* 28:289–304.

"

280 References

Argyle, M., R. Ingham, F. Alkema, and M. McCallin. 1973. The different functions of gaze. *Semiotica* 7:19–31.

Baddeley, A., N. Thomson, and M. Buchanan. 1975. Word length and the structure of short-term memory. *Journal of Verbal Learning and Verbal Behavior* 14:575–89.

Baker, C. 1977. Regulators and turn-taking in American Sign Language discourse. In *On the other hand: New perspectives in American Sign Language* ed. L. Friedman, 215–36. New York: Academic Press.

———. 1980. How does "sim com" fit into a bilingual approach to education? In *Proceedings of the Second NSSLRT,* ed. F. Caccamise and D. Hicks, 3–12. Silver Spring, Md.: National Association of the Deaf.

Baker, C., and D. Cokely. 1980. *American Sign Language: A teacher's resource text on grammar and culture.* Silver Spring, Md.: T. J. Publishers.

Baker, C., and C. Padden. 1978. Focusing on the nonmanual components of American Sign Language. In *Understanding language through sign language research,* ed. P. Siple, 27–57. New York: Academic Press.

Baker-Shenk, C. 1983. A microanalysis of the non-manual components of questions in American Sign Language. Ph.D. diss., University of California, Berkeley.

Bates, E., L. Benigni, I. Bretherton, L. Camaioni, and V. Volterra. 1979. *The emergence of symbols: Cognition and communication in infancy.* New York: Academic Press.

Bates, E., L. Camaioni, and V. Volterra. 1975. The acquisition of performatives prior to speech. *Merrill-Palmer Quarterly* 21:205–26.

Battison, R. 1974. Phonological deletion in American Sign Language. *Sign Language Studies* 5:1–19.

———. 1978. *Lexical borrowing in American Sign Language.* Silver Spring, Md.: Linstok Press.

Beery, K. E., and N. A. Buktenica. 1967. *Developmental test of visual-motor integration.* Chicago: Follett Educational Corporation.

Bellugi, U. 1980. Clues from the similarity between signed and spoken language. In *Signed and spoken language: Biological constraints on linguistic form,* ed. U. Bellugi and M. Studdert-Kennedy, 115–40. Weinheim: Verlag Chemie.

Bellugi, U., and S. Fischer. 1972. A comparison of sign language and spoken language. *Cognition* 1:173–200.

Bellugi, U., S. Fischer, and D. Newkirk. 1979. The rate of speaking and signing. In *The signs of language,* ed. E. Klima and U. Bellugi, 181–94. Cambridge: Harvard University Press.

Bellugi, U., and E. S. Klima. 1972. The roots of language in the sign talk of the deaf. *Psychology Today* 6:60–76.

———. 1982a. From gesture to sign: Deixis in a visual-gestural language. In *Speech, place and action: Studies of language in context,* ed. R. J. Jarvella and W. Klein, 297–313. Chichester: John Wiley.

———. 1982b. The acquisition of the three morphological systems in American Sign Language. *Papers and Reports on Child Language Development* (Stanford University) 21:1–35.

Bellugi, U., E. Klima, and P. Siple. 1975. Remembering in signs. *Cognition* 3:93–125.

Bellugi, U., and M. Studdert-Kennedy, eds. 1980. *Signed and spoken language: Biological constraints on linguistic form.* Deerfield Beach, Fla.: Verlag Chemie.

Bender, L. 1938. *A visual motor gestalt test and its clinical use.* New York: American Orthopsychiatric Association.

Bernstein, M., M. Maxwell, and K. Matthews. 1985. Bimodal or bilingual communication. *Sign Language Studies* 47:127–40.

Bickerton, D. 1975. *Dynamics of a creole system.* New York: Cambridge University Press.

———. 1981. *Roots of language.* Ann Arbor, Mich.: Karoma.

———. 1982. Learning without experience the creole way. In *Exceptional language and linguistics,* ed. L. K. Obler and L. Menn, 15–29. New York: Academic Press.

———. 1984. The language bioprogram hypothesis. *Behavioral and Brain Sciences* 7:173–88.

Bienvenu, M. J., and B. Colonomos. 1985. *An introduction to American deaf culture: Rules of social interaction.* videotape. Silver Spring, Md.: Sign Media.

Billman, D., and M. Shatz. 1984. Interactive devices of two-year-old dyads: A twin and nontwin comparison. *Discourse Processes* 7:301–19.

Bilovsky, D., and J. Share. 1965. The ITPA and Down's syndrome: An exploratory study. *American Journal of Mental Deficiency* 70:78–82.

Blanchard, I. 1964. Speech pattern and etiology in mental retardation. *American Journal of Mental Deficiency* 68:612–17.

Bonvillian, J. D., and R. J. Folven. 1990. The onset of signing in young children. In *SLR 87: Papers from the Fourth International Symposium on Sign Language Research,* ed. W. Edmondson and F. Karlsson, 183–89. Hamburg: Signum Press.

Bonvillian, J. D., and K. E. Nelson. 1976. Sign language acquisition in a mute autistic boy. *Journal of Speech and Hearing Disorders* 41:339–47.

———. 1982. Exceptional cases of language acquisition. In *Children's language,* ed. K. E. Nelson, 3:322–91. Hillsdale, N.J.: Lawrence Erlbaum.

Bonvillian, J. D., K. E. Nelson, and J. M. Rhyne. 1981. Sign language and autism. *Journal of Autism and Developmental Disorders* 11:125–37.

Bonvillian, J. D., Orlansky, M. D., Novack, L. L., and Folven, R. J. 1983. Early sign language acquisition and cognitive development. In *The acquisition of symbolic skills,* ed. D. R. Rogers and J. A. Sloboda, 207–14. New York: Plenum Press.

Bonvillian, J. D., C. A. Rea, M. Orlansky, and L. Slade. 1987. The effect of sign language rehearsal on deaf subjects' immediate and delayed recall of English word lists. *Applied Psycholinguistics* 8:33–54.

Bornstein, H. 1974. Signed English: A manual approach to English language development. *Journal of Speech and Hearing Disorders* 39:330–43.

Bornstein, H., and I. K. Jordan. 1984. *Functional signs.* Baltimore: University Park Press.

Bornstein, H., and K. L. Saulnier. 1984. *Signing.* Washington, D.C.: Gallaudet College.

Bornstein, H., K. L. Saulnier, and L. B. Hamilton. 1980. Signed English: A first evaluation. *American Annals of the Deaf* 125:467–81.

Bornstein, M. H., and M. G. Ruddy. 1984. Infant attention and maternal stimulation: Prediction of cognitive and linguistic development in singletons and twins. In *Atten-*

tion and performance X: Control of language processes, ed. H. Bouma and D. G. Bouwhuis, 433–45. London: Erlbaum.

Bowerman, M. 1982. Reorganizational processes in lexical and syntactic development. In *Language acquisition: The state of the art,* ed. E. Wanner and L. R. Gleitman. New York: Cambridge University Press.

———. 1986. First steps in acquiring conditionals. In *On conditionals,* ed. E. C. Traugott, A. Ter Meulen, J. S. Reilly, and C. A. Ferguson. Cambridge: Cambridge University Press.

Brigance, A. 1978. *Brigance diagnostic inventory of early development.* North Billerica, Mass.: Early Development Curriculum Associates.

Brown, S. 1986. Etiological trends, characteristics, and distributions. In *Deaf children in America,* ed. A. Schildroth and M. Karchmer. San Diego, Calif.: College-Hill Press.

Bruner, J. S. 1975. The ontogenesis of speech acts. *Journal of Child Language* 2:1–19.

———. 1978. On prelinguistic prerequisites of speech. In *Recent advances in the psychology of language: Language development and mother-child interaction,* ed. R. N. Campbell and P. T. Smith, 199–214. New York: Plenum Press.

Bruning, J. L., and B. L. Kintz. 1977. *Computational handbook of statistics,* 2d ed. Glenview, Ill.: Scott Foresman.

Caccamise, F. 1973. An analysis of hearing-impaired persons' responses to C/i/ syllables under three test modes. Ph.D. diss., University of Washington.

———. 1979. Reliability of CID Everyday Sentence Lists for performance assessment of receptive English simultaneous and manual communication skills. *American Annals of the Deaf* 124:726–30.

Caccamise, F., L. Brewer, and B. Meath-Lang. 1983. Selection of signs and sign languages for use in clinical and academic settings. *Audiology* 8:31–44.

Campos, J., K. C. Barrett, M. E. Lamb, H. H. Goldsmith, and C. Stenberg. 1983. Socioemotional development. In *Handbook of child psychology,* ed. P. Mussen, vol. 2, *Infancy and development: Psychobiology,* ed. M. Haith and J. Campos. New York: John Wiley.

Card, S., P. Spector, and G. Walter. 1980. Comparison of three measures of speech intelligibility of the hearing-impaired. Paper presented at the annual convention of the New York Speech, Language, and Hearing Association.

Carmel, S. 1975. *International hand alphabet charts.* Rockville, Md.: Carmel.

Carr, E. G., J. A. Binkoff, E. Kologinsky, and M. Eddy. 1978. Acquisition of sign language by autistic children: I. Expressive labeling. *Journal of Applied Behavior Analysis* 11:489–501.

Carr, E. G., and P. A. Dores. 1981. Patterns of language acquisition following simultaneous communication with autistic children. *Analysis and Intervention in Developmental Disabilities* 1:347–61.

Carr, E. G., E. Kologinsky, and S. Leff-Simon. 1987. Acquisition of sign language by autistic children: III. Generalized descriptive phrases. *Journal of Autism and Developmental Disorders* 17:217–29.

Carroll, J., P. Davies, and B. Richmond. 1971. *The American Heritage word frequency book.* Boston: Houghton Mifflin.

Caselli, M. C. 1983. Communication to language: Deaf children's and hearing children's development compared. *Sign Language Studies* 39:113–44.

Chomsky, N. 1986. *Knowledge of language: Its nature, origin, and use.* New York: Praeger.

Clark, L. E., and F. Grosjean. 1982. Sign recognition processes in American Sign Language: The effect of context. *Language and Speech* 25:325–40.

Cokely, D., and R. Gawlik. 1973. Options: A position paper on the relation between manual English and sign. *Deaf American* 25:7–11.

Collis, G. M., and H. R. Schaffer. 1975. Synchronization of visual attention in mother-infant pairs. *Journal of Child Psychology and Psychiatry* 16:315–20.

Comrie, B. 1981. *Language universals and linguistic typology.* Chicago: University of Chicago Press.

Conrad, R. 1979. *The deaf child.* London: Harper and Row.

Conway, D., H. Lytton, and F. Pysh. 1980. Twin-singleton language differences. *Canadian Journal of Behavioural Science* 12:264–71.

Coulter, G. R. 1979. American Sign Language typology. Ph.D. diss., University of California, San Diego.

———. 1980. Continuous representation in American Sign Language. In *Proceedings of the First National Symposium on Sign Language Research and Teaching,* ed. W. C. Stokoe, 247–57. Silver Spring, Md.: National Association of the Deaf.

———. 1990. One aspect of ASL stress and emphasis: Emphatic stress. In *Theoretical issues in sign language research,* vol. 1, *Linguistics,* ed. S. D. Fischer and P. Siple. Chicago: University of Chicago Press.

Crandall, K. 1978a. Reading and writing skills and the deaf adolescent. *Volta Review* 80:319–32.

———. 1978b. Inflectional morphemes in the manual English of young hearing-impaired children and their mothers. *Journal of Speech and Hearing Research* 21:372–86.

Creak, E. M. 1964. Schizophrenic syndrome in childhood: Further progress report of a working party. *Developmental Medicine and Child Neurology* 6:530–35.

Creedon, M. P. 1973. Language development in nonverbal autistic children using a simultaneous communication system. Paper presented at the meeting of the Society for Research in Child Development, Philadelphia.

Cross, T. G. 1977. Mothers' speech adjustments: The contributions of selected child listener variables. In *Talking to children: Language input and acquisition,* ed. C. Snow and C. Ferguson. Cambridge: Cambridge University Press.

Cunningham, C. C., S. M. Glenn, and P. Wilkinson. 1985. Mental ability, symbolic play and receptive and expressive language of young children with Down's syndrome. *Journal of Child Psychology and Psychiatry* 26:255–65.

Davis, E. A. 1937. *Linguistic skill in twins, singletons with siblings and only children from 5 to 10 years.* Monograph series 14. Minneapolis: University of Minnesota Institute in Child Welfare.

Day, E. J. 1932. The development of language in twins: I. A comparison of twins and single children. *Child Development* 3:179–99.

DeMatteo, A. 1977. Visual imagery and visual analogs in American Sign Language. In *On the other hand: New perspectives on American Sign Language,* ed. L. Friedman, 109–36. New York: Academic Press.

DeMyer, M., J. Hingtgen, and R. Jackson. 1981. Infantile autism reviewed: A decade of research. *Schizophrenia Bulletin* 7:388–451.

Deuchar, M. 1983. Negative incorporation in sign language as creoles. Paper presented at the annual meeting of the Linguistic Society of America, Minneapolis.

deVilliers, J. G., and P. A. deVilliers. 1978. *Language acquisition.* Cambridge: Harvard University Press.

Doll, E. A. 1953. *The Vineland Social Maturity Scale.* Circle Pines, Minn.: American Guidance Service.

Dore, J. 1975. Holophrases, speech acts and language universals. *Journal of Child Language* 2:21–40.

Duncan, S., and D. W. Fiske. 1977. *Face-to-face interaction: Research, methods, and theory.* Hillsdale, N.J.: Lawrence Erlbaum.

Dunn, L. M., and L. M. Dunn. 1981. *Peabody Picture Vocabulary Test: Revised.* Circle Pines, Minn.: American Guidance Service.

Dyson, A. 1986. Symbol weaving: Interrelationships between the drawing, talking and dictating of young children. Paper presented at the American Education Research Association, San Francisco.

Eisenberg, L. 1956. The autistic child in adolescence. *American Journal of Psychiatry* 112:607–12.

Ekman, P. 1972. Universals and cultural differences in facial expressions of emotion. In *Nebraska symposium on motivation, 1971,* ed. J. K. Cole. Lincoln: University of Nebraska Press.

———. 1979. About brows: Emotional and conversational signals. In *Human ethology,* ed. M. von Cranach, K. Foppa, W. Lepenies, and D. Ploog. Cambridge: Cambridge University Press.

Ekman, P., and W. Friesen. 1978. *Facial Action Coding System.* Palo Alto, Calif.: Consulting Psychologists Press.

Ellis, N., and R. Hennelly. 1980. A bilingual word-length effect: Implications for intelligence testing and the relative ease of mental calculation in Welsh and English. *British Journal of Psychology* 71:43–51.

Engen, T. 1971. Psychophysics: II. scaling methods. In *Woodworth and Schlosberg's experimental psychology,* ed. J. W. Kling and L. A. Riggs, 47–86. New York: Holt, Rinehart, and Winston.

Erber, N. 1979a. Auditory-visual perception of speech with reduced optical clarity. *Journal of Speech and Hearing Research* 22:212–23.

———. 1979b. Speech perception by profoundly hearing-impaired children. *Journal of Speech and Hearing Disorders* 44:255–70.

Erting, C. 1985a. Linguistic variation in a school for deaf children: An analysis of the communicative behavior of preschoolers with deaf and hearing adults. In *SLR '83: Proceedings of the Third International Symposium on Sign Language Research,* ed. W. C. Stokoe and V. Volterra, 38–47. Silver Spring, Md.: Linstok Press.

———. 1985b. Sociocultural dimensions of deaf education: Belief systems and communicative interaction. *Sign Language Studies* 47:111–26.

Ervin-Tripp. S. 1973. An analysis of the interaction between language, topic, and listener. In *Language acquisition and communicative choice,* ed. A. Dil, 239–61. Stanford: Stanford University Press.

Fant, L. J. 1972. *Ameslan: An introduction to American Sign Language*. Silver Spring, Md.: National Association of the Deaf.

Farran, D. C., P. Hirschbiel, and S. Jay. 1980. Toward interactive synchrony: The gaze patterns of mothers and children in three age groups. *International Journal of Behavior Development* 3:215–24.

Feldman, H., S. Goldin-Meadow, and L. Gleitman. 1978. Beyond Herodotus: The creation of language by linguistically deprived deaf children. In *Action, symbol, and gesture: The emergence of language*, ed. A. Lock. New York: Academic Press.

Ferreiro, E. 1984. The underlying logic of literacy development. In *Awakening to literacy*, ed. H. Goelman, A. Oberg, and F. Smith. London: Heinemann.

Fischbein, S. 1978. School achievement and test results for twins and singletons in relation to social background. In *Twin research: Psychology and methodology*, ed. W. E. Nace, 101–9. New York: Alan R. Liss.

———. 1981. Intelligence-test results in opposite-sex twins. In *Twin research 3: Intelligence, personality, and development*, ed. L. Gedda, P. Parisi, and W. E. Nance. 34–50. New York: Alan R. Liss.

Fischer, S. D. 1973a. Verb inflections in American Sign Language and their acquisition by the deaf child. Paper presented at the Linguistic Society of America annual meeting, San Diego, California.

———. 1973b. Two processes of reduplication in American Sign Language. *Foundations of Language* 9:469–80.

———. 1974a. Sign language and linguistic universals. In *Actes du colloque Franco-Allemand de grammaire transformationelle*, vol. 2, *Etudes de sémantique et autres*, ed. C. Rohrer and N. Ruwet, 187–204. Tubingen: Max Niemeyer.

———. 1974b. The ontogenetic development of language. In *Language and language disturbances: The Fifth Lexington Conference on Pure and Applied Phenomenology*, ed. E. W. Straus. Pittsburgh: Duquesne University Press.

———. 1975. Influences on word order change in ASL. In *Word order and word order change*, ed. C. Li, 1–25. Austin: University of Texas Press.

———. 1978. Sign language and creoles. In *Understanding language through sign language research*, ed. P. Siple, 309–31. New York: Academic Press.

———. 1985. The effects of age on the acquisition of sign language: A critical period? In *Proceedings of the Tenth Japanese Symposium on Sign Language Studies*, ed. K. Kanda, 66–71. Tokyo: Japan Sign Language Research Association.

Fischer, S., and B. Gough. 1978. Verbs in American Sign Language. *Sign Language Studies* 18:17–48.

Fisher, H. 1966. *Improving voice and articulation*. Boston: Houghton Mifflin.

Foley, W. A., and R. D. Van Valin, Jr. 1984. *Functional syntax and universal grammar*. Cambridge: Cambridge University Press.

Folven, R. J., J. D. Bonvillian, and M. D. Orlansky. 1984–85. Communicative gestures and early sign language acquisition. *First Language* 5:129–44.

Frankenburg, W. K., J. B. Dodds, A. W. Fandal, E. Kazuk, and M. Cohrs. 1975. *Denver Developmental Screening Test: Revised*. Denver: Ladoca Project and Publishing Foundation.

Friedman, S., M. A. Thompson, S. Crawley, A. Criticos, D. Drake, M. Iacobbo, P. P. Rogers, and L. Richardson. 1976. Mutual visual regard during mother-infant play. *Perceptual and Motor Skills* 42:427–31.

Fristoe, M., and L. L. Lloyd. 1978. A survey of the use of non-speech systems with the severely communication impaired. *Mental Retardation* 16:99–103.

Gardner, L., and J. M. Zorfass. 1983. From sign to speech: The language development of a hearing-impaired child. *American Annals of the Deaf* 128:20–23.

Garvey, C. 1984. *Children's talk.* Cambridge: Harvard University Press.

Gee, J. P. 1985. The narrativization of experience in the oral style. *Journal of Education* 167:9–35.

———. 1989. Two styles of narrative construction and their linguistic and educational implications. *Discourse Processes* 12:287–307.

Gee, J. P., and W. Goodhart, 1985. Nativization, linguistic theory, and deaf language acquisition. *Sign Language Studies* 49:291–342.

———. 1988. American Sign Language and the biological capacity for language. In *Language learning and deafness,* ed. M. Strong, 49–74. New York: Cambridge University Press.

Gee, J. P. and J. A. Kegl. 1982a. Semantic perspicuity and the locative hypothesis. In *Proceedings of the eighth annual meeting of the Berkeley Linguistic Society.* Berkeley: Berkeley Linguistics Society.

———. 1982b. Semantic perspicuity and the locative hypothesis: Implications for acquisition. *Journal of Education* 164:185–209.

———. 1983a. ASL structure: Towards the foundation of a theory of case. Paper presented to special session on sign language, Annual Boston University Conference on Language Development, Boston, Massachusetts.

———. 1983b. Narrative/story structure, pausing, and American Sign Language. *Discourse Processes* 6:243–58.

Geers, A. E., J. S. Moog, and B. Schick. 1984. Acquisition of spoken and signed English by profoundly deaf children. *Journal of Speech and Hearing Disorders* 49:378–88.

Givon, T. 1976. Topic, pronoun, and grammatical agreement. In *Subject and topic,* ed. C. Li. New York: Academic Press.

———. 1979. *On understanding grammar.* New York: Academic Press.

Glover, M. E., J. L. Preminger, and A. R. Sanford. 1981. *The early learning accomplishment profile: Birth to thirty-six months.* Chapel Hill, N.C.: Kaplan Press.

Goldin-Meadow, S. 1979. Structure in a manual communication system developed without a conventional language model: Language without a helping hand. In *Studies in neurolinguistics,* vol. 4, ed. H. Whitaker and H. A. Whitaker. New York: Academic Press.

———. 1982. The resilience of recursion: A study of a communication system developed without a conventional language model. In *Language acquisition: The state of the art,* ed. L. R. Gleitman and E. Wanner. New York: Cambridge University Press.

Goldin-Meadow, S., and H. Feldman. 1975. The creation of a communication system: A study of deaf children of hearing parents, *Sign Language Studies* 8:275–334.

———. 1977. The development of language-like communication without a language model. *Science* 197:401–3.

Goldin-Meadow, S., and M. Morford. 1985. Gesture in early child language: Studies of deaf and hearing children. *Merrill-Palmer Quarterly* 31:145–76.

Goldin-Meadow, S., and C. Mylander. 1983. Gestural communication in deaf children: The non-effects of parental input on language development. *Science* 221:372–74.

———. 1984. Gestural communication in deaf children: The effects and noneffects of parental input on early language development. *Monographs of the Society for Research in Child Development* 49, nos. 3–4.

———. 1991. Levels of structure in a communication system developed without a language model. In *Brain maturation and cognitive development: Comparative and cross cultural perspectives*, ed. K. Gibson and A. Peterson, 315–44. Hawthorn, N.Y.: Aldine. Forthcoming.

Goodhart, W. 1984. Morphological complexity, ASL, and the acquisition of sign language in deaf children. Ph.D. diss., Applied Psycholinguistics Program, Boston University.

Gregory, S. 1985. *The social context of early sign language development*. Final report to the Nuffield Foundation. Nuffield, England: Nuffield Foundation.

Grosjean, F. 1977. The perception of rate in spoken and sign languages. *Journal of Psycholinguistic Research* 22:408–13.

———. 1979. A study of timing in a manual and a spoken language: American Sign Language and English. *Journal of Psycholinguistic Research* 8:379–405.

———. 1981. Sign and word recognition: A first comparison. *Sign Language Studies* 32:195–220.

Gruber, J. S. 1976. *Studies in lexical relations*. Amersterdam: North-Holland.

Gustason, G., D. Pfetzing, and E. Zawolkow. 1972. *Signing Exact English*. Silver Spring, Md.: National Association of the Deaf.

———. 1980. *Signing Exact English*. Los Alamitos, Calif.: Modern Signs Press.

Haiman, J. 1978. Conditionals are topics. *Language* 54:565–89.

Hanson, V. 1982a. Short-term recall by deaf signers of American Sign Language: Implications of encoding strategy for order recall. *Journal of Experimental Psychology: Learning, Memory, and Cognition* 8:572–83.

———. 1982b. Use of orthographic structure by deaf adults: Recognition of fingerspelled words. *Applied Psycholinguistics* 3(4): 343–56.

Hanson, V., D. Shankweiler, and F. Fischer. 1983. Determinants of spelling ability in deaf and hearing adults: Access to linguistic structure. *Cognition* 14:323–44.

Harris, M., J. Clibbens, J. Chasin, and R. Tibbitts. 1989. The social context of early sign language development. *First Language* 9:81–97.

Hartelius, M. 1975. *The chicken's child*. New York: Scholastic Book Services.

Hiskey, M. S. 1966. *Hiskey-Nebraska Test of Learning Aptitude*. Lincoln, Nebr.: M. S. Hiskey.

Hoffmeister, R. J. 1977. The influential POINT. Paper presented at the National Symposium on Sign Language Research and Training, Chicago.

———. 1978. The development of demonstrative pronouns, locatives and personal pronouns in the acquisition of American Sign Language by deaf children of deaf parents. Ph.D. diss., University of Minnesota.

Hoffmeister, R., and R. Wilbur. 1980. Developmental: The acquisition of sign language. In *Recent perspectives on American Sign Language*, ed. H. Lane and F. Grosjean, 61–78. Hillsdale, N.J.: Lawrence Erlbaum.

Howlin, P. A. 1981. The effectiveness of operant language training with autistic children. *Journal of Autism and Developmental Disorders* 11:89–105.

Hulme, C., N. Thomson, C. Muir, and A. Lawrence, 1984. Speech rate and the development of short-term memory span. *Journal of Experimental Child Psychology* 38:241–53.

Huttenlocher, J. 1984. Word recognition and word production in children. In *Attention and performance X,* ed. H. Bouma and D. G. Bouwhuis. Hillsdale, N.J.: Lawrence Erlbaum.

Huttenlocher, J., and D. Burke. 1976. Why does memory span increase with age? *Cognitive Psychology* 8:1–31.

Izard, C. E. 1971. *The face of emotion.* New York: Appleton-Century-Crofts.

Jackendoff, R. S. 1978. Grammar as evidence for conceptual structure. In *Linguistic theory and psychological reality,* ed. M. Halle, J. Bresnan, and G. Miller. Cambridge: MIT Press.

————. 1983. *Semantics and cognition.* Cambridge: MIT Press.

James, W. 1890. *The principles of psychology.* Vol. 1. New York: Henry Holt.

Johnson, D. D. 1976. Communication characteristics of a young deaf adult population: Techniques for evaluating their communication skills. *American Annals of the Deaf* 121:409–24.

Kahn, J. 1981. A comparison of sign and verbal language training with nonverbal retarded children. *Journal of Speech and Hearing Research* 24:113–19.

Kantor, R. M. 1982a. Communicative interaction in American Sign Language between deaf mothers and their deaf children: A psycholinguistic analysis. Ph.D. diss., Applied Psycholinguistics Program, Boston University.

————. 1982b. Communicative interaction: Mother modification and child acquisition of American Sign Language. *Sign Language Studies* 36:233–82.

Karmiloff-Smith, A. 1979. *A functional approach to child language.* Cambridge: Cambridge University Press.

Kay, P., and G. Sankoff. 1974. A language-universals approach to pidgins and creoles. In *Pidgins and creoles: Current trends and prospects,* ed. D. DeCamp and I. Hancock. Washington, D.C.: Georgetown University Press.

Keenan, E. O. 1974. Conversational competence in children. *Journal of Child Language* 1:163–83.

————. 1977. Making it last: Repetition in children's discourse. In *Child discourse,* ed. S. Ervin-Tripp and C. Mitchell-Kernan, 125–38. New York: Academic Press.

Keenan, E. O., and E. Klein. 1975. Coherency in children's discourse. *Journal of Psycholinguistic Research* 4:365–80.

Kegl, J. A. 1985. Locative relations in American Sign Language. Ph.D. diss., MIT.

Kendon, A. 1967. Some functions of gaze-direction in social interaction. *Acta Psychologica* 26:22–63.

Kiernan, C., B. Reid, and L. Jones. 1982. *Sign and symbols: A review of literature and survey of the use of non-vocal communication systems.* London: Heinemann.

Klein, R. M. 1976. Attention and movement. In *Motor control: Issues and trends,* ed. G. Stelmach, 143–73. New York: Academic Press.

Klein, W. 1986. *Second language acquisition.* Cambridge: Cambridge University Press.

Kleinke, C. 1986. Gaze and eye contact: A research review. *Psychological Review* 100:78–100.

Klima, E., and U. Bellugi. 1979. *The signs of language*. Cambridge: Harvard University Press.

Klima, E., U. Bellugi, D. Newkirk, C. Pedersen, and S. Fischer. 1979. The structured use of space and movement: Morphological processes. In *The signs of language*, ed. E. Klima and U. Bellugi, 272–315. Cambridge: Harvard University Press.

Kluwin, T. 1981. The grammaticality of manual representations of English in classroom settings. *American Annals of the Deaf* 126:417–21.

Koch, H. L. 1966. *Twins and twin relations*. Chicago: University of Chicago Press.

Konstantareas, M. M. 1985. Review of evidence on the relevance of sign language in the early communication training of autistic children. *Australian Journal of Human Communication Disorders* 13:77–97.

Konstantareas, M. M., J. Oxman, and C. D. Webster. 1977. Simultaneous communication with autistic and other severely dysfunctional nonverbal children. *Journal of Communication Disorders* 10:267–82.

Krakow, R., and V. Hanson. 1985. Deaf signers and serial recall in the visual modality: Memory for signs, fingerspelling, and print. *Memory and Cognition* 13:265–72.

Kyle, J. G., and B. Woll. 1985. *Sign language: The study of deaf people and their language*. Cambridge: Cambridge University Press.

Labov, W. 1966. *The social stratification of English in New York City*. Washington, D.C.: Center for Applied Linguistics.

———. 1972a. *Sociolinguistic patterns*. Philadelphia: University of Pennsylvania Press.

———. 1972b. *Language in the inner city*. Philadelphia: University of Pennsylvania Press.

———. 1972c. Methodology. In *A survey of linguistic science*, ed. W. Dingwall. College Park: University of Maryland.

Lane, H., P. Boyes-Braem, and U. Bellugi. 1976. Preliminaries to a distinctive feature analysis of handshapes in American Sign Language. *Cognitive Psychology* 8:263–89.

Lane, H., and F. Grosjean. 1980. *Recent perspectives on American Sign Language*. Hillsdale, N.J.: Lawrence Erlbaum.

Launer, P. 1982a. A plane is not to fly: Acquiring the distinction between related nouns and verbs in American Sign Language. Ph.D. diss., City University of New York.

———. 1982b. Early signs of motherhood: Motherese in American Sign Language. Paper presented to the American Speech-Language-Hearing Association, Toronto.

Laver, J. 1970. The production of speech. In *New horizons in linguistics*, ed. J. Lyons. Baltimore: Penguin Books.

Layton, T. L. 1987. Manual communication. In *Language and treatment of autistic and developmentally disordered children*, ed. T. L. Layton, 189–213. Springfield, Ill.: Charles C Thomas.

Lenneberg, E. H. 1964. The capacity for language acquisition. In *The structure of language: Readings in the philosophy of language*, ed. J. A. Fodor and J. J. Katz. Englewood Cliffs, N.J.: Prentice-Hall.

290   References

————. 1967. *Biological foundations of language.* New York: John Wiley.

Levelt, J. M., G. Richardson, and W. La Heij. 1985. Pointing and voicing in deictic expressions. *Journal of Memory and Language* 24:133–64.

Levine, M. H., and B. Sutton-Smith. 1973. Effects of age, sex, and task on visual behavior during dyadic interaction. *Developmental Psychology* 9:400–405.

Liddell, S. 1978. Nonmanual signals and relative clauses in American Sign Language. In *Understanding language through sign language research,* ed. P. Siple, 59–90. New York: Academic Press.

————. 1980. *American Sign Language syntax.* The Hague: Mouton.

————. 1984. THINK and BELIEVE: Sequentiality in American Sign Language. *Language* 60:372–99.

————. 1986. Head thrust in ASL conditional marking. *Sign Language Studies* 52:243–62.

Liddell, S., and R. Johnson. 1989. American Sign Language: The phonological base. *Sign Language Studies* 64:195–278.

Lillo-Martin, D., and E. Klima. 1990. Pointing out differences: ASL pronouns in syntactic theory. *Theoretical issues in sign language research,* vol. 1, *Linguistics,* ed. S. D. Fischer and P. Siple, 191–210. Chicago: University of Chicago Press.

Ling, D. 1976. *Speech and the hearing-impaired child: Theory and practice.* Washington, D.C.: Alexander Graham Bell Association for the Deaf.

Livingston, S. 1983. Levels of development in the language of deaf children. *Sign Language Studies* 40:193–286.

Lockyer, L., and M. Rutter. 1970. A five- to fifteen-year follow-up study of infantile psychosis: 4. Patterns of cognitive ability. *British Journal of Social and Clinical Psychology* 9:152–63.

Loew, R. 1982. Roles and reference. In *Teaching American Sign Language as a second/foreign language,* ed. F. Caccamise, M. Garretson, and U. Bellugi, 40–58. Silver Spring, Md.: National Association of the Deaf.

————. 1984. Roles and reference in American Sign Language: A developmental perspective. Ph.D. diss., University of Minnesota.

Lotter, V. 1978. Follow-up studies. In *Autism: A reappraisal of concepts and treatment,* ed. M. Rutter and E. Schopler, 475–95. New York: Plenum Press.

Luria, A. R., and F. I. Yudovich. 1971. *Speech and the development of mental processes in the child.* Trans. O. Kovasc and J. Simon. Middlesex: Penguin Books. Originally published 1956.

Lytton, H. 1980. *Parent-child interaction: The socialization process observed in twin and singleton families.* New York: Plenum Press.

Lytton, H., D. Conway, and R. Sauve. 1977. The impact of twinship on parent-child interaction. *Journal of Personality and Social Psychology* 35:97–107.

McCune-Nicolich, L. 1981. Toward symbolic functioning: Structure of early pretend games and potential parallels with language. *Child Development* 52:785–97.

McDonald, B. 1982. *Aspects of the American Sign Language predicate system.* Ann Arbor, Mich.: University Microfilms.

MacGillivray, I., P. P. S. Nylander, and G. Corney, eds. 1975. *Human multiple reproduction.* London: Saunders.

McIntire, M. L. 1977. The acquisition of American Sign Language hand configurations. *Sign Language Studies* 16:247–66.

McIntire, M. L, and J. Groode. 1982. Hello, goodbye, and what happens in between. In *Social aspects of deafness*, vol. 1, *Deaf children and the socialization process*, ed. C. Erting and R. Meisegeier, 299–347. Washington, D.C.: Gallaudet College.

McIntire, M. L., J. Reilly, and U. Bellugi. 1987. Hands and faces: The evidence from conditionals in ASL. Paper presented at the Fourth International Conference for the Study of Sign Language, Lappeenranta, Finland.

McNeill, D. 1985. So you think gestures are nonverbal? *Psychology Review*, 92:350–71.

McNeill, D., and E. Levy. 1982. Conceptual representations in language activity and gesture. In *Speech, place and action: Studies in deixis and related topics*, ed. R. Jarvella and W. Klein, 271–95. Chichester: John Wiley.

MacWhinney, B. 1976. Hungarian research on the acquisition of morphology and syntax. *Journal of Child Language* 3:397–410.

———. 1978. The acquisition of morphophonology. *Monographs of the Society for Research in Child Development* 43(1–2): 1–122.

Maestas y Moores, J. 1980. Early linguistic environment: Interactions of deaf parents with their infants. *Sign Language Studies* 23:99–136.

Malmstrom, P. M., and M. N. Silva. 1986. Twin talk: Manifestations of twin status in the speech of toddlers. *Journal of Child Language* 13:293–304.

Marks, L. E. 1974. *Sensory processes: The new psychophysics*. New York: Academic Press.

Marmor, G., and L. Petitto. 1979. Simultaneous communication in the classroom: How well is English grammar represented? *Sign Language Studies* 23:99–136.

Matheny, A. P., Jr., and C. Bruggemann. 1972. Articulation proficiency in twins and singletons from families of twins. *Journal of Speech and Hearing Research* 15:845–51.

Matthews, P. H. 1974. *Morphology: An introduction to the theory of word structure*. Cambridge: Cambridge University Press.

Maxwell, M. 1983a. Language acquisition in a deaf child of deaf parents: Speech, sign variations, and print variations. In *Children's Language*, vol. 4, ed. K. E. Nelson. Hillsdale, N.J.: Lawrence Erlbaum.

———. 1983b. Some functions and uses of literacy in the deaf community. *Language in Society* 14(2): 205–22.

———. 1984. A deaf child's natural development of literacy. *Sign Language Studies* 44:191–224.

———. 1987. The acquisition of English bound morphemes in sign form. *Sign Language Studies*, 57:323–52.

———. n.d. Code-switching across sign languages: A case study of an eight-year-old deaf child. In preparation.

Maxwell, M., and M. Bernstein. 1985. The synergy of sign and speech in simultaneous communication. *Applied Psycholinguistics* 6:63–82.

Mayberry, R. I. 1991. The importance of childhood to language acquisition. In *The transition from recognizing speech sounds to spoken words*, ed. H. C. Nusbaum and J. C. Goodman. Cambridge: MIT Press.

Mayberry, R., and S. Fischer. 1989. Looking through phonological shape to lexical meaning: The bottleneck of non-native sign language processing. *Memory and Cognition* 17:740–54.

Mayberry, R., S. Fischer, and N. Hatfield. 1983. Sentence repetition in American Sign Language. In *Language in sign: An international perspective on sign language,* ed. J. G. Kyle and B. Woll, 206–14. London: Croom Helm.

Mayberry, R., and R. Wodlinger-Cohen. 1987. After the revolution: Educational practice and the deaf child's communication skills. In *They grow in silence,* 2d ed., ed. E. Mindel and M. Vernon. San Diego: College-Hill Press.

Meadow, K. 1968. Early manual communication in relation to the deaf child's intellectual, social, and communicative functioning. *American Annals of the Deaf* 113:29–41.

Mear, K., M. Maxwell, and M. Bernstein. 1991. Simultaneous communication codes in different settings: Hearing teachers. *Sign Language Studies.* Forthcoming.

Meier, R. 1981. Icons and morphemes: Models of the acquisition of verb agreement in ASL. *Papers and Reports on Child Language Development* 20:92–99.

———. 1982. Icons, analogues and morphemes: The acquisition of verb agreement in American Sign Language. Ph.D. diss., University of California, San Diego.

———. 1984. Sign as creole. *Behavioral and Brain Sciences* 7:201–02. (A reply to Bickerton 1984.)

Miller, A., and E. E. Miller. 1973. Cognitive-development training with elevated boards and sign language. *Journal of Autism and Childhood Schizophrenia* 3:65–85.

Milroy, L. 1980. *Language and social networks.* Oxford: Blackwell.

Mindel, E. D., and McC. Vernon. 1971. *They grow in silence: The deaf child and his family.* Silver Spring, Md.: National Association of the Deaf.

Mittler, P. 1970. Biological and social aspects of language development in twins. *Developmental Medicine and Child Neurology* 12:741–57.

———. 1971. *The study of twins.* Harmondsworth: Penguin.

Moores, D. F. 1974. Nonvocal systems of verbal behavior. In *Language perspectives: Acquisition, retardation, and intervention,* ed. R. L. Schiefelbusch and L. L. Lloyd. Baltimore: University Park Press.

Moskowitz, B. A. 1978. The acquisition of language. *Scientific American* 239: 92–108.

Mounty, J. 1984. Nativization and grammaticalization in American Sign Language: An analysis of the "FINISH" sign. Unpublished manuscript, Program in Applied Psycholinguistics, Boston University.

———. 1986. Nativization and input in the language development of two deaf children of hearing parents. Ph.D. diss., Applied Psycholinguistics Program, Boston University.

Muhlhauser, P. 1980. Structural expansion and the process of creolization. In *Theoretical orientations in creole studies,* ed. A. Valdman and A. Highfield. New York: Academic Press.

Mundy, P., M. Sigman, J. Ungerer, and T. Sherman. 1987. Nonverbal communication and play correlates of language development in autistic children. *Journal of Autism and Developmental Disorders* 17:349–64.

Munsinger, H., and A. Douglass II. 1976. The syntactic abilities of identical twins, fraternal twins, and their siblings. *Child Development* 47:40–50.

Nelson, K. 1973. Structure and strategy in learning to talk. *Monographs of the Society for Research in Child development* 38 (1–2, serial no. 149).

Newell, W., F. Caccamise, K. Boardman, and B. Holcomb. 1983. Adaptation of the Language Proficiency Interview (LPI) for assessing sign communicative competence. *Sign Language Studies* 41:311–52.

Newport, E. L. 1981. Constraints on structure: Evidence from American Sign Language and language learning. In *Aspects of the development of competence,* ed. W. A. Collins, Minnesota Symposium on Child Psychology 14. Hillsdale, N.J.: Lawrence Erlbaum.

———. 1982. Task specificity in language learning? Evidence from speech perception and American Sign Language. In *Language acquisition: The state of the art,* ed. E. Wanner and R. L. Gleitman, 450–86. New York: Cambridge University Press.

———. 1984. Constraints on learning: Studies in the acquisition of American Sign Language. *Papers and Reports on Child Language Development* 23:1–22.

———. 1990. Maturational constraints on language learning. *Cognitive Science* 14:11–28.

Newport, E. L., and E. G. Ashbrook. 1977. The emergence of semantic relations in American Sign Language. *Papers and Reports on Child Language Development* 13:16–21.

Newport, E. L., H. Gleitman, and L. Gleitman. 1977. Mother, I'd rather do it myself: Some effects and non-effects of maternal speech style. In *Talking to children: Language input and acquisition,* ed. C. Snow and C. A. Ferguson. Cambridge: Cambridge University Press.

Newport, E. L., and R. P. Meier. 1986. The acquisition of American Sign Language. In *The cross-linguistic study of language acquisition,* ed. D. I. Slobin, 881–938. Hillsdale, N.J.: Lawrence Erlbaum.

Newport, E. L., and T. Supalla. 1980. The structuring of language: Clues from the acquisition of signed and spoken language. In *Signed and spoken language: Biological constraints on linguistic form,* ed. U. Bellugi and M. Studdert-Kennedy, 187–211. Dahlem Konferenzen. Deerfield Beach, Fla.: Verlag Chemie.

Nicholson, R. 1979. The relationship between memory span and processing speech. In *Intelligence and learning,* ed. M. P. Friedman, J. P. Das, and N. O'Connor. New York: Plenum Press.

Nielson, G. 1964. *Studies in self confrontation.* Copenhagen: Munksgaard.

Norman, D. 1976. *Memory and attention.* 2d ed. New York: John Wiley.

Ochs, E., and B. Schieffelin. 1984. Language acquisition and socialization: Three developmental stories and their implications. In *Culture theory: Essays on mind, self, and emotion,* ed. R. A. Shweder and R. A. LeVine. New York: Cambridge University Press.

Offir, C. W. 1976. Visual speech: Their fingers do the talking. *Psychology Today* 10:71–78.

Orlansky, M. D., and J. D. Bonvillian. 1985. Sign language acquisition: Language development in children of deaf parents and implications for other populations. *Merrill-Palmer Quarterly* 31:127–43.

Padden, C. 1983. The interaction of morphology and syntax in American Sign Language. Ph.D. diss., University of California, San Diego.

———. 1988. Grammatical theory and signed languages. In *Linguistics: The Cambridge survey*, ed. F. Newmeyer. Cambridge: Cambridge University Press.

———. n.d. The emergence of spelling in young deaf children. Manuscript, University of California, San Diego.

Padden, C., and B. LeMaster. 1985. An alphabet on hand: The acquisition of fingerspelling in deaf children. *Sign Language Studies* 47:161–72.

Padden, C. A., and D. M. Perlmutter. 1987. American Sign Language and the architecture of phonological theory. *Natural Language and Linguistic Theory* 5:335–76.

Peck, C. A., and A. L. Schuler. 1987. Assessment of social/communicative behavior for students with autism and severe handicaps: The importance of asking the right question. In *Language and treatment of autistic and developmentally disordered children*, ed. T. L. Layton, 35–62. Springfield, Ill.: Charles C Thomas.

Perlmutter, D. 1990. On the segmental representation of transitional and bidirectional movements in ASL phonology. In *Theoretical issues in sign language research*, vol. 1, *Linguistics*, ed. S. D. Fischer and P. Siple, 67–80. Chicago: University of Chicago Press.

Petitto, L. 1981. On the acquisition of anaphoric reference in American Sign Language. Unpublished manuscript, Salk Institute for Biological Studies, La Jolla, California.

———. 1983a. From gesture to symbol: The acquisition of personal pronouns in American Sign Language. Ph.D. diss., Harvard University.

———. 1983b. From gesture to symbol: The relationship between form and meaning in the acquisition of ASL. *Papers and Reports on Child Language Development* (Stanford University) 22:100–107.

———. 1985a. From gesture to symbol: The relation of form to meaning in ASL personal pronoun acquisition. In *SLR '83: Proceedings of the Third International Symposium on Sign Language Research*, ed. W. Stokoe and V. Volterra, 55–63. Silver Spring, Md.: Linstok Press.

———. 1985b. "Language" in the pre-linguistic child. In *The development of language and language researchers*, ed. F. Kessel. Hillsdale, N.J.: Lawrence Erlbaum.

———. 1986. Language vs. gesture: Why sign languages are *not* acquired earlier than spoken languages. Paper presented at the conference on Theoretical Issues in Sign Language Research, Rochester, New York.

Poizner, H., U. Bellugi, and R. Tweney. 1981. Processing of formational, semantic, and iconic information in ASL. *Journal of Experimental Psychology: Human Perception and Performance* 7:1146–59.

Prinz, P. M., and E. A. Prinz. 1979. Simultaneous acquisition of ASL and spoken English. *Sign Language Studies* 25:283–96.

Quigley, S. P., and P. V. Paul. 1984. *Language and Deafness*. San Diego, Calif.: College-Hill Press.

Raffin, M. J. M., J. M. Davis, and L. A. Gilman, 1978. Comprehension of inflectional morphemes by deaf children exposed to a visual English sign system. *Journal of Speech and Hearing Research* 21(2): 387–400.

Read, C. 1971. Pre-school children's knowledge of English phonology. *Harvard Educational Review* 41:1–34.

————. 1975. *Children's categorization of speech sounds in English.* Urbana, Il.: National Council of Teachers of English.

Reich, P., and M. Bick. 1977. How visible is visible English? *Sign Language Studies* 14:59–72.

Reilly, J. S. 1982. The acquisition of conditionals in English. Ph.D. diss., University of California, Los Angeles.

————. 1986. The acquisition of temporals and conditionals. In *On conditionals,* ed. E. C. Traugott, A. ter Meulen, J. S. Reilly, and C. A. Ferguson. Cambridge: Cambridge University Press.

Reilly, J. S., and U. Bellugi. 1988. Competition on the face: Affect and language. Paper presented at the Fourth International Conference on Infant Studies, Washington, D.C.

Reilly, J. S., M. L. McIntire, and U. Bellugi. 1987. The role of isomorphy in development: Topics and conditionals in American Sign Language. Paper presented at the Fourth International Congress for the Study of Child Language, Lund, Sweden.

————. 1990. Faces: The relationship between language and affect. In *From gesture to language in hearing and deaf children,* ed. V. Volterra and C. Erting, 128–41. Springer-Verlag. Forthcoming.

Ritvo, E., and B. J. Freeman. 1977. National Society for Autistic Children definition of the syndrome of autism. *Journal of Pediatric Psychology* 2:146–48.

Romaine, S. 1982. *Sociolinguistic variation in speech communities.* London: Edward Arnold.

————. 1984. *The language of children and adolescents: The acquisition of communicative competence.* Oxford: Basil Blackwell.

Rutter, M. 1978. Diagnosis and definition of childhood autism. *Journal of Autism and Developmental Disorders* 8:139–61.

————. 1983. Cognitive deficits in the pathogenesis of autism. *Journal of Child Psychology and Psychiatry* 24:513–31.

Sachs, J., B. Bard, and M. L. Johnson. 1981. Language learning with restricted input: Case studies of two hearing children of deaf parents. *Applied Psycholinguistics* 2(1): 33–54.

Sachs, J., and M. L. Johnson. 1976. Language development in a hearing child of deaf parents. In *Baby talk and infant speech,* ed. W. von Raffler-Engel and Y. Lebrun, 246–52. Lisse, Netherlands: Swets and Zeitlinger.

Sameroff, A. J. 1975. Early influences on development: Fact or fancy? *Merrill-Palmer Quarterly* 21:267–94.

Sameroff, A. J., and M. J. Chandler. 1975. Reproductive risk and the continuum of caretaking casualty. In *Review of child development research,* vol. 4, ed. F. D. Horowitz, E. M. Hetherington, S. Scarr-Salapatek, and G. M. Siegel, 187–244. Chicago: University of Chicago Press.

Sandler, W. 1986. The spreading hand autosegment of American Sign Language. *Sign Language Studies* 50:1–28.

Sankoff, G. 1980. *The social life of language.* Philadelphia: University of Pennsylvania Press.

Sankoff, G., and S. Laberge. 1973. On the acquisition of native speakers by a language. *Kivung* 6:32–47.

Savic, S. 1979. Mother-child verbal interaction: The functioning of completions in the twin situation. *Journal of Child Language* 6:153–58.

———. 1980. *How twins learn to talk.* London: Academic Press.

Savic, S., and M. Jocic. 1975. Some features of dialogue between twins. *International Journal of Psycholinguistics* 4:34–51.

Schaeffer, B., G. Kollinzas, A. Musil, and P. McDowell. 1977. Spontaneous language for autistic children through signed speech. *Sign Language Studies* 17:287–328.

Schein, J., and M. Delk. 1974. *The deaf population of the United States.* Silver Spring, Md.: National Association of the Deaf.

Schiavetti, N., D. Metz, and R. Sitler. 1981. Construct validity of Direct Magnitude Estimation in interval scaling of speech intelligibility: Evidence from a study of the hearing-impaired. *Journal of Speech and Hearing Research* 24:441–45.

Schieffelin, B. B., and E. Ochs. 1986. Language socialization. *Annual Review of Anthropology* 15:163–91.

Schlesinger, H. S., and K. P. Meadow. 1972. *Sound and sign.* Berkeley: University of California Press.

Schopler, E., R. Reichler, R. F. DeVellis, and K. Daly. 1980. Toward objective classification of childhood autism: Childhood Autism Rating Scale (CARS). *Journal of Autism and Developmental Disorders* 10:91–103.

Scollon, R., and S. B. K. Scollon. 1981. *Narrative, literacy and face in interethnic communication.* Norwood, N.J.: Ablex.

Scroggs, C. 1983. An examination of the communicative interactions between hearing impaired infants and their families. In *Language in sign,* ed. J. Kyle and B. Woll, 126–32. London: Croom Helm.

Shand, M. 1982. Sign-based short-term coding in American Sign Language signs and printed English words by congenitally deaf signers. *Cognitive Psychology* 14:1–12.

Siegel, L. S. 1982. Reproductive, perinatal, and environmental factors as predictors of the cognitive and language development of preterm and full-term infants. *Child Development* 53:963–73.

Siple, P., ed. 1978a. *Understanding language through sign language research.* New York: Academic Press.

———. 1978b. Visual constraints for sign language communication. *Sign Language Studies* 19:95–110.

———. 1978c. Linguistic and psychological properties of American Sign Language: An overview. In *Understanding language through sign language research,* ed. P. Siple, 3–23. New York: Academic Press.

Siple, P., and L. Brewer. 1985. Individual differences in coding strategies for short-term retention of signs. In *SLR '83: Proceedings of the Third International Symposium on Sign Language Research,* ed. W. Stokoe and V. Volterra, 109–19. Silver Spring, Md.: Linstok Press.

Siple, P., F. Caccamise, and L. Brewer. 1982. Signs as pictures and signs as words: The effects of language knowledge on memory for new vocabulary. *Journal of Experimental Psychology: Learning, Memory and Cognition* 8:619–25.

Sisco, F., and R. Anderson. 1980. Deaf children's performance on the WISC-R relative to hearing status of parents and child-rearing experiences. *American Annals of the Deaf* 125:923–30.

Slobin, D. I. 1973. Cognitive prerequisites for the development of grammar. In *Studies of child language development*, ed. C. A. Ferguson and D. I. Slobin. New York: Holt, Rinehart and Winston.

———. 1977. Language change in childhood and in history. In *Language learning and thought*, ed. J. Macnamara. New York: Academic Press.

———. 1981. The origins of the grammatical encoding of events. In *The child's construction of language*, ed. W. Deutsch. New York: Academic Press.

———. 1982. Universal and particular in the acquisition of language. In *Language acquisition: The state of the art*, ed. E. Wanner and L. R. Gleitman. Cambridge: Cambridge University Press.

———. 1983. What the natives have in mind. In *Pidginization and creolization as language acquisition*, ed. R. Andersen, 246–56. Rowley, Mass.: Newbury House.

———, ed. 1986. *The cross-linguistic study of language acquisition*. Hillsdale, N.J.: Lawrence Erlbaum.

Snow, C. 1984. Parent-child interaction and the development of communicative ability. In *The acquisition of communicative competence*, ed. R. Schiefelbusch and J. Pickar, 69–107. Baltimore: University Park Press.

Spelke, E., W. Hirst, and U. Neisser. 1976. Skills of divided attention. *Cognition* 4:215–30.

Stern, D. 1977. *The first relationship*. Cambridge: Harvard University Press.

Stewart, D. A., C. T. Akamatsu, and N. Bonkowski. 1990. Synergy effect: Sign driven and speech driven simultaneous communication. In *SLR 87: Papers from the Fourth International Symposium on Sign Language Research*, ed. W. Edmondson and F. Karlsson, 235–42. Hamburg: Signum Press.

Stigler, J., S. Lee, and H. Stevenson. 1986. Digit memory in Chinese and English: Evidence for a temporarily limited store. *Cognition* 23:1–20.

Stokes, W., and P. Menyuk. 1975. A proposal for the investigation of the acquisition of American Sign Language and signed English by deaf and hearing children enrolled in integrated nursery school programs. Unpublished manuscript, Boston University, Boston.

Stokoe, W. C. 1960. *Sign language structure: An outline of the visual communications systems*. Studies in Linguistics Occasional papers 8. Buffalo, N.Y.: Department of Anthropology and Linguistics, University of Buffalo. (Reprinted Silver Spring, Md.: Linstok Press, 1978.)

Stokoe, W. C., D. Casterline, and C. Croneberg, 1965. *A Dictionary of American Sign Language on linguistic principles*. Washington, D.C.: Gallaudet College Press. (Reprinted 1976.)

Strong, M. 1985. The language of young deaf children: ASL and English. Paper presented at the annual TESOL convention, New York.

Strong, M., and E. Charlson. 1988. Simultaneous communication: Are teachers attempting an impossible task? *American Annals of the Deaf* 132:376–82.

Supalla, S. 1986. Manually coded English: An understanding of modality's role in signed language. Paper given at the conference on Theoretical Issues in Sign Language Research, University of Rochester.

————. 1988. Getting back on the track: Toward an understanding of the role modality plays in signed language development. Keynote speech, Conference on Theoretical Issues in Sign Language Research, 2, Gallaudet University.

————. 1990. The arbitrary name sign system in American Sign Language. *Sign Language Studies* 67:99–126.

Supalla, S., and E. Newport. n.d. Possible languages: Modality constraints in the acquisition of a non-natural gestural communication system. Manuscript in preparation, University of Arizona.

Supalla, T. 1978a. Morphology of verbs of motion and location in American Sign Language. In *Proceedings of the Second National Symposium on Sign Language Research and Teaching,* ed. F. Caccamise and D. Hicks. Washington, D.C.: National Association of the Deaf.

————. 1978b. Morphophonology of hand classifiers in American Sign Language. working paper, University of California, San Diego.

————. 1982. Structure and acquisition of verbs of motion and location in American Sign Language. Ph.D. diss., University of California, San Diego.

Supalla, T., and E. Newport. 1978. How many seats in a chair? The derivation of nouns and verbs in American Sign Language. In *Understanding language through sign language research,* ed. P. Siple, 91–132. New York: Academic Press.

Suty, K., and S. Friel-Patti. 1982. Looking beyond Signed English to describe the language of two deaf children. *Sign Language Studies* 35:153–66.

Swisher, L. P., and E. J. Pinsker. 1971. The language characteristics of hyperverbal, hydrocephalic children. *Developmental Medicine and Child Neurology* 13: 746–55.

Swisher, M. V. 1984. Signed input of hearing mothers to deaf children. *Language Learning* 34:69–85.

————. 1985. Characteristics of hearing mothers' manually coded English. In *SLR '83: Proceedings of the Third International Symposium on Sign Language Research,* ed. W. C. Stokoe and V. Volterra, 38–47. Silver Spring, Md.: Linstok Press.

————. 1989. Visual reception of sign language in young deaf children: Is peripheral vision functional for receiving linguistic information? In *Second International Symposium on Cognition, Education, and Deafness, Working Papers,* vol. 1. Washington, D.C.: Gallaudet University.

Swisher, M. V., and K. Christie. 1989. Communication using a signed code for English: Interaction between deaf children and their mothers. In *Language development and sign language,* ed. B. Woll. Bristol: International Sign Linguistics Association.

Swisher, M. V., K. Christie, and S. L. Miller. 1989. The reception of signs in peripheral vision by deaf persons. *Sign Language Studies* 63:99–125.

Swisher, M. V., and M. Thompson. 1985. Mothers learning simultaneous communication: The dimensions of the task. *American Annals of the Deaf* 130:212–17.

Tedlock, D. 1983. *The spoken word and the work of interpretation.* Philadelphia: University of Pennsylvania Press.

Tervoort, B. T. 1961. Esoteric symbolism in the communication behavior of young deaf children. *American Annals of the Deaf* 106(5): 436–80.

Tomasello, M., S. Mannle, and A. C. Kruger. 1986. Linguistic environment of one-to two-year-old twins. *Developmental Psychology* 22:169–76.

Traugott, E. C., and S. Romaine. 1983. The problem of style in sociohistorical linguistics. In *Proceedings of the Sixth International Conference on Historical Linguistics*, ed. J. Fisiak. Amsterdam: Benjamins.

Traugott, E. C., A. ter Meulen, J. S. Reilly, and C. A. Ferguson, eds. 1986. *On conditionals*. Cambridge: Cambridge University Press.

Trevarthen, C. B. 1979. Instincts for human understanding and for cultural cooperation: Their development in infancy. In *Human ethology: Claims and limits of a new discipline*, ed. M. Cranach et al. New York: Cambridge University Press.

Vernon, M. 1967. Relationship of language to the thinking process. *Archives of General Psychiatry* 16:325–33.

Volterra, V. 1983. Gestures, signs and words at two years. In *Language in sign*, ed. J. Kyle and B. Woll, 109–15. London: Croom Helm.

Volterra, V., and M. C. C. Caselli. 1985. From gestures and vocalizations to signs and words. In *SLR '83: Proceedings of the Third International Symposium on Sign Language Research*, ed. W. Stokoe and V. Volterra, 1–9. Silver Spring, Md.: Linstok Press.

Wallace, M. 1986. *The silent twins*. Englewood Cliffs, N.J.: Prentice-Hall.

Wanner, E., and L. R. Gleitman, eds. 1982. *Language acquisition: The state of the art*. Cambridge: Cambridge University Press.

Washington State School for the Deaf. 1972. *An introduction to manual English*. Vancouver, Wash.: Washington State School for the Deaf.

Waterman, P., and M. Shatz. 1982. The acquisition of personal pronouns and proper names by an identical twin pair. *Journal of Speech and Hearing Research* 25:149–54.

Watts, D., and H. Lytton. 1981. Twinship as handicap: Fact or fiction. In *Twin research 3: Intelligence, personality, and development*, ed. L. Gedda, P. Parisi, and W. E. Nance, 283–86. New York: Alan R. Liss.

Webster, C. D., H. McPherson, K. Sloman, M. A. Evans, and E. Kuchar. 1973. Communicating with an autistic boy by gestures. *Journal of Autism and Childhood Schizophrenia* 3:337–46.

Wechsler, D. 1974. *Manual for the WISC-R*. New York: Psychological Corporation.

Weir, R. 1962. *Language in the crib*. The Hague: Mouton.

Wilbur, R. B. 1979. *American Sign Language and sign systems*. Baltimore: University Park Press.

———. 1986. Interaction of linguistic theory and sign language research. In *The real world linguist: Linguistic applications for the 1980's*, ed. P. Bjarkman and V. Raskin. Norwood, N.J.: Ablex.

———. 1987. *American Sign Language: Linguistic and applied dimensions*. Boston: Little, Brown.

Wilbur, R. B., and M. L. Jones. 1974. Some aspects of the acquisition of American Sign Language and English by three hearing children of deaf parents. In *Papers from the tenth regional meeting, Chicago Linguistic Society*, ed. M. W. LaGaly, R. A. Fox, and A. Bruck, 742–49. Chicago: Chicago Linguistics Society.

Wilson, R. S. 1975. Twins: Patterns of cognitive development as measured on the Wechsler Preschool and Primary Scale of Intelligence. *Developmental Psychology* 11:126–34.

———. 1977. Twins and siblings: Concordance for school-age mental development. *Child Development* 48:211–16.

———. 1981. Mental development: Concordance for same-sex and opposite-sex dizygotic twins. *Developmental Psychology* 17:626–29.

———. 1983. The Louisville twin study: Developmental synchronies of behavior. *Child Development* 54:298–316.

Wimsatt, W. C. 1981. Robustness, reliability, and overdetermination. In *Scientific inquiry and the social sciences,* ed. M. B. Brewer and B. E. Collins, 124–63. San Francisco: Jossey-Bass.

Woodward, J. 1973a. Some characteristics of Pidgin Sign English. *Sign Language Studies* 3:39–46.

———. 1973b. Inter-rule implications in ASL. *Sign Language Studies* 3:47–56.

———. 1982. *How you gonna get to heaven if you can't talk with Jesus?* Silver Spring, Md.: T. J. Publishers.

Zajonc, R. B., and G. B. Markus. 1975. Birth order and intellectual development. *Psychological Review* 82:74–88.

Zazzo, R. 1978. Genesis and peculiarities of the personality of twins. In *Twin research: Psychology and methodology,* ed. W. E. Nance, 1–11. New York: Alan R. Liss.

Author Index

Subject Index